U.S. STAMP YEARBOOK 2004

A comprehensive record of technical data, design development and stories behind all of the stamps and postal cards issued by the United States Postal Service in 2004.

By
George Amick

Published by *Linn's Stamp News*, the largest and most informative stamp newspaper in the world. *Linn's* is owned by Amos Press, 911 Vandemark Road, Sidney, Ohio 45365. Amos Press also publishes *Scott Stamp Monthly* and the Scott line of catalogs.

ISSN 0748-996X

ACKNOWLEDGMENTS

Once again, I must thank many persons whose help made another *Linn's U.S. Stamp Yearbook* possible.

Foremost among them are Terrence McCaffrey, manager of stamp development for the U.S. Postal Service, and his art directors: Carl Herrman, Phil Jordan, Ethel Kessler, Derry Noyes, Howard Paine and Richard Sheaff. Year after year, they recount for me the stories of how these remarkable stamps were planned and designed.

Willing help was provided by USPS officials David Failor, Bill Gicker, Rita Peer, Faustino Romero, Lauren Sposato and many others, and from Robert Williams of the Federal Duck Stamp Office. At PhotoAssist, Louis Plummer, Sidney Brown and their associates are always available to answer my questions promptly and fully.

Thanks also to the illustrators, designers and photographers who shared their experiences in creating stamp art, including John Boyd, Sally Andersen-Bruce, Lonnie Busch, Michael Deas, James Gurney, Philip Handleman, Michael Osborne, Richard Schlecht and Scot Storm. I am grateful also to Diane Boyce of D. Blumchen & Company, Christopher Rowson of the USS Constellation Museum, Joe Sheeran of Ashton-Potter (USA) Ltd., and Sandra Lane and Don Woo of Sennett Security Products.

I'm indebted to many philatelic colleagues, including Jay Bigalke, Robert Dumaine, Lloyd de Vries, Stephen Esrati and the entire editorial staff of *Linn's Stamp News.* I owe special thanks to Angie Stricker, who was responsible for the layout of *Yearbook 2004.*

No writer ever had a better editor than Donna Houseman of *Linn's Stamp News,* or a more willing, knowledgeable and supportive helper than my wife, Donna Amick. My gratitude, as always, to them both.

George Amick

CONTENTS

Legend for Linn's Yearbook Specification Charts

The following is an explanation of the terminology used in the charts that appear at the beginning of each chapter in this *Yearbook*:

Date of Issue: The official first-day-sale date designated by the Postal Service.

Catalog Number: The number or numbers assigned to the stamp or other postal item by the Scott *Specialized Catalogue of United States Stamps & Covers*.

Colors: The color or colors in which the stamp is printed. A number in parentheses preceded by the letters PMS refers to the color's designation under the Pantone Matching System.

First-Day Cancel: The post office location that is identified in the official first-day cancellations.

FDCs Canceled: This figure represents the total number of first-day covers hand-canceled and machine-canceled for collectors and dealers by Stamp Fulfillment Services in Kansas City, Missouri. It does not include covers canceled at the first-day site on the day of issue.

Format: The number and arrangement of stamps in the panes and printing plates.

Perf: The number of teeth or holes per 2 centimeters, as measured with a perforation gauge, and the type of perforator or die cutter used.

Selvage Inscriptions: Informational or promotional material printed in the selvage of certain sheet stamps.

Selvage Markings: Standard markings, other than plate numbers, of the kind found on most sheet stamps.

Cover Markings: Material printed on the inside and outside of booklet covers.

Illustrator or Photographer: The person commissioned by USPS to provide the artwork for the stamp.

Designer: The specialist who adapts the illustration or photograph to a stamp design.

Art Director: The USPS staff member or private-sector graphic arts specialist assigned to work with the illustrator and designer. Often the art director is also the designer.

Typographer: The specialist who selects and arranges the kind and size of type for the letters and numbers in the stamp design.

Engraver: The person who engraves the die for a stamp with an intaglio component.

Modeler: The specialist who takes the artwork and typography and makes any adaptations that are necessary to meet the requirements of the printing process. After completing this work, the modeler makes a stamp-size, full-color model of the design, which must be approved by USPS before production begins.

Stamp Manufacturing: The agency or company that manufactured the stamp, and the process by which it was made.

Quantity Ordered: The number of stamps or other postal items ordered by USPS.

Plate/Sleeve/Cylinder Number Detail: The number and location of plate, sleeve and/or cylinder numbers on the selvage of sheet stamps, on the peel-off strips, covers or stamps of booklet panes, and on coil stamps at constant intervals along the strip.

Plate/Cylinder Numbers Reported: The numbers or combinations of numbers of plates or cylinders used to print the stamp.

Counting Number Detail: The progressive numbers that are printed on the back of some coil stamps or their liner paper at constant intervals for counting purposes.

Tagging: The method used to add phosphor to the stamp or postal stationery in order to activate automated mail-handling equipment in post offices.

INTRODUCTION

In 2004, stamp collectors savored a second consecutive year in which the Postal Service held its output of collectible new varieties of stamps and postal stationery to a manageable level — manageable, at least, in comparison to some of the excesses of the recent past, such as the record 242 varieties issued by USPS in 2002.

The total count for 2004 was 148, up from the 121 of the year before. The difference was accounted for in part by the unusually high number of postal cards, of which 31 were issued this year.

Among the year's 113 stamps were 65 commemoratives. These included a se-tenant pair bearing portraits of Meriwether Lewis and William Clark, in two 10-stamp panes bound in a prestige booklet celebrating the 200th anniversary of the explorers' expedition across the American West.

The prestige booklet was the Postal Service's third, and the first to sell at more than face value. Collectors and philatelic writers complained that they had to spend $8.95 to obtain $7.40 worth of stamps, but postal officials replied that the premium was justified by the value added in the booklet and illustrated text.

USPS also issued a single 37¢ commemorative for the Lewis and Clark expedition in a pane of 20 — with no price markup. The designs of all three Lewis and Clark stamps imitated the look of 1920s stamps, and their frames were printed by intaglio, a process that appeals to stamp-collecting traditionalists.

The first of three annual "Art of Disney" blocks of four depicted Mickey Mouse, Donald Duck and other familiar animated cartoon characters from the Walt Disney Studios. Each block will have a specific theme; that of the 2004 stamps was "friendship." USPS accompanied the Disney stamps with a matching set of picture postal cards, which is standard practice, and with a set of letter sheets bearing the imprinted images of the stamps, which was new. The sheets were sold in packets of 12 for $14.95, more than triple their face value, and the protests that followed from collectors and others were even more intense than for the Lewis and Clark prestige-booklet surcharge.

Other highlights among the commemorative stamps were a 15-stamp "Cloudscapes" pane depicting different cloud formations, a 10-stamp "Art of the American Indian" pane featuring artwork of various Indian tribes, and five black-and-white stamps in a pane of 20 reproducing sculptures of Isamu Noguchi.

Several ongoing series were continued. The sixth entry in the Nature of America series, and the first to feature an underwater biome, was a 10-stamp pane illustrating the flora and fauna of a Pacific coral reef. A convertible booklet in the American Treasures series reproduced Martin Johnson Heade's painting *Giant Magnolias on a Blue Velvet Cloth*.

Black Heritage, the longest-running commemorative series in U.S.

history, got its 28th entry with a stamp depicting singer-actor-civil rights activist Paul Robeson, a highly controversial figure because of his outspoken pro-Stalinist views. The Lunar New Year series' 12th and final stamp commemorated the Year of the Monkey. John Wayne, who had been waiting in the wings to be on a Legends of Hollywood stamp, finally got his due when Spencer Tracy was bumped from the 2004 schedule. The Literary Arts entry for 2004 was author James Baldwin.

A block of four commemoratives depicted noted American choreographers. Single stamps honored other prominent figures in popular culture: playwright and director Moss Hart, children's author Dr. Seuss, film composer Henry Mancini and architect-inventor R. Buckminster Fuller.

The Postal Service continued its tradition of public-health "message" stamps with a single urging early detection of sickle cell anemia. Other singles marked the 50th anniversary of the U.S. Air Force Academy and the opening of the National World War II Memorial on the Mall in Washington, D.C. The sesquicentennial of the *USS Constellation*, the Navy's last all-sail warship, was marked with an all-intaglio, monochrome commemorative. Differences between the Postal Service and the International Olympic Committee over stamp designs and other issues that led to a USPS stamp boycott of the 2000 Summer Games were laid to rest, and a U.S. commemorative was issued for the 2004 Summer Games in Athens.

Four contemporary Christmas stamps depicting Santa Claus ornaments were issued in four different formats, accounting for 16 of the year's 22 special stamps. A new category, wedding-invitation stamps, was introduced, and a new Love stamp was issued. USPS retired the Hanukkah and Kwanzaa designs that it had recycled through three different rate changes, and issued new stamps with a fresh look for those holidays.

The number of definitives (26) was low because there was no rate change to send new varieties featuring flags and other patriotic icons pouring from the presses of the Postal Service's contract printers. However, collectors and catalog makers were caught off balance by the emergence of seven new varieties of nondenominated Sea Coast stamps, some of them unannounced. Other old designs were used for new varieties as well, including 10 color variations of the nondenominated American Eagle first-class presort-rate coil stamp, now out in a water-activated version. Only three new designs for definitives appeared: low-value stamps in the American Design series depicting a Chippendale chair and a Navajo necklace, and a 23¢ Distinguished Americans stamp in three formats honoring track star Wilma Rudolph.

In 2004, USPS again offered selected commemorative stamps to collectors in uncut press sheets. Four issues were available in that form: Pacific Coral Reef, John Wayne, Isamu Noguchi and the Lewis and Clark single. Only one stamp, the Air Force Academy commemorative, incorporated a Scrambled Indicia hidden image of the kind that can only be seen with a special acrylic decoder sold by Stamp Fulfillment Services.

37¢ PACIFIC CORAL REEF (10 DESIGNS)
NATURE OF AMERICA SERIES

Date of Issue: January 2, 2004

Catalog Numbers: Scott 3831, pane of 10; 3831a-3831j, stamps

Colors: yellow, magenta, cyan, black, blue (PMS 294), green (PMS 5635)

First-Day Cancel: Honolulu, Hawaii

First-Day Cancellations: 523,559

Format: Pane of 10, vertical and horizontal. Gravure printing cylinders printing 80 subjects per revolution, 2 panes across, 4 panes around, manufactured by Keating Gravure. Also sold in uncut press sheets of 8 panes (4 across by 2 down).

Gum Type: self-adhesive

Stamp Size: horizontal stamps, 1.56 by 1.225 inches (39.624 by 31.115mm); vertical stamps, dimensions reversed

Pane Size: 9.125 by 6.75 inches (231.775 by 171.45mm)

Uncut Press Sheet Size: 36¼ by 14¼ inches

Perforations: 10¾ (die-cut simulated perforations) (Comco Commander rotary die cutter)

Selvage Inscription: "PACIFIC CORAL REEF/SIXTH IN A SERIES" "NATURE OF AMERICA"

Liner Back Markings: "PACIFIC CORAL REEF/Coral reefs and their surrounding waters are complex/ecosystems supporting thousands of dif-

9

ferent life-forms./But like the biologically rich rain forests of the tropics, they/are also fragile realms, sensitive to temperature changes/and highly vulnerable to human activities that exploit/their resources./Reefs can stretch for miles in the clear, shallow waters/of the tropics and subtropics. Built up primarily by coral/polyps, tiny organisms that secrete calcium carbonate,/these massive structures protect the shores of nearby/landmasses from wave-induced erosion while providing/food and shelter for countless creatures./The stamp pane depicts a coral reef near Guam, a United/States territory in the western Pacific Ocean. In this scene,/a large humphead wrasse eyes its neighbors as a blacktip/shark prowls in the distance. Meanwhile, a spectacular/lionfish — one of many reef dwellers characterized by/elaborate patterns and bright colors — forages among/ the coral for shrimps, crabs, and small fish."

Numbered illustration. "1. Blue Coral/Heliopora coerulea/2. Mound Coral/Porites sp./3. Antler Coral/Pocillopora eydouxi/4. Clown Triggerfish/Balistoides conspicillum/5. Magnificent Sea Anemone/Heteractis magnifica/6. Pink Anemonefish/Amphiprion perideraion/7. Reef Blacktip Shark/Carcharhinus melanopterus/8. Emperor Angelfish/Pomacanthus imperator/9. Threadfin Butterflyfish/Chaetodon auriga/10. Black-spotted Puffer/Arothron nigropunctatus.11. Staghorn Coral/Acropora sp./12. Snowflake Moray Eel/ Echidna nebulosa/13. Spanish Dancer/Hexabranchus sanguineus/14. Humphead Wrasse/Cheilinus undulatus/15. Lionfish/Pterois volitans/16. Moorish Idol/Zanclus cornutus/17. Triton's Trumpet/Charonia tritonis/18. Hawksbill Turtle/Eretmochelys imbricata/19. Crown-of-thorns Sea Star/ Acanthaster planci/20. Bumphead Parrotfish/Bolbometopon muricatum/ 21. Palette Surgeonfish/Paracanthurus hepatus/22. Prickly Red Sea Cucumber/Thelenota ananas/23. Orangeband Surgeonfish/Acanthurus olivaceus/24. Oriental Sweetlips/Plectorhinchus vittalus/25. Bluestreak Cleaner Wrasse/Labroides dimidiatus/26. Mushroom Coral/Fungia sp./27. Wedge Picassofish/Rhinecanthus rectangulus."

"©2003 USPS/NATURE OF AMERICA/THIS SERIES OF STAMPS FEATURES THE BEAUTY AND COMPLEXITY OF PLANT AND ANIMAL COMMUNITIES IN THE UNITED STATES." Universal Product Code (UPC) "457100."

Illustrator: John Dawson of Hilo, Hawaii

Designer, Typographer and Art Director: Ethel Kessler of Bethesda, Maryland

Stamp Manufacturing: Stamps printed by Avery Dennison Security Printing Division, Clinton, South Carolina, on a Dia Nippon Kiko gravure press. Stamps finished by Avery Dennison.

Quantity Ordered: 76,000,000 stamps

Plate Number Detail: no plate numbers

Paper Supplier: Fasson Division of Avery Dennison

Tagging: unphosphored paper, block tagging over stamps

The Stamps

The first U.S. stamp issue of 2004 was a pane of 10 commemoratives depicting the marine life of a Pacific Ocean coral reef. Issued January 2 in Honolulu, Hawaii, it was the sixth in an annual series called "Nature of America" and the first to feature an underwater biome or major ecological community.

Like its predecessors, the pane displays a colorful murallike picture containing 10 self-adhesive, die-cut stamps that form part of the mural and can be peeled out of it. The stamps are laid out in a staggered fashion to correspond to the location of their subjects in the overall illustration. Four of the stamps stand alone, while each of the remaining stamps partially abuts at least one other stamp.

Each has a design that bleeds off the tips of the simulated perforations and depicts at least one identifiable species native to a coral reef. The only typography on each stamp is "USA 37" in two lines of dropout white Eras type (which helps the user locate the stamp on the pane) and the tiny 2004 year date in black in the lower left corner.

The stamps are semijumbo in size. Five are vertically oriented and five are horizontal. At no point on the pane does the die cutting run to the edges, and there are no cuts in the backing paper, which makes it somewhat difficult to extract individual stamps. The pane has no plate numbers.

The paper is unphosphored. Tagging was applied on press and covers each stamp, extending just beyond the tips of its die-cut simulated perfs.

As with the previous panes, the back of the liner displays an outline drawing of the scene on the front, with the species numbered and keyed to a list giving their common and scientific names. The caption notes that

Pacific Coral Reef pane viewed under shortwave ultraviolet light, showing block tagging over each of the 10 stamps.

11

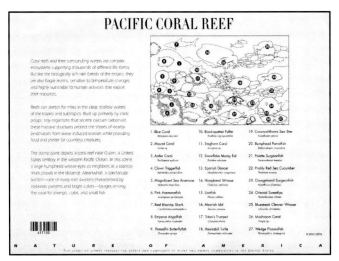

PACIFIC CORAL REEF

Coral reefs and their surrounding waters are complex ecosystems supporting thousands of different life-forms. But like the biologically rich rain forests of the tropics, they are also fragile realms, sensitive to temperature changes and highly vulnerable to human activities that exploit their resources.

Reefs can stretch for miles in the clear shallow waters of the tropics and subtropics. Built up primarily by coral polyps, tiny organisms that secrete calcium carbonate, these massive structures protect the shores of nearby landmasses from wave-induced erosion while providing food and shelter for countless creatures.

The stamp pane depicts a coral reef near Guam, a United States territory in the western Pacific Ocean. In this scene, a large humphead wrasse eyes its neighbors as a blacktip shark prowls in the distance. Meanwhile, a spectacular lionfish—one of many reef dwellers characterized by elaborate patterns and bright colors—ranges among the coral for shrimp, crabs, and small fish.

1. Blue Coral
2. Mound Coral
3. Antler Coral
4. Clown Triggerfish
5. Magnificent Sea Anemone
6. Pink Anemonefish
7. Reef Blacktip Shark
8. Emperor Angelfish
9. Threadfin Butterflyfish

10. Black-spotted Puffer
11. Staghorn Coral
12. Snowflake Moray Eel
13. Spanish Dancer
14. Humphead Wrasse
15. Lionfish
16. Moorish Idol
17. Triton's Trumpet
18. Hawksbill Turtle

19. Crown-of-thorns Sea Star
20. Bumphead Parrotfish
21. Palette Surgeonfish
22. Prickly Red Sea Cucumber
23. Orangeband Surgeonfish
24. Oriental Sweetlips
25. Bluestreak Cleaner Wrasse
26. Mushroom Coral
27. Wedge Picassofish

NATURE OF AMERICA

The back of the Pacific Coral Reef pane's liner paper contains descriptive text and a key to the species shown on the front of the pane.

"This series of stamps features the beauty and complexity of plant and animal communities in the United States." On the previous five panes, the caption referred to "plant and animal communities in North America," but Pacific Coral Reef required a change in the wording.

For uniformity, it was decided that the entire series would be created by the same design team: illustrator John Dawson of Hilo, Hawaii, and Ethel Kessler, a Postal Service art director, designer and typographer. However, different printers and printing methods have been used. The Pacific Coral Reef pane was printed by the gravure process by Avery Dennison Security Printing Division.

Each Nature of America issue has been offered for sale in uncut press sheets at face value through Stamp Fulfillment Services. The price of a Pacific Coral Reef press sheet of eight panes, four across by two down, was $29.60.

USPS increased its print order for Pacific Coral Reef (76 million stamps) from that of the previous year's pane, Arctic Tundra (60 million).

12

A large amount of John Dawson's illustration remains after the 10 stamps are removed from the pane.

It was the largest printing in the series since the Great Plains Prairie pane of 2001 (89.6 million).

Some of the species depicted in Dawson's paintings are outside the borders of the 10 stamps. When the stamps are extracted, these species remain behind in the large selvage, which covers a total area of approximately 43 square inches, more than twice the approximately 19 square inches accounted for by the stamps. That ratio has remained constant through the series.

At the time the first pane, Sonoran Desert, was issued in 1999, Terrence McCaffrey, manager of stamp development for USPS, acknowledged that there is "waste within the illustration area, but we felt it was a good tradeoff." The alternative, he said, would have been to create five more stamps within the mural for a total of 15. Keeping the number of stamps on a pane at 10 keeps a large stamp program from becoming even larger.

The Postal Service originally planned to issue six panes in the series,

with no underwater biome included. Later, officials decided there were enough subjects, and the marketing potential was favorable enough, for the series to be expanded to 12 panes.

"We made the decision to include underwater communities, and asked John Dawson to sketch the first of these, for a Pacific coral reef," said Ethel Kessler. "When we saw the sketch, the [Citizens' Stamp Advisory] Committee's reaction was like, 'How fast can he do the finished painting, because this is going to be gorgeous.'

"Rather than have him finish the Northern Deciduous Forest artwork, which was just about complete, we decided to jump this one ahead of it." The Northern Deciduous Forest pane was pushed back to 2005.

The 2004 pane depicts a coral reef near Guam, a U.S. territory in the western Pacific Ocean, according to the text on the backing paper. It is daytime, and sunlight filters down from the surface, illuminating the marine life below. The dominant image is of a large humphead wrasse, a type of fish, swimming at the upper center. Altogether, 27 species in the illustration are identified in the key on the back.

The stamps themselves and the species that appear on them in whole or part are (starting at the upper left): Scott 3831a, emperor angelfish, mound coral, blue coral; 3831b, humphead wrasse, Moorish idol; 3831c, bumphead parrotfish; 3831d, black-spotted puffer, threadfin butterflyfish, staghorn coral; 3831e, hawksbill turtle, palette surgeonfish; 3831f, pink anemonefish, magnificent sea anemone; 3831g, snowflake moray eel, Spanish dancer; 3831h, lionfish; 3831i, Triton's trumpet; 3831j, Oriental sweetlips, bluestreak cleaner wrasse, mushroom coral, wedge Picassofish, prickly red seacucumber (portions of only the latter two are visible).

Five of the identified species appear in the selvage but not on stamps: reef blacktip shark, clown triggerfish, antler coral, crown-of-thorns sea star, orangeband surgeonfish.

Several other species are shown in the picture but were arbitrarily omitted from the key because there was room for only 27 listings. These include Gorgonian fan coral (extreme upper left), bristleworm (bottom left, just beneath the Spanish dancer), fan tube worm (bottom center, just beneath the lionfish), bluefin trevally (the two fish just above and to the right of the humphead wrasse), scissortail sergeant (the school of striped fish just to the left of the hawksbill turtle) and Christmas tree worm (bottom right, just below the prickly red sea cucumber).

One previous U.S. stamp issue with an underwater theme was the 15¢ Coral Reefs se-tenant block of four of 1980 (Scott 1827-1830). These stamps picture various corals and fish of the South Atlantic and Pacific oceans, including the Moorish idol, a fish that also is on a stamp on the Pacific Coral Reef pane. The 25¢ Creatures of the Sea se-tenant block of four of 1990 (Scott 2508-2511) depicts four sea mammals, while the 29¢ Wonders of the Seas se-tenant block of four of 1994 (Scott 2863-2866) shows scenes from above and below the ocean's surface: birds, boats, divers, dolphins and fish. Among the fish are three species of butterflyfish similar to the threadfin butterflyfish that can be found on the Pacific Coral Reefs pane.

John Dawson's original pencil sketch for the Pacific Coral Reef stamp, dated February 4, 2002, included several species that didn't appear on the finished version, including a manta ray and two swimming jellyfish (upper right corner). The working caption is "Pacific Coral Reef, Guam USA."

15

The Designs

John Dawson is a veteran wildlife and nature artist whose other U.S. stamp credits, besides the first five Nature of America panes, include the Cats block of four of 1988, the Idaho Statehood commemorative of 1990 and the four Flowering Trees stamps of 1997. He paints with acrylics.

The Nature of America assignments call for him to crowd a large amount of detail into a relatively small (8¾ by 5⅝-inch) space. The need to include flora and fauna of widely varying sizes requires that he position the small creatures in the foreground and the large ones in the distance, making their apparent size the same.

"John Dawson is just astonishing," enthused Ethel Kessler. "We ask him to do these wonderful paintings, and to place in each one each of these little characters that will go on a stamp of its own, and have every stamp look a little different, and deal with the problems of scale, perspective, lighting, all of that, and he just loves it!

"Pacific Coral Reef was like backyard for him. He lives in Hawaii, and he and his wife love to snorkel and they see all this underwater stuff. He had a great time with this one."

PhotoAssist, the Postal Service's research firm, hired two experts in the ecology of Pacific coral reefs as consultants for the project: Robert Richmond of the Marine Laboratory at the University of Guam and Charles Birkeland of the Hawaii Cooperative Fishery Research Unit at the University of Hawaii. They gave their opinions as to the appropriateness of the selected species, advised on the nomenclature, and reviewed Dawson's color sketches for accuracy. Their recommendations were relayed to the artist and Kessler by PhotoAssist staff member Carol Highsaw.

Dawson's painting shows "more abundance and biodiversity than one would normally see," Richmond told the design team, "but this is a beautiful and striking illustration of why coral reefs should be protected. It's a very striking piece of art that will attract a lot of attention and highlight the exceptional beauty of coral reefs."

This is the upper left corner of a preliminary color sketch. For the final artwork, on the advice of the Postal Service's consultants, Dawson changed the species of fish from blue-girdled angelfish to emperor angelfish and made the Gorgonian fan less bushy.

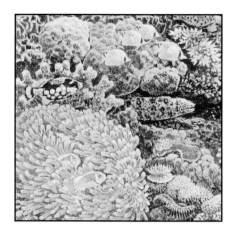

This is another segment of the preliminary color sketch, showing an upside-down jellyfish between the Spanish dancer and bristleworm. For his finished painting, Dawson eliminated the jellyfish, which the consultants said prefers sandy sea bottoms.

Added Birkeland: "In general, the painting is beautiful and represents the way Guam's reefs looked in the 1970s, the way they should look. I really like the general design, especially with the prevalence of humphead wrasse and bumphead parrotfish. These are so important to Guam's reefs, although they've become rare over the past 20 years or so."

Dawson made a number of changes at the consultants' recommendations, including these:

• He substituted an emperor angelfish for the blue-girdled angelfish he originally had painted. The blue-girdled angelfish is not found on Guam, Birkeland said, and its inclusion would invite corrections from sport divers and fish hobbyists. The emperor angelfish has the same shape and position in the painting, but has a different color pattern.

• He reduced the sizes of the cleaner wrasse that is shown inside the mouth of the Oriental sweetlips and the mushroom coral just below.

• He repainted the Christmas tree worm. "The two spires belong to the same worm and should be touching each other," Richmond noted. "It is also a bit larger than it should be; featherduster worms [such as the fan tube worm] have a larger 'footprint' than Christmas tree worms."

Shown here is the lower right corner of the preliminary color sketch. Dawson later revised it to reduce the number of stripes in the Oriental sweetlips and reduce the sizes of the bluestreak cleaner wrasse at the sweetlips' mouth and the mushroom coral just below.

• He made the color of the Spanish dancer more orange and less red.

• He gave greater prominence to the black fin tips and white side stripes of the reef blacktip shark. "They are quite attractive sharks," Birkeland noted.

• He revised the Gorgonian fan to make it less bushy after consulting a reference photo provided by Birkeland.

• He reduced the number of stripes on the Oriental sweetlips from eight to six.

• He eliminated some species that he had included in his preliminary sketches, such as an upside-down jellyfish, which prefers sandy sea bottoms, and a long-spined sea urchin and pin cushion sea star that had been in the lower right corner.

On the stamp pane, Dawson's painting is framed in white. Above the picture, in a typeface called Didot, is the inscription "PACIFIC CORAL REEF." "SIXTH IN A SERIES," in the upper right corner, and "NATURE OF AMERICA," across the bottom, are smaller and set in Eras type.

In addition to the standard four process colors used to print the stamps, Avery Dennison used a PMS blue for the wording in the selvage, as well as a PMS green.

First-Day Facts

Postmaster General John E. Potter dedicated the Pacific Coral Reef stamps in a July 2 ceremony at Honolulu's Waikiki Aquarium.

Dr. Cynthia Hunter, interim director of the aquarium, welcomed the guests. Speakers were Charles Birkeland of the University of Hawaii, one of the design consultants, and John Dawson, the stamps' illustrator. Edward Broglio, Honolulu District manager for USPS, was master of ceremonies. U.S. Senator Daniel Akaka of Hawaii, ranking Democrat on the Senate Postal Subcommittee, also was present.

The Waikiki Aquarium, which celebrated its 100th anniversary in 2003, is the third oldest public aquarium in the United States. A part of the University of Hawaii since 1919, it is located next to a living reef on the Waikiki shoreline.

With the Pacific Coral Reef pane, USPS introduced a new format for its first-day ceremony programs. Instead of a generic folder, the new programs feature a gummed 6-inch by 9-inch envelope that contains the ceremony program card. On the envelope, in normal first-day cover position, is the stamp, tied with the first-day cancellation. Faint outlines of generic stamps are printed on the left side of the envelope, and the USPS eagle and the words "First day of issue ceremony" are near the bottom.

For a limited time, Stamp Fulfillment Services offered uncacheted first-day covers of the Pacific Coral Reef pane for $6.20.

37¢ YEAR OF THE MONKEY
LUNAR NEW YEAR SERIES

Date of Issue: January 13, 2004

Catalog Number: Scott 3832

Colors: magenta, yellow, cyan, green (PMS 321)

First-Day Cancel: San Francisco, California

First-Day Cancellations: 104,434

Format: Panes of 20, horizontal, 4 across, 5 down. Gravure printing cylinders printing 360 stamps per revolution (30 across, 12 around) manufactured by Armotek Industries.

Gum Type: self-adhesive

Overall Stamp Size: 1.56 by 0.99 inches; 39.21 by 25.14mm

Pane Size: 7.25 by 5.94 inches; 184.15 by 150.81mm

Perforations: 10¾ (die-cut simulated perforations) (Comco Custom rotary die cutter)

Selvage Markings: "© 2003/USPS" ".37/x20/$7.40" "PLATE/POSITION" and diagram.

Back Markings: Universal Product Code (UPC) "455300" in 4 locations.

Designer, Illustrator and Typographer: Clarence Lee of Honolulu, Hawaii

Art Director: Terrence McCaffrey (USPS)

Modeler: Donald H. Woo of Sennett Security Products, Chantilly, Virginia

Stamp Manufacturing: Stamps printed for Sennett Security Products by American Packaging Corporation, Columbus, Wisconsin, on Rotomec 4 gravure press. Stamps finished by Unique Binders of Fredericksburg, Virginia.

Quantity Ordered: 80,000,000

Cylinder Number Detail: 1 set of 4 cylinder numbers preceded by the letter S in selvage above or below each corner stamp

Cylinder Number Combination Reported: S1111

Paper Supplier: Mactac

Tagging: phosphored paper

The Stamp

On January 13, in San Francisco, California, the Postal Service issued a 37¢ stamp commemorating the Year of the Monkey in the modified lunar (lunisolar) calendar that is used in China and other parts of Asia.

The self-adhesive stamp was the 12th and last in an annual sequence of stamps that celebrate the arrival of the Lunar New Year and feature the animals for which the years are named. It was printed by American Packaging Corporation for Sennett Security Products by the gravure process and distributed in panes of 20.

Its dedication in San Francisco marked the return to a city in a state bordering the Pacific Ocean, where the first nine stamps in the series were issued because of the region's large Asian-American populations. The 10th and 11th stamps were dedicated in New York City and Chicago, respectively.

Many non-Asian countries now issue Lunar New Year stamps and souvenir sheets. The first such stamp from USPS bore a 29¢ denomination, appeared late in 1992 and marked the forthcoming Year of the Rooster. It proved so popular with Asian Americans and overseas buyers that USPS committed itself to a series. Subsequent stamps commemorated the years of the Dog and Boar (also 29¢), Rat, Ox and Tiger (32¢), Hare and Dragon (33¢), Snake and Horse (34¢), and Ram (37¢).

On December 30, 2003, Postmaster General John E. Potter unveiled the design of what he called "a spectacular grand finale" to the series: a two-sided souvenir sheet, to be issued in 2005, containing two of each of the 12 previously used designs set off by a bright orange selvage. The denominations would be revised where necessary to give each one a 37¢ postal value, USPS said.

Each design in the series has been the work of the same illustrator, Clarence Lee, a Chinese American from Honolulu, who prepared all 12 in the 1990s. Each bears a stylized image of the creature that gave its name to the year, along with the appropriate Chinese New Year inscription in Kanji characters and the words "HAPPY NEW YEAR!" in English.

Several of the Postal Service's private printing firms have produced the stamps, using a variety of methods. The Year of the Rooster stamp was the work of American Bank Note Company, which printed it by a combination of intaglio and offset. The next six, Dog, Boar, Rat, Ox, Tiger and Hare, were gravure-printed by Stamp Venturers or its successor firm, Sennett Security Products. Then came the Dragon and Snake stamps, which were printed by offset lithography by Sterling Sommer for Ashton-Potter (USA) Ltd., and the Horse and Ram stamps, produced by Banknote Corporation of America, also using the offset process.

The design of the Year of the Monkey stamp was first made public in the Winter 2003 issue of *USA Philatelic,* the catalog of the Stamp Fulfillment Services mail-order center, which was mailed to subscribers in October 2003.

"It's been a brilliant series," said Terrence McCaffrey, manager of stamp development for USPS and art director for all the Lunar New Year stamps after the first one. "It's been very popular."

The traditional Chinese calendar, unlike the Islamic calendar, isn't based solely on the moon, but is based on both the moon and sun, to keep it close to seasonal changes. The lunisolar New Year occurs during the first new moon in the Far East after the sun enters Aquarius. The Year of the Monkey (year 4702 in the lunisolar calendar) began January 22, 2004, the earliest commencement date in the cycle in more than a century.

The monkey is the ninth of the 12 animals associated with the calendar, but its position in the stamp series is 12th because the series began with the rooster. Past Years of the Monkey have been 1920, 1932, 1944, 1956, 1968, 1980 and 1992.

According to the Postal Service, "The Lunar New Year is a family affair that holds great importance to those of Asian descent around the world. It is a time to cast away the bad blood of the previous year and to wish for good fortune in the coming year.

"Lively, witty, inventive, intelligent and good at problem solving, the Monkey is the sign of the inventor, the improviser and the motivator in the Chinese zodiac. Legend says a person born during the Year of the Monkey is fated for success at whatever he or she chooses to do. No challenge will be too great.

"The traditional Chinese New Year marks the beginning of a new season, also called Spring Festival. It is a time of renewed hope for a prosperous future often celebrated through family reunions."

The Design

Clarence Lee, who has headed his own graphic design firm in Honolulu for more than three decades, has depicted the animal on each Lunar New Year stamp in a way that suggests traditional Chinese cut paper art. He cuts the figure from paper with an Exacto knife, photographs the cutout and overlays the negative on an airbrushed background so the background color shows through the transparent parts of the figure.

The Kanji characters are done in grass-style calligraphy by Lau Bun of Honolulu, a member of a family of Chinese calligraphers. On the Year of the Monkey stamp, the upper and middle characters on the left signify "monkey." The character beneath it, which is common to all the stamps, signifies "year." All the typography, Kanji and English, is in white, dropped out of the background.

As with the previous stamps in the series, the featured creature is shown in subtle gradations of rose, orange, yellow, green and blue, which American Packaging Corporation created using three process colors, cyan, magenta and yellow. There is no black on the stamp. The solid background is blue-green, in keeping with a plan established early in the series by Lee and Terrence McCaffrey, USPS manager of stamp development. They decided to move through the dark colors of the spectrum for the first six stamps, beginning with the bright red of the Year of the Rooster stamp and ending with the blue-green of the Year of the Tiger, then repeat the sequence for the final six.

The stylized monkey is shown standing and waving its arms; its tail loops upward, over and down behind the Kanji characters. Clarence Lee depicted the animal's features and decorated its body with cut-out curves, circles and jagged-line patterns.

First-Day Facts

Donna Peak, USPS controller and vice president for finance, dedicated the Year of the Monkey stamp at the Nob Hill Masonic Center in San Francisco.

David Louie, reporter-anchor for KGO-TV (ABC) in San Francisco, was master of ceremonies. Speakers included Walter Wong, president, San Francisco Chinese Chamber of Commerce; Bill Wong, president, Chinese Consolidated Benevolent Association; Claudine Cheng, past president, Organization of Chinese Americans Inc.; Scott Tucker, San Francisco District manager, USPS; and stamp designer Clarence Lee. A surprise attendee and speaker was newly inaugurated San Francisco Mayor Gavin Newsom, in his fifth day on the job.

For a limited period, Stamp Fulfillment Services sold uncacheted first-day covers of the Year of the Monkey stamp for 75¢.

37¢ PAUL ROBESON
BLACK HERITAGE SERIES

Date of Issue: January 20, 2004

Catalog Number: Scott 3834

Colors: gray, black, cool gray, red (PMS 181)

First-Day Cancel: Princeton, New Jersey

First-Day Cancellations: 82,251

Format: Panes of 20, vertical, 5 across, 4 down. Gravure printing cylinders printing 360 stamps per revolution (30 across, 12 around) manufactured by Southern Graphics Systems.

Gum Type: self-adhesive

Overall Stamp Size: 0.99 by 1.56 inches; 25.146 by 39.624mm

Pane Size: 5.94 by 7.25 inches; 150.87 by 184.15mm

Perforations: 10¾ (die-cut simulated perforations) (Comco Custom rotary die cutter)

Selvage Markings: "© 2003/USPS" ".37/x20/$7.40" "PLATE/POSITION" and diagram.

Back Markings: On selvage liner: Universal Product Code (UPC) "455400" in 4 locations. On stamp liner: "A world-renowned actor,/singer, activist, and athlete,/Paul Robeson (1898-1976)/was a man ahead of his time./Whether performing/spirituals and folk songs or/interpreting Shakespeare's/*Othello,* Robeson infused/his life and work with his/principled stand against/ racism and his outspoken/commitment to social justice."

Photographers: photo attributed to Annette and Basil Zarov, Montreal, Canada

Designer, Art Director and Typographer: Richard Sheaff of Scottsdale, Arizona

Modeler: Donald H. Woo of Sennett Security Products, Chantilly, Virginia

Stamp Manufacturing: Stamps printed for Sennett Security Products by American Packaging Corporation, Columbus, Wisconsin, on Champlain Roto 3 gravure press. Stamps finished by Unique Binders of Fredericksburg, Virginia.

Quantity Ordered: 130,000,000

Cylinder Number Detail: 1 set of 4 cylinder numbers preceded by the letter S in selvage above or below each corner stamp

Cylinder Number Combination Reported: S1111

Paper Supplier: Mactac

Tagging: phosphored paper

The Stamp

On January 21, the Postal Service issued a Black Heritage stamp honoring Paul Robeson, a multitalented American who was widely admired for his achievements as a singer, actor, scholar and civil rights activist but also was vilified for his outspoken support of the Soviet Union and its dictator, Josef Stalin, during the Cold War.

For Robeson's admirers, the stamp was very late in coming. They had campaigned, unsuccessfully, for its issuance in 1998, the centennial year of his birth.

According to philatelic writer Ken Lawrence, the stamp campaign may have begun in 1995 with LeRoy Wolins of South Haven, Michigan, who admired and worked for Robeson. It gained momentum the following year under the direction of Dr. Margaret Burroughs, founder of the DuSable Museum of African American History in Chicago. Supporting her initiative, six members of the Congressional Black Caucus introduced a resolution in the 104th Congress calling for a commemorative for the actor-singer.

Lawrence himself participated in the lobbying effort. "From these beginnings," he wrote in *Scott Stamp Monthly*, "the Paul Robeson 100th Birthday Committee launched a petition drive from its headquarters at Columbia College in Chicago. The names of celebrity sponsors in fine print filled the letterhead margin from top to bottom: actors, authors, educators, poets, politicians, labor leaders, musicians, socialists and communists. Among these luminaries were Ossie Davis, Ruby Dee, Edward Asner, Pete and Toshi Seeger, Studs Terkel, Sonia Sanchez and John Hope Franklin. Mark Rogovin, founder of the Chicago Peace Museum, staffed the headquarters and coordinated activities.

"Eventually more than 50,000 signatures were gathered on petitions to [the Citizens' Stamp Advisory Committee], and countless individual letters also were submitted. Artists painted portraits of Robeson as proposed designs for stamps. New York Friends of the *People's Weekly World* (the

Communist Party's newspaper) issued pinback buttons and panes of stickers suggestive of stamps picturing Robeson, headed 'We Demand!'

"Despite the energy and enthusiasm we devoted to this campaign, we came up empty. No stamp was issued to commemorate Robeson's 100th birthday in 1998."

The omission of a Robeson stamp from that year's U.S. stamp program drew criticism in the press of his home state, New Jersey. "Indefensible," said *The Star-Ledger* of Newark. "Robeson's accomplishments should outweigh any reservations about his politics. If the Postal Service sees fit to honor cartoon characters like Sylvester and Tweety, it's ludicrous to ignore a gifted American." *The Times* of Trenton called the Postal Service's neglect of Robeson "hard to understand."

"Belatedly in January 1999," continued Ken Lawrence, "we received letters of apology from James Tolbert, manager of stamp development for [USPS], regretting that our proposal had not been acknowledged in a timely manner, but stating that the proposal was still under consideration."

In fact, USPS staff members and CSAC had favored a stamp for Robeson all along, Terrence McCaffrey, manager of stamp development, told *The Yearbook.* But it was vetoed by the postmaster general, the late Marvin T. Runyon, because of Robeson's pro-Soviet positions.

"He said, 'Not on my watch,' " McCaffrey said.

There was an inconsistency in Runyon's attitude, McCaffrey acknowledged. In 1998, the year of Robeson's centennial, Runyon sanctioned the issuance of a Celebrate the Century stamp honoring W.E.B. DuBois, a black historian and civil rights leader who in his later years joined the Communist Party (something Robeson swore he never did) and renounced his U.S. citizenship. It was the second U.S. stamp to picture DuBois, for whom a Black Heritage commemorative was issued a few months before Runyon took office. Runyon also had approved a 1998 stamp honoring folk singer Woody Guthrie, whose left-wing views led to accusations, never confirmed, that he was a member of the Communist Party. "I guess [Runyon] knew more about Robeson and had this personal thing against him," McCaffrey said.

After Runyon resigned as postmaster general in May 1998, CSAC revisited the idea of Robeson as a Black Heritage series subject. Its members recalled that they recently had authorized commemorative stamps honoring Malcolm X,

Despite Postmaster General Marvin Runyon's refusal to approve a stamp for Robeson because of his pro-Stalin sentiments, Runyon approved this stamp (Scott 3181l) in the Celebrate the Century series depicting W.E.B. DuBois, who joined the Communist Party and renounced his U.S. citizenship.

Robeson was depicted on a 20-pfennig stamp of the communist German Democratic Republic (Scott 2330) in 1983 and a 500-franc airmail stamp from Mali (Scott C522) in 1986.

another controversial black American, and Mexican artist Frida Kahlo, also a Stalin apologist, and "survived," McCaffrey said. "They asked, why not do Robeson?" he said. "Yes, he did have those beliefs, but we honor people not for their political beliefs but for their contributions to society.'"

The design of Robeson's stamp was unveiled September 29, 2003, at Columbia University in New York City, where he earned a law degree. And now, predictably, the Postal Service was hit by criticism from the right.

Eight days before the stamp's issuance, Arnold Beichman, a columnist for the conservative *Washington Times*, listed several Robeson quotations in which he praised Stalin, defended Stalin's oppression of his own people and those of the Soviet satellite countries, and called the USSR "the country I love above all." "Let's put it simply," Beichman wrote. "The radical left in America has won a great propaganda victory in getting an arm of our government to honor a man who dedicated his artistry to a bloody tyrant just as Leni Riefenstahl dedicated her moviemaking talents to Adolf Hitler."

After the column was published, Terrence McCaffrey said, "we started getting letters, and we had congressmen calling and complaining. We sent a form letter saying we stood behind our decision to issue the stamp, and [the criticism] did subside."

Robeson previously was postally honored by at least two other countries. He was depicted on a 20-pfennig stamp of the communist German Democratic Republic (Scott 2330) in 1983 and a 500-franc airmail stamp from Mali (Scott C522) in 1986.

Paul Bustill Robeson was born April 9, 1898, in Princeton, New Jersey, the son of a minister who had been a slave. His extraordinary talents were evident as early as high school, where he was an outstanding student and athlete.

In 1915, Robeson became only the third black American to enter Rutgers College, after achieving the highest score ever recorded on the qualifying exam. At Rutgers, he won the oratory contest four years in a row, was elected to Phi Beta Kappa as a junior, won 14 varsity sports letters and was twice named to the All-America football team chosen by Walter Camp, who called him a "veritable superman." He was valedictorian of the Class of 1919.

Robeson helped pay his way through Columbia Law School by playing professional football, coaching college football and acting on the stage. After graduation in 1923, he worked briefly in a law firm, but resigned after a white secretary refused to take dictation from him. He became a full-time actor and singer, playing the lead role in productions of two Eugene O'Neill plays, *All God's Chillun Got Wings* and *The Emperor Jones.*

He starred in Shakespeare's *Othello* in London in 1931 and reprised the role in New York in 1943. Renowned for his resonant bass-baritone singing voice, he helped establish black American spirituals as an American art form. He appeared in the London production of the musical *Show Boat* in 1928 and made its greatest song, *Ol' Man River,* his own. He also appeared in films in Great Britain and the United States.

Robeson's fundamental belief in human dignity led him to rebel against racism in America and colonialism abroad, and he used his public appearances as a platform to denounce these injustices, performing at labor union and civil rights rallies. In 1934, he made his first trip to the Soviet Union, and embarked on his long and unfortunate romance with Soviet communism. As *Linn's Stamp News* writer Rick Miller wrote:

"Blinded by his own galling experiences of racial prejudice and the hero's welcome he received from the Soviet government, Robeson made himself available to Stalin on all fronts, toeing the party line on every issue from the persecution of Trotskyite dissenters to the Non-Aggression Pact with Nazi Germany. ...

"After World War II, when Stalin's artificially contrived famines, genocide against non-Russian ethnic minorities, political purges and other crimes against humanity became generally known, many American leftists and communists denounced Stalin. Far from denouncing him, Robeson remained a stalwart supporter."

He paid a heavy personal cost as the Cold War deepened and fear of communism gripped the country. The FBI labeled Robeson a member of the Communist Party, and the State Department withdrew his passport and that of his wife, Eslanda. Leaders of the National Association for the Advancement of Colored People attacked him as a "Kremlin stooge." Blacklisted at home and unable to tour abroad, he saw his income reportedly drop from $104,000 in 1947 to $2,000 in 1950.

At a 1956 House Un-American Activities Committee hearing, Robeson was asked why he did not stay in the USSR, where he had received the Stalin Peace Prize in 1952. Robeson replied, 'Because my father was a slave, and his people died to build this country, and I am going to stay here and have a part of it just like you. And no fascist-minded people will drive me from it." He also told the committee, "I am not being tried for whether I am a communist; I am being tried for fighting for the rights of my people, who are still second-class citizens in this United States of America."

The Supreme Court restored the Robesons' passports in 1958, and they spent much of the next five years abroad. Paul's health failed and they returned to the United States in 1963. After Eslanda's death two years later, Paul Robeson lived with his sister in Philadelphia. He died in that city January 23, 1976, at the age of 77. Posthumously, he was recognized by the United Nations in 1978 for his opposition to apartheid in South Africa, was inducted into the College Football Hall of Fame in 1995 and received a Grammy Award for Lifetime Achievement in 1998.

In the Postal Service's carefully edited news release announcing the stamp, there was no hint of the controversy that consumed much of Robeson's life. The same was true for the brief biography on the official program at the first-day ceremony. One would assume from reading the news release that Robeson's career was universally lauded, commented *Linn's Stamp News* editor Michael Schreiber.

"The postal announcement deftly airbrushes away all frailties, much as Soviet propagandists removed images of undesirables from historic photographs," Schreiber wrote in *Linn's*. However, he conceded, "the talented Robeson ... deserves to be on a U.S. stamp."

The stamp was the 27th in the Black Heritage series, which began in 1978. A self-adhesive, it was printed by the gravure process by American Packaging Corporation for Sennett Security Products and distributed in panes of 20. A paragraph of text about Robeson is printed on the back of the liner paper; it, too, omits any mention of the controversy with which he lived for more than half his life.

On February 6, 17 days after the Robeson stamp was issued, the Postal Service officially denied what it called "recent newspaper articles and fast-spreading Internet rumors stating that the U.S. Postal Service will discontinue its long-standing Black Heritage stamp series." The reports were "totally untrue," the USPS news release said, "as is the allegation that the Postal Service has directed that current stamps be destroyed." USPS had issued similar denials in the past, most recently in 2001, when it commented that the rumors were "quickly turning into an urban legend."

The Design

Although the first 16 Black Heritage stamps showed full-color illustrations of their subjects, the stamps issued since 1996 have featured photographs in monotone or duotone. This has prompted some black Americans to complain that the men and women honored in the series were slighted by not being pictured in full color and to ask for a restoration of the series' original look. The dissenting letters and e-mails came not from organizations but from individuals, and reflected the views of some Postal Service staff members as well, Terrence McCaffrey said.

On the other hand, he said, the minority-group members of CSAC have had no problem with the design style of the recent Black Heritage stamps. "They were fine with it," he said. "They defended it. They felt it was a superb series, very elegant and dignified, but they understood the wants of the American public, and they were willing to entertain a change."

Meanwhile, Richard Sheaff, the USPS art director who created the current design format, had developed some proposed Paul Robeson designs in that format based on different photographs. The photo that CSAC members liked best, a black-and-white, was taken circa 1943 and showed a smiling Robeson. "Although the photographer is unknown, an inscription by Robeson in the lower left corner of the print suggests that Montreal-based photographers Annette and Basil Zarov made the original photograph," said the Postal Service news release.

Now, to satisfy the members of the public who felt the Black Heritage portraits should be in full color, CSAC asked Sheaff to commission a color painting based on the photograph attributed to the Zarovs. The job was done by Albert Slark, a digital illustrator from Toronto, Canada, who specializes in book covers and advertising and also paints from life. In his color interpretation of the photo, Slark gave Robeson a light blue jacket and turned his patterned necktie into solid red.

In the interim, however, USPS officials had contacted Paul Robeson's son, Paul Jr., who approved Sheaff's design using the black-and-white photograph. Later, when the son saw the painted version, he turned it down. "He said, 'No, I prefer the black-and-white photo. I don't want the color painting,' " McCaffrey said.

Because the family's wishes are given precedence, the photograph was used, and the Robeson stamp conforms in design to its recent predecessors. The words "BLACK HERITAGE" and "37 USA," in a font called

Art director Richard Sheaff prepared these alternative designs using photographs of a uniformed Robeson in the role of the menacing Brutus Jones in Eugene O'Neill's The Emperor Jones *(1933), taken by Edward Steichen; a beaming Robeson in a business suit, taken by Yousuf Karsh; and a stern-faced actor as Shakespeare's* Othello, *taken by Sasha.*

Because some black Americans felt the Black Heritage stamps should be in full color rather than monotone or duotone, Albert Slark was commissioned on CSAC's instructions to prepare this painting of Robeson based on a black-and-white photo attributed to Montreal photographers Annette and Basil Zarov. Robeson's son, Paul Jr., preferred the photo, and it, rather than the painting, is shown on the stamp.

Impact, are at the top. "Paul Robeson," in Futura Extra Bold, is across the bottom, on a panel that resembles a transparent overlay across Robeson's lapel and tie. The name line, in red, provides the only dash of color on the stamp; the rest of the typography and the portrait are printed in gray, black and cool gray inks.

First-Day Facts

U.S. Representative Rush Holt, Democrat of New Jersey, suggested to USPS officials and Paul Robeson Jr. that the stamp have its first-day sale in Princeton. Although the town of his birth was "spiritually located in Dixie," the singer-actor had written in his autobiography, his days there were his "happier" days, and its close-knit black American community gave him "an abiding sense of comfort and security." Holt's idea was approved, and the ceremony was held in Richardson Auditorium in Princeton University's Alexander Hall, a building that had been pictured on the 1996 postal card marking the university's 250th anniversary (Scott UX263).

Holt was a featured speaker, along with Robeson's son, Paul Jr.; Regena L. Thomas, New Jersey secretary of state; and actor Avery Brooks. Murry E. Weatherall, USPS vice president for diversity development, dedicated the stamp. Amy Gutmann, Princeton University provost, presided, and Shirley Tilghman, the university's president, gave the welcome. Henry Foner, president of the Paul Robeson Foundation, was an honored guest.

Paul Robeson Jr. and Avery Brooks also had been present when the stamp's design was unveiled in September 2003, along with Vinnie Malloy, district manager and postmaster for the Postal Service's New York District, and Manning Marable of Columbia University's Center for Contemporary Black History.

For a limited time, Stamp Fulfillment Services sold uncacheted first-day covers of the Robeson stamp for 75¢.

The earliest known prerelease use of a Robeson stamp was on an envelope machine-canceled in Sacramento, California, January 17, three days before the first-day sale.

37¢ THEODORE SEUSS GEISEL (DR. SEUSS)

Date of Issue: March 2, 2004

Catalog Number: Scott 3835

Colors: magenta, yellow, cyan, black, line red, line blue

First-Day Cancel: La Jolla, California

First-Day Cancellations: 68,052

Format: Pane of 20, horizontal, 4 across, 5 down. Gravure printing cylinders printing 180 stamps per revolution (12 across, 15 around) manufactured by Southern Graphics Systems.

Gum Type: self-adhesive

Overall Stamp Size: 1.56 by 1.23 inches; 39.62 by 31.24mm

Pane Size: 7.25 by 8 inches; 184.15 by 203.2mm

Perforations: 12 by 11½ (die-cut simulated perforations) (Comco custom rotary die cutter)

Selvage Inscription: "Dr. Seuss" "Dr. Seuss properties™ & ©2003 Dr. Seuss Enterprises, L.P./All Rights Reserved."

Selvage Markings: "©2003/USPS." ".37/x 20/$7.40." "PLATE/POSITION" and diagram.

Back Markings: Universal Product Code (UPC) "455500" in 4 locations on back of liner paper.

Designer, Art Director and Typographer: Carl Herrman of Carlsbad, California

Modeler: Donald H. Woo of Sennett Security Products, Chantilly, Virginia

Stamp Manufacturing: Stamps printed for Sennett Security Products by American Packaging Corporation, Columbus, Wisconsin, on Rotomec 3000 gravure press. Stamps finished by Unique Binders of Fredericksburg, Virginia.

Quantity Ordered: 172,000,000

Cylinder Number Detail: 1 set of 6 cylinder numbers preceded by the letter S in selvage beneath each lower corner stamp

Cylinder Number Combination Reported: S111111

Paper Supplier: Mactac

Tagging: phosphored paper

The Stamp

On March 2, the Postal Service issued a stamp honoring Theodor Seuss Geisel, the world's best-selling children's author, who wrote and illustrated his books under the name "Dr. Seuss." The date was the 100th anniversary of his birth.

The stamp had its first-day sale at the Geisel Library of the University of California San Diego in La Jolla, California. The library is the repository of Geisel's papers.

One of the author's best-known characters, the Cat in the Hat, was depicted on a 33¢ stamp of the Celebrate the Century pane for the 1950s, issued in 1999 (Scott 3187h). Its verso text reads in part: "This masterpiece uses repeated syllables, rhythmic verse and fanciful drawings to teach children to read and to use their imaginations."

The idea for a Dr. Seuss stamp originated with the Citizens' Stamp Advisory Committee, according to Terrence McCaffrey, manager of stamp development for USPS.

"A couple of committee members brought it up," McCaffrey said. "The Cat in the Hat was one of our more popular Celebrate the Century stamps, and I think that probably triggered the thought that we needed to honor Dr. Seuss."

The self-adhesive stamp, semijumbo in size, was printed by American Packaging Corporation for Sennett Security Products by the gravure process and distributed in panes of 20.

The design was unveiled October 27, 2003, in Springfield, Massachusetts, where Geisel (pronounced GUYS-ell) was born March 2, 1904. On hand at the Dr. Seuss National Memorial Sculpture Garden were Jon Steele, vice president of the Postal Service's Northeast Area; Audrey Geisel, the writer's wife; U.S. Representative Richard Neal, Democrat of Massachusetts; and other officials.

Geisel graduated from Dartmouth College in 1925 and studied literature at Oxford University. He then began a career as an artist and writer. His first published cartoon appeared in *The Saturday Evening Post* for July 16, 1927. Soon afterward, he and his wife, Helen Palmer Geisel, moved to New York City, where he joined the staff of the humor magazine *Judge*. It was here that he first used the pen name Dr. Seuss, his mother's maiden name and his own middle name.

In 1928, Geisel was employed by Standard Oil of New Jersey to design an advertising campaign for its insecticide. The slogan he invented, "Quick, Henry, the Flit!" became a national catchphrase. He supported himself and Helen during the Great Depression by drawing ads for General Electric, NBC, Standard Oil and other companies.

Geisel made his first venture into book illustration in 1931 when he provided the artwork for two collections of children's sayings. His first children's-book manuscript, *And To Think That I Saw It on Mulberry Street*, was rejected by 27 publishers before Vanguard Press accepted it for publication in 1937. Its rhyming text combined with illustrations was unusual in children's books at the time. Reviewers recognized that "Dr. Seuss" had created a new kind of book that appealed to a child's imagination and sense of humor.

During World War II, Geisel was a soldier in Frank Capra's Army Signal Corps unit in Hollywood, writing films for the U.S. armed forces. After the war, he and Helen moved to La Jolla, California, where he resumed writing children's books. He wrote 44 in all, including *The 500 Hats of Bartholomew Cubbins* (1938), *Horton Hatches the Egg* (1940), *How the Grinch Stole Christmas* and *The Cat in the Hat* (both 1957), *One Fish Two Fish Red Fish Blue Fish* and *Green Eggs and Ham* (both 1960) and *The Lorax* (1971).

The Cat in the Hat was written in response to a challenge from a publishing executive to create a popular reading primer using a vocabulary of only 225 words. The book was an immediate success and became the prototype for Dr. Seuss' best-selling Random House series, Beginner Books, in which he made reading fun by combining engaging stories, bizarre illustrations and playful sounds to teach basic reading skills.

Geisel had no children of his own. He attributed his rapport with youngsters to his early decision to "be a child" all his life, and he approached them with frankness and a healthy respect for their fantasies. "A person's a person no matter how small," he said. "Children want the same things we want. To laugh, to be challenged, to be entertained and delighted."

Among other distinctions, Geisel is credited with inventing the word "nerd." The Merriam-Webster dictionary says the word originated as "a creature in the children's book *If I Ran the Zoo* (1950) by Dr. Seuss (Theodor Geisel)."

In 1984, Geisel received a Pulitzer Prize "for his special contribution over nearly half a century to the education and enjoyment of America's children and their parents." His final book, *Oh, the Places You'll Go!* (1990), offered encouragement to the young as they set out on the journey of life. A best-seller, the book became a popular graduation gift.

Geisel also worked in film and television. With animator Chuck Jones, he produced Peabody Award-winning TV adaptations of *How the Grinch Stole Christmas* in 1966 and *Horton Hears a Who* in 1970, and wrote the lyrics to the songs for both programs. He received an award from the International Animated Cartoon Festival for the 1972 TV version of *The Lorax*, and won Emmys for four specials he produced between 1975 and 1982.

After Helen Geisel's death in 1967, Geisel married Audrey Diamond. Geisel himself died September 24, 1991, in La Jolla. At the time of his passing, his books had sold more than 200 million copies. In 2000, a Seuss-themed musical, *Seussical*, ran on Broadway. Later, Hollywood made live-action film versions of *How the Grinch Stole Christmas*, with Jim Carrey in the title role, and *The Cat in the Hat*, with Mike Myers as the Cat.

The Design

With the Dr. Seuss stamp, the portrait came first. Art director Carl Herrman chose a color photograph of the subject as a mature man, with gray hair and beard, that was taken by the Associated Press when Geisel visited Dallas, Texas, to deliver a speech April 3, 1987.

But the design needed more than just a face to tell the Dr. Seuss story. It needed some reference to his work. Herrman educated himself about the author by visiting his local library in Carlsbad, California, and borrowing

every Dr. Seuss book in the collection.

Next, Herrman went to the Geisel Library in La Jolla, a 25-minute drive from his home. The building, a spectacular six-story stepped tower that was built in the 1960s and renamed in 1995 for

The photograph of Theodor Seuss Geisel shown on the stamp was made by the Associated Press April 3, 1987, in Dallas, where Geisel was on a speaking trip.

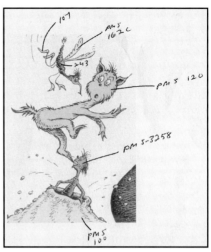

Shown here are reproductions of two pages from Dr. Seuss's works from which Carl Herrman borrowed original art for the stamp. The title page of Oh Say Can You Say? *shows the Glotz, which Herrman flopped, or reversed. The illustration from* I Had Trouble in Getting to Solla Sollew *depicts the book's hero, the anonymous "young fellow," being tormented by the Skritz and the Skrink. The numbers added by Herrman are of the PMS colors that had to be matched to accurately represent the pictures in the books.*

Theodor and Audrey Geisel, houses the Mandeville Special Collections Library, which has custody of the Dr. Seuss papers, notebooks, sketch pads and original drawings.

"I met with the person in charge and was astounded at what she was able to provide for me," Herrman said. "There were the mechanicals that Geisel prepared for the printer, the black-and-white pen-and-ink drawings with no color — the publisher would add it — and the original tissues with his notations on them.

"Whatever I decided to use, I could scan directly into the computer and add the color myself. That's much better than shooting the art from the pages of a book where the color is screened and perhaps not in perfect register."

Herrman prepared a working design to show to CSAC, in which he surrounded the head-and-shoulders photograph of Geisel with six of his characters: the Cat in the Hat; the Grinch; the Glotz from *Oh Say Can You Say?* (1979); and the Skritz, the anonymous "young fellow" and the Skrink, three characters from *I Had Trouble in Getting to Solla Sollew* (1965). He chose and arranged the artwork so that the characters not only were posing with Geisel, but interacting with him.

"I flopped [reversed] the Glotz, which was teetering on some wobbly blue pilings, so he would be looking right into Dr. Seuss's eyeglasses, as if he was meant to be there," Herrman said. "I found the three characters from the other book, the hero being tormented by the Skritz and the Skrink. It filled up the space and left a lovely amount of white space.

"The Grinch looks as if he is teasing Dr. Seuss by pulling on his bow tie. And the Cat in the Hat had to be there, too. He seems to be looking over Dr. Seuss's shoulder admiring the whole gang and being very pleased with himself."

Herrman had considered his layout only "a quick first attempt to see how this worked," but CSAC "loved the interaction," he said, and he made no changes in the characters or their relationship to their creator. Nor did he commission an illustrator to make a painting of Geisel based on the photograph, as he had intended to do.

"The photo was nice and sharp, and the committee said 'No, leave it that way. A photo of him works better as a contrast to his drawings,' " Herrman said. Because the original print had an excess of yellow and showed Geisel with a very ruddy complexion, Dodge Color, the company that does prepress stamp work for the Postal Service, electronically moderated the tones.

However, a comparison of the actual stamp with its reproduction in the Postal Service's *USA Philatelic* catalog — made from the same electronic file — shows that the stamp printer made Geisel's face considerably darker than the designer had intended it to be.

Herrman placed the name "THEODOR SEUSS GEISEL" in Futura Bold capitals in a red band across the bottom of the stamp, with the first and last names in yellow and the middle name, "SEUSS," in white for emphasis. "USA 37," in black, is in the upper right corner.

The addition of a header, or decorative top selvage, to the pane was a late decision. Its centerpiece is the author's hand-drawn "Dr. Seuss" from his books' title pages, in colors that shade from dark blue on the left to red on the right. Around the words swim four creatures from the title page of *One Fish Two Fish Red Fish Blue Fish*, while a fifth fish, the blue one, smiles from the selvage in the lower right corner.

"It was a lot of fun," Herrman said. "I was able to get the original art for this, too. Everything fit, but the blue fish was like one fish too many, so I slipped him in at the bottom. It was as if, 'Oops, we made

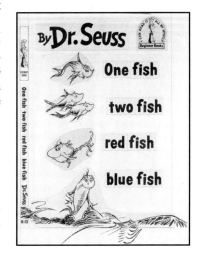

This is the "mechanical," or pasted-up sheet, for the cover of One Fish Two Fish Red Fish Blue Fish *that Geisel sent to the printer. Prominently featured are the five fish images that Herrman borrowed for the selvage of the Dr. Seuss stamp pane.*

a mistake, we forgot one of the fish — oh, there it is!' "

In addition to the four standard process colors, the printer used two self-colors, a line red and line blue, to print the stamps and selvage art.

Varieties

Shortly after the stamp was issued, a Colorado collector purchased a pane with no die cuts. He sold the pane to Colorado dealer Shayne Clinard, who notified *Linn's Stamp News*. Clinard said the same collector returned to his store several days later and sold him another pane with the same error.

First-Day Facts

Angelo Wider, manager of finance administration for USPS, dedicated the stamp in a ceremony at the Geisel Library.

Also participating were Dennis P. Smith, executive director of the San Diego Council on Literacy; Marsha A. Chandler, acting chancellor of UC San Diego; Carl Herrman, the stamp's art director and designer; Al Iniguez, USPS vice president for Pacific Area operations; and John E. Platt, the Postal Service's San Diego District manager.

For the 33¢ Cat in the Hat stamp of 1999, Dr. Seuss Enterprises declined to license the use of the Cat or of Dr. Seuss's name for cachets. This time, the firm decided to award the rights for a cachet, without cost, only to the American First Day Cover Society, a non-profit organization.

Stamp Fulfillment Services offered uncacheted first-day covers of the Dr. Seuss stamp for sale for 75¢.

37¢ UNITED STATES AIR FORCE ACADEMY

Date of Issue: April 1, 2004

Catalog Number: Scott 3838

Colors: magenta, yellow, cyan, dark blue (PMS 273), orange (PMS 135), purple (PMS 272)

First-Day Cancel: Colorado Springs, Colorado

First-Day Cancellations: 134,263

Format: Panes of 20, horizontal, 4 across, 5 down. Gravure printing cylinders printing 360 stamps per revolution (30 across, 12 around) manufactured by Armotek Industries.

Gum Type: self-adhesive

Scrambled Indicia: falcon silhouette

Overall Stamp Size: 1.56 by 0.99 inches; 39.62 by 25.14mm

Pane Size: 7.25 by 5.94 inches; 184.15 by 150.87mm

Perforations: 10¾ (die-cut simulated perforations) (Comco custom rotary die cutter)

Selvage Markings: "© 2003/USPS" ".37/x20/$7.40" "PLATE/POSITION" and diagram.

Back Markings: Universal Product Code (UPC) "455600" in 4 locations.

Photographer: Philip Handleman of Birmingham, Michigan

Designer, Art Director and Typographer: Phil Jordan of Falls Church, Virginia

Modeler: Donald H. Woo of Sennett Security Products, Chantilly, Virginia

Stamp Manufacturing: Stamps printed for Sennett Security Products by American Packaging Corporation, Columbus, Wisconsin, on Rotomec 4 gravure press. Stamps finished by Unique Binders of Fredericksburg, Virginia.

Quantity Ordered: 60,000,000

Cylinder Number Detail: 1 set of 6 cylinder numbers preceded by the letter S in selvage above or below each corner stamp

Cylinder Number Combination Reported: S111111

Paper Supplier: Mactac

Tagging: phosphored paper

The Stamp

On April 1, the Postal Service issued a 37¢ stamp commemorating the 50th anniversary of the establishment of the United States Air Force Academy near Colorado Springs, Colorado, and featuring a dramatic photograph of the institution's cadet chapel.

The stamp was the third within a decade to honor one of the nation's three major armed forces academies. In 1995 USPS issued a 32¢ commemorative for the 150th anniversary of the U.S. Naval Academy at Annapolis, Maryland, and in 2002 it marked the 200th anniversary of the U.S. Military Academy at West Point, New York, with a 34¢ stamp.

The three stamps technically violated Item 11 of the Citizens' Stamp Advisory Committee's criteria for stamp subject selection, as amended, which reads: "Requests for commemoration of universities and other institutions of higher education shall be considered only for stamped cards and only in connection with the 200th anniversaries of their founding."

However, CSAC decided that the service academies occupy a category of their own, unlike ordinary colleges and universities, and that as the principal producer of officers for the armed forces, they merit commemorative stamps on significant anniversaries.

American Packaging Corporation printed the Air Force Academy stamp by the gravure process for Sennett Security Products. It was distributed in panes of 20.

On April 1, 1954, President Dwight D. Eisenhower signed a congressional bill that established the U.S. Air Force Academy. Such an institution had been advocated by aviation leaders for some 40 years. Momentum grew after 1948, when the armed forces were unified in a cabinet-level Department of Defense and an Air Force separate from the Army was created.

James Forrestal, the first secretary of defense, appointed a panel to recommend a general method of education for the Army, Navy and Air Force. It was co-chaired by Eisenhower, then president of Columbia University, and Robert L. Sterns, president of the University of Colorado. The board reported in 1950 that expanding the older service academies at West Point and Annapolis would not meet the needs of the Air Force.

Following congressional authorization of the Air Force Academy in 1954, Secretary of the Air Force Harold E. Talbott named a commission to help him choose a site for the new institution. A total of 580 possible sites in 45 states was reduced to three, from which Talbott selected the site in Colorado.

The first class was sworn in July 11, 1955, at a temporary location at

Lowry Air Force Base near Denver. (The author of this book, then an Air Force sergeant, was an instructor in the intelligence technical training school at Lowry, which was one of the units that had to vacate the base to make room for the academy.) This first class moved to the Colorado Springs location August 29, 1958, and graduated the following spring, in June 1959.

Women were admitted in June 1976. Under present federal law, total annual enrollment at the academy is limited to 4,000 men and women, the same restriction that applies to enrollments at the two other major service academies.

More than 34,000 men and women have graduated from the academy since its establishment, and more than half of those who received USAF commissions remain on active duty. The academy has produced a Medal of Honor winner, Captain Lance P. Sijan, who died in North Vietnam in 1968; more than 325 general officers; 32 astronauts; two combat aces; and numerous Rhodes Scholars, Guggenheim Fellows and National Science Foundation Fellows.

Each year, thousands of people visit the academy. Many come to see the chapel, which received the 25-Year Award of the American Institute of Architects in 1996. Done in expressionist modern style, it has been called one of the icons in American ecclesiastical architecture and is said to be Colorado's number one man-made tourist attraction.

The aluminum, glass and steel structure was designed by Walter A. Netsch Jr. of Skidmore, Owings and Merrill of Chicago, Illinois, built at a cost of $3.5 million and completed in 1962. It features 17 spires 150 feet in height, massed like a phalanx of fighter jets shooting vertically into the sky. There is no significance to the number 17, according to the academy's Web site: "Original designs were judged to be too expensive, so changes were made, among them a reduction in the number of spires. The changes did not alter the basic design of the chapel."

The building contains separate chapels for Protestant, Catholic and Jewish cadets, plus two all-faiths worship rooms.

The Design

The horizontally arranged commemorative-size stamp reproduces a photograph of the chapel against a violet sky crossed by four parallel white lines representing the contrails of high-flying USAF jets. It was designed by Phil Jordan, a Postal Service art director who specializes in stamps featuring aviation and space subjects.

"Early in the formative stages, Philip Handleman contacted me about a stamp idea he had unrelated to the Air Force Academy," Jordan said. "I asked whether he had some photos. He didn't, but was planning a personal trip out there and said he would take some."

Handleman, of Birmingham, Michigan, is a pilot, air-show performer and prolific aviation writer, editor and photographer. In 1997, his photograph of the Thunderbirds, the precision flying team, was featured on a Jordan-designed 32¢ stamp commemorating the 50th anniversary of the Air Force. His trip to the academy became the first of at least four he would take there on his own in 2002 as he became absorbed in the stamp project.

"I can't say enough nice things about Philip," Jordan said. "He went to one hell of a lot of trouble and personal expense just to be a part of the stamp."

Handleman, in a Veterans' Day 2004 talk to military reservists in the Postal Service, explained that his commitment "evolved in the aftermath of the September 11, 2001, attacks with a personal quest of mine to bolster the spirit and strengthen the resolve of everyone who clings to the belief that freedom offers humankind the best chance to realize its full potential."

In the cadet chapel, he continued, "the American values of tolerance, pluralism and universality conspicuously manifest themselves. I fervently hope that the 60 million stamps emblazoned with this image, when affixed to envelopes sent to the far corners of the globe, will serve as a reminder that an American service academy has as its centerpiece a religious facility whose sanctuaries are open to the prayers of every faith."

Each time Handleman visited the campus, he was joined by a designated escort, Master Sergeant Ken Carter of the academy staff, who helped him in his search for subjects, angles and lighting conditions. Handleman

Phil Jordan created these two designs using Philip Handleman photographs of the chapel with the academy's statue honoring the Tuskeegee Airmen of World War II in the foreground. The vertically arranged photograph shows a DeHavilland Twin Otter that went aloft at Handleman's request to test the feasibility of showing a bomber or fighter plane in a flyover at 1,000 feet, the lowest permitted altitude. The test showed that a plane in the picture would have been only a speck at stamp size, and the idea was dropped.

Jordan developed these design concepts from Handleman photographs of the chapel with a Republic F-105, one of the academy's aircraft displays, in the foreground and the Rocky Mountains in the background.

shot "a few thousand" images, he told *The Yearbook,* of the academy's icons — mostly of the chapel. He and Carter worked under difficult conditions; the building was undergoing "tons of restorative work, inside and outside," Handleman said, "and it was a daily struggle to try to get a clean shot without construction workers, cranes and scaffolding in the way."

Jordan reviewed Handleman's color slides as they arrived at his studio and narrowed the field to a few of the most promising. He worked up these as stamp designs, including some images of the chapel with other objects in the foreground, such as the academy's statue honoring the Tuskegee Airmen of World War II and a Republic F-105, one of the institution's permanent aircraft displays. "It became clear to me, as well as the [CSAC] Design Subcommittee, that a good photo of the chapel alone would do the job," Jordan said.

However, he and Handleman wanted an element in the picture that spoke of aviation, and felt that an Air Force fighter or bomber in flight over the chapel would be just the thing. They suspected, however, that a plane flying at the minimum-allowed altitude — 1,000 feet above the highest surface on the campus — would be too small to "read" at stamp size. No lower-altitude flyover would be permitted, even for a postage stamp.

As a test, Handleman persuaded academy officials to send the school's largest aircraft, a DeHavilland Twin Otter used for the cadets' parachute jumps, on a flight over the chapel at the prescribed altitude while he photographed it. "We worked out a system by which Ken would call the control tower from his cell phone as we stood down in the Honor Court, and the tower would relay our requests to the aircraft," Handleman said.

The resulting photographs confirmed what they had feared. When the photos were reduced, the Twin Otter was merely a speck. There was no point in asking for a bomber or fighter plane to "pose" over the chapel, and the flyover idea was abandoned.

The chapel photograph chosen for the stamp — the favorite of everyone involved in the decision — was made from ground level, roughly 50 feet from the southeast corner of the building, at sunrise on a summer morning. Handleman used a handheld Nikon camera body with an F100 wide-angle zoom lens, a low f-stop and $^1/_{125}$ second shutter speed.

"The colors are natural," he said. "I was fascinated by the purplish glow against the glass wall and, at the base, the amber tone against the granite.

"The purple carried over into the sky. If the top part of the original image hadn't been cropped for the stamp, you would see the frame going higher and higher into the morning sky, and the pronounced purple tone turn into blue and darker blue."

Jordan was reluctant, however, to give up the idea of showing a plane over a chapel, and tried to accomplish it electronically. From Handleman's portfolio, he selected several shots of the Northrop Grumman B-2 Spirit stealth bomber, with its distinctive flying-wing configuration, taken at air shows. "I tried to combine some of Philip's B-2 photos with his chapel photo," Jordan said. "[Computer artist] Gretchen Maxwell did the combos for me, using Photoshop software. While they looked real, there were too many problems for it to work well, and we discarded it as a serious solution.

"It became obvious to all of us that the chapel photo was enough to symbolize the institution. I tried to use colored rules under the type to suggest the class-coding by color that the academy uses, but it was a stretch. Finally, after trying a number of type arrangements, I hit on one that pleased me and the subcommittee — but it still lacked something 'aerial.'

"I stumbled on the concept of contrails to symbolize the four under-graduate classes and suggest high-altitude planes without specifically showing a plane. Philip agreed to having his photo altered, and Gretchen added the contrails. It worked!"

The contrails separate the words "United States Air Force Academy," in orange and white, and the dates "1954-2004," in dark blue, in the upper left quadrant. "USA 37," in orange, is in the upper right. Jordan chose a font called Agfa Rotis Serif for the words and Times New Roman for the

After Jordan chose Handleman's close-up view of the chapel for the stamp design, he created several versions in which he electronically added one of the photographer's pictures of a B-2 stealth bomber in flight. "While they looked real, there were too many problems for it to work well, and we discarded it as a serious solution," Jordan said. These designs also show a variety of type treatments and Jordan's attempt to use yellow, red, light blue and dark blue lines under the type to suggest the academy's practice of coding classes by color.

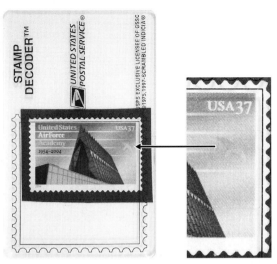

The stamp's "Scrambled Indicia," visible only through a special decoder, is a falcon, mascot of the Air Force Academy, in the sky on the right side.

numerals. The printer employed three process colors and three PMS colors to produce the stamp; no black ink was used.

The stamp incorporates "Scrambled Indicia," a patented process by which an image is hidden in the design and can be seen only by using a special acrylic decoder sold by the Postal Service. It is the silhouette of a flying falcon, the Academy mascot, designed by Jordan and printed by the magenta cylinder on the right side below the denomination. (The decoder must be positioned at right angles to the design for the image to be visible.)

USPS has a contractual agreement with Graphic Security Systems Corporation of Lake Worth, Florida, to use Scrambled Indicia on three stamp issues annually. Hidden images are primarily intended to provide additional security against counterfeiting, but USPS also considers them a bonus feature for stamp collectors and young people who might become collectors.

First-Day Facts

William T. Johnstone, an Air Force veteran and secretary of the USPS Board of Governors, dedicated the stamp in a ceremony in the Honor Court on the academy campus in Colorado Springs.

Also participating were Lieutenant General John Rosa, superintendent of the academy, and Duane Boyle, its chief of program development and command architect. Lieutenant Colonel Lori Salgado was master of ceremonies.

For a limited time, Stamp Fulfillment Services sold uncacheted first-day covers of the stamp for 75 cents.

37¢ HENRY MANCINI

Date of Issue: April 13, 2004

Catalog Number: Scott 3839

Colors: pink, magenta, yellow, cyan, black, gray (PMS 430)

First-Day Cancel: Los Angeles, California

First-Day Cancellations: 88,747

Format: Panes of 20, horizontal, 4 across, 5 down. Gravure printing cylinders printing 360 stamps per revolution (30 across, 12 around) manufactured by Armotek Industries.

Gum Type: self-adhesive

Overall Stamp Size: 1.56 by 0.99 inches; 39.62 by 25.14mm

Pane Size: 7.25 by 5.94 inches; 184.15 by 150.87mm

Perforations: 10¾ (die-cut simulated perforations) (Comco custom rotary die cutter)

Selvage Inscription: "THE PINK PANTHER and associated marks and characters™ &/©2003 UNITED ARTISTS CORPORATION. All rights reserved."

Selvage Markings: "© 2003/USPS." "37/x 20/$7.40." "PLATE/POSITION" and diagram.

Back Markings: On selvage liner: Universal Product Code (UPC) "455800" in 4 locations. On stamp liner: "Henry Mancini (1924-1994) was one of/the most successful composers in the/history of television and film and also a/popular pianist and conductor. He won/20 Grammys and 4 Oscars; his albums/have sold more than 30 million copies."

Artist: Victor Stabin of Jim Thorpe, Pennsylvania

Designer, Art Director and Typographer: Carl Herrman of Carlsbad, California

Modeler: Donald H. Woo of Sennett Security Products, Chantilly, Virginia

Stamp Manufacturing: Stamps printed for Sennett Security Products by American Packaging Corporation, Columbus, Wisconsin, on Rotomec 4 gravure press. Stamps finished by Unique Binders of Fredericksburg, Virginia.

Quantity Ordered: 80,000,000	
Cylinder Number Detail: 1 set of 6 cylinder numbers preceded by the letter S in selvage above or below each corner stamp	
Cylinder Number Combination Reported: S111111	
Paper Supplier: Mactac	
Tagging: phosphored paper	

The Stamp

On April 13, in Los Angeles, California, the Postal Service issued a stamp honoring Henry Mancini, a composer whose songs and themes for films and television programs are known around the world. The date was three days before the 80th anniversary of his birth.

Mancini, who wrote comfortably in a variety of musical styles, won 20 Grammy Awards for his recordings and four Academy Awards for his movie music. Had he been eligible, he doubtless would have been depicted on a stamp in the Legends of American Music series, which ran from 1993 to 1999 and comprised 93 varieties and 80 designs in 14 musical categories, including film music. But when the series was current, Mancini had not been deceased for the minimum 10 years that would have qualified him for stamp honors. The same situation applied to conductor Leonard Bernstein and songwriter Irving Berlin, both of whom passed the 10-year mark and were pictured on commemorative stamps after the Legends series was concluded.

The stamp, a self-adhesive, was printed by the gravure process by American Packaging Corporation for Sennett Security Products and distributed in panes of 20. A paragraph of text about Mancini appears on the back of each stamp's liner paper.

Postmaster General John E. Potter unveiled the design August 16, 2003, at the 2003 Mancini Musicale at the University of California at Los Angeles. On hand were Virginia (Ginny) Mancini, the composer's wife; actor-director Clint Eastwood, who received the 2003 "Hank" Award from the Henry Mancini Institute for distinguished service to American music; and jazz trumpeter, composer and producer Quincy Jones, who presented the award.

Enrico Nicola Mancini was born to Italian immigrant parents April 16, 1924, in Cleveland, Ohio. His given name was Anglicized to Henry at an early age. He was raised in West Aliquippa, Pennsylvania, where he was taught to play the piccolo by his father, took formal flute and piano lessons, and began writing music arrangements on his own. He met famed bandleader Benny Goodman and, with his encouragement, entered New York's Julliard School of Music on a scholarship at age 17.

His education was interrupted the next year when he was drafted into the Army Air Corps and assigned to a military band led by Norman Leyden. After World War II, he returned to New York, where Tex Beneke, leader of the reorganized Glenn Miller Orchestra, hired him as a pianist.

In 1947, Mancini married Ginny O'Connor, a singer with the band whose audition he had accompanied on the piano. They moved to Burbank, California, where he found work performing, composing and arranging music. Five years later, he wrote music for an Abbott and Costello film, *Lost in Alaska*, which led to more assignments, including arranging for *The Glenn Miller Story* (1954). One of his earliest complete scores was for *Man Afraid* in 1957.

The following year, he wrote a Latin rock score for Orson Welles' *Touch of Evil* and composed the music for *Peter Gunn*, a television drama produced and directed by Blake Edwards. His jazzy theme for the stylish film noir private-eye series became a pop standard, and it remains familiar today, long after the TV series itself has been largely forgotten. Mancini's first record album, music from *Peter Gunn*, sold more than one million copies, won Grammys for best arrangement and as album of the year, and made Mancini a recording star. His albums today have combined sales of more than 30 million copies.

From the 1950s to the early 1990s, Mancini wrote complete scores for more than 70 films. He collaborated with Blake Edwards on several of these movies, notably *Breakfast at Tiffany's* (1961), which won two Oscars, for best song — *Moon River*, with lyrics by Johnny Mercer — and best score. His other two Oscars also came for his work with Edwards: the title song to *Days of Wine and Roses* (1962) and the musical score for *Victor/Victoria* (1982). Other Mancini-Edwards film collaborations were the long-running *Pink Panther* series that began in 1964, *The Great Race* (1965), *Darling Lili* (1970) and *10* (1979). His films with other directors included *Charade* (1963), a thriller in which a rare stamp is the key to the plot; *Dear Heart* (1964); and *Wait Until Dark* (1967). His incidental music for *Hatari!* (1962) produced a surprise hit, *Baby Elephant Walk*. Mancini's TV theme credits include *Mr. Lucky, Newhart, Remington Steele, The Thorn Birds,* and *Hotel*.

Mancini died of pancreatic cancer June 14, 1994. His legacy continues through the Henry Mancini Award, presented by the American Society of Composers, Authors and Publishers each year to a contributor to film or television music, and the Henry Mancini Institute, a nonprofit organization based in Los Angeles that was established in 1997 to honor its namesake, provide comprehensive professional training for emerging musicians and conduct community outreach programs.

Ginny Mancini viewed the stamp as more than a commemoration of Henry Mancini's career. "For me, this stamp is a marketing tool for arts education programs — music education, in particular," she told *Playback*, ASCAP's online magazine. "Frankly, if [Mancini] hadn't had music education as a child, he'd never have ended up on a postage stamp, and that's why I get on my soapbox all the time."

The Design

To illustrate the stamp, Carl Herrman, art director for the project, first turned to Michael Deas, whose strikingly lifelike portraits have graced a dozen U.S. commemoratives beginning with the Marilyn Monroe and Tennessee Williams stamps of 1995. Deas found a photographic reference that suited him, showing Mancini in a tuxedo, and made a pencil sketch.

"Unfortunately for Michael, this came right after I had presented the Dr. Seuss stamp design to the [Citizens' Stamp Advisory] Committee," Herrman said. "They loved its interactivity of the background and the portrait that showed what the man did, what his achievements were. When they saw Michael's sketch of just a guy in a tux with no indication of music or a piano or anything else, their reaction was, 'Why can't you do something like you did with Dr. Seuss, and show some of the interesting things Henry Mancini has done?'"

Herrman then turned to a new artist, Victor Stabin. The art director had seen a Stabin portrait of Charles Dickens showing the writer with a whirlwind of manuscripts and realized that it was the kind of artistic treatment that he and CSAC were looking for.

"Victor is a fine-arts painter who also happens to be a genius at image manipulation with the computer," Herrman said. "He first paints a picture, then does things with it electronically. He was thrilled with the assignment and instantly rattled off more than anyone should spontaneously know about Mancini, including about half his songs."

Working with photographs of the composer provided by PhotoAssist, the Postal Service's research firm, Stabin developed several different design approaches incorporating bars of music and props that evoked

In this Victor Stabin design, a smiling Mancini sits at the piano surrounded by reminders of three of his best-known compositions. A lounging Pink Panther holds up the piano lid, wine and roses sit on the keys and Moon River ripples in the background.

These two Stabin design approaches are based on the photograph of Mancini that was the basis for the finished stamp. One incorporates weblike musical staffs and the Moon River and Pink Panther props, while the other, also with staffs, shows a close-up of the composer against a cloud-filled blue sky.

three of Mancini's best-known compositions, *Moon River* and the themes from *The Pink Panther* and *Days of Wine and Roses.* The solution ultimately chosen by Herrman and CSAC shows Mancini in a conducting pose against a white background that suggests a movie screen. The composer's arms and head cast shadows on the screen, and the silhouetted heads of singles and couples across the bottom of the picture represent the audience. A dark frameline at the top and sides, bleeding to the tips of the simulated perforations, completes the cinema-theater effect.

Stabin painted the picture in oil on board, using a reference photo supplied by the Center for Motion Picture Study of the Academy of Motion Picture Arts and Sciences. The date and place it was taken are unknown. It shows the composer conducting an unseen orchestra in a studio, with a microphone suspended in front of him. He wears a turtleneck sweater and has a wristwatch on his left wrist. There is no baton in the photo, but to clarify the action on the stamp, Stabin inserted one in Mancini's right hand.

It was Herrman's idea to add two elements to complete the design. One was the cartoon figure of the Pink Panther; the other was a list of some of the films and TV shows that were scored by the composer.

The art director first placed the Panther on the movie screen itself, peer-

Victor Stabin based his painting of Mancini on this photograph of the composer conducting an unseen orchestra in a studio. (Source: Center for Motion Picture Study).

Carl Herrman made a preliminary list of 16 films and TV shows scored by Mancini, choosing some on the basis of their letter count, and superimposed the list over the composer's arm, as shown here. The list was revised by Terrence McCaffrey and finalized after a few changes requested by the Mancini family were made. It was placed behind Mancini's arm to suggest credits rolling past on a movie screen. United Artists requested a different pose for the Pink Panther in the lower left corner, saying that the pose in this design made the Panther appear to be walking away from the audience and leaving the theater.

ing out of the frame at the audience. CSAC thought the character in that location was too intrusive. Herrman then put him in the lower left corner, with his back to the screen. But United Artists Corporation, which holds the rights to the character, vetoed the pose.

"They said it looked almost as if he was walking away from the audience and leaving the theater," Herrman said. "They wanted him in what they thought was a more positive situation, standing and pointing to Mancini. I made the change, but I liked my original much better."

Herrman drew up a preliminary list of 16 of Mancini's works, choosing a variety of title lengths for visual interest. His list included some relatively obscure Mancini films, including *Abbott and Costello Lost in Alaska, Creature from the Black Lagoon, The Glass Menagerie, W.C. Fields and Me* and *Mommie Dearest*. He set the titles in gray Europa capitals and ran them from top to bottom on the right side of the design, over the composer's outstretched left arm. CSAC later suggested that the titles be placed behind Mancini, like credits rolling past on the screen.

Terrence McCaffrey, manager of stamp development and a devoted movie fan, told Herrman that the selection of titles would have to be approved by Ginny Mancini. "I said, 'I can't go to the Mancini family with a list that includes *Abbott and Costello Lost in Alaska* and *Creature From the Black Lagoon* rather than some of the great ones,' " McCaffrey said. "So I made another list with some of the better known titles, understanding that the family would have the final call."

McCaffrey's list, which replaced Herrman's in the working design, consisted of *Breakfast at Tiffany's, Days of Wine and Roses, Charade, Peter Gunn, The Pink Panther, Victor/Victoria, The Glenn Miller Story, Darling Lili, The Great Race, Experiment in Terror, Two For The Road, Dear Heart* and *Mr. Lucky*. He took the design to Ginny Mancini's penthouse on

Los Angeles' Wilshire Boulevard, where he met with the composer's wife and two of their children, Felice and Christopher.

"Ginny was very excited about it. She thought the concept, with the screen and credits and the Pink Panther, was brilliant," McCaffrey recalled. "I left the design with her and told her, 'This is the number of slots we have for the film and TV credits. Let me know what you want included on the final list.'"

McCaffrey pointed out to her that one of the films he had included, *Dear Heart*, was the story of two people, played by Glenn Ford and Geraldine Page, who meet at a postmasters' convention and fall in love, which gave it an appropriate postal connection. "She loved that," he said.

Soon afterward, McCaffrey received Ginny Mancini's final choices. He relayed the information to Herrman with instructions to drop *Darling Lili*, *Mr. Lucky* and *The Glenn Miller Story*, replace them with *Touch of Evil*, *Hatari!* and *The Thorn Birds*, and move *Two for the Road*, which was partly obscured by Mancini's arm, higher on the list. On April 9, 2003, McCaffrey met again with the composer's wife and received her approval of the finished design.

Herrman superimposed the name HENRY MANCINI on the composer's maroon sweater in dropout white Europa capitals. Some printers dislike dropping letters out of a process-color background because it requires close registration of the colors, so Herrman purposely made the letters "chunky," he said, to help American Packaging Corporation hold the edges. To no avail; the company decided on its own to outline the letters with a black line that would mask any slight misregistration.

Registration problems also interfered with a Postal Service attempt to fix a quirk in the design that some had considered undignified. In the stamp image that first was made public, the Pink Panther appears to be tickling Mancini under his right arm. Postal officials noticed this juxtaposition, changed the design electronically to create a small gap between the paw and the composer, and released the revised image in December 2003. However, on many specimens of the actual stamp, the colors that make up Mancini's sweater are slightly out of register, which is all that is needed to restore the contact and the "tickle."

Herrman purposely made the dropped-out letters of the name HENRY MANCINI on the composer's sweater "chunky," he said, to facilitate American Packaging Corporation's task of holding the edges of the process colors used to print the sweater. However, the printing firm made its job easier still by unilaterally deciding to outline the letters in black to mask any slight misregistration. Shown here are close-ups of the original artwork, with no outline on the letters, and the actual stamp, with the outline.

On the left is the image of the Pink Panther on the design of the Mancini stamp that was released to the public. The Panther is pointing to Mancini, but he is placed so closely to the composer that he appears to be tickling him under the arm. In December 2003, USPS released a revised design (right) in which the cartoon cat has been moved slightly to open a gap between paw and armpit. On the actual stamp, however, any slight misregistration of colors in Mancini's sweater causes the paw to again appear to be in contact with the composer.

Herrman placed the mandatory 2004 year date inside the dark frameline on the right, where it is virtually invisible.

Although Sennett Security Products and the Postal Service reported that five colors were used in the printing, there actually were six used, as indicated by the six-digit cylinder numbers in the pane selvage. The colors were process magenta, cyan and black; pink; gray; and the unreported sixth color, process yellow.

First-Day Facts

One of the most elaborate first-day events in many years was organized for the Mancini stamp, thanks in large part to Ginny Mancini, who oversaw the planning of an all-star tribute to her husband that accompanied the outdoor first-day ceremony at Music Center Plaza in Los Angeles and continued that evening at the Walt Disney Concert Hall.

Postmaster General John E. Potter dedicated the stamp. Participants in the ceremony included former U.S. senator and astronaut John Glenn, Henry Mancini's fellow Ohioan and long-time friend of the family; Ginny Mancini; the couple's daughter, singer Monica Mancini, who performed *The Star Spangled Banner*; and S. David Fineman, chairman of the USPS Board of Governors. The composer's work was performed by 100 student flutists from Los Angeles area schools led by Sir James Galway, one of the world's best known flutists, and the University of Southern California Marching Trojan Band, featuring the Pink Panther himself.

The concert that evening was hosted by John Glenn and Julie Andrews, the female star of *Darling Lili* and *Victor/Victoria*. Monica Mancini sang *Charade* and *Days of Wine and Roses* to open and close the event, and Patrick Williams, artistic director of the Henry Mancini Institute, directed the institute's alumni orchestra. James Galway and his wife Jeanne re-created a Mancini-Galway flute duet of Meredith Willson's *76 Trombones*

Postmaster General John E. Potter, the Pink Panther, Ginny Mancini and Senator John Glenn stand in front of a blowup of the Henry Mancini stamp at the April 13 first-day ceremony in Los Angeles. (USPS photo)

from a years-ago July 4 celebration in Washington, D.C. Other performers included Quincy Jones, Michael Feinstein, Stevie Wonder and John Williams.

For a limited time, Stamp Fulfillment Services sold uncacheted first-day covers of the Mancini stamp for 75¢.

37¢ AMERICAN CHOREOGRAPHERS
(4 DESIGNS)

Date of Issue: May 4, 2004

Catalog Numbers: Scott 3840-3843, stamps; 3843a, horizontal strip of 4

Colors: black, cyan, magenta, yellow, beige (PMS 7506), purple (PMS 2776)

First-Day Cancel: Newark, New Jersey

First-Day Cancellations: 270,129

Format: Pane of 20, horizontal, 4 across, 5 down. Offset printing plates printing 240 stamps per revolution (12 across, 20 around).

Gum Type: self-adhesive

Stamp Size: 1.56 by 0.99 inches; 39.625 by 25.146mm

Pane Size: 7.24 by 6.47 inches; 183.896 by 164.433mm

Perforations: 10¾ (die-cut simulated perforations) (IDC two-station die cutter)

Selvage Inscription: "AMERICAN CHOREOGRAPHERS" "Martha Graham is a registered trademark" "Alvin Alley is a trademark of Alvin Alley Dance Foundation, Inc." "The appellation *Agnes de Mille* belongs to de Mille Productions." "BALANCHINE is a trademark of The George Balanchine Trust."

54

Selvage Markings: "©2003/USPS." ".37/x20/$7.40." "PLATE/POSITION" and diagram.

Back Markings: Universal Product Code (UPC) "456000" in 4 locations on back of liner paper

Designer, Art Director and Typographer: Ethel Kessler of Bethesda, Maryland

Modeler: Joseph Sheeran of Ashton-Potter (USA) Ltd., Williamsville, New York

Stamp Manufacturing: Stamps printed by Ashton-Potter on a Mueller Martini A76 modified offset press. Stamps processed by Ashton-Potter.

Quantity Ordered: 57,000,000

Plate Number Detail: 1 set of 6 plate numbers preceded by the letter P in selvage below each bottom corner stamp

Plate Number Combination Reported: P111111

Paper Supplier: Paper Corporation of the United States/Glatfelter

Tagging: phosphored paper

The Stamps

On May 4, the Postal Service issued four se-tenant stamps honoring Alvin Ailey, George Balanchine, Agnes de Mille and Martha Graham, four distinguished American choreographers of the 20th century.

The project originated with a campaign by admirers of Balanchine for a stamp to mark his 100th birth year in 2004. "Peter Martins, director of the New York City Ballet, and numerous other luminaries were writing to us," recalled Terrence McCaffrey, manager of stamp development for USPS. "We also had received letters asking for stamps for Alvin Ailey and Martha Graham.

"We decided to explore the possibility of a set of stamps honoring those three, plus Agnes de Mille, who the experts told us was a powerhouse of choreography and would be a natural if we wanted to round it out to four."

The Citizens' Stamp Advisory Committee had followed a similar expansion process on two prior occasions. In 2000, CSAC satisfied a long-standing public demand by approving stamps for war heroes Audie Murphy and Sergeant Alvin York, then added two other subjects to create a Distinguished Soldiers block of four. Two years later the committee decided to honor journalists Nellie Bly and Ida M. Tarbell, and subsequently enlarged the issue into a block of four for Women in Journalism.

The self-adhesive American Choreographers stamps were printed by the offset process by Ashton-Potter (USA) Ltd. and distributed in panes of 20, four stamps across by five down. The varieties are arranged in horizontal strips rather than blocks. Each horizontal strip of four contains one of each variety, while each vertical column of five comprises stamps of the same design. A decorative top selvage, or header, bears the words "AMERICAN CHOREOGRAPHERS."

All four of the honored choreographers were recipients of the Kennedy Center Honors, considered the U.S. equivalent of knighthood in Great Britain or the French Legion of Honor.

Ailey was born January 5, 1931, near Waco, Texas, and his works often reflected his Texas roots, combining blues and gospel with ballet, modern dance, jazz, and African and Caribbean movements — different styles that made great demands on his dancers. He began studying with the Lester Horton Dance Theater in 1953 and became the company's choreographer  after Horton's death. He formed his own company, the Alvin Ailey Dance Theater, in 1958. His 1960 masterpiece *Revelations* brought the company international acclaim. Ailey received many honors, including the NAACP's Spingarn Medal and the United Nations Peace medal. He died December 1, 1989, in New York City.

"Perhaps the best known American choreographer in many parts of the world, Alvin Ailey helped to bridge the gap between modern dance and the general public in the United States and abroad," says the Kennedy Center's Web site.

George Balanchine was born Georgi Melitonovitch Balanchivadze in St. Petersburg, Russia, January 22, 1904, and graduated from that city's Imperial Theatre School. In 1933 he  came to the United States, where he co-founded the School of American Ballet in 1935 and the New York City Ballet in 1948. Called "the father of American ballet," Balanchine created more than 400 ballets, including a celebrated staging of Tchaikovsky's *Nutcracker* in 1954, and also worked in Broadway theater and the movies. He died April 30, 1983, at the age of 79.

He said of ballet, "The choreographer and the dancer must remember that they reach the audience through the eye — and the audience, in turn, must train itself to see what is performed upon the stage. It is the illusion created which convinces the audience, much as it is with the work of a magician. If the illusion fails, the ballet fails, no matter how well a program note tells the audience that it has succeeded."

Agnes de Mille was born September 18, 1905, in New York City, into a theatrical family that included motion-picture producer and director Cecil B. de Mille, her uncle. The Web site of the University of Southern California says of the school's 1926 alumna: "Few could imagine that the tiny woman with child-sized feet — older and heavier than most dancers, with holes in her tights and masses of uncontrollable red hair — would make history in the ballet world and become the queen of Broadway."

De Mille created her first ballet, *Black Ritual*, in 1940 after joining the American Ballet Theater. She was able to blend the language of classical ballet, the expressive quality of modern dance and the traditions of American folk dance; for example, her ballet *Rodeo* (1942), to the music of Aaron Copland, featured the movement of American cowboys.

She choreographed several now-legendary Broadway musicals, beginning with *Oklahoma!* (1943), using dance to advance the plot. Also an engaging writer, de Mille published several books, including two autobiographical volumes. She suffered a stroke in 1975, but continued to work until her death in New York City October 7, 1993.

A scene from *Oklahoma!*, showing the principal characters Laurey and Curly dancing, was shown on sheet and booklet stamps in the Legends of American Music series in 1993 (Scott 2722, 2769).

Martha Graham was the principal founder of modern dance in America and was named one of the 100 most important people of the 20th century by *Time* magazine. She described dance as the hidden language of the soul. "Every

This block of diamond-shaped stamps of 1978 celebrated four forms of American dance: ballet, theater, folk and modern.

dance is a kind of fever chart, a graph of the heart," she said. "… The instrument through which the dance speaks is also the instrument through which life is lived … the human body."

Graham was born near Pittsburgh, Pennsylvania, in May 1894, and began dancing at the age of 22. A decade later, she founded her own dance company, starring in productions that were distinguished by their sharp, angular movements and blunt gestures. Her last dance performance, at age 76, was in *Cortege of Eagles*. She continued to choreograph, teach and travel with her company until her death April 1, 1991, at the age of 96. Graham choreographed more than 180 works in her lifetime.

American dance first was postally commemorated in 1978 with a block of four diamond-shaped 13¢ stamps featuring four forms of dancing: ballet, theater, folk and modern (Scott 1749-1752). In 1998, American ballet was honored with a single 32¢ stamp (Scott 3237) and 20¢ picture postal card (Scott UX297).

The Designs

To create the designs, Postal Service art director Ethel Kessler enlisted the services of Paula Scher of New York City, a graphic designer and teacher who is well known for a style of decorative typography combined with imagery. Working with photographs of the four subjects provided by PhotoAssist, the Postal Service's research firm, Scher created four stamps with full-length or half-length images of the choreographers, set against pastel backgrounds of yellow, green, orange and blue and framed by heavy lettering. But Kessler was disappointed in the result.

"I felt that the graphic style took over and overwhelmed the unique individual choreography of each of these four people," she said. "The 37 [denomination] was so large, and the wording around the stamps — yes, it did make a frame, but it also was pretty intense." CSAC reacted to the designs in the same way, and Kessler asked Scher to try again.

In her second effort, the designer used the same images of the choreographers, but this time each image was in a distinc-

This was Paula Scher's first attempt to create a block of four stamps honoring the designated choreographers, using full-length or half-length images, set against pastel backgrounds and bordered by heavy typography. Art director Ethel Kessler "felt that the graphic style took over and overwhelmed the unique individual choreography of each of these four people," she said.

Scher's next effort incorporated the same images of the choreographers that were used in the first designs, but in distinctive colors, against white backgrounds and with enclosed strips of type over the images that CSAC members referred to as Band-Aids. The new design attempts were strikingly similar to the American Dance commemoratives of 1978, down to the same four colors used for the dancing figures.

tive color — blue, green, red-violet and orange — while the backgrounds were white inside black stamp margins. She superimposed on the dancers the words "American Choreographers" in enclosed strips, which CSAC members jokingly referred to as Band-Aids.

By coincidence, the revised design concepts were quite similar to the four diamond-shaped American Dance commemoratives of 1978, which also showed full-length dancing figures in blue, green, red-violet and orange against white backgrounds. "What I didn't want to do, 26 years later, was four more stamps about dance with the same colors against the same white backgrounds," Kessler said. "It just didn't make sense."

At this point, Kessler decided to take over the design job herself with the help of Greg Berger, whose private design firm shares office space with Kessler's in Bethesda, Maryland. Berger had assisted Kessler in previous stamp design projects and had received sole design credit for the Adoption stamp and picture postal card of 2000.

"I wanted to help people understand the distinctions among the choreographers," Kessler said. "I wanted to show the epitome of each person's work on his or her stamp.

"We did Martha Graham first. We had a portrait of her that looked great, and an image of her dancing, and put the two together. It was like the ultimate merging of the mind of the choreographer and the dancer! We wondered if it was possible to do the same thing with the others."

The result of their efforts was four commemorative-size stamps, horizontally arranged, with a common design style featuring a photographic portrait of the choreographer on the left and a photo representing the person's work on the right. The names of the choreographers, in dropped-out Frutiger capitals with a slight beige screen, are integrated into the design in curved or angled lines that complement the movement of the dancers in the photographs. The small, vertical "37 USA," tucked in the lower left

Judith Jamison, Alvin Ailey's successor as director of his dance company, urged that this portrait of Ailey be used on his stamp. "I said to her, 'He looks so angry!' " recalled Ethel Kessler. "Judith answered, 'But he WAS angry!' We compromised on a picture in which he has a milder expression."

or right corner, seems virtually an afterthought.

Alvin Ailey's picture on the stamp is a studio portrait made by Deborah Feingold in 1988, when Ailey was 57, and was one of three photos available for the purpose. One was furnished by Judith Jamison, a close associate of Ailey and his successor as director of the company, who urged Ethel Kessler to use it. "I said to her, 'He looks so angry!' " Kessler recalled. "Judith answered, 'But he WAS angry!' We compromised on a picture in which he has a milder expression."

To the right of the portrait, six dancers face the viewer, their faces lifted and arms upraised. The six are cropped from a photograph of a larger number performing a movement from Ailey's *Revelations*. They are Hope Boykin, Glenn A. Sims, Tina M. Williams, Linda-Denise Fisher-Harrell, Laura Rossini and Wendy Sasser. The photo was taken in 2000 by Paul Kolnick of New York City. In an earlier version of the design, Kessler used a different photo, a staged shot of three dancers leaping.

The photograph of Balanchine was made by his wife, the ballerina Tanaquil Le Clercq, whom he married in 1952. He was probably in his 50s when the picture was taken. The dance photo was made around 1970 by David Lindner of New York and shows Delia Peters, Bonita Borne and Karin von Aroldingen of the New York City Ballet, with their backs to the camera, performing in *Serenade*, the first ballet created in the United States by Balanchine and the first important work of ballet ever made for American dancers. The picture is cropped from a larger photo showing five dancers.

This early design for the Alvin Ailey stamp incorporated a photograph of three of the Ailey Company's dancers in a synchronized leap. In the photo, made by Andrew Eccles in 2001, the trio is not performing a particular work but simply is moving for the camera.

An early version of the Agnes de Mille stamp shows three dancing de Milles in photographer Gjon Mili's multiple exposure. In the final design, only two are shown.

The photo portrait of Agnes de Mille was found in a scrapbook owned by de Mille and now in the collection of the New York Public Library. No further information on it is available. The two dancing de Milles on the stamp are multiple exposures of the choreographer made by Gjon Mili in 1944; in an earlier version of the stamp design, Kessler displayed three images from the photographic print.

Martha Graham's portrait is from a photograph by Barbara Morgan, taken in 1935, the year Graham turned 41. The other photo on the stamp was made in 1940, also by Morgan, and shows Graham performing *Letter to the World*, a dance-drama based on the life and work of Emily Dickinson.

The picture demonstrates the dancer's remarkable grace and flexibility. She stands on her right leg, her body forward in a horizontal position, her left leg thrust backward, high above her waist. As *Linn's Stamp News* reader Harold Short pointed out, because the photo is cropped, the graceful sweeping line and flow of Graham's skirt on the right and bottom sides are not seen, which caused some viewers to mistakenly think that Graham was standing upright and the picture had been laid out sideways on the stamp.

Originally, Kessler planned to include the words "American Choreographer" in each design along with the subject's name. "I was hoping that

This is the full photograph of Martha Graham by Barbara Morgan that was cropped at top, right and bottom to fit in the stamp design. At first glance, some viewers mistakenly assumed that the picture was sideways on the stamp.

the type would actually dance across the stamps, in a way re-emphasizing the kind of choreography that these people did," she said. "But I think it kind of got in the way." In the end, she decided to limit the stamp typography to the names, and convey the fact that the subjects were American choreographers in the pane header. This simplified the designs, but it also resulted in a loss of information, Kessler conceded. "When people see the stamps on envelopes, are they going to know who Agnes de Mille is?" she asked rhetorically. "Creating a design that will be reduced to stamp size and still communicate effectively is always a balancing job."

Once the design style was determined, Kessler addressed the question of color. Her first plan was to make the choreographers' portraits black and white and set them off with framelines in four metallic inks, gold, silver, bronze and copper, that would be echoed in the shading of the dancers' photographs. However, CSAC's design subcommittee wanted color added. One of the members, Meredith Davis, pointed out that adding a different color background to each stamp would help emphasize the differences in the four dance styles. Accordingly, Kessler made the Balanchine background a pinkish lavender, shading into blue ("It seemed to me that classical ballet needed a gentle, beautiful color"). She used an almost aggressive red for Alvin Ailey ("His color needed to be intense"), a gold shade for Martha Graham and blue-green for Agnes de Mille.

Normally, panes of stamps incorporating four designs are laid out in blocks of four, but when Kessler tried this arrangement with her choreographers, the result looked "very jumpy," she said. "It was all over the place." Her solution was to reorganize the four varieties as horizontal strips and vertical columns.

Her original header design included a paragraph of text about each

Ethel Kessler's original header design contained a paragraph of text about each choreographer. These were eliminated in the final version. Instead of arranging the four designs in blocks on the pane, as shown here, she arranged them in horizontal strips of four so that each vertical column contained stamps of the same design.

choreographer, but the text was dropped in the final version, in which "AMERICAN CHOREOGRAPHERS" in curving black lines is set against the same words, in a different alignment, dropped out of a light purple tone. "The header shows movement, it shows something about light, and it's very calm, compared to the earlier efforts," Kessler said.

Ashton-Potter printed the stamps in the four standard process colors, plus beige and purple.

First-Day Facts

Linda A. Kingsley, USPS vice president for strategic planning, dedicated the stamps in a ceremony at the New Jersey Performing Arts Center's Victoria Theater in Newark, New Jersey.

Lawrence P. Goldman, president and chief executive officer of the Performing Arts Center, gave the welcome. Dr. Bob Lee, director of community affairs for WBLS Radio of New York City, was master of ceremonies. Also on hand were Agnes de Mille's son, Jonathan Prude, professor of history at Emory University; Sylvia Waters, former Alvin Ailey American Dance Theater company member and current artistic director of Ailey II; Marvin Preston, executive director, Martha Graham Dance; David Lindner of David Lindner Photography, New York City; and Newark Mayor Sharpe James.

The ceremony featured live performances by the School of American Ballet, Ailey II, the American Ballet Theater and Martha Graham Dance, showcasing the style of each of the honored choreographers.

For a limited time, Stamp Fulfillment Services sold sets of four uncacheted first-day covers for $3.

37¢ LEWIS AND CLARK BICENTENNIAL

Date of Issue: May 14, 2004

Catalog Number: Scott 3854

Colors: cyan, magenta, yellow, black, green (PMS 454), offset; dark green (PMS 5535), intaglio

First-Day Cancel: Astoria, Oregon; Atchison, Kansas; Great Falls, Montana; Hartford, Illinois; Ilwaco, Washington; Orofino, Idaho; Omaha, Nebraska; Pierre, South Dakota; Sioux City, Iowa; St. Charles, Missouri; Washburn, North Dakota

First-Day Cancellations: 384,382 (includes 37¢ Lewis and Clark Bicentennial prestige booklet)

Format: Panes of 20, horizontal, 4 across, 5 down. Offset and intaglio printing plates printing 180 stamps per revolution (12 across, 15 around). Also sold in uncut press sheets of 9 panes (3 across by 3 down).

Gum Type: self-adhesive

Overall Stamp Size: 1.56 by 0.98 inches; 39.62 by 24.89mm

Pane Size: 7.26 by 5.9 inches; 184.4 by 149.86mm

Uncut Press Sheet Size: 21¾ by 17¾ inches

Perforations: 10¾ (die-cut simulated perforations) (Heidelberg rotary die cutter)

Selvage Markings: "© 2003/USPS" ".37/x20/$7.40" "PLATE/POSITION" and diagram.

Back Markings: Universal Product Code (UPC) "455900" in 2 locations

Illustrator, Typographer and Designer: Michael J. Deas of Brooklyn Heights, New York

Art Director: Phil Jordan of Falls Church, Virginia

Modeler: Donald H. Woo of Sennett Security Products, Chantilly, Virginia

Stamp Manufacturing: Stamps printed for Sennett Security Products by Banknote Corporation of America, Browns Summit, North Carolina, on Roland 300 intaglio-offset press. Stamps finished by BCA.

Quantity Ordered: 62,200,000

Plate Number Detail: 1 set of 5 offset plate numbers and 1 intaglio plate number preceded by the letter S in selvage above or below each corner stamp

Plate Number Combination Reported: S11111-1

Paper Supplier: Paper Corporation of the United States/Spinnaker Coatings

Tagging: unphosphored paper; large block tagging covering stamps

37¢ LEWIS AND CLARK BICENTENNIAL PRESTIGE BOOKLET (2 DESIGNS)

Date of Issue: May 14, 2004

Price: $8.95

Catalog Numbers: Scott 3855-3856, single stamps; 3856a, horizontal or vertical pair; 3856b, booklet pane of 10; BK297, complete booklet

Colors: black, cyan, magenta, yellow, beige (PMS 454), offset; red (PMS 200), blue (PMS 288), intaglio

First-Day Cancel: Astoria, Oregon; Atchison, Kansas; Great Falls, Montana; Hartford, Illinois; Ilwaco, Washington; Orofino, Idaho; Omaha, Nebraska; Pierre, South Dakota; Sioux City, Iowa; St. Charles, Missouri; Washburn, North Dakota

First-Day Cancellations: 384,382 (includes 37¢ Lewis and Clark Bicentennial stamp)

Format: 32-page booklet of text and pictures, including 2 panes, each containing 10 stamps, vertical, 5 of each variety, in 2 horizontal rows of 5 stamps. Stamp panes are pages 3 and 30, backed by pages 4 and 29, respectively. Offset and intaglio printing plates printed 90 stamps, 6 across, 15 around.

Gum: self-adhesive

Overall Stamp Size: 1.105 by 1.44 inches; 28.067 by 36.576mm

Pane and Booklet Size: 6.8125 by 3.75 inches; 173.037 by 95.25mm

Perforations: 10½ by 10¾ (die-cut simulated perforations) (IDC 22-inch die cutter)

Selvage Markings: none

Cover Markings: On front: "LEWIS & CLARK/The Corps of Discovery/1804-1806." On back: "This 32 page/booklet also/contains twenty/37-cent stamps./$8.95." USPS logo and Universal Product Code (UPC) "0 15645 16646 2." Caption to accompany cover photograph.

Stamp Illustrator, Designer and Typographer: Michael Deas of Brooklyn Heights, New York

Art Director and Booklet Designer: Phil Jordan of Falls Church, Virginia

Modeler: Joseph Sheeran of Ashton-Potter (USA) Ltd., Williamsville, New York

Stamp Manufacturing: Stamps printed by Ashton-Potter on Stevens Variable Size Security Documents webfed 6-color offset, 3-color intaglio press. Covers and text printed by Sterling Sommer, Tonawanda, New York, on Heidelberg 840 offset press. Stamps and booklets processed by Ashton-Potter.

Quantity Ordered: 1,000,000 booklets (20,000,000 stamps)

Plate Number Detail: no plate numbers

Paper Supplier: Fasson/Glatfelter (stamps); Sappi Magnostar (cover and text)

Tagging: phosphored paper

The Stamps

On May 14, the Postal Service issued three 37¢ stamps commemorating the 200th anniversary of the westward expedition of the "Corps of Discovery" led by Captains Meriwether Lewis and William Clark.

The stamps had simultaneous first-day sales in 11 cities and towns in 11 states along the route taken by the explorers as they crossed the newly purchased Louisiana Territory on their way to the Pacific Ocean. The sites included Hartford, Illinois, and Astoria, Oregon, where the outbound trip began and ended.

Two of the three stamps are semijumbos, one depicting Lewis, the other Clark. They are in a prestige booklet containing 20 se-tenant stamps, 10 of each design. The third stamp is commemorative size and was distributed

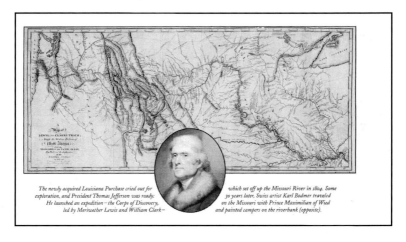

The newly acquired Louisiana Purchase cried out for exploration, and President Thomas Jefferson was ready. He launched an expedition – the Corps of Discovery, led by Meriwether Lewis and William Clark – *which set off up the Missouri River in 1804. Some 30 years later, Swiss artist Karl Bodmer traveled on the Missouri with Prince Maximilian of Wied and painted campers on the riverbank (opposite).*

LEWIS AND CLARK Like Gilbert and Sullivan or Currier and Ives, the names "Lewis and Clark" have entered the English language as a single phrase. Meriwether Lewis was a 26-year-old Army veteran of the western frontier when President Thomas Jefferson brought him to Washington in 1801 to serve as his personal secretary. They lived together in the President's House "like two mice in a church," according to Jefferson. There Lewis learned more about the President's wide-ranging interests, especially his curiosity about the West.

When Jefferson was ready to launch an expedition to the Pacific Ocean, he chose Lewis to lead it. And Lewis turned to an old friend, William Clark, another Virginian, to be his co-captain. Clark was four years older than Lewis and had once been his commanding officer, but during their entire time together they apparently never quarreled or seriously disagreed. Their names will be forever linked.

THE EXPEDITION Between 1804 and 1806 the "Corps of Volunteers on an Expedition of North Western Discovery," under the command of Lewis and Clark, journeyed from St. Louis to the mouth of the Columbia River on the Pacific Coast of North America. Their mission, given them by President Jefferson, was to find a water route across the country – the elusive Northwest Passage – if it existed. The party

included a slave named York; Lewis's dog, Seaman; and, later on, a teenaged Indian girl, Sacagawea, and her infant son. They would map and chart; counsel with Indians; suffer from heat and cold and hunger; flee grizzly bears; discover new plants and animals; and, on many evenings, dance to fiddle music around their campfire.

Forty-odd "robust...helthy hardy young men" gathered on a bank of the Wood River, a tributary of the Missouri, not far upstream from St. Louis. It was 4:00 p.m. on May 14, 1804, when the Corps of Discovery set off–"men in high Spirits." Their three craft–a 55-foot-long keelboat named *Discovery* and two pirogues, or flat-bottomed dugouts–struggled upriver against the powerful Missouri current.
It was "a Cloudy rainey day," Clark wrote, but they "proceeded on under a jentle brease up the Missourie...." It took them two and a half months to reach "Council Bluff" in present-

day Nebraska. There they met with members of the Oto and Missouri tribe–their first official council with Indians. Game was plentiful, but so were the pesky "Misquitors."

LIFE–AND DEATH–ON THE RIVER
On July 31, Sergeant Charles Floyd complained of a stomachache: "I am verry Sick and Has ben for Somtime," he wrote in his journal. On August 20 he died, "with a great deel of Composure," Clark wrote; "before his death he Said to me, 'I am

going away. I want you to write me a letter.'" Probably he died of a ruptured appendix and peritonitis, afflictions unknown at the time that would have been fatal anywhere; appendectomies were not practiced until the late 1800s.

The wide Missouri River served as the expedition's highway, their 55-foot-long keelboat, here as sketched by Clark, their chief vessel. Rowed, sailed, pushed, and pulled, it carried the Corps of Discovery alongside a bluff a few miles below the mouth of the Platte River (opposite) and later past the mouth of the Big Sioux River (above).

Two years later, as the corps passed by on their way home, they paused to pay respects at his grave. Today a monument to Sergeant Floyd–the only man lost on the expedition and the first U.S. soldier to die west of the Mississippi–stands in downtown Sioux City, Iowa.

A DIVERSE GROUP The presence of the Shoshone woman Sacagawea, and her baby Jean Baptiste; of Clark's slave York; and Lewis's Newfoundland dog Seaman, the unofficial member of the party, surely makes the corps' diversity noteworthy in the annals of exploration.
Later writers tended to romanticize the role Sacagawea played in guiding the expedition, though certainly her knowledge of geography near today's Bozeman Pass was a help. She went uncomplaining all the way to the coast and back,

carrying Jean Baptiste and pitching in when needed. Clark called her "Janey," and Lewis wrote of her "fortitude and resolution." She died in 1812 at a fur-trading post in present-day South Dakota, soon after giving birth to a daughter.

Tough little Jean Baptiste evidently was little trouble: Except during a period of fever and illness – possibly mumps or tonsillitis – he gets few mentions in the journals. Clark later saw to his education, taking him into his home in St. Louis. In 1823, Jean Baptiste met Prince Paul of Württemberg and accompanied him back to Europe. He returned to the U.S. in 1829 and took up a career as mountain man, fur trader, and explorers' guide, dying in Oregon in 1866.

York caused a stir among the Plains Indians – they were "much astonished," Clark wrote, because they had never seen a black man. A Hidatsa chief even spit on his finger and tried to rub the black off. Clark eventually freed York, who reportedly died of cholera around 1830.

Seaman appears occasionally in the journals, catching squirrels and beavers and even an antelope; sounding the alarm when grizzlies came too close to camp; diverting a panicked "buffaloe" from charging over the sleeping men; howling with torture from the attack of "musquetoes." Even Clark referred to him as "our dog."

The Lewis and Clark expedition included an unlikely supporting cast: York, Clark's slave; Sacagawea, a teenage Shoshone girl, and her baby Jean Baptiste; and Seaman, Lewis's Newfoundland dog. Clark named Pompy's Tower (above) after Jean Baptiste, whom he affectionately called Pomp or Pompy. Located in present-day Montana, the sandstone outcrop is now called Pompeys Pillar.

INDIANS ⌁ "Brave active young men...likely fellows," Clark thought warriors of the Yankton Sioux, when the Corps of Discovery met up with them in present-day South Dakota. Jefferson's instructions regarding the Indians had been specific: Meet them and observe their ways carefully, paying particular attention to their populations, languages, food, clothing, housing, laws, customs, trading practices, agriculture, fishing, hunting, war, and many other aspects. "In all your intercourse with the natives,

Lewis and Clark presented symbolic Jefferson Peace Medals to Indian chiefs along the way.

treat them in the most friendly & conciliatory manner which their own conduct will admit...." During the journey, the explorers would encounter some 50 wonderfully diverse tribes. Clark seemed most comfortable among Indians, but Lewis was the more careful observer of their societies.

At each encounter the routine was similar: First the captains would persuade the tribe's chiefs to join them for a council. They would

parade their men, show some of the wonders of western technology – the magnet, the compass, the spyglass – and Lewis would fire his air gun. They presented Peace Medals; distributed gifts such as beads and cloth and mirrors; and everyone sat for a lengthy, prepared speech that explained U.S. sovereignty over the territory and encouraged trade.

They had a tense and frustrating confrontation with the Teton Sioux that nearly ended with bloodshed. The Arikara, the first of the Northern Plains tribes they met, were "Dirty, Kind, pore, & extra-vegent." They knew of the Assiniboine by their "turbulent and

---

A Piegan Blackfeet man (opposite) adorns himself with blue face paint and red clay or vermilion smeared in his hair. Among the Indians of the Northwest, the expedition found canoes with "curious images at bough and Stern," according to Lewis. Clark sketched this canoe in his journal. His box compass showed the way.

faithless" reputation. After their winter with the Mandan, they pushed on and encountered Indians barely known to Euro-Americans. The Shoshone provided horses when the corps most needed them. The "Stout likely men, handsom women" of the

Beautifully painted robe and a cap made from the hide of a rare white buffalo attest to this Hidatsa's high status. Sunburst-like images represent a warrior's feather bonnet. At left, three horizontal feathers in a Teton Sioux's hair indicate he has touched three fallen foes in battle. The painted buffalo robe records an incident of Mandan history – a battle among several Plains tribes.

Nez Perce tribe gave them dried salmon and camas roots and showed them how to burn out logs to make canoes. To the curious President back in Washington, the explorers sent boxes of Indian artifacts – and even Indians. Several chiefs made the perilous trip to visit Jefferson.

Lewis and Clark as Naturalists

Partly due to Lewis's untimely death in 1809, a promised volume on the natural history

discoveries of the expedition didn't appear until nearly a century later. So Lewis and Clark were rightly celebrated as adventurers and geographers, but their scientific contributions were slighted. In fact, during their trip to the coast and back, the two men discovered and described hundreds of species of plants and animals new to science. A list of

Lewis and Clark collected flora and fauna new to the science of the day. Left to right: Lewis's monkey flower (Mimulus lewisii), a coho salmon, a prairie dog, Lewis's woodpecker (Melanerpes lewis), bitterroot (Lewisia rediviva), a grizzly bear, and ragged robin (Clarkia pulchella).

them would fill pages and would include: the grizzly bear, the prairie dog, the sage grouse, the cutthroat trout, the salmonberry, the bitterroot, the cottonwood, Clark's nutcracker, and Lewis's woodpecker. Careful scientific descriptions of these species fill page after page of the journals.

Grizzly Country

The corps had heard about grizzly bears *(Ursus arctos horribilis)* but doubted their fearsome reputation among the Indians, who after all had only "their bows and arrows or indifferent fuzees [fusils, or muskets]." But soon they recognized their danger.

William Bratton wounded one and had to flee from the enraged beast. Lewis found himself face to face with a charging bear and, his rifle unloaded, ran "haistily" into the river. He presented the point of his espontoon and the bear retreated. The creatures customarily took several shots to kill, and Lewis shortly conceded: "These bear being so hard to die reather intimedates us all…I…had reather fight two Indians than one bear…."

The winter of 1804-05 found the expedition deep in frigid North Dakota. They built a fort on the Missouri near the Knife River villages of the Mandan and Hidatsa. Typical earth lodges have been reconstructed at On-A-Slant, a Mandan village decimated by smallpox and already abandoned when Lewis and Clark passed by.

Winter with the Mandan

The corps halted for the winter in present-day North Dakota, in the country of the Mandan and Hidatsa Indians. They built a fort of log huts and settled in. As winter storms howled, the captains kept busy cataloguing their ethnographic notes and preparing natural history specimens to send back to Jefferson in the spring. Here too they worked on

their journals, books destined to become classics of both American history and American literature. Clark was the more consistent

journal keeper; educated to the standards of his time and place, his spelling ricochets across the pages: He once wrote of conferring with some Indians "ounder a orning" and used at least 15 different spellings for "musketoors." The journals were first published – with the spelling corrected – in 1814 and have appeared in various editions ever since.

The Louisiana Purchase

By winter the corps was deep into the Louisiana Purchase – the newest addition to the nation. In 1803, strapped for cash, Napoléon Bonaparte had offered to sell Louisiana – the mammoth chunk of land west of the Mississippi –

A Mandan chief wears a feather bonnet and a leather shirt trimmed with ermine tails. At far left, a Mandan village sits on a bluff across the frozen Missouri. Snug lodges kept out the cold; this reconstruction is located at the Knife River National Historic Site.

Darkening clouds brood above the White Cliffs of the Missouri, where, Lewis thought, "...it seemed as if those seens of visionary inchantment would never have and end...."

to the U.S. Jefferson's emissaries, delighted to have the port of New Orleans in American hands, leaped at the offer. With one stroke, the purchase doubled the size of the country. Not everyone approved. A letter to an opposition newspaper read, "We are to give money of which we have too little for land of which we already have too much." But the Corps of Discovery was intent on finding out just what the President had bought.

Life on the Missouri

On April 7, 1805, the corps left their winter home among the Mandan. The keelboat returned downstream and the 33-member "permanent party" pushed on up the Missouri. Crossing Montana, they saw "emence" herds of bison and were awestruck by the "seens of visionary inchantment" among the White

Cliffs of the Missouri. When they came unexpectedly to a fork in the river – the mouth of today's Marias River – they correctly deduced which was the true Missouri. A more difficult barrier loomed ahead – the thunderous Great Falls of the Missouri. Here five cataracts within ten miles – "hising flashing and sparkling" – delayed them for a month as they laboriously portaged men, canoes, and matériel for 18 miles across steep slopes, deep gullies, and acres of prickly-pear cactus.

At Decision Point, the junction of the Missouri and Marias Rivers (top), the men explored, and at the Great Falls (left) they portaged. Clark mapped the route (above).

through the Rockies would entail weeks of hardship and difficulty. Battling across the Bitterroots alone took 11 days of stumbling through snow, across fallen timber and slippery boulders. Some of the horses tumbled down steep hillsides. The corps ran low on food, surviving on portable soup and three colts. By mid-September

MOUNTAINS—AND MORE MOUNTAINS ☞ On June 20, the explorers described "a chain of mountains to the west Some part of which…are Covered with Snow and appear verry high." The Rockies. Lewis and Clark knew about the Rocky Mountains, but on maps the range appeared as a thin line, easily and quickly portaged. In reality, the struggle

---

Sacagawea's tribe, the Shoshone, supplied much-needed horses, for soon after passing Three Forks (right), the river became too shallow for boats. Bodmer painted this Shoshone woman in 1833 (far right). Charles M. Russell's painting (below) depicts a friendly party of Flathead Indians greeting the corps shortly before their brutal crossing of the Bitterroot Mountains (opposite).

they were across, but they still had the Cascade Range ahead of them. There though, river currents for once would be with them, not against.

AN AMAZING COINCIDENCE ☞ At the age of 12, Sacagawea had been kidnapped near the Three Forks of the Missouri in present-day Montana. She spent a few years with her Hidatsa captors before the French-Canadian trapper Toussaint Charbonneau purchased her as his wife. Badly in need of horses

to cross the mountains, the Corps of Discovery had hoped to obtain them in trade from her former tribe, the Shoshone. For days they had searched fruitlessly among the mountains for the Indians. Finally, shortly after crossing the Continental Divide, the party located the Shoshone and began negotiating for horses. It was August 17, 1805. Suddenly Sacagawea "jummped up, and ran and embraced" the chief, "weeping profusely." They had stumbled onto the very band she had been stolen from. And the chief was Cameahwait, her brother.

DOWNSTREAM AT LAST ☞ With horses beneath them and another winter approaching, the explorers now searched for navigable waters that would carry them to the Pacific Ocean. The route they chose took them down the Clearwater to the Snake and down the Snake to the Columbia and down the Columbia to the sea. These rivers introduced a new hazard: rapids the likes of which they had never seen. But they made

five dugouts from ponderosa pines and gamely launched themselves into the white water. Alternately hurtling through rapids, portaging, or getting into the frigid water and hauling the canoes over "sholes," the men made slow but steady progress. Clark described one stretch's

Downstream at last! The expedition descended the Clearwater River (left), the Snake, and the Columbia (above), where Mount Hood rises in the distance. In November 1805 they reached the coast: "Great joy in camp—we are in view of the ocean." On the morning of the 12th they saw Saddle Mountain (opposite) covered with snow.

"horrid appearance of this agitated gut Swelling, boiling & whorling in every direction…." But there were salmon in the water. They were getting close.

THE VOTE 🖙 Through the first weeks of November – in constant rain and wind, soaked to their skins – the Corps of Discovery struggled toward the Pacific. They found evidence of white contact with tribes of the Northwest: Chinook men wore "Salors old Clothes;" entering one house, Clark saw "a British musket, a cutlash and Several brass Tea kittles." They debated about a suitable spot for wintering: They could remain on the north shore of the Columbia, though hunting was bad there; they could retreat a ways back up the river, but that would put them farther from the sea; or they could cross to the

south side of the Columbia, where there were reportedly more elk. The captains canvassed the party and everyone expressed an opinion,

even York and Sacagawea. For the first time a black slave and a woman voted in an American election.

Another winter, another fort: In the drizzly rain forest of the Pacific Northwest, Fort Clatsop (detail of reconstruction, above) arose near present-day Astoria, Oregon. Not far away, fog blankets Tillamook Head, whose highest point was officially named Clark's Mountain in 2002.

WINTER AT FORT CLATSOP 🖙 They crossed the river and built Fort Clatsop, naming it after a local tribe. By the end of December it was completed. Here they spent a cold,

hungry, and miserable winter, constantly wet from the endless coastal rain and drizzle and seldom with anything to eat but elk. On Christmas they had "pore Elk

boiled, Spilt [spoiled] fish & Some roots, a bad Christmass diner."
They put a detachment to work on the beach about 15 miles away, making salt to replenish their supply.

Lewis compiled his zoological, botanical, and ethnographic notes on the fauna, flora, and Indian cultures; Clark worked on his geographical data, drawing many small-scale maps of features west of the Great Falls of the Missouri.

In the captains' view, the local Indians – who were accustomed to bargaining with traders rather than explorers – were prone to pilfering and had to be constantly watched. Hunting parties went out nearly every day and just managed to keep the corps fed. Monotony and fleas tormented the party.

A beached whale brought diversion. When word of it reached the fort, Clark put together a party to go and attempt to purchase "a parcel of the blubber." Sacagawea voiced her only recorded protest: She "was very impatient to be permitted to go with me…

She observed that She had traveled a long way with us to See the great waters, and that now that monstrous fish was also to be Seen, She thought it verry hard that She Could not be permitted to See either (She had never yet been to the Ocian)." She went along.

Surf washes the shore at Ecola State Park in northwest Oregon. The whale that beached nearby brought visitors – including Sacagawea – from Fort Clatsop in January 1806 and also gave the park its name: Ecola is derived from a Chinook word for "whale." The corps' saltmaking camp was located not far away at present-day Seaside, Oregon.

HOMEWARD BOUND ᵔᵔ As the dreary winter of 1805-06 dragged to a close, thoughts and plans turned toward home. "Not withstanding the repeeted fall of rain," as Clark noted, Fort Clatsop had served them well. Still, they abandoned it with no reluctance on Sunday, March 23, 1806. They fought their way back up the

Columbia and by mid-May were ready again to tackle the Bitterroots, but the mountains lay deep in snow. They whiled away impatient weeks, waiting. They ran footraces with the Nez Perce and treated them for various illnesses. It was the end of June before they had successfully recrossed the Rockies. And here another wrinkle was introduced: For one long leg of the homeward journey, the party would split up.

Eager for home, the expedition began retracing their steps in March 1806, passing such familiar landmarks as Two Sisters (left) on the Columbia River in present-day Washington and again crossing the Bitterroot Mountains (above). For part of the return journey, Lewis and Clark separated. While Lewis went north, Clark explored along the Bitterroot River (opposite) and the Yellowstone.

DEATH ON THE TRAIL ᵔᵔ The plan called for Lewis to travel east to the Great Falls with nine men, then turn north with a smaller party to explore the Marias River. Clark and the rest of the corps would retrace the 1805 route back to Three Forks. From there, some men would descend the Missouri; Clark and the others would continue overland to the Yellowstone

and descend that river to its confluence with the Missouri. The entire corps would meet up again at the mouth of the Yellowstone.

Lewis hoped to avoid the fierce Blackfeet, but on July 26, he saw "a very unpleasant sight"– eight Piegan of the Blackfeet Confederacy. The two parties camped together and in the morning a scuffle over the rifles and the horses led to violence:

Two Piegan were killed, the only Indians to die at the hands of the corps.

The Missouri River (opposite), now a benign downstream highway, carried the men toward civilization: away from Western Indians, such as this Piegan man; away from the Yellowstone River; away from the now familiar elk.

A HUNTING ACCIDENT ᵔᵔ With the strong Missouri current behind them, the Corps of Discovery raced for home. Mileage that had taken them days to accomplish on the outbound journey now was covered in hours. Lewis was enjoying the trip less than the others: He was lying face down in a canoe, shot in the buttocks. On August 11, he and Pierre Cruzatte went ashore to replenish their supply of elk. Cruzatte, ordinarily a fine

hunter–though blind in one eye and nearsighted in the other–mistook his captain for an elk and blazed away. "Damn you, you have shot me," yelled Lewis. Though painful, the wound soon healed. A little more than a month later, on September 20, 1806, Clark wrote: "we Saw Some cows on the bank which was a joyfull Sight…and Caused a Shout to be raised for joy." They were nearly home.

THEIR LASTING LEGACY ⚬ On September 23, wrote Sergeant John Ordway, "we arived in Site of St. Louis, fired three Rounds as we approached… people gathred on the Shore and Huzzared.…" The Lewis and Clark expedition was finished. They could reflect on a trip of unparalleled excellence. They had done as ordered: journeyed 8,000 miles to the Pacific and back; found the "most practicable rout…across the continent by means

of the…Missouri and Columbia," though in the process they laid to rest the dream of a Northwest Passage; and brought back incredible tales of Indians and grizzlies, of raging rivers and snowbound mountain trails, material in their journals to enthrall readers 200 years later. Whenever exploration is spoken of, the names of Meriwether Lewis and William Clark–and their hardy Corps of Discovery–will always be honored.

Names forged in iron and etched in stone stand the test of time. A branding iron Lewis carried was found nearly a century after the expedition; Clark's name and date survive still, carved on Pompeys Pillar. Lewis and Clark failed in one of their principal missions: to find an all-water route to the Pacific Ocean. But their expedition set the stage for Manifest Destiny and the sea-to-sea nation that America would become.

ACKNOWLEDGMENTS

We would like to thank the following individuals for their generous assistance: Robert N. Bergantino, Montana Tech, The University of Montana; Mario Davignon, F.M.R. Costumes, Montreal; Jon Kukla, Patrick Henry National Memorial, Bob Moore, Jefferson National Expansion Memorial; Gary E. Moulton, University of Nebraska; and photographer Wayne Mumford, Kalispell, Montana.

PHOTO AND ILLUSTRATION CREDITS

Unless otherwise noted, all photographs are ©Wayne Mumford.

©Chuck Haney: *Front & back covers*

Harvard Museum of Natural History, photo by Mark Sloan, ©President and Fellows of Harvard College: *p. 13 (top left)*

©Michael Haynes: *p. 8 (left & right)*

©Mike & Lisa Husar/DRK Photo: *p. 13 (center)*

Joslyn Art Museum, Omaha, Nebraska, Gift of Enron Art Collection: *p. 5 (bottom right); p. 6; p. 7 (top right); p. 10 (bottom right); p. 12 (left & right); p. 15 (bottom left); p. 25 (top); p. 29 (right); p. 26 (left)*

Library of Congress: *p. 4*

Montana Historical Society: *pp. 18-19 (center)*

Missouri Historical Society, St. Louis: *p. 10 (top center); p. 12 (top center)*

National Museum of American History, Smithsonian Institution, Behring Center: *p. 10 (top right)*

Collection of the New-York Historical Society: *p. 4 (inset)*

Oregon Historical Society: *p. 10 (bottom left & bottom center); p. 28 (bottom left)*

Peabody Museum, Harvard University: *p. 12 (center)*

©U.S. Postal Service: *p. 3 (all); p. 5 (top left & top right); p. 30 (all); p. 32 (inset)*

Yale Collection of Western Americana, Beinecke Rare Book and Manuscript Library: *p. 7 (bottom left); p. 17 (bottom right)*

PRODUCTION

Stamp Illustrator, Designer & Typographer: Michael J. Deas

Art Director & Booklet Designer: Phil Jordan

Creative Director: Terrence W. McCaffrey

Stamp Art Research: Louis P. Plummer

Author, Booklet & Captions: Ron Fisher

Text Research & Editing: Victoria Cooper

Rights & Permissions: Sidney T. Brown

Production & Typography: John Boyd

Inside covers: Rugged but peaceful, serene but charged with drama, this landscape from the upper Missouri River was home to Native Americans. Euro-American exploration would change everything.

A new day dawns over the confluence of the Missouri and Marias Rivers in Montana. At this unexpected fork, the Lewis and Clark expedition paused to reconnoiter for several days in June 1805, en route to the Pacific Ocean.

UNITED STATES POSTAL SERVICE®

This 32 page booklet also contains twenty 37-cent stamps.
$8.95

in panes of 20. All three are self-adhesives and were produced by a combination process, with frames printed in single-color intaglio and multicolor vignettes printed by offset lithography, for the booklet stamps, or gravure, for the single.

The prestige booklet was the third such product produced by USPS, following booklets featuring U.S. Navy Submarines in 2000 and Old Glory in 2003, and the first to be priced at more than the face value of the stamps inside. Its cost was $8.95, a $1.55 markup over the postage value of $7.40.

Only 1 million booklets (20 million stamps) were ordered, compared to printings of 1.5 million for the Submarines booklet and 3 million for the Old Glory booklet, and distribution was highly limited. USPS said shipments would go "to each of the 11 first-day-of-issue locations, to stamp distribution offices along the Lewis and Clark Trail, and to any post office doing a special event. Purchases may also be made online, through the catalog, at philatelic centers and postal stores."

Similar distribution plans initially had been announced for the Subma-

rines and Old Glory booklets, but in both cases collectors' complaints prompted the Postal Service to eventually lift the restrictions. This didn't happen in the case of the Lewis and Clark booklet, however.

Ashton-Potter (USA) Ltd. printed the booklet stamps, while subcontracting the job of printing the booklet itself to Sterling Sommer. The booklet consists of 28 pages of text, historic illustrations and scenic photographs, plus front and back covers and two 10-stamp panes. The panes are the first and last pages of the booklet and are collectibly different: The back of the liner-release paper of one pane pictures Thomas Jefferson and a map of the Louisiana Purchase, while production and related information is printed on the back of the second pane.

The text was written by Ron Fisher, a Lewis and Clark enthusiast who first wrote about the Corps of Discovery in 1970 and has visited many of the expedition's camps. Fisher's article, "Lewis and Clark: Naturalist-Explorers," appeared in the October 1998 *National Geographic*.

The covers display a wraparound color photograph by Chuck Haney of the confluence of the Missouri and Marias rivers in Montana at sunset. Another continuous photograph, showing the rugged landscape of the upper Missouri, is on the inside of the front and back covers. It was taken by Wayne Mumford of Kalispell, Montana, who made several of the booklet's other scenic photos as well.

The single Lewis and Clark stamp was printed by Banknote Corporation of America for Sennett Security Products, the prime contractor. Sennett purchased BCA in January 2004 after the latter lost its own printing contract with USPS. The print order was 62.2 million stamps.

The single also was made available in uncut press sheets of nine panes at face value, $66.60. The Scott *Specialized Catalogue of United States Stamps & Covers* lists three position pieces from the uncut sheet: a cross-gutter block of four, a horizontal pair with vertical gutter and a vertical pair with horizontal gutter.

This stamp was an afterthought, said Terrence McCaffrey, manager of stamp development for USPS. The Citizens' Stamp Advisory Committee decided at the outset that the historical significance of the expedition merited the special treatment of a prestige booklet, McCaffrey said. However, the committee realized that the stamps in the booklet would mostly be collected rather than used, and approved the issuance of a third stamp that would carry the Lewis and Clark story into the general mailstream.

Collectors reported finding many panes from the prestige booklet with small but distracting printing flaws. Most of the flaws involve stray ink

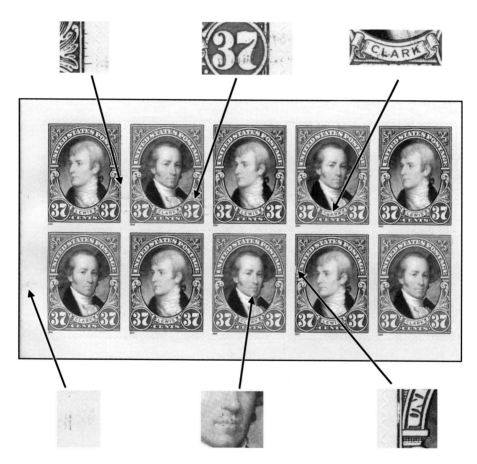

Some of the panes in the Lewis and Clark souvenir booklets display numerous small but distracting printing flaws. Close-up images and arrows point to six such flaws on this pane. Stray ink marks are found on the selvage (bottom-left close-up) and the stamps themselves (top-middle, top-right and bottom-middle close-ups). The top-left close-up shows ink streaks that run perpendicular to the vertical frameline of the stamp; the bottom-right close-up shows how the red and blue inks of the intaglio frames are susceptible to flaking away from the somewhat glossy stamp paper.

Collectors found it a challenge to remove a pane from a booklet for mounting in an album without damaging both the pane and the booklet. Removing the two panes leaves evidence of the glue that was used to bind the panes into the booklet. The page beneath each pane detaches from the booklet's spine when a pane is removed.

marks, both on the selvage and on the stamps themselves. Other flaws appear to be the result of the intaglio process used to print the red and blue frames. (See illustration.)

Donna Rajotte, the stamp-savvy philatelic clerk of the Providence, Rhode Island, main post office, told *Linn's Stamp News*, "I have looked at several hundred booklets, and all of them have some flaws. Some flaws are worse than others.

"About 75 percent are the more common flaws, such as obvious ink smears and spatters. Of the rest, about half are worse — misregistration of the 2004 year date, badly dented booklet covers and so on — and the rest have less noticeable flaws."

Linn's reported seeing some booklets in which the offset-printed 2004 year date on each stamp in a pane is shifted so that it appears almost entirely within the bottom frameline.

Removing a pane from a booklet for mounting in an album without damaging both pane and booklet turned out to be a challenge. A removal operation can leave glue and paper from the booklet cover on the left selvage (see illustration) and also can cause one or more pages to fall out. One *Linn's* reader, Roger Skulsky of Canton, Michigan, reported a successful extraction of both panes after running a hot iron over the front bound edge of the booklet for five to 10 seconds. *Linn's* cautioned readers using this procedure to start with a low-heat setting below mid-range to avoid damaging the stamps.

Collectors of used stamps found that the stamps of the booklet were difficult to soak from envelopes. The problem is with the center portions, behind the oval portraits, which clings to the envelope paper after the outer portions behind the frames come loose. *Linn's* Stamp Soaker columnist, "J.A. Watercutter," advised using warm water. After 25 minutes or so, he wrote, "the stamps [can] be pulled gently off, leaving the entire adhesive layer on the paper clippings."

"I suspect that the solid layers of ink used to print the vignettes significantly reduced the penetration of water through the front of the stamp paper to the water-soluble layer sandwiched between the stamp paper and the adhesive layer," Watercutter wrote. "The monochrome frames of the stamps, in contrast, exhibit numerous areas bearing no ink whatsoever, which helps the water-soluble layer dissolve in short order."

The surcharge imposed by the Postal Service for the stamps in the prestige booklet drew criticism. "The extra charge turns the stamps into unsanctioned semipostals (charity stamps) whose cost will be borne almost exclusively by stamp collectors," wrote *Linn's* editor Michael Schreiber in his Open Album column. "The extra charge poses the behemoth Postal Service as a charity case, a beggar looking for a paltry $1.55 million for its $70 billion annual budget. It's like throwing a penny into the Grand Canyon. ...

"The Lewis and Clark stamp surcharge should be canceled. ... If the Postal Service can't sell basic commemorative stamps at face value (that used to be the law), then the stamps should not be issued."

Wayne Youngblood, editor/publisher of *Stamp Collector*, deplored the surcharges on both the prestige booklet and the Art of Disney letter sheets. In his For The Record column, he wrote that "the United States Postal Service — which has the institutional memory of a fruit fly — is once again trying to sell postal products at huge premiums over face value to the very stamp collectors who support that branch ... [T]his approach has just never paid off for USPS."

Postal officials defended the surcharge as appropriate for the "value added" to the stamps by the booklet's text and pictures. A questionnaire sent with 5,000 of the booklets by Stamp Fulfillment Services included this question: "Are you satisfied with the price you paid for the booklet and its quality?" Of the 4,500 customers who returned the questionnaires, 68 percent "didn't mind paying the premium" for the booklet, David Failor, executive director of stamp services for USPS, told a meeting of philatelic journalists. "We are still exploring [souvenir] booklets," Failor said. He added that "no final decisions have been made" regarding the future of the format.

The single Lewis and Clark stamp issued for general postal use proved to be very popular. It was sold out at Stamp Fulfillment Services around the end of August 2004, except in uncut press sheets, which remained on sale for another few months. As of mid-2005, however, the prestige booklet still could be purchased.

Even before President Thomas Jefferson had closed the deal with France for the Louisiana Territory, he had obtained funding from Congress for a trip to the Missouri River headwaters and beyond. The expedition's principal objective, he said, would be to find "the most direct and practicable water communication across this continent, for the purposes of commerce."

To lead it, Jefferson chose his personal secretary, Meriwether Lewis, a 29-year-old Army officer and veteran of the western frontier. Lewis turned to an old friend, William Clark, a Virginian like himself, to be his co-captain. Clark was four years older than Lewis and was his former commanding officer, but the two worked in harmony together on the expedition.

The Corps of Discovery consisted of some 44 men, including Clark's slave, York. They spent the winter of 1803-1804 at Camp DuBois, near what is now Hartford, Illinois. On May 14, 1804, they pushed a 55-foot keelboat and two pirogues — flat-bottomed dugouts — off the eastern bank of the Mississippi River, crossed over and entered the mouth of the Missouri River.

The explorers worked their way upstream against the current through the summer and fall. En route, they lost a member of the party, Sergeant Charles Floyd, who died, apparently of a burst appendix, near present-day Sioux City, Iowa, August 20, 1804. Remarkably, his was the only fatality of the entire expedition.

In North Dakota, the Corps went into winter camp with the Mandan Indians. Here, to the explorers' good fortune, they met a Shoshone teenager named Sacagawea. At age 12, the girl had been sold into slavery with the Mandans who, in turn, sold her to a French-Canadian fur trader, Toussaint Charbonneau. Lewis and Clark hired Charbonneau to accompany their expedition as an interpreter, and Sacagawea and the couple's infant son, Jean-Baptiste, went with him. In Montana the expedition met a Shoshone band led by Sacagawea's brother Cameahwait, and she was instrumental in obtaining horses and guides for the expedition. As the journey continued, the suspicions of other Indian tribes were allayed by the presence of the woman and her child.

The expedition's trip to the Pacific Ocean and back lasted two years, four months and 10 days and covered more than 8,000 miles. As Ron Fisher wrote in the prestige booklet, by the time the explorers returned to St. Louis they had mapped and charted, counseled with Indians, suffered from heat and cold and hunger, fled grizzly bears, discovered new plants and animals and, on many evenings, danced to fiddle music around their campfire.

But they failed, through no fault of their own, to discover President Jefferson's hoped-for water route to the Pacific. A navigable water route with an easy portage over the Rocky Mountains didn't exist. The explorers followed the Missouri River to its headwaters in the mountains of Montana, where snow-capped peaks blocked the route. To find streams flowing westward to the Columbia River and the Pacific, they had to portage some 340 miles. "Of this distance," Lewis reported to Jefferson, "200 miles is along a good road, and 140 over tremendious [sic] mountains which for 60 mls. are covered with eternal snows."

At the end of the expedition, Lewis announced that their journals would be published, including a volume "confined exclusively to scientific research, and principally to the natural history of those hitherto unknown regions." However, the journals were perhaps not fully appreciated until their 2002 publication in a 13-volume set that was edited by Gary E. Moulton, professor of history at the University of Nebraska. The Moulton edition is regarded as the first complete edition edited to modern standards.

After the Corps' return, President Jefferson appointed Lewis governor of the Louisiana Territory. Lewis, a man given to episodes of depression and intemperance, still occupied that post when he committed suicide October 11, 1809, at age 37. By contrast, Clark served as governor of the Missouri Territory and thereafter had a long stint as superintendent of Indian affairs. He died at age 68 September 1, 1838, one of the last survivors of the Corps of Discovery, and his funeral, with a mile-long procession of carriages and mounted troops, was the biggest ever seen in St. Louis.

The U.S. Mint joined the commemoration of the 200th anniversary of the Lewis and Clark expedition by issuing two new nickels and a silver dollar in 2004 and announcing that a third and fourth nickel would appear in 2005.

The silver dollar shows on the obverse Captains Lewis and Clark on a stream bank, making plans for the following day. The reverse depicts the Peace Medal, surrounded by 17 stars representing the number of states in the Union in 1804. Two feathers symbolize the many Indian cultures touched by the Corps of Discovery.

Two of the 2004 nickels bear on the obverse the familiar bust of Thomas Jefferson that first appeared on the coin in 1938. The reverse of the first coin reproduces the Peace Medal, which Jefferson ordered to be made as a token of peace to give to Indian leaders they would meet on their journey. The reverse of the second depicts their keelboat, *Discovery*.

The Lewis and Clark Bicentennial silver dollar shows on the obverse the two leaders standing on a stream bank. Lewis is holding his journal, and Clark holds a rifle. The reverse depicts the Jefferson Peace Medal, with 17 stars representing the number of states in the Union in 1804 and two feathers to represent the many American Indian cultures touched by the expedition. The coin was designed by U.S. Mint sculptor/engraver Donna Weaver.

Shown here are the reverses of the two new nickels issued in 2004 to commemorate the Lewis and Clark expedition. One features the Peace Medal that President Jefferson ordered to be made for distribution to Native American chiefs whom the explorers would encounter. It shows the hands of a Native American and a European-American clasped in a friendly handshake below a crossed pipe and tomahawk. The coin's designer was Norman E. Nemeth, a U.S. Mint sculptor/engraver. The other depicts the keelboat that was part of the expedition's transportation, with Captains Lewis and Clark standing on deck at the start of their trip. It was designed by Mint sculptor/engraver Al Maletsky.

The new nickels for 2005 show a new likeness of Jefferson on the obverse, with the word "Liberty" based on his own handwriting. The first shows on the reverse an image of the American bison, recalling the wildlife encountered by the expedition. The second features a scene of the Pacific Ocean and the inscription "Ocean in view! O! The joy!", based on an excited entry in Clark's journal for November 7, 1805. (In fact, the explorers were still a few days away from the Pacific; what they first sighted was the broad Columbia River estuary.)

These images are on the two new nickels announced by the U.S. Mint for 2005. The obverse shows a new profile portrait of Thomas Jefferson, with the word "Liberty" in a replica of his handwriting. Designer Joe Fitzgerald based it on a 1789 bust by Jean-Antoine Houdon and made it age-appropriate to Jefferson's presidency by referring to later paintings by Gilbert Stuart and Rembrandt Peale. Mint sculptor/engraver Don Everhart sculpted the portrait. The first reverse design, by Jamie Franki, depicts the American bison and was sculpted by the Mint's Norman E. Nemeth. The second reverse features a Pacific Ocean scene and an inscription, "Ocean in view! O! The joy!" adapted from William Clark's journal of November 7, 1805. It was designed by Joe Fitzgerald and sculpted by the Mint's Donna Weaver.

The U.S. Post Office Department issued this 3¢ stamp in 1954 to commemorate the 150th anniversary of the Lewis and Clark expedition (Scott 1063). It depicts Lewis, Clark and Sacagawea on a bank of the Missouri River.

The 2004 stamps were not the first U.S. postal recognition of the Lewis and Clark expedition.

On July 28, 1954, the Post Office Department issued a 3¢ violet-brown stamp to mark the Corps of Discovery's 150th anniversary (Scott 1063). The stamp, designed by Bureau of Engraving and Printing artist Charles R. Chickering, depicts Lewis, Clark and Sacagawea on a bank of the Missouri River. It had its first-day sale in Sioux City, Iowa.

And on September 23, 1981, USPS produced a 12¢ postal card for the expedition's 175th anniversary (Scott UX91). The first-day city was St. Louis, Missouri. The card's stamped imprint, designed by David Blossom, shows a close-up of the explorers standing side by side surveying the landscape. Other members of the Corps and their boats are behind them, on the river's edge. Because the postcard rate rose to 13¢ November 1, 1981, the card was usable without additional postage for only 38 days.

Sacagawea alone is pictured on a 29¢ stamp of the 1994 Legends of the West pane of 20 (Scott 2869s) and on its matching 19¢ picture postal card (Scott UX176). The illustrator was Mark Hess.

This 12¢ postal card (Scott UX91) with an illustration by David Blossom was issued in 1981 to mark the expedition's 175th anniversary.

The expedition's Shoshone guide, Sacagawea, is pictured on this 29¢ stamp from the Legends of the West pane of 1994 (Scott 2869s). The artwork is by Mark Hess.

The Designs

To illustrate the two stamps that were planned at the outset, USPS art director Phil Jordan chose Michael Deas, a master portrait artist whose oil paintings have been reproduced on several stamps in the Legends of Hollywood and Literary Arts series.

"Metaphorically, we too were swept up in a long journey across uncharted territory," Jordan said. "My role in this ever-changing journey seemed to be constantly declaring, 'Let's not go up that river!'

"We started the active work in January 2001. I originally thought of a se-tenant pair, with Lewis on one stamp and Clark on the other, perhaps with other figures and a great scenic background, continuous across the two stamps.

"I wasn't wedded to the idea, and Michael talked me out of that concept. He wanted to do portraits of each man — evocative period paintings. He also wanted to design frames based on classic engraved U.S. stamps, that would themselves be engraved. I told him to proceed along that line, and he did sketches of portraits that had so much potential that we forgot about any other approach."

Both men are shown in formal wear. Deas based his portrait of Wil-

Deas' principal sources for his portraits of Meriwether Lewis and William Clark were these portraits from life by Charles Willson Peale, circa 1807. For Lewis, he also worked from a circa 1803 or 1807 crayon-on-paper portrait by Charles Saint-Memin, also shown here. The latter shows Lewis with his hair in a small queue, as Deas shows him on the stamp.

liam Clark on two portraits from life: a circa 1807 Charles Willson Peale painting belonging to the Independence National Historical Park in Philadelphia, and a circa 1809 painting that is attributed to Gilbert Stuart or J.W. Jarvis.

For the Lewis stamp, he relied on two portraits as well. The primary source was another Peale painting, also circa 1807 and also belonging to the Independence National Historical Park. The other was a circa 1803 or 1807 crayon-on-paper portrait by Charles Balthazar-Julien Febret De Saint-Memin now owned by the Missouri Historical Society.

Deas explained his thinking to a Postal Service interviewer. "I knew that I wanted to create fresh and original paintings in the style of a painter from that period," he said. "Charles Peale painted famous portraits of Lewis and Clark, but they've been reproduced ad infinitum. However, I've always been fond of Gilbert Stuart and his portraits; he was alive during the time of Lewis and Clark, and I greatly admire his work. So I took existing portraits and combined them to create new, authentic pictures — a new third portrait of each explorer in the style of Gilbert Stuart."

The artist painted Lewis with his hair in a small queue. One of the expert consultants retained by PhotoAssist, the Postal Service's research firm, commented that an 1800 Army general order had forbidden officers to wear queues, and argued that if Lewis had grown the queue while on his trip to the west, he would have cut it off upon his return. However, Jordan declined to have Deas revise his artwork, pointing out that the queue is clearly present in the Saint-Memin portrait.

"Clark is a little skinnier in Michael's portrait than in the Peale painting, a little more intense, even a little more red-haired," Jordan said. "But this is the way Michael felt these people would have looked.

These are Michael Deas' original pencil sketches for the portrait stamps.

"Late in the process, I bought a book titled *Dear Brother*, which is a collection of letters from William Clark to his brother, Jonathan [edited by James Holmberg, Yale University Press, 2002]. As I thumbed through it, I came face to face with what seemed to be Michael's portrait of Clark for the stamp! It was a circa 1855 photograph of Clark's eldest son, Meriwether Lewis Clark. The son, according to the caption, bore 'a strong resemblance to his father.' I said to myself, 'Michael has nailed this.' Michael told me he never had seen the photograph.

"I never questioned the spiritual fidelity of Michael's portraits, and it was nice to see the literal fidelity confirmed as well!"

The completed portraits sat on Jordan's worktable for several months, "looking down on the constantly evolving commemorative stamp art and the prestige booklet concept," Jordan said. As it turned out, at the end of that evolution, the illustration for the third stamp — the commemorative single — would be a byproduct of the booklet design process.

Earlier, Jordan had asked Deas, besides illustrating the two booklet stamps, to illustrate a wraparound cover for the booklet as well. "Michael sketched a beautiful, sweeping panorama landscape with Lewis, Clark and Sacagawea on a cliff overlooking the winding Missouri, with great heaps of his patented cumulus clouds building in the setting sun," Jordan said. "The scene was a most evocative artist's impression of the immense wilderness the Corps of Discovery encountered. It was an imagined location,

Phil Jordan was struck by the resemblance of Deas' painting of William Clark to this circa 1855 photograph of Clark's son, Meriwether Lewis Clark, surrounded by his own six sons, which he found in the book Dear Brother, *a collection of William Clark's letters to his brother Jonathan. The picture caption reads: "Clark was known as Lewis and was said to bear a strong resemblance to his father." Jordan affixed a copy of the Clark stamp to the book page for comparison.*

Art director Phil Jordan originally wanted stamp artist Michael Deas to illustrate the wraparound cover of the prestige booklet, and Deas created this rough sketch showing Lewis, Clark and Sacagawea on a high cliff looking over the route ahead. However, CSAC demanded that the illustration show an identifiable scene where the two expedition leaders could be historically placed together. The necessary research that followed was time-consuming, and Jordan decided to use a present-day photograph for the cover, while Deas adapted his design idea for use on the third, stand-alone Lewis and Clark stamp. The only element of Deas' sketch that survived on the finished booklet cover was the title logo.

to be based on a collection of typical scenes along the route."

The design subcommittee of CSAC was pleased with the sketch, but insisted that the scene should be an actual identifiable place. This requirement sent Jordan, PhotoAssist and the project consultants searching through the journals for a time and place when Lewis and Clark were verifiably together — and in a suitably attractive setting.

"Naturally, I wanted Michael to do the third stamp, the mail-use stamp," Jordan said. "But this posed a dilemma, as he was loaded down with the booklet-cover assignment, which in itself posed a daunting set of research obstacles to be resolved before it could even be restarted.

"The search for a location for the cover wasn't as easy as first thought. Most locations where both Lewis and Clark could be conclusively shown together were difficult to illustrate, or insignificant pauses along the route.

"There's one place called the Three Forks of the Missouri, where the journal showed that Lewis had stood and looked out over gorgeous scenery. But it turned out that Clark was away up the western fork at the time.

"We were told, 'You can place them together at the Beaver's Head rock, or the Horse Prairie,' two sites in southwest Montana near the Continental Divide. But I found out that although Lewis was on the Beaver's Head, Clark had a severe infection in his ankle and couldn't walk, so you can be sure he wasn't up there with Lewis." And the site of the Corps' encampment at Horse Prairie now is under water, according to consultant Robert N. Bergantino of the University of Montana's Montana Tech, who has studied the Corps of Discovery's route and stopping places and has mapped the area's rivers as they were in 1805. "We surely weren't going to get any reference photos of that location," Jordan said.

Ultimately, the design team found its site: the juncture of the Missouri and Marias rivers in north central Montana. Here, Lewis' journal entry for June 3, 1805, places the two together on a cliff overlooking the rivers, and describes in detail the entire scene: 'Capt. C. & myself stroled out to the top of the hights in the fork of these rivers from whence we had an extensive and most inchanting view. ... To the South we saw a range of lofty mountains which we supposed to be a continuation of the S. Mountains.' " These probably were the Highwood Mountains, near present-day Great Falls.

(The explorers' arrival here marked a critical moment in the journey. It was unclear which branch was the Missouri River, which the Mandan Indians had assured them would take them toward the headwaters of the Columbia River. Choosing the wrong one would extract a heavy cost in lost time and morale and perhaps "defeat the expedition altogether," as Lewis wrote. After Lewis and Clark led scouting expeditions up the north and south forks, respectively, they concluded — correctly, as it turned out — that the north fork was the tributary and the south was the true Missouri.)

For Jordan and Deas, the design process became even more complicated when consultant Bergantino explained that the two rivers were much wider in 1805 than they are today, and their beds had a different location and configuration. The landscape and horizons remained unchanged, however. "We asked ourselves, 'Do we illustrate the rivers as they were in 1805? And, if we do, what reference do we use?' " Jordan said.

Bergantino provided drawings of how the intersection of the rivers probably looked to Lewis and Clark. The designers also studied satellite photos on which details of the former riverbeds could be discerned, as well as contemporary ground-level photos by their Montana photographer, Wayne Mumford, arranged in various panoramas as the explorers might have seen them from their clifftop vantage point.

Ultimately, however, Jordan decided that to ask Deas to continue to work on the booklet-cover illustration, as well as create a painting for the third stamp — "which was not part of the original deal" — would overburden the artist and make it unlikely that he could complete the assignments on time. "I felt it would be in the best interests of everyone that we not go through with doing a painting for the cover, and default to a photograph of the Missouri and Marias rivers," Jordan said. "Michael then could use his preliminary art for the cover as a basis for the stamp, and we could amortize the great amount of research and time we had invested." Fortunately, he added, the cover photograph that was chosen, by Chuck Haney, "turned out to be spectacular."

The only part of Michael Deas' preliminary sketches for the booklet cover that survived in the finished product was the booklet title: the words "LEWIS & CLARK" in capital letters, "The Corps of Discovery" in calligraphy inside an ornamental cartouche, and the dates "1804-1806."

Deas sketched his proposed design for the single stamp in semijumbo size as well as the commemorative size that was ultimately selected. He noted with this sketch: "Figures are slightly large for image area and will likely be reduced somewhat."

For his stamp illustration, Deas borrowed and revised the figures of Lewis and Clark from his booklet cover sketches, but omitted Sacagawea. Where they are standing is south of the intersection of the rivers, which are not seen in the painting, and they are looking east. Deas used the same male model for both explorers. Their shirts were based on a re-creation of a period leather shirt, made by F.M.R. Costumes. The leggings, belts and other items were fashioned from props in the artist's studio, while the hats, scarves and other pieces of clothing were obtained from a junk shop. The rifle held by one of the explorers is based on photos of a vintage gun, circa 1804, and the telescope held by the other explorer "is made up," Deas told the Postal Service.

Deas based the bluff in the foreground on a Mumford photograph. For the view of the mountains in the background he used several images, including an 1833 painting of the Highwoods by Karl Bodmer and a photograph of the same area by George Thomas. He filled his sky with billowing clouds glowing with reflected sunlight.

The artist sketched the design in both semijumbo and commemorative sizes. "We liked the commemorative better because it allowed more of the scope of the landscape to be shown," said the Postal Service's Terrence McCaffrey. "The image in the semijumbo is too tight and rounded off too

This is Michael Deas' finished painting for the single Lewis and Clark stamp, curved at the top where it will fit inside the engraved frame.

The frame of the Lewis and Clark stamp issued in pane form (center) bears a strong similarity to the 2¢ Liberty Bell Sesquicentennial Exposition commemorative of 1926 (Scott 627) (left), but also borrows design elements of the three Huguenot-Walloon Tercentenary stamps of 1924, the high-value 5¢ stamp (Scott 616) of which is at right.

much."

Deas designed the frames for all three stamps, creating the lettering and ornamentation by hand. His artwork then was converted to recess-engraved dies by a photochemical process. *Linn's* associate editor Rick Miller was able to deconstruct the frame designs to identify their sources.

The basic design of the single stamp's frame, Miller wrote, "is strikingly similar" to the 1926 2¢ Liberty Bell Sesquicentennial Exposition stamp (Scott 627). However, it also borrows elements from the 1924 three-stamp Huguenot-Walloon Tercentenary issue (Scott 614-616), including the size and placement of the denominations in the circular tablets at both sides of the bottom of the frame, the word "CENTS" at the base of the frame between the denominations, and the scrolls at the upper corners containing the anniversary year dates. The inscription "LEWIS & CLARK BICENTENNIAL" on a ribbon across the bottom of the vignette is evocative of a third stamp design from the same period, the Lexington-Concord issue of 1925.

The two portrait stamps reuse design elements from the Fourth Bureau definitive series of 1922 (Scott 551-573), such as the name of the stamp subject in the curved scroll beneath the portrait, and from the 2¢ carmine rose George Washington stamp of the Washington Bicentennial issue of 1932 (Scott 707), with its fleur-de-lis devices in the upper corners and the words "UNITED STATES POSTAGE" above the portraits in a framed arc resting on pedestals.

All the stamps cited above were designed by Clair Aubrey Huston of the Bureau of Engraving and Printing, BEP's most prolific stamp designer for 30 years until his retirement in 1933.

Because the process-color illustrations on the three stamps could be expected to shift somewhat in relation to the engraved frames during printing, Deas made the inside of the frames heavier than normal to trap any straying colors. "They are a little bit thicker than we wanted," Jordan acknowledged.

Deas chose the frame colors: blue for Lewis and red for Clark in the prestige booklet, green for the single. "I met with Don Woo [of Sennett

The 37¢ Clark and Lewis stamps, center left and right, reuse design elements from the Fourth Bureau definitive series issue of 1922 and the Washington Bicentennial issue of 1932. A ½¢ Nathan Hale stamp (Scott 551) from the 1922 series is shown at left and a 2¢ George Washington stamp (Scott 707) from the Bicentennial series is at right.

Security Products, the modeler of the single stamp] on the final proofs and gave him a color reference to reiterate that we didn't want the frame to go too green," Jordan said. "Michael was afraid it would come out the color of Monopoly money. We got it just the way he wanted, I think, really dark, almost more black than green."

To enhance the impression of classic stamp designs, the printers tinted the paper — a light beige for the portrait stamps and a light green for the single.

Jordan expressed pride in the stamps and booklet. "The vision of Michael Deas and his dedication to details and immense talent made this project, in retrospect, the most satisfying of all the stamps I've been privileged to art-direct, and ensured its success," he said.

First-Day Facts

The 11 cities and towns chosen to host the first-day ceremonies range in population from 335,000 (Omaha, Nebraska) to 800 (Ilwaco, Washington). Following is a list of the communities, the locations of the events and the principals listed as participants:

Hartford, Illinois, Camp River Dubois Festival Grounds. Dedicating official: Patrick R. Donahoe, chief operating officer and executive vice president, USPS. Welcome: William Moore, mayor, Hartford. Master of Ceremonies: Donn Johnson, director of communications, Missouri Historical Museum. Honored guest: Danita Aquiningoc, Gateway District manager, USPS.

St. Charles, Missouri, boardwalk of old train depot (moved from the Lewis and Clark Monument, Frontier Park, because of rain). Dedicating official: Danita Aquiningoc, Gateway District manager, USPS (also present at Hartford, Illinois, ceremony 3½ hours earlier). Speakers: Peyton C. "Bud" Clark, great-great-great-grandson of William Clark; Peter Rexford, syndicated columnist. Welcome: Patti York, mayor, St. Charles. Master of Ceremonies: Venetia McEntire, chair, St. Charles Lewis and Clark Bicentennial Commission. Honored guest: William Clark, eighth-generation descendant of William Clark.

Sioux City, Iowa, Southern Hills Mall Center Court. Dedicating official: Susan M. LaChance, acting district manager, Hawkeye District, USPS. Speakers: Tom Vilsack, governor of Iowa; Steve King, U.S. representative, Iowa. Introduction of governor: Mark Monson, chairman, Iowa Lewis and Clark Bicentennial Commission. Welcome: Dave Ferris, mayor, Sioux City. Master of ceremonies: Christa Henton, anchor, Channel 9 KCAU-TV.

Atchison, Kansas, Riverhouse Restaurant. Dedicating official: Ormer Rogers Jr., Mid-America District manager, USPS. Speakers: Mike Hayden, secretary, Kansas Wildlife and Parks; Karen Seaberg, chairman, Kansas Lewis and Clark Bicentennial Commission. Welcome: Dan Garrity, mayor, Atchison. Master of ceremonies: Karen Fuller, reporter/anchor, KCTV Channel 5.

Omaha, Nebraska, Lewis and Clark Landing. Dedicating official: Irene A. Lericos, manager, field communications, USPS. Speakers: Mike Fahey, mayor, Omaha; Ron Hull, chairman, Nebraska Lewis and Clark Bicentennial Commission; Carol Russel, president, Nebraska Foundation for the Humanities; Darrek Draper, performing the role of George Drouillard, Lewis and Clark's interpreter. Master of ceremonies: EvaJon Sperling, postmaster, Omaha.

Pierre, South Dakota, South Dakota Capitol rotunda. Dedicating official: Laree K. Martin, Dakotas District manager, USPS. Speakers: Dennis Eisnach, mayor, Pierre; Sam Tidball, mayor, Fort Pierre, South Dakota; Jay Vogt, director, South Dakota State Historical Society. Master of ceremonies: Ronald L. Vail, manager, post office operations, USPS.

Washburn, North Dakota, Fort Mandan, two miles west of the North Dakota Lewis and Clark Interpretive Center. Dedicating official: David E. Failor, executive director, stamp services, USPS. Speakers: John Hoeven, governor of North Dakota; Byron Dorgan, U.S. senator, North Dakota; Tex Hall, chairman, Mandan, Hidatsa, Arihara Nation; Kevin Kirkey, interpretative coordinator, Lewis and Clark Fort Mandan Foundation. Master of ceremonies: David Borlaug, president, Lewis and Clark Fort Mandan Foundation.

Great Falls, Montana, Lewis and Clark National Historic Trail Interpretive Center. Dedicating official: Robert G. Klein, Big Sky District manager, USPS. Speakers: Max Baucus, U.S. senator, Montana; Conrad Burns, U.S. senator, Montana; Dennis Rehberg, U.S. representative, Montana; Karl Ohs, lieutenant governor, Montana; Darrell Kipp, member, Montana Lewis and Clark Bicentennial Commission; Larry Epstein, past president, Lewis and Clark Trail Heritage Foundation. Welcome: Randy Gray, mayor, Great Falls. Master of ceremonies: Jane Schmoyer-Weber, director, Lewis and Clark Historic Trail Interpretive Center, U.S. Department of Agriculture, Forest Service.

Orofino, Idaho, Pink House Recreation Site. Dedicating official: Joyce H. Carrier, manager, public affairs, USPS. Speakers: Keith Petersen, coordinator, Idaho Governor's Lewis and Clark Trail Committee; Anthony Johnson, chairman, Nez Perce Executive Committee; John Wayne, Clearwater County Historical Society. Welcome: Ben Carpenter, postmaster, Orofino. Master of ceremonies: Ron Carroll, manager, post office operations, USPS.

Ilwaco, Washington, Lewis and Clark Interpretive Center, Cape Disappointment State Park. Dedicating official: Richard J. Strasser Jr., chief financial officer and executive vice president, USPS. Speaker: Rex Ziak, author and historian. Welcome: Paul Malmberg, Southwest regional director, Washington State Parks. Master of ceremonies: Dallas W. Keck, Portland District manager, USPS.

Astoria, Oregon, Fort Clatsop National Memorial. Dedicating official: Richard J. Strasser Jr., chief financial officer and executive vice president, USPS (also was dedicating official at Ilwaco, Washington, three hours earlier). Speakers: Joe Scovell, chairman, Tribal Council, Clatsop Nehalem Confederated Tribes; Richard Basch, National Park Service. Welcome: Chip Jenkins, superintendent, Fort Clatsop National Memorial. Master of ceremonies: Dallas W. Keck, Portland District manager, USPS (also was M.C. at Ilwaco, Washington).

Because the Postal Service does not break down the total first-day cancellations applied by Stamp Fulfillment Services' Cancellation Services unit in Kansas City, Missouri, or keep a record of hand cancellations applied at the sites themselves on the issue date, there is no way to determine the relative numbers of cancellations from the 11 first-day sites. Lloyd de Vries, who writes the Modern FDCs column in *Linn's Stamp News,* reported that cachetmakers participating in the bourse at the 2004 Napex show in McLean, Virginia, said the Great Falls, Montana, postmark easily outsold the other 10 sites by mail and Internet, but no explanation for its popularity was offered.

For a limited time, Stamp Fulfillment Services sold uncacheted first-day covers of the Lewis and Clark single stamp in sets of 11 for $8.25. Random single first-day covers were sold for 75¢.

37¢ ISAMU NOGUCHI (5 DESIGNS)

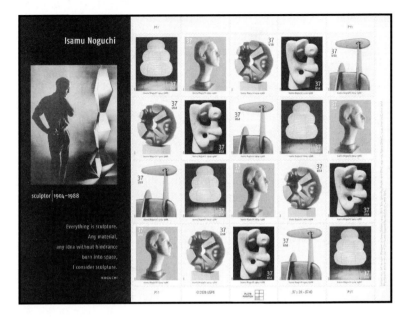

Date of Issue: May 18, 2004

Catalog Numbers: Scott 3857-3861, stamps; 3861a, horizontal strip of 5

Colors: black in unit No. 1, black in unit No. 2

First-Day Cancel: Long Island City, New York

First-Day Cancellations: 312,187

Format: Pane of 20, vertical, 5 across, 4 down. Offset printing plates printing 120 stamps per revolution (10 across, 12 around). Also sold in uncut press sheets of 6 panes (2 across by 3 down).

Gum Type: self-adhesive

Stamp Size: 1.225 by 1.56 inches; 31.115 by 39.624mm

Pane Size: 9.5 by 7.125 inches; 241.3 by 180.975mm

Uncut Press Sheet Size: 21 by 27 inches

Perforations: 10½ by 10¾ (die-cut simulated perforations) (IDC two-station die cutter)

Selvage Inscription: "Isamu Noguchi/sculptor 1904-1988/Everything is sculpture./Any material,/any idea without hindrance/born into space,/I consider sculpture./NOGUCHI" "bottom row, left to right: *Margaret La Farge Osborn*, 1937; *Black Sun*, 1960-63; *Mother and Child*, 1944-47; *Figure* (detail), 1945; *Akari 25N*, circa 1968./Reproduced with permission of The Isamu Noguchi Foundation Inc., New York."

96

Selvage Markings: "© 2003 USPS." ".37x20=$7.40." "PLATE/POSITION" and diagram.

Back Markings: Universal Product Code (UPC) "456100" in 4 locations on back of liner paper

Designer, Art Director and Typographer: Derry Noyes of Washington, D.C.

Modeler: Joseph Sheeran of Ashton-Potter (USA) Ltd., Williamsville, New York

Stamp Manufacturing: Stamps printed by Ashton-Potter on a Mueller Martini A76 modified offset press. Stamps processed by Ashton-Potter.

Quantity Ordered: 57,000,000

Plate Number Detail: 1 set of 2 plate numbers preceded by the letter P in selvage above or below each corner stamp

Plate Number Combinations Reported: P11, P22

Paper Supplier: Paper Corporation of the United States/Glatfelter

Tagging: phosphored paper, with block tagging on eight stamps

The Stamps

On May 18, the Postal Service issued a set of five self-adhesive stamps honoring Japanese-American sculptor Isamu Noguchi in the 100th anniversary year of his birth. Noted for merging Western and Eastern influences and expanding the definition of sculpture, Noguchi created a varied body of work, from busts, abstract pieces and furniture to graceful meditation gardens, theatrical sets and sprawling landscapes.

The set was the sixth entry in an unnamed, de facto series of stamps with similar formats that feature the work of 20th-century painters and sculptors: Georgia O'Keeffe (1996), Alexander Calder (1998), Louise Nevelson (2000), Frida Kahlo (2001) and Andy Warhol (2002). The stamps come in panes of 20, five across by four down, are semijumbo in size and vertically arranged, and depict one or more of their subject's works. A wide selvage on one side of the pane bears his or her photograph and a representative quotation.

Isamu Noguchi 1904–1988

Isamu Noguchi 1904–1988   Isamu Noguchi 1904–1988

The Noguchi stamps were produced by the offset process by Ashton-Potter (USA) Ltd. The six vertical rows of die-cut simulated perfs on the pane extend to the edges of the selvage at the top and bottom to facilitate separation by postal clerks, but the five horizontal rows of die cuts do not go beyond the stamps.

Collectors could also buy uncut press sheets of six panes, two across by three down. The Scott *Specialized Catalogue of United States Stamps & Covers* lists the following position pieces from a press sheet: horizontal pair with vertical gutter (wide selvage), vertical pair with horizontal gutter (narrow selvage), block of eight with vertical gutter, block of 10 with horizontal gutter, and cross-gutter block of eight. A cross-gutter block consists of one stamp from each of two upper panes and three stamps vertically from each of two lower panes.

The Noguchi pane is the first in the series to be printed in no color other than black. The stamps have two tagging types, overall and block. The overall tagging results from the stamps being printed on phosphored paper. In addition, eight stamps, the four depicting the bust of *Margaret La Farge Osborn* and the four depicting the sculpture *Mother and Child*, are block-tagged because their dark backgrounds require additional taggant to activate the automatic mail-processing equipment used by USPS.

Isamu Noguchi was born Isamu Gilmour in Los Angeles November 17, 1904. His mother, Leonie Gilmour, was an American writer, and his father, Yonejiro Noguchi, was a Japanese poet.

The father abandoned the family soon after Isamu's birth, and the boy was taken to Japan by his mother when he was 2. In Japan he attended Japanese and Jesuit schools and was apprenticed at a young age to a cabinetmaker, where he learned woodworking and the love of tools.

When he was 13, his mother sent him to a progressive boarding school in Indiana. In 1922, he enrolled in the premedical program at Columbia University in New York City, where he also attended Leonardo da Vinci Art School.

He dropped out of Columbia in 1924, changed his name from Gilmour to Noguchi, and took a studio in Manhattan where he could sculpt full time. He quickly moved beyond traditional sculpture and was influenced by surrealism and other schools of abstract art.

Studying in Paris on a Guggenheim fellowship, Noguchi worked with Romanian abstract sculptor Constantin Brancusi and met Alexander Calder and Alberto Giacometti. In 1929 he returned to New York, where he supported himself by producing representational busts of well-known people such as R. Buckminster Fuller and George Gershwin, although he considered this type of work artistically limiting.

During World War II, in sympathy with Japanese-American internees, Noguchi was briefly interned at his own request. After several months, he petitioned the U.S. government and was released. In 1950, he traveled to Japan to help bridge the cultural gap between the former enemies and re-establish artistic relations.

Throughout his career, Noguchi strove to expand the role of the sculptor. He worked with a wide range of materials, including wood, stone, marble, steel, bamboo, paper and even water, and created works on an ever-expanding scale, including gardens that were inspired by Japanese tradition but marked by Western influence.

Noguchi also designed building interiors, courtyards and large-scale landscapes around the world. His corporate commissions in the United States included courtyards for Connecticut General Life Insurance Company (now CIGNA) in Bloomfield, Connecticut; two symbolic gardens for IBM headquarters in Armonk, New York; and the Horace E. Dodge Fountain, a Detroit landmark that incorporates water as a prominent sculptural element. He created two monumental concrete bridge railings for the Peace Park in Hiroshima, Japan.

Strongly attracted to the theater, Noguchi designed stage sets for choreographer Martha Graham, in a collaboration that began in 1935 and lasted 40 years. He created sets and costumes for other choreographers, including George Balanchine, and designed the set for the Royal Shakespeare Company's production of *King Lear* in 1955.

Noguchi married Japanese film star Yoshiko (Shirley) Yamaguchi in 1952. The union ended in divorce five years later.

In 1986, Noguchi represented the United States in the Biennale, a prestigious art exhibition in Venice. The following year, he was awarded the National Medal of Arts by President Ronald Reagan, and in 1988 he received the Award for Distinction in Sculpture from the Sculpture Center in New York and the Third Order of the Sacred Treasure in Japan.

He died December 30, 1988, at the age of 84. In a symbol of his lifetime attempt to fuse his Japanese and American artistic and cultural heritages, his body was cremated, with half the ashes interred in his sculpture garden at Mure, on the island of Shikoku, Japan, and the other half in Long Island City, New York, at the Isamu Noguchi Garden Museum.

Shown here are two alternative stamp designs depicting a bust of a woman and an abstract sculpture. They were replaced on the pane by the bust of **Margaret La Farge Osborn** *and* **Figure** *(detail), respectively.*

Isamu Noguchi 1904–1988

Isamu Noguchi 1904–1988

The Designs

USPS art director Derry Noyes had a special reason to volunteer for the design assignment. She was a long-time admirer of Noguchi's work and had a memorable meeting with him two decades earlier.

"In 1980, I designed a brochure, logo, maps and a number of other graphic elements for an international sculpture conference in Washington," she said in a Postal Service interview. "Noguchi was the honorary chair and an exhibitor. We had lunch and spent a while discussing his work. Because I talked to him and saw him alongside his own sculpture, I found myself with a stronger understanding of the amazing things he was doing."

However, as Noyes had discovered when she designed the Alexander Calder pane in 1998, depicting sculpture on stamps isn't easy.

"I did a tremendous amount of research," she told *The Yearbook*. "I looked at everything Noguchi had done. The breadth of work is mammoth, and the scale of it ranges from stage sets to portrait busts. I wanted to show a cross-section of these things, and also to get across what set him apart — that he tried to put the beauty of his sculpture into everyday things we use, like furniture and lamps.

"I also wanted to use details to show the structure of some of his sculptures, how they are put together, almost like puzzle pieces. But I was worried that the images wouldn't hold up when they were reduced, and that if it all was too abstract, people wouldn't be able to identify with it."

Noyes narrowed the universe of Noguchi's work to a handful of pieces that she felt would show best at stamp size. Of these, five made the final cut. Although some of the pictures she selected were in color, she decided to make the stamps black and white.

"Doing it that way sort of tied the images together," she said. "I tried color, making each stamp a different color, but it all was too distracting. Using black and white, and the gray tones in between, makes you focus on the objects themselves. It's more soothing, and it really brings out the dimensions and textures of the objects."

PhotoAssist, the Postal Service's research firm, contacted the Isamu Noguchi Foundation for clearances and help in obtaining satisfactory photographic prints or transparencies. "Usually, when you deal with fine-arts foundations, there are rights problems and problems with cropping the images," Noyes said. "But the Noguchi Foundation people were really nice to work with. They were so happy that this was going to happen that we didn't run into any roadblocks."

Of the five objects shown on the stamps, four are entire and one is a detail of a larger work. They are identified in a line of type on the narrow selvage on the right side of the pane. The pieces are:

The bust of *Margaret La Farge Osborn*, 1937, from a private collection in Connecticut. Its subject was the granddaughter of the painter John La Farge; the daughter of C. Grant La Farge, the initial architect for the Episcopal Cathedral of St. John the Divine in New York City; and the sister of Christopher La Farge, an architect who was better known as poet and novelist, and Oliver La Farge, an archaeologist who won a Pulitzer Prize in 1929 for his first novel, *Laughing Boy*. Her husband was William Osborn, an executive of the Phelps Dodge Corporation. The author of one published novel, Margaret was a friend of young artists, including Noguchi and R. Buckminster Fuller (another 2004 stamp subject). The stamp's photograph of the bust was made by Rudolph Burckhardt.

Black Sun, 1960-1963. This nine-foot doughnut in Swedish black granite is part of the collection of the Rockefeller Foundation and is displayed at Kykuit, the Rockefeller estate in Tarrytown, New York. It was photographed by Nicolas Eckstrom. A similar *Black Sun*, in Brazilian granite, is at the Seattle, Washington, Art Museum, where panoramic views of the city skyline and the Space Needle can be seen through its center hole.

Mother and Child, 1944-1947. This abstract onyx sculpture, 19¼ inches high, is in the collection of the Isamu Noguchi Garden Museum in Long Island City. "It was hard to hold onto the detail on the photograph

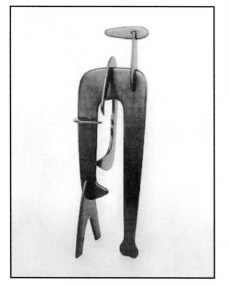

and not lose a lot of it into shadow," Noyes said. "Dodge Color [the company that does the Postal Service's preprint work] had to help with this one." The photograph is by Rudolph Burckhardt.

This is the bronze sculpture Figure, *of which the top right portion is shown as a detail on one of the stamps. The sculpture, which stands 60 inches high, is in the Isamu Noguchi Garden Museum.*

Figure (detail), 1945. The stamp depicts the upper right portion of a 60-inch bronze abstract sculpture in the Noguchi museum. Bill Jacobson was the photographer.

Akari 25N, a table lamp, circa 1968, also from the museum collection. "I was determined to get an Akari lamp on the pane, because that's how people know him best," Noyes said. Akari lamps, constructed of mulberry paper, bamboo and wires, were inspired by the lanterns of the fishermen of Gifu on the coast of Japan. The light sculpture rests on a three- or four-legged base that makes it appear to float in space. "Inherent in Akari are lightness and fragility," Noguchi wrote. "They seem to me the magical unfolding away from the material world." The photograph is by Kevin Noble.

Along the bottom of each stamp are the words: "Isamu Noguchi 1904-1988" in black. Elsewhere in the design is "37 usa," in black or dropout white. The typeface is called Fago. The lowercase "usa" "just seemed to look right," Noyes said. "No one complained! Sometimes uppercase becomes clunky looking, and I wanted to keep the type as minimal as possible."

The wide pictorial selvage on the left side of the pane displays a photograph of Noguchi by Eliot Elisofon circa 1950 in which the sculptor is contemplating a prototype for a tall, segmented Akari light sculpture that has been called "Column of Light." The photo is in the collection of the Harry Ransom Humanities Research Center at the University of Texas at Austin. Beneath it is an oft-quoted Noguchi comment: "Everything is sculpture. Any material, any idea without hindrance born into space, I consider sculpture." PhotoAssist supplied the quotation but was unable to determine the date and context of it.

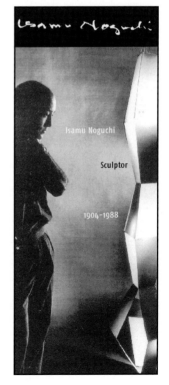

"The photo captured his interaction with his work, rather than just being a portrait of him, and it fit in a vertical format," Noyes said. "I tried blowing it up really big, but it became grainy, and also it seemed a little overpowering at that size." She included a replica of Noguchi's signature in the latter version, but omitted it in the finished design.

This alternative selvage design incorporates a larger picture and a replica of the sculptor's signature, and has no quotation.

First-Day Facts

Donna M. Peak, vice president of finance and controller for USPS, dedicated the stamps in a ceremony at the Isamu Noguchi Garden Museum in Long Island City, New York.

Also participating were Jenny Dixon, director of the Noguchi museum; Helen Marshall, Queens, New York, borough president; Richard Schwartz, chairman of the New York State Council on the Arts; and Catherine Cassidy, marketing manager for the USPS Triboro District.

The museum had been closed for more than two years for renovations and was scheduled to officially reopen June 12, 2004. Noguchi founded the two-story facility in a former photoengraving plant three years before his death. It has a small garden and contains more than 250 works covering all his creative periods.

For a limited time, Stamp Fulfillment Services sold a set of five uncacheted first-day covers for $3.75.

37¢ NATIONAL WORLD WAR II MEMORIAL

Date of Issue: May 29, 2004

Catalog Number: Scott 3862

Colors: black, cyan, magenta, yellow

First-Day Cancel: Washington, D.C. Stamp had nationwide sale on its first-day date.

First-Day Cancellations: 114,835

Format: Panes of 20, horizontal, 4 across, 5 down. Offset printing plates printing 180 stamps per revolution (15 across, 12 around).

Gum Type: self-adhesive

Scrambled Indicia: U.S. flag

Overall Stamp Size: 1.56 by 0.99 inches; 39.625 by 25.146mm

Pane Size: 7.135 by 5.9 inches; 181.229 by 149.86mm

Perforations: 10¾ (die-cut simulated perforations) (IDC two-station die cutter)

Selvage Markings: "©2003/USPS" ".37/x20/$7.40" "PLATE/POSITION" and diagram.

Back Markings: Universal Product Code (UPC) "456200" in 4 locations.

Artist: Tom Engeman of Brunswick, Maryland

Art Director and Typographer: Howard Paine of Delaplane, Virginia

Modeler: Joseph Sheeran of Ashton-Potter (USA) Ltd., Williamsville, New York

Stamp Manufacturing: Stamps printed by Ashton-Potter on offset portion of Stevens Variable Size Security Documents A76 modified webfed 6-color offset, 3-color intaglio press. Stamps processed by Ashton-Potter.

Quantity Ordered: 96,400,000

Plate Number Detail: 1 set of 4 plate numbers preceded by the letter P in selvage above or below each corner stamp

Plate Number Combination Reported: P1111

Paper Supplier: Paper Corporation of the United States/Glatfelter

Tagging: phosphored paper

The Stamp

On May 29, the Postal Service issued a 37¢ stamp commemorating the dedication of the National World War II Memorial in Washington, D.C. The stamp, picturing a portion of the memorial, was sold nationwide that day, but its first-day city was Washington, where its unveiling officially opened the dedication ceremony for the memorial itself.

Two previous commemoratives also had depicted war memorials in the nation's capital. The Vietnam Veterans Memorial appeared on a 20¢ stamp in 1984 (Scott 2109), and the Korean War Veterans Memorial was the subject of a 37¢ stamp in 2003 (Scott 3803).

The World War II Memorial stamp, a self-adhesive, was printed by the offset process by Ashton-Potter (USA) Ltd. and distributed in panes of 20. Its design first appeared in public in a grainy color image published in Issue No. 3 (Vol. 2, year 2003) of *American Commemorative Collectibles*, a newsletter published by USPS in conjunction with its commemorative stamp panel program.

The memorial is on the National Mall between the Lincoln Memorial and the Washington Monument, on the site of the old Rainbow Pool. It honors the 16 million Americans who served in the armed forces during history's greatest conflict, the more than 400,000 military personnel who gave their lives in defense of their country, and the millions who supported them on the home front.

Nearly 59 years elapsed between the end of the war in August 1945 and the memorial's dedication. President Bill Clinton signed the law authorizing the memorial on May 25, 1993, after which came a lengthy period of fund-raising, public hearings and various official approvals. More than $195 million in cash and pledges was raised, including $16 million from the federal government.

An open national competition to choose the design drew more than 400 entries. The winning team, assembled by Leo A. Daly, an international architecture firm, included Friedrich St. Florian of Providence, Rhode Island, design architect; Raymond J. Kaskey, sculptor; James A. van Sweden, landscape architect; and Nicholas Benson, stone carver and letterer. The joint venture of Tompkins Builders and Grunley-Walsh Construction was the general contractor.

Many persons objected to the planned location of the memorial, saying it would be a disruptive visual element in the classic axis defined by the Capitol, the Washington Monument, the Reflecting Pool and the Lincoln Memorial. But the original plan prevailed, and construction began in September 2001. The memorial was opened to the public April 29, 2004, exactly one month before its dedication.

Its unifying elements are a plaza and a rebuilt Rainbow Pool. Twenty-four bronze bas-relief sculptures along the ceremonial entrance balustrades depict America's war years, at home and overseas. Two 43-foot pavilions, one for the Atlantic theater, the other for the Pacific, serve as markers and entries on the north and south ends of the plaza. Inside each 23-foot-square pavilion are four bronze columns supporting American eagles that hold a suspended victory laurel.

Each pavilion stands in the center of a curving row of 28 granite pillars, 56 in all, one for each of the World War II-era states, territories and the District of Columbia. The 17-foot pillars are adorned with oak and wheat bronze wreaths, two to a pillar. Each is open in the center and connected to the others by a bronze sculpted rope symbolic of the nation's wartime unity.

The Freedom Wall on the western side of the memorial is decorated with 4,000 gold stars in remembrance of the Americans who gave their lives during the conflict, when the gold star was the symbol of family sacrifice. There are small fountains at the base of the two memorial pavilions, larger fountains in the Rainbow Pool and waterfalls flanking the Freedom Wall.

World War II itself, the people who fought in it and the weapons they used have been the subjects of a large number of U.S. stamps over the years, including several that were issued while the conflict was raging. From 1991 through 1995, USPS marked the 50th anniversary of the war with a set of 50 commemoratives issued in annual panes of 10 stamps each to recall the events of the years 1941 through 1945 (Scott 2559, 2697, 2765, 2828 and 2981).

The Design

Howard Paine had served as art director for the World War II 50th anniversary series and volunteered to fill that role for the World War II Memorial stamp. For his illustrator, he chose Tom Engeman, whose computer-generated art features bold, simple areas of light and shade and whose previous work for USPS has included the nondenominated Butte, Mountain and Sea Coast coils of 1995-2002; the 23¢ Ohio University card of 2003; and the 23¢ Columbia University card issued earlier in 2004.

It was obvious that the stamp must depict the memorial, but in the spring of 2002, when the design team began work, construction was in only the earliest stages. Paine recalled his experience as art director for *National Geographic* magazine when he was asked to provide a panoramic picture of Expo '67 long before the vast fairgrounds in Montreal was completed. "The artist, William H. Bond, had to work from plans, models, sketches and artists' renderings from countries around the world," he said. The same strategy would be needed here, and Louis Plummer of PhotoAssist, the Postal Service's research firm, arranged for Paine, Engeman and himself to pay a visit to the construction site on the Mall.

"We met with the builders and people from the National Park Service," Paine said. "They had a trailer with plans and drawings on the walls, and three models. One, at very small scale, showed the entire Mall, with the memorial in place. A second model, at larger scale, showed details of the

Stamp artist Tom Engeman is shown visiting the World War II Memorial site during construction and photographing a model of the memorial on the National Mall inside the builder's trailer.

memorial itself, the 56 columns or pillars, the two pavilions, the steps, the pool and so on. A third model was at even greater scale and showed one of the pavilions close up, so the details and inscriptions could be seen.

"Outside, where we tramped around wearing hard hats, there was a single column at full scale — not of painted wood or styrofoam, but of real stone. It was being assembled so the contractors could get a good idea of exactly how to hoist each slab of granite into place. Eventually, they would have to do that 56 times."

The visitors took numerous photographs, to capture detail and to try to frame a composition for an effective stamp design. Later, Engeman made a series of rough sketches picturing the memorial from different angles and distances.

"We decided that we wanted a three-quarters perspective that showed one pavilion and an arc of columns, indicating how the columns come out like arms embracing the pool, with trees in the background," Paine said.

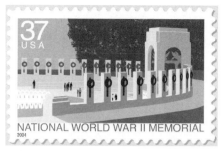 

In these two unused designs, a day and night view, the pavilion that dominates the picture is seen from outside the curving row of granite pillars rather than inside, as on the finished stamp.

"We decided, too, that we didn't want to show the Washington Monument in the distance, which some people suggested that we do to fix the memorial's location. We had shown the monument many times on stamps, and we wanted to focus on the memorial. We didn't want the 'competition' of the monument in the design."

Working from the photographs he made at the construction site, Engeman came up with designs from two slightly different perspectives. Each depicted one of the two 43-foot memorial arches and a section of the curving row of pillars that flanks it. After experimenting with a night scene, in shades of blue with solid darkness behind, the artist and art director decided on a daytime setting.

In Engeman's finished picture, 11 pillars and a portion of a 12th can be seen. Stylized jets of water curve upward in front of the pavilion and from the pool in the foreground. Three visitors, presumably a father, mother and teen-age child, stand within the memorial and provide scale. Behind the pavilion, the lacy branches of a grove of trees are silhouetted against a crimson sky that shades to a darker tone at the top of the design.

The word on the pavilion above the arch is only suggested, and cannot be identified as "Atlantic" or "Pacific." "We didn't want to favor one over the other on the stamp," Paine said.

Engeman placed the words "NATIONAL WORLD WAR II MEMO-

The stamp's "Scrambled Indicia," visible only through a special acrylic decoder, is a U.S. flag in the open sky at the upper left.

RIAL" in blue Universe capitals on a white strip across the bottom. The inscription "37 USA," also in blue, is in the upper left corner.

The stamp includes "Scrambled Indicia," a patented process in which a printed design element can be seen only through a special acrylic decoder sold by the Postal Service. It consists of a U.S. flag in the open sky at the upper left.

On his own initiative, Engeman prepared a stamped envelope incorporating the stamp design in three colors, black, blue and red. However, postal officials decided that the stamp alone would be sufficient to commemorate the event.

First-Day Facts

Postmaster General John E. Potter dedicated the stamp before an audience estimated at 140,000 that was gathered for the day's events on the Mall. This portion of the program took place on a small stage to the left of the main stage where the dedication of the memorial itself was scheduled.

Speaking of the uniformed men and women who served in World War II, Potter said: "As postmaster general, I take pride in knowing that 'mail

Postmaster General John E. Potter and John E. Walsh, vice chairman of the Postal Service Board of Governors, unveil the design of the World War II National Memorial stamp at the dedication ceremony for the stamp and the memorial. (Photo by Daniel Afzal, U.S. Postal Service)

call' was the sound of home, no matter where they served. I am gratified that a simple letter, sealed with a kiss, was a powerful reminder of what they were fighting for on those distant oceans and battlefields."

After his remarks, Potter joined John Walsh, vice chairman of the USPS Board of Governors and a World War II veteran of the U.S. Army's 78th Infantry Division, in unveiling a large replica of the stamp.

The ceremony for the memorial featured speeches by President George W. Bush; former U.S. Senator Bob Dole, a wounded World War II veteran, who had chaired the fund-raising campaign; actor Tom Hanks; and NBC news anchor Tom Brokaw, whose book *The Greatest Generation* saluted the Americans who fought in the war. Retired Marine Corps General P.X. Kelley, the chairman of the American Battle Monuments Commission, officially presented the memorial on behalf of the nation. Among those attending were former President George H.W. Bush, a Navy pilot during the war, and former President Bill Clinton.

For a limited time, Stamp Fulfillment Services offered uncacheted first-day covers for sale at 75¢.

37¢ OLYMPIC GAMES

Date of Issue: June 9, 2004

Catalog Number: Scott 3863

Colors: black, cyan, magenta, yellow

First-Day Cancel: Philadelphia, Pennsylvania

First-Day Cancellations: 80,760

Format: Pane of 20 stamps, horizontal, 4 across, 5 down. Offset printing plates printing 240 stamps per revolution (12 across, 20 around).

Microprinting: "XXVIII Olympiad" along instep of running figure's right foot

Gum Type: self-adhesive

Overall Stamp Size: 1.56 by 0.99 inches; 39.625 by 25.146mm

Pane Size: 7.24 by 5.92 inches; 183.896 by 150.638mm

Perforations: 10¾ (die-cut simulated perforations) (IDC two-station die cutter)

Selvage Inscription: "36 U.S.C. Sec. 220506/Official Licensed Product of the/United States Olympic Committee."

Selvage Markings: "©2003/USPS" ".37/x20/$7.40" "PLATE/POSITION" and diagram

Back Markings: Universal Product Code (UPC) "456300" in 4 locations on liner paper.

Artist: Lonnie Busch of Franklin, North Carolina

Art Director, Designer and Typographer: Richard Sheaff of Scottsdale, Arizona

Modeler: Joseph Sheeran of Ashton-Potter (USA) Ltd., Williamsville, New York

Stamp Manufacturing: Stamps printed by Ashton-Potter on Mueller Martini A76 Modified offset press. Stamps processed by Ashton-Potter.

Quantity Ordered: 71,800,000

Plate Number Detail: 1 set of 4 plate numbers preceded by the letter P in selvage above or below each corner stamp

Plate Number Combination Reported: P1111

Paper Supplier: Paper Corporation of the United States/Glatfelter
Tagging: unphosphored paper, block tagging over stamps

The Stamp

On June 9, the Postal Service issued a stamp commemorating the forthcoming 2004 Olympic Games in Athens, Greece. Because its design was influenced by a Greek artifact in the University of Pennsylvania Museum of Archaeology and Anthropology, the first-day ceremony was held at the museum in Philadelphia.

U.S. stamps for the Olympics have a long tradition behind them. In recent years, however, the Postal Service has found working with the Olympic committees extremely frustrating. The Summer Games in Atlanta, Georgia, in 1996, was marked by bitter disagreements over stamp designs, licensing rights, post office facilities at the Games and other issues. As a result, USPS refused to issue stamps honoring the 1998 Winter Games in Japan and the 2000 Summer Games in Australia, choosing instead to produce single, generic Winter Sports and Summer Sports stamps that made no reference to the Olympics.

In 2002, after a rapprochement of sorts, USPS produced a block of four Winter Sports stamps that also paid tribute to the Winter Games in Utah by once more incorporating in the designs the Olympic symbol, five interlocking rings. But as the 2004 Summer Games approached, Olympian rule-making and procrastination complicated the Postal Service's planning, to the point that officials considered the possibility of canceling a stamp that had been announced and its design made public.

"The [Citizens' Stamp Advisory] Committee had told us to try to get approval to use the Olympic rings again," said Terrence McCaffrey, manager of stamp development. "Their position was that if we couldn't get the rings, there would be no stamp. They refused to play the game again of issuing just a 'summer sports' stamp." CSAC's determination not to reuse that tactic was reinforced by its choice of a design that was evocative of ancient Greece. A summer sports stamp that had a Greek look would be "a little too blatant" snub of the Olympics, McCaffrey explained.

After several months of intermittent communication with the International Olympic Committee, USPS found that it would need approval from the U.S. Olympic Committee as well, even though the Games would be held on foreign soil. The necessary signed agreements took additional months to obtain. Then, after Olympic officials saw the proposed design, they vetoed its wording and type style — "It had to be a little more standard, and not as Greek-looking as we had made it," McCaffrey said — and specified the inscription to be used.

Meanwhile, the Postal Service had published a poster bearing the designs of its 2004 commemoratives, including a simplified Olympic Games design with no Olympic rings and no wording other than "37

USA." "We didn't have the approval we needed, so we couldn't legally reproduce the rings or the words 'Olympic Games,' even as a promotion for an upcoming stamp," McCaffrey explained. If no agreement had been forthcoming, the stamp would have been scratched from the program, but shortly thereafter the Olympic committees signed off on the final design.

The stamp, a self-adhesive, was printed by Ashton-Potter (USA) Ltd. by the offset process and distributed in panes of 20, with block tagging over the stamps but not the selvage. The design and its solid background color cover the entire surface of the stamp to the tips of the die-cut simulated perfs and flow into the adjacent stamps. Collectors of used stamps quickly became aware of an unusual problem related to this feature.

The pseudonymous J.A. Watercutter, author of the "Stamp Soaker" column in *Linn's Stamp News*, was prompted by a reader's complaint to conduct an experimental soak of some Olympic Games stamps clipped from envelopes. After soaking for about 15 minutes in relatively hot water, the printed design of one stamp (shown in an accompanying illustration) "literally separated from the underlying paper, much like plastic wrap peeled from a piece of processed cheese," Watercutter reported.

"During drying, the design veneer shrinks slightly, causing the underlying paper to curl and ripple," he continued. "Once dry, the thin printed layer is very brittle and easily cracks and flakes off the stamp paper. I did manage to soak and dry one stamp ... with the entire design intact, but a number of hairline cracks are visible in the bottom right corner of this stamp."

Later, Watercutter wrote, a reader sent him another soaked Olympic Games stamp (also illustrated) with more severe damage. "[S]o much of the design was missing that it's difficult to determine the stamp's subject or its country of origin," he commented. "Almost all of the '37 USA' in the top left corner is gone.

Two of the more extreme examples of what can happen when used specimens of the 2004 Olympic Games stamps are soaked from envelope paper. On the left is a stamp soaked by Linn's *columnist J.A. Watercutter on which the right side of the printed design peeled away and the remainder of the design veneer shrank slightly, causing the underlying paper to curl and ripple. On the right is a stamp submitted by a* Linn's *reader, which soaking damage rendered almost unrecognizable.*

"... In all my years of soaking stamps, I'd never seen anything like this. ... At this point, I think it's wise to leave on piece any used examples of the 37¢ Summer Olympic Games stamp."

The writer of *The Yearbook* had better luck soaking a few Olympics stamps, which came off their envelopes after half an hour or more in cool water and were pressed dry between pieces of cardboard (with waxed paper beneath the gum side to prevent sticking). The designs survived intact.

The first recorded Olympic Games took place in the Greek Sanctuary of Zeus at Olympia in 776 B.C. The Games were held every four years for nearly 12 centuries. Beginning with a single footrace called the stadion, the competition grew to include other events, including boxing, javelin and discus.

The Roman emperor Theodosius I banned the Olympics at the end of the 4th century A.D. More than 1,500 years later, they were revived in Athens in 1896 under the leadership of French sportsman Baron Pierre de Coubertin. The Summer Games have been held every four years since then, with the exception of 1916, 1940 and 1944, when World Wars I and II forced their cancellation.

The Games of the XXVIII Olympiad — an Olympiad is the four-year interval between Games — were held from August 13 to 29, 2004, in the country where they were born and the city where they were revived, with events taking place in the shadow of the Acropolis and other ancient sites. In all, 11,099 athletes representing 202 countries participated; both totals were new records. For the first time, the Olympic flame traveled to

In developing his illustration for the 2004 Olympic Games stamp, Lonnie Busch referred to these photographs of a bowl and amphora on which athletes and warriors in black act out strenuous scenes against a brick-colored background. The amphora, from the University of Pennsylvania Museum, shown on the right, is described as circa 530-525 B.C. and depicts a mythological battle between Hercules (left) and two Amazon women.

every continent on its way to light the torch signaling the opening of the Games.

In the final tally, the United States led all other nations in gold medals (35) and total medals (103), followed by China (32, 63); Russia (27, 92); Austria (17, 49); Japan (16, 37) and Germany (14, 48).

The Design

Art director Richard Sheaff chose an old associate, Lonnie Busch of Franklin, North Carolina, to illustrate the stamp. The two had worked together most recently on the 50-variety Greetings From America pane in 2002 that included a distinctive design for each state.

It was Sheaff's suggestion that the Olympic Games stamp pay tribute to the host country by depicting a runner in the style of the black-on-red silhouettes that decorated Attic vases during a period approximately from 630 to 470 B.C. For reference, he sent Busch color photographs of appropriate artifacts, including a bowl and amphora from the University of Pennsylvania museum that depicted ancient athletes and warriors.

Busch experimented with a vertical design, but it was obvious that a horizontal layout was more compatible with the running figure he wanted to use. On his computer, the artist created the image of a stylized racer in full stride, in black against a brick-colored background. Light-toned linework within the silhouette mimics that found on ancient art; a slight chipping and mottling effect suggests the weathered appearance of excavated pottery.

The same silhouette, but in red, is repeated in front of and behind the black central image, with the duplicates crossing the die cuts and into the stamps on either side. Thus, each row of a full pane gives the visual impression of a crowded field of runners competing in a footrace from the left selvage to the right. A classical design element called a meander, or key pattern, runs along the top and bottom of each stamp and spans the full pane.

Busch's original typography was a distinctive font called Cirrus. He placed the "37 USA" and a small set of Olympic rings in the upper left corner, in dropout white, and "2004 Summer Olympic Games * Athens" across the bottom. After the design went to Dodge Color, which does the Postal Service's prepress work, the Olympic commit-

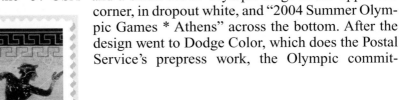

During the design development process, Busch created this vertical design, but decided that a horizontal layout would better enable him to depict the racer in full stride.

The microprinting on the stamp consists of the inscription "XXVIII Olympiad" along the instep of the running figure's right foot.

tees asked that the bottom inscription be changed to "2004 OLYMPIC GAMES * ATHENS, GREECE." In putting in the new wording, Eric Kriemelmeyer, a Dodge Color computer graphics specialist, altered the font to a more conventional sans-serif type.

Because the stamp is offset-printed, its design includes microprinting for security purposes. "XXVIII Olympiad" in black characters can be seen with a magnifying glass along the instep of the black running figure's right foot.

The Postal Service announced that the design also would incorporate a so-called Scrambled Indicia image of the kind that can be viewed only through a special decoder lens. However, there is no Scrambled Indicia on the stamp.

First-Day Facts

The Postal Service tentatively planned to hold the first-day ceremony in three U.S. cities named Athens: in Georgia, Ohio and Texas. The plan was dropped, and the ceremony was held in Philadelphia.

S. David Fineman, chairman of the USPS Board of Governors, and board member Alan C. Kessler jointly dedicated the stamp at the University of Pennsylvania Museum of Archaeology and Anthropology. Speakers were Judith Rodin, president of the university, and David Gilman Romano, senior research scientist for the museum's Mediterranean Section. Jeremy A. Sabloff, Williams director of the museum, gave the welcome. Master of ceremonies was Paul Todd Makler, a member of the U.S. Olympic fencing team in 1952 and its captain in 1964. The honored guests included six other former U.S. Olympians: Brenda Bartlett, swimmer, 1976; Elliott Denman, race walker, 1952; Barbara Kirch Grudt, rowing, 1984 and 1988; Stephen Kirk, team handball, 1984 and 1988; Paul Todd Makler Jr., fencing, 1972; and David Micahnik, fencing, 1960, 1964 and 1968.

For a limited time, Stamp Fulfillment Services sold uncacheted first-day covers of the 2004 Olympics stamp for 75¢.

116

37¢ THE ART OF DISNEY: FRIENDSHIP (4 DESIGNS)

Date of Issue: June 23, 2004

Catalog Numbers: Scott 3865-3868, stamps; 3868a, block or vertical strip of 4

Colors: cyan, magenta, yellow, black)

First-Day Cancel: Anaheim, California

First-Day Cancellations: 340,448 (includes Disney stamped stationery and postal cards)

Format: Pane of 20, vertical, 5 across, 4 down. Offset printing plates printing 180 stamps per revolution (15 across, 12 around).

Gum Type: self-adhesive

Stamp Size: 1.23 by 1.56 inches; 31.24 by 39.62mm

Pane Size: 7.13 by 8 inches; 181.1 by 203.2mm

Perforations: 10½ by 10¾ (die-cut simulated perforations) (Heidelberg rotary die cutter)

Selvage Inscription: "The Art of Disney/FRIENDSHIP." "Disney Materials ©Disney."

Selvage Markings: "©2003/USPS." ".37/x20/$7.40." "PLATE/POSITION" and diagram.

Back Markings: On selvage liner: "THE ART OF DISNEY: FRIENDSHIP/ Every good story has heroes and villains, but friends play a part, too. From the friendships in Disney films, we've/learned how to share, trust, laugh in spite of difficulties, and sometimes, just have fun." Universal Product Code (UPC) "566700" in 4 locations.

On stamp liners: "Mickey Mouse/and Friends/Mickey first appeared in/Steamboat Willie in 1928,/while Goofy started playing/for laughs in 1932, and/Donald added fuel to the fun/in 1934. Since then, the/pals have shared adventures/and misadventures/while always keeping their/ friendship intact." "Bambi and Thumper/Irrepressible Thumper/isn't awed by Bambi's/status as the 'young prince/of the forest' but simply/sees a new playmate./Generations have treasured/this coming-of-age story/for its natural beauty/and gentle, laughter-filled/depiction of/childhood friend-ships." "Mufasa and Simba/When we grow up we/make new friends who/share different parts of our/lives. But if we are fortunate/like the lion cub Simba, who/idolizes his father Mufasa,/our parents are our first/'best' friends who anchor/us with friendship that/grows from love no one/else can match." "Pinocchio and/Jiminy Cricket/Sometimes a friend has to/play the role of 'Official/Conscience' for us./Although Pinocchio doesn't/always want to hear what/Jiminy Cricket has to say,/the chipper little fellow is a/steady, stalwart mentor/when Pinocchio needs/him most."

Designer: David Pacheco, Burbank, California

Illustrator: Peter Emmerich, New York, New York

Art Director: Terrence McCaffrey

Modeler: Donald Woo of Sennett Security Products

Stamp Manufacturing: Stamps printed by Banknote Corporation of America/ Sennett Security Products, Browns Summit, North Carolina, on Roland 300 offset press. Stamps processed by Unique Binders, Fredericksburg, Virginia.

Quantity Ordered: 284,000,000

Plate Number Detail: 1 set of 4 plate numbers preceded by the letter S in selvage below each lower corner stamp

Plate Number Combinations Reported: S1111, S2222

Paper Supplier: Paper Corporation of the United States/Spinnaker Coatings

Tagging: block tagging over stamps

Previous U.S. stamps with themes related to Walt Disney Studios were a 6¢ stamp of 1968 honoring Disney himself (Scott 1355) and a 32¢ stamp in the Celebrate the Century series recalling the first full-length animated film, Snow White and the Seven Dwarfs *of 1937 (Scott 3185h).*

The Stamps

Since 1970, some two dozen small countries have produced sets of stamps and souvenir sheets featuring animated cartoon characters from the films of the Walt Disney Studios. Most of these items were produced by Inter-Governmental Philatelic Corporation of New York City under contract with Disney and are considered exploitive issues that some collectors regard with disdain.

For a long time, however, no U.S. stamp pictured a Disney character, because of the restrictions imposed by the studio on such reproductions. Even the 6¢ stamp issued by the U.S. Post Office Department to honor Walt Disney himself two years after his death in 1966 showed only a generic "Children of the World" procession.

The first break in the Disney policy came in 1998 when a 32¢ Celebrate the Century stamp in the pane for the 1930s depicted *Snow White*, the title character of the first full-length animated cartoon film. But even that project initially met with a "negative" response from Disney officials, according to Terrence McCaffrey, manager of stamp design for USPS. "They didn't want to do the stamp," McCaffrey said. The studio cooperated only after Karl Malden, a veteran film actor and member of the Citizens' Stamp Advisory Committee, asked Roy E. Disney, vice chairman of Disney's board of directors, to intervene.

So it represented a full policy reversal by the company when on June 23, 2004, the Postal Service issued four self-adhesive stamps in a se-tenant pane of 20 depicting familiar animated cartoon characters from the films of the Walt Disney Studios.

The pane was the first of three that will be issued annually to celebrate "The Art of Disney." Each set will have a theme, the first of which was "Friendship." The friends depicted on the stamps were Mickey Mouse, Goofy and

Donald Duck; Bambi and Thumper; Simba and his father, Mufasa; and Pinocchio and Jiminy Cricket. The subsequent years' themes will be "Celebration" and "Romance."

Accompanying the stamps were companion sets of stamped picture postal cards and letter sheets (see separate chapters).

The new attitude at Disney was signaled in February 2002, when studio officials informed Kelly Spinks, a Postal Service lawyer specializing in obtaining rights to use protected names and images on stamps, that they wanted to discuss a possible stamp project. Spinks and McCaffrey met with the officials and concluded that they were serious and would be cooperative.

"The committee [CSAC] was skeptical," McCaffrey recalled. "They said, 'OK, you went through five years of Looney Tunes. That wasn't enough for you. You want to go back for more?'" From 1997 through 2001, USPS had issued annual stamps picturing characters from Warner

The pane bears descriptive text on the reverse on the liner paper.

Bros.' Looney Tunes animated cartoons, beginning with Bugs Bunny and ending with Porky Pig.

"I said, 'This is different. It's not as big a program, and I really think it could work,'" McCaffrey continued. "They said, 'Remember all the times we had to go to Capitol Hill and explain why we were doing a Bugs Bunny stamp and not commemorating the Spanish settlement of the Southwest and other subjects that Congress wanted?' I said, 'I understand!'"

However, CSAC member Jean Picker Firstenberg, who is director and chief executive officer of the American Film Institute, expressed enthusiasm for the idea, and McCaffrey was asked to meet again with the Disney studio and return with some answers and a specific proposal.

Disney's motivation in reaching out to the Postal Service turned out to be purely commercial. The studio was about to launch a marketing drive to revitalize Disney's signature character, Mickey Mouse, whose 75th anniversary was coming up in 2003, and wanted to use a U.S. stamp issue as an element of the campaign.

"Mickey is not the icon he used to be," McCaffrey explained. "You don't see him on the Saturday morning cartoons, you don't see him in movies, you don't see him anywhere except in the Disney theme parks. They're trying to bring Mickey back. In our talks with the studio, they were quite honest with us about it.

"We felt that the stamps would generate good revenue for us, just as Bugs Bunny, Daffy Duck and Wile E. Coyote did. For us, it would be a revenue generator; for them, it would help raise awareness of Mickey."

Originally, CSAC and postal officials thought in terms of a one-time stamp issue featuring Mickey and some of his better-known colleagues. Later, they decided to expand it to a three-year series. "We didn't want to go any further than that," McCaffrey said. "We found that with Looney Tunes, after the third year, interest began to drop off, and by the fifth year it was just like 'OK, this is so over now!' The studio agreed; they didn't want to overextend it."

The plan that emerged was to issue a block of four stamps each year, one stamp starring Mickey Mouse, two others depicting other characters that Disney describes as "classics" (in the 2004 set, these were the Pinocchio-Jiminy Cricket and Bambi-Thumper stamps), and a fourth featuring characters, in McCaffrey's words, "that are fairly contemporary but rapidly becoming classic" (Simba-Mufasa).

"We didn't want to feature films as such, but feature the relationships between the characters," McCaffrey said. "The committee said explicitly that we weren't going to endorse movies. That's why we came up with

our themes: friendship, romance and celebration. These are not a *Bambi* movie stamp, a *Lion King* movie stamp or a *Pinocchio* movie stamp."

The first four stamps were announced August 7, 2003, at the annual meeting of postal officials and the philatelic press. The Postal Service unveiled their designs December 30, 2003, in Washington, D.C.

However, both disclosures were anticlimactic. On July 24, 2003, *Hollywood Reporter*'s web site had posted an article by Jesse Hiestand on Disney's plans to restore Mickey Mouse to center stage, and reported that USPS "will recognize Mickey and his friends with a three-year stamp campaign." The article described the company's plans for "Mickey to play a more prominent role" as it sought to revive a "lackluster" consumer products division. "The mouse, at least in our opinion, is an underutilized branding tool," one analyst told the publication. And the design of the Mickey-Goofy-Donald stamp was displayed November 24, 2003, on *The New York Times'* Web site accompanying a similar article on Mickey's future.

The stamps, semijumbo in size, were printed for Sennett Security Products/Banknote Corporation of America by American Packaging Corporation using the offset process and distributed in panes of 20 with decorative selvage. The panes are laid out in four horizontal rows of five, with each horizontal row consisting of two alternating designs. Any block or vertical strip of four from the pane comprises all four varieties.

In anticipation of the stamps' popularity, the Postal Service ordered a printing of 284 million, which was almost five times the 57 million printing quantity for the four American Choreographers stamps that were issued May 4.

Mickey Mouse was born in the mind of the 26-year-old Walt Disney when he was traveling from New York to California by train in 1928, according to the filmmaker's own account. The character's jaunty personality and his name, Mortimer, were taken from a mouse Disney had adopted as a pet while working for a Kansas City, Missouri, film ad company. His wife rejected the name Mortimer as too pretentious and suggested the name Mickey instead.

While Disney supplied Mickey Mouse's personality and, for many years, his screen voice, the character's physical appearance was the creation of Disney's first partner, the legendary animator Ub Iwerks. Mickey's film debut,

Steamboat Willie, released November 18, 1928, exploited the movies' brand-new sound technology; the short was synchronized to two songs — "Steamboat Bill" and "Turkey in the Straw" — that Mickey performed on various improvised instruments. *Steamboat Willie* was a smash hit, and led a parade of dozens of Mickey Mouse animated cartoons that helped ease the gloom of the Depression for film audiences.

Goofy, originally known as Dippy Dawg, made his film debut as a hayseed in the crowd in *Mickey's Revue* (1932). The Disney Web site describes Goofy as "good-natured but not that bright." Donald Duck first appeared on the screen in the Silly Symphonies cartoon *The Wise Little Hen* (1934) as a rather dumpy little bird with a long beak and a sailor suit. In time, the temperamental duck would be featured in more animated cartoons than his friend Mickey.

"In Walt Disney's *Bambi* (1942), an energetic rabbit named Thumper becomes a lifelong friend to a young deer," the Postal Service said in a news release. "Thumper accompanies Bambi in both pleasurable pursuits, such as their winter adventures on ice, and in adversity.

"Our parents can be our best friends, as the cub Simba learns in *The Lion King* (1994) when his father, Mufasa, comes to his rescue after Simba is chased by hyenas. Simba idolizes Mufasa and hopes to grow up to be just like him.

"Sometimes, as in Walt Disney's animated film classic *Pinocchio* (1940), a friend acts as our conscience and keeps us out of trouble — or, at least, tries to. After he is magically brought to life, the wooden marionette Pinocchio is assisted by diminutive Jiminy Cricket in his effort to become a real boy."

The Designs

The Looney Tunes stamps had been designed by Warner Bros. artists, and in the same way, artists from the Disney Studios provided the illustrations for the Disney stamps. The process was neither swift nor simple.

Choosing the subjects and developing the designs involved some two years of "shuttle diplomacy" between the Postal Service and Disney, during which Terrence McCaffrey and other Stamp Services officials made frequent flights to California to discuss and review design concepts with a creative team from the studio headed by Brian Siegel.

"One of the first things I made clear was that I didn't want to see any animation cel art," McCaffrey said. "Most foreign countries have used cels. I said, 'If we're going to do Disney stamps, they're going to be unique, original.' They totally agreed."

The illustrators assigned to the project were David Pacheco, creative director of Walt Disney Art Classics, who served as art director, and Peter Emmerich of New York City, a former Disney animator who now is a freelance illustrator. Working in pencil, Pacheco developed the design concepts, from which Emmerich created the finished art. Emmerich's

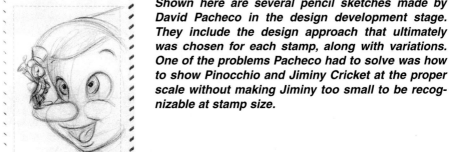

Shown here are several pencil sketches made by David Pacheco in the design development stage. They include the design approach that ultimately was chosen for each stamp, along with variations. One of the problems Pacheco had to solve was how to show Pinocchio and Jiminy Cricket at the proper scale without making Jiminy too small to be recognizable at stamp size.

124

In this Peter Emmerich color rough, Jiminy Cricket is perched on Pinocchio's nose. However, at stamp size, Jiminy and his blue top hat would have been lost against Pinocchio's black hair. Besides, said Terrence McCaffrey, "Pinocchio's nose would have had to be a little longer than normal to give Jiminy room to stand, and that would mean he was lying."

acrylic-on-canvas paintings conveyed a "retro look, with a texture and three-dimensionality that was just what we were looking for," McCaffrey said.

Pacheco drew at least a dozen different scenarios for each stamp, the studio official told *Disney Insider*, an online publication. Postal officials "went over the rough concepts one at a time and made a choice as to which one they felt worked best," Pacheco continued. "Everyone was very pleasant to work with, and they were very open to our ideas."

"We wanted real tight close-ups," McCaffrey said. "We didn't want full body illustrations; those would be just too distant.

"Our biggest problem was with Pinocchio and Jiminy Cricket and their size relationship. Jiminy is so small and Pinocchio is so big. We liked an approach in which Jiminy is standing on Pinocchio's nose, but at stamp size he would have been lost against the background of Pinocchio's black hair. Besides, Pinocchio's nose would have had to be a little longer than normal to give Jiminy room to stand, and that would mean he was lying. Did we want Pinocchio lying on the stamp? No!

"David went back to the sketch pad, and we came up with the solution in which Jiminy is floating down beneath his umbrella near Pinocchio's head."

Emmerich provided some visual context for two of the stamps — grass and flowers for Bambi and Thumper, the Pride Rock for Mufasa and

These color roughs by Peter Emmerich incorporate visual context: flowers and grass for Bambi and Thumper, Pride Rock for Mufasa and Simba. In the finished art, all four stamps have plain backgrounds.

125

Simba — but removed them from the finished art so that all four stamps would have the same plain beige-colored background.

Pacheco's favorite of the four stamps was Mickey and his friends. "The design stemmed from a childhood memory," he said. "When I was asked to include all three characters in the tiny format, I thought to myself, 'So how do I get all three in and still make it entertaining?'

"I remembered going to those automatic photo booths with friends where everyone squeezes into the narrow booth and everyone is pushing each other to get in the front before the flash goes off. This is the moment I tried for. Mickey has made it to the center at the last second. His arms are slightly out, still trying to keep Goofy back (who really doesn't mind), and Donald is in the process of jumping up, trying (as always) to get in the best spot — his hat slipping off and his hand in mid-wave."

Emmerich's favorite is Bambi and Thumper. "My biggest challenge was giving Dave's concepts form and volume without losing their spontaneity," he told the Postal Service. "I tend to work in very vivid color, but I toned it down for a more realistic feeling.

"I tried to express emotion through the rendering of the characters' eyes, and I concentrated less on texture and more on the light reflecting off them. For Bambi and Thumper, I used subtle blues to enhance the image and create a warm moment."

The only typography on the stamps is a blue "37" and red "USA" in one corner, in a studio font called Mickey's Wacky.

From the outset, Terrence McCaffrey had wanted the pane to have decorative selvage. Some early concept sketches for the selvage by Derry Noyes, a Postal Service art director, were simple: a header bearing a picture of Tinkerbell, the diminutive fairy from Disney's *Peter Pan*, and the pane title, all against a white background.

Brian Siegel and his creative team then took over the selvage project, retaining Tinkerbell — who also will appear on the two later Disney panes — but adding a blue background and other design elements.

"We talked about placing pencil sketches across the top, showing the evolution of one of the characters from a real rough pencil to a more refined pencil to a finished piece of art to show how a piece of art is created," McCaffrey said. "We couldn't get that to work, because it kept

USPS art director Derry Noyes developed this early concept of a simple header design with a white background, featuring Tinkerbell as the Disney character.

Paper streamers and a burst of confetti accompanied the June 23 first-day ceremony for the four The Art of Disney Friendship stamps at Disneyland.

fighting the stamp pane. We decided that the stamps needed to be the focal point, and the selvage design should be supporting."

Another version by the Disney team included line drawings of Mickey, Bambi, Thumper and Lady and the Tramp, from the Disney film of that name, all in dark blue against the lighter blue of the background. "We chose not to use this because it got really busy," McCaffrey said. "You had to look hard at it to see what everything was."

In the end, the selvage decorations on the four sides consisted of what McCaffrey called "stars, swishes and pixie dust." Across the top, in dropout white, are the words "The Art of" in Stempel Garamond italic, and the Disney logo. Below, in red capitals with a blue dropped shadow, is "FRIENDSHIP" in the Mickey's Wacky font.

First-Day Facts

Postmaster General John E. Potter dedicated the Disney stamps and postal stationery in a ceremony in front of Sleeping Beauty's Castle at the Disneyland resort in Anaheim, California.

Speakers were Michael Eisner, Walt Disney Company chief executive officer, and actor George Wendt, best known as Norm in the television sitcom *Cheers*.

Persons wishing to enter Disneyland only to view the ceremony were allowed to make reservations by telephone. Regular admission to Disneyland was not included.

For a limited time, Stamp Fulfillment Services sold sets of uncacheted first-day covers of the four Disney stamps for $3.

37¢ USS CONSTELLATION

Date of Issue: June 30, 2004

Catalog Number: Scott 3869

Color: brown (PMS 4625)

First-Day Cancel: Baltimore, Maryland

First-Day Cancellations: 84,540

Format: Panes of 20, square, 4 across, 5 down. Intaglio printing plates printing 180 stamps per revolution (12 across, 15 around).

Gum Type: self-adhesive

Overall Stamp Size: 1.225 by 1.225 inches; 31.115 by 31.115mm

Pane Size: 5.9 by 7.12 inches; 149.86 by 180.848mm

Perforations: 10½ (die-cut simulated perforations) (IDC two-station die cutter)

Selvage Markings: "© 2003/USPS" ".37/x20/$7.40" "PLATE/POSITION" and diagram.

Back Markings: Universal Product Code (UPC) "456700" in 4 locations.

Designer and Art Director: Howard Paine of Delaplane, Virginia

Typographer: John Boyd of New York, New York

Engraver: Christopher Broadbridge

Modeler: Joseph Sheeran of Ashton-Potter (USA) Ltd., Williamsville, New York

Stamp Manufacturing: Stamps printed by Ashton-Potter on intaglio portion of Stevens Variable Size Security Documents A76 modified webfed 6-color offset, 3-color intaglio press. Stamps processed by Ashton-Potter.

Quantity Ordered: 45,000,000

Plate Number Detail: 1 intaglio plate number preceded by the letter P in selvage above or below each corner stamp

Plate Number Reported: P1

Paper Supplier: Paper Corporation of the United States/Glatfelter

Tagging: phosphored paper

The Stamp

On June 30, the Postal Service marked the 150th anniversary of the launching of *USS Constellation* by issuing a 37¢ stamp in Baltimore, Maryland, where the sloop-of-war now serves as a docked museum.

The stamp was requested in July 2001 by Christopher Rowsom, executive director of the USS Constellation Museum, on behalf of the museum's anniversary steering committee, and approved by the Citizens' Stamp Advisory Committee. No petition campaign or string-pulling by influential citizens was necessary. "We fit the guidelines perfectly," Rowsom told *The Yearbook*. "An event of national significance, an anniversary year that was falling correctly, and all of that. We were very pleased that [the stamp] did happen."

The ship and its anniversary were important for several reasons, Rowson told CSAC. "*Constellation* is the last naval vessel afloat that was on active duty during the Civil War, making her the only intact representative of the Union Navy surviving today," he wrote. "She is the last all-sail ship built by the U.S. Navy, representing the pinnacle of sailing technology just before the rise of steam power.

"*Constellation*'s service as flagship of the African Squadron just before the Civil War, and her rescue of over 700 souls from the defilement of slavery, is a story that the American public knows little about, but needs to be told. The humanitarian mission to Ireland to deliver food to that beleaguered nation suffering under the political oppression of the English Crown is another untold story.

"*USS Constellation*'s roles as rescuer, protector, flagship and training ship over the course of 100 years of naval service are just cause for a celebration commemorating the launch of this incredible vessel — incredible because of her great history, and incredible because she is still here for us to appreciate."

The self-adhesive stamp was printed by intaglio by Ashton-Potter (USA) Ltd. and distributed in panes of 20.

A full understanding of *Constellation*'s history has been possible only recently. For a long time, the vessel was confused with its namesake, the U.S. frigate *Constellation*, which was launched in 1797 and earned distinction in battle — a confusion that was abetted over the years by the U.S. Navy and the Postal Service.

"For decades, naval authorities disagreed on whether *Constellation* was a new ship built in 1854 or a modification of the 1797 frigate of the same name," USPS said in a press release announcing the stamp. "In 1991, scientific examination of the ship and a recently discovered half-hull model confirmed that the ship berthed in Baltimore and known as the *USS Constellation* was indeed a new ship built in 1854."

Construction on the present *Constellation* began in 1853, just as the original ship was deemed beyond repair and broken up at the same location, the Gosport Navy Yard (now the Norfolk, Virginia, Naval Shipyard).

According to the Constellation Museum, the new *Constellation* "was built with eight pieces of the original vessel contained somewhere in her timbers, giving her the esteemed provenance from the famous frigate." The mixup of identities may have stemmed in part from the coincidence of timing.

Although no previous stamp had depicted *Constellation*, the vessel had been shown on four U.S. postal cards and a stamped envelope. Some of these earlier postal stationery items are inscribed "U.S. Frigate Constellation" or "U.S.F. Constellation" for the 1797 38-gun frigate, but they picture the 1854 *USS Constellation*, which was armed with a main battery of 20 guns.

The Postal Service press releases for these items did nothing to diminish the confusion. On April 7, 1988, in announcing the upcoming issuance of an 8.4¢ nonprofit-rate precanceled stamped envelope depicting *Constellation* at sea (Scott U612), USPS provided the following tangled history:

"The frigate *Constellation* was launched in Baltimore in 1797. Included among its exploits were the capture of the *Insurgente* (in 1799) and action with the *Vengeance* (in 1800) during a naval war with France. After being idle for many years, the ship was fully commissioned in 1940 and was a flagship of the Atlantic Fleet in World War II. Since 1955, it has been anchored in Baltimore, where it is now a featured tourist attraction in that city's popular Inner Harbor." (Information based on that erroneous press release was included in the 1988 *Linn's U.S. Stamp Yearbook*.)

In fact, the ship now permanently docked in Baltimore was designed by John Lenthall, chief of the Navy Bureau of Construction, and launched August 26, 1854. At 186 feet in length, it was 22 feet longer than the original *Constellation* and was built to be manned by a crew of some 300.

Commissioned July 28, 1855, the ship served with the Mediterranean Squadron until 1858. As the flagship of the African Squadron from 1859 to 1861, on anti-slavery patrol, it captured three slave vessels: the brigs *Cora* and *Triton* and the *Delicia*.

During the Civil War, *Constellation* saw diplomatic service in the Mediterranean Sea and searched for Confederate raiders. Later, the ship was part of the West Gulf Coast Blockading Squadron and ended the war as a floating barracks. Afterward, it served as a training vessel at the U.S. Naval Academy in Annapolis, Maryland, and occasionally was used for other missions, including transporting works of American art to the Paris Exposition of 1878 and food to Ireland during the 1880 famine.

Over the next 50 years, *Constellation* was a stationary training ship at the Newport, Rhode Island, Naval Training Station, and participated in the 1914 Star-Spangled Banner Centennial Tour and the commemoration of the 150th anniversary of the Declaration of Independence July 5, 1926.

Decommissioned by the Navy in 1933, *Constellation* returned to active duty during World War II. For a brief time in 1942, the vessel was flag-

U.S.F. CONSTELLATION

U.S. POSTAGE 6 CENTS

8.4 NONPROFIT

USA

US FRIGATE CONSTELLATION

Shown here are the stamped areas of three items of postal stationery depicting Constellation: *a 6¢ Tourism Year of the Americas postal card of 1972, an 8.4¢ nonprofit-rate envelope of 1988 and a 15¢ America the Beautiful postal card of 1989. At the time these items were issued, it was not known for certain that the* USS Constellation *(1854 to the present day) was an altogether different ship from the U.S. frigate* Constellation *(1797 to 1853).*

America the Beautiful   USA 15

ship for the U.S. Atlantic Fleet and the headquarters of Vice Admiral Royal E. Ingersoll. In 1955, once again decommissioned, *Constellation* was brought to Baltimore and donated by the Navy to a local non-profit foundation. When it finally was opened to the public nearly a decade later, it had been configured to resemble its namesake, the Baltimore-built frigate *Constellation.*

In November 1996, *Constellation* was towed to drydock for extensive restoration, and on July 2, 1999, the venerable ship, a National Historic Landmark now restored to its own original 1854 configuration, returned to its permanent berth in Baltimore's Inner Harbor and reopened its decks to the public.

A third U.S. Navy ship to bear the name *Constellation* was an aircraft carrier commissioned in 1961 and decommissioned in 2003. The carrier participated in several engagements, from the Vietnam War to Operation Iraqi Freedom.

Two of the four postal cards to show a ship identified as *Constellation* were issued in 1972 to mark Tourism Year of the Americas. The first (Scott UX61) shows a line drawing of the docked vessel, its sails furled, in the imprinted stamp design. Although the image is captioned "U.S.F. Constellation," it actually is of *USS Constellation*, in Baltimore. The other card (Scott UX62) pictures Gloucester, Massachusetts, in the stamp design, but shows on the reverse an enlargement of the same *Constellation* illustration from Scott UX61, along with three other line-drawn images.

A 15¢ America the Beautiful postal card issued October 7, 1989, (Scott UX136) reproduces a Bart Forbes painting of Baltimore's Inner Harbor in its imprinted stamp, with the National Aquarium in the background and *Constellation* floating at anchor — not at a dock — in the harbor. "The dock would have just absolutely destroyed a nice clean image, so we eliminated it," Joe Brockert, the Postal Service project manager for the card, explained. The same card (Scott UX140) later was issued on a sheet se-tenant with three other America the Beautiful cards.

The Design

CSAC and the USPS staff make an occasional gesture to stamp-collecting traditionalists by directing that the intaglio process (recess engraving) be used in printing a new stamp. As noted in preceding chapters, the three commemoratives issued earlier in 2004 for the 200th anniversary of the Lewis and Clark expedition were printed with engraved frames. The choice of design subject for the *Constellation* stamp was a picture of the historic ship under full sail, and this was "a natural" for engraving in a single color, said Terrence McCaffrey, USPS manager of stamp development.

It was suggested that the stamp be designed by Richard Schlecht of Frederick, Maryland, whose paintings had been the basis for several previous U.S. stamps and postal cards depicting ships, beginning with the 20¢ German Immigration stamp of 1983. But after PhotoAssist, the Postal Service's research firm, found an appropriate 1893-vintage photograph in the collection of the U.S. Naval Historical Center, the decision was made to have the stamp's engraver work directly from the photo rather than from an intervening illustration. Ultimately, however, Schlecht was called on to clarify and modify some of the ship's features in the ancient print.

The modifications were prompted by Ken Hickman, curator and historian at the Constellation Museum, who suggested to PhotoAssist that the photograph be made to show the ship as it looked during its "fighting" career, from 1854 to 1871, with a white stripe from bow to stern surround-

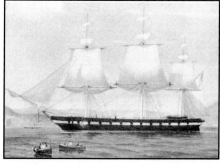

Richard Schlecht referred to these two paintings by Tomaso DeSimone when he electronically altered the photograph of Constellation *to add a white stripe to the hull. The painting of the ship with its sails furled was made in 1856 when* Constellation *visited Naples, Italy, on its first cruise. The other painting, made in 1862, shows the ship entering the harbor in Naples.*

ing the gun ports. For guidance on the latter, Schlecht consulted two paintings of *Constellation* in Naples, Italy, by Tomaso DeSimone.

"The photograph was almost unreadable, it was so poor in quality," Schlecht said. "I scanned it into Photoshop and made some corrections just to bring out some of the detail, and add some detail where there was none but I knew there should have been some. This included four or five gun ports aft of those that were visible.

"So it was sort of a corrected and improved version of a not-so-great photograph. It worked. We gave the engraver something to go by. He would not have had anything to go by before."

Art director Howard Paine is partial to square stamps, and made this one square, as well. "Our photo fit happily into it," he said. The words "USS Constellation" in condensed Galliard type are across the top, with "37 USA" on the right.

For the stamp's single color, "we tried dark green, purple, several blues, and brown," Paine said. "It came down to a dark blue, PMS 541, and a dark brown, PMS 4625.

"Richard Schlecht said, 'Well, the water is blue, and the ship is brown, and we're honoring the ship, aren't we?' That thought stuck with me, and the [CSAC] design subcommittee agreed, so we have a brown stamp, which evokes an old sepia-toned photo and gives the scene all the more feeling of history. It adds a quiet elegance to any envelope."

First-Day Facts

The *Constellation* stamp originally was scheduled for release on the 150th anniversary of the ship's launching, August 26, but the ceremony was moved up to June 30 to coincide with the start of Baltimore's five-day Tall Ships "Sailabration" featuring sailing vessels from several nations.

Deputy Postmaster General John Nolan dedicated the stamp in a ceremony on a stage in front of the docked ship at Baltimore's Inner Harbor. Speakers included Christopher Rowson, the USS Constellation Museum's executive director, who wrote the letter that led to the stamp's issuance; David J. Beck, chairman of the museum board; Baltimore Mayor Martin O'Malley; and U.S. Representative C.A. "Dutch" Ruppersberger, Democrat of Baltimore.

For a limited time, Stamp Fulfillment Services sold uncacheted first-day covers of the *Constellation* stamp for 75¢.

37¢ R. BUCKMINSTER FULLER

Date of Issue: July 12, 2004

Catalog Number: Scott 3870

Colors: black, cyan, magenta, yellow, blue (PMS 7450)

First-Day Cancel: Stanford, California

First-Day Cancellations: 70,303

Format: Panes of 20, vertical, 5 across, 4 down. Offset printing plates printing 120 stamps per revolution (8 across, 15 around).

Gum Type: self-adhesive

Microprinting: "USPS" beside left leg of structure supporting Fuller's head

Overall Stamp Size: 1.225 by 1.56 inches; 31.115 by 39.624mm

Pane Size: 7.24 by 7.12 inches; 183.896 by 180.848mm

Perforations: 10½ by 10¾ (die-cut simulated perforations) (IDC two-station die cutter)

Selvage Markings: "©2003/USPS" ".37/x20/$7.40" "PLATE/POSITION" and diagram.

Selvage Inscription: "Buckminster Fuller™ Licensed by the Estate of Buckminster Fuller./This license represented by The Roger Richman Agency, Inc."

Back Markings: "Renowned as the mind/behind the geodesic dome,/R. Buckminster Fuller/(1895-1983)/was an inventor, architect,/engineer, designer, geometrician,/cartographer, and philosopher./His pioneering solutions to the/world's problems reflected/his commitment to using/innovative design to/improve human lives," plus Universal Product Code (UPC) "456400" in 4 locations, on liner paper.

Artist: Boris Artzybasheff

Designer, Art Director and Typographer: Carl Herrman of Carlsbad, California

Modeler: Joseph Sheeran of Ashton-Potter (USA) Ltd., Williamsville, New York

Stamp Manufacturing: Stamps printed by Ashton-Potter on offset portion of Stevens Variable Size Security Documents A76 modified webfed 6-color offset, 3-color intaglio press. Stamps processed by Ashton-Potter.

Quantity Ordered: 60,000,000

Plate Number Detail: 1 set of 5 plate numbers preceded by the letter P in selvage above or below each corner stamp

Plate Number Combinations Reported: P11111, P22222

Paper Supplier: Paper Corporation of the United States/Glatfelter

Tagging: phosphored paper

The Stamp

On July 12, the Postal Service issued a stamp honoring R. Buckminster Fuller, inventor, architect, engineer, designer, geometrician, cartographer and philosopher, who is best known as the creator of the geodesic dome.

Fuller's family had asked for the stamp, and when the request reached the Citizens' Stamp Advisory Committee, it was embraced by CSAC member Michael Heyman, who is secretary emeritus of the Smithsonian Institution. "He jumped on it right away and said, 'This man deserves a stamp,' " said Terrence McCaffrey, manager of stamp development for USPS.

The self-adhesive semijumbo commemorative was printed by the offset process by Ashton-Potter (USA) Ltd. and distributed in panes of 20. Descriptive text is printed on the back of the liner paper behind each stamp.

Its date of issue was the 109th anniversary of Fuller's birth in 1895 and the 50th anniversary of the patent for his geodesic dome. The dome, pound for pound, is the lightest, strongest and most cost-effective structure ever conceived. It is created from triangles, arranged in pentagons and hexagons, that distribute stress and enclose space without internal support. The larger it is, the proportionally lighter and stronger it becomes.

Geodesic domes represent "a breakthrough in shelter, not only in cost-effectiveness, but in ease of construction," says the Buckminster Fuller Institute Web site. "In 1957, a geodesic dome auditorium in Honolulu was put up so quickly that 22 hours after the parts were delivered, a full house was comfortably seated inside enjoying a concert."

More than 300,000 domes of various sizes are standing today. Plastic and fiberglass "radomes" house delicate radar equipment along the Arctic perimeter, and weather stations withstand winds up to 180 mph. Corrugated metal domes have given shelter to African families at a cost of $350 each. The U.S. Marine Corps has called the geodesic dome "the first basic improvement in mobile military shelter in 2,600 years."

Among the biggest domes is the one that held the *Spruce Goose*, the huge flying boat built by Howard Hughes and displayed in Long Beach Harbor, California, from 1982 to 1992. The dome later became a Warner Bros. movie studio. Still another large and famous Fuller dome housed the U.S. Pavilion at Expo 67 in Montreal in 1967; 200 feet high and 250 feet in diameter, it was dubbed "Buckminster Cathedral" by actor Peter Ustinov. Fuller carried expansive thinking to new extremes with his assertion that a two-mile-diameter dome could be built over midtown Manhattan and pay back its construction costs in 10 years by eliminating the expense of snow removal.

Richard Buckminster "Bucky" Fuller was born July 12, 1895, in Milton, Massachusetts. He attended Harvard University, served as a Navy lieutenant in World War I, then held several managerial and executive positions in private industry.

In 1927, bankrupt, discredited and jobless, Fuller contemplated suicide. In an epiphany, however, he decided that his life belonged not to himself but to the world at large. In the institute Web site's words, he decided "to embark on what he called 'an experiment to discover what the little, penniless, unknown individual might be able to do effectively on behalf of all humanity.' "

Fuller was "truly a man ahead of his time," the institute says. "His lifelong goal was the development of what he called 'Comprehensive Anticipatory Design Science,' — the attempt to anticipate and solve humanity's major problems through the highest technology by providing 'more and more life support for everybody, with less and less resources.' " The coiner of the term "Spaceship Earth," he was one of the earliest proponents of renewable energy sources, such as solar, wind and wave, which he incorporated into his designs. "There is no energy crisis, only a crisis of ignorance," he said.

Fuller's inventions — some built as prototypes, others existing only on paper — stemmed from a concept he called "Dymaxion," derived from the words "dynamic," "maximum" and "ion." His 4D house, later called the Dymaxion house, was suspended from a central, prefabricated mast with all the utilities factory-installed. He created a prefabricated, fully equipped bathroom; a 10-seat, three-wheeled Dymaxion car that could turn in its own length; and a Dymaxion 2-D map of the world with no detectable distortion of the continents, now known as the Fuller projection.

In all, Fuller collected 25 patents, wrote 28 books and traveled more than 14.5 million miles advancing his ideas in lectures and interviews around the world. His work is in the permanent collections of many museums. He received 47 honorary doctorates and dozens of major architectural and design awards, including the gold medal of the American Institute of Architects and the gold medal of the Royal Institute of British Architects.

Late in life, Fuller was awarded the Presidential Medal of Freedom. On July 1, 1983, while at the bedside of his critically ill wife Anne, he suffered a heart attack and died at age 87. Anne died two days later.

Artist Braldt Bralds made these two portraits of Fuller, showing him outside and inside a geodesic dome. Art director Carl Herrman mocked up each of them in both standard semijumbo and hexagonal formats.

The Design

USPS art director Carl Herrman had been an admirer of R. Buckminster Fuller since he saw a Dymaxion automobile exhibited at the Museum of Modern Art in the 1960s, and he welcomed the assignment to design the stamp. At the outset, CSAC members advised him to think outside the box. "They said that this man was a wild thinker, a philosopher, and that I should not just do something straightforward," he said.

For the illustration, Herrman chose Braldt Bralds, a Dutch-born realistic artist whose diverse credits include magazine and book covers, Celestial Seasoning tea boxes, United Nations stamps and a block of as-yet-unissued U.S. stamps. Unfortunately, Herrman said, "It was hard to find great photographs of Fuller for Braldt to work with. They showed him either very young or very old, and they didn't generate a lot of energy."

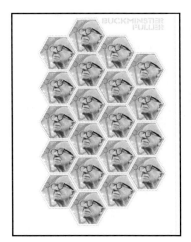

Shown here are Carl Herrman's layouts for two 20-stamp panes incorporating his hexagonal treatment of the Braldt Bralds illustrations.

Bralds' first effort was a detailed drawing of Fuller, his face lined with age, standing in front of a geodesic dome. CSAC turned it down as too conventional, even after Herrman worked it up as a hexagonal stamp design in a honeycomb pane layout that was intended to evoke the dome's structural pattern.

Committee member Meredith Davis suggested that an appropriately eccentric illustration would show Fuller inside a dome, with the interior reflected in his eyeglasses. Bralds dutifully produced an oil painting to these specifications, but CSAC didn't like this effort either. The problem, Herrman said, was that the design didn't explain itself. "Unless you knew who Buckminster Fuller was, and understood what the geodesic dome was, he looked like some old man in a cage," he said. "The idea just didn't translate."

At this point, Herrman returned to a proposal he had made at the beginning, one that truly honored CSAC's "outside-the-box" mandate. He suggested a design based on a memorably fanciful *Time* magazine cover portrait of the inventor in which his bald head mimicked a geodesic dome. The painter was Boris Artzybasheff, a prolific producer of portraits that typically were imaginative combinations of human and machine imagery.

"They told me the image wouldn't fit the stamp format," Herrman said. "I said, 'Yes, it will.'" Its dimensions proved to be a nearly perfect fit for a semijumbo stamp arranged vertically. Committee members also feared that the design would be too unorthodox to win the necessary approval of the Fuller family. However, after Herrman learned that the original painting had been donated to the National Portrait Gallery in Washington, D.C., and was available for stamp use, CSAC agreed to let him proceed.

Boris Artzybasheff was born in Russia in 1899, came to America in 1919 to escape the Bolsheviks, and died in 1965 after a distinguished career in commercial art. Over a 24-year span, he painted more than 200 cover illustrations

The Boris Artzybasheff painting of R. Buckminster Fuller shown on the Fuller stamp first appeared on the cover of Time *magazine's January 10, 1964, issue.*

for *Time* and illustrated some 50 books. During World War II, he created a popular series of satirical and powerful images for *Life* magazine.

In Artzybasheff's *Time* cover of January 10, 1964, the geodesic Fuller gazes at the viewer through heavy horn-rimmed glasses. His head is elevated by a series of supporting struts and is surrounded by geodesic domes, including one being airlifted by helicopter; a Dymaxion Car; a 4D Apartment House; and an assortment of objects and models representing the geometric and structural principles he discovered.

Adapting the illustration to the stamp proved to be a simple task. Herrman cropped the image slightly at the top, eliminating a nonessential moon and flying jet plane. Using a font called Europa, he inserted the name "R. BUCKMINSTER FULLER" in capitals above and behind the inventor's head and centered a smaller "USA 37" across the bottom.

When the design was completed, Terrence McCaffrey flew to California to show it to Fuller's daughter, Allegra Fuller Snyder, who is professor emerita of dance and dance ethnology at the University of California at Los Angeles, and John Ferry, a family friend who represents the estate. "I was very nervous," McCaffrey admitted. "I thought Allegra would be displeased and ask for a literal portrait of her father. But when she saw it, she said, 'Oh, the *Time* magazine cover! That's my favorite!' I walked out very relieved."

Later, McCaffrey gave a sneak preview of the design to impromptu focus groups of postal employees and others. "It was interesting to get their reaction, because they're not used to seeing a portrait interpreted in this fashion," he said. "There were hoots from the audience — people saying, 'What on earth is this?' — but after I explained it to them, they understood it and were favorably impressed."

Because the stamp was offset-printed, microprinting was included in the design for security reasons. It consists of the letters "USPS" beside the supporting strut on the left side.

The microprinted letters "USPS" can be found beside the left strut of the structure supporting Fuller's head.

The Fuller commemorative was the most literal transfer of a *Time* magazine cover portrait to a U.S. stamp, but it wasn't the first. The painting of the racehorse Secretariat for the 33¢ Secretariat Wins Triple Crown stamp, issued in 1999 as part of the Celebrate the Century pane for the 1970s, was based on a photograph that appeared on the cover of *Time* June 11, 1973. *Time* covers depicting General Claire Chennault in 1943 and Henry Luce in 1967 were based on photos that later were used as reference by the illustrators of the 40¢ Chennault and 32¢ Luce stamps in the Great Americans series.

First-Day Facts

Anita Bizzotto, USPS senior vice president and chief marketing officer, dedicated the stamp in a ceremony at Stanford University, where Fuller's papers are archived. The event was held in the Cubberley Auditorium of the School of Education.

Other participants included Fuller's daughter, Allegra Fuller Snyder; Dr. Buzz Aldrin, astronaut on *Gemini 12* and *Apollo 11* and the second man to stand on the moon; Michael A. Keller, Stanford University librarian; Joshua Arnow, president of the board of directors of The Buckminster Fuller Institute; Carolyn Johnson, reporter and anchor, KGO-TV ABC; and Scott Tucker, San Francisco District manager for USPS.

For a limited time, Stamp Fulfillment Services sold uncacheted first-day covers of the Fuller stamp for 75¢.

37¢ JAMES BALDWIN
LITERARY ARTS SERIES

Date of Issue: July 23, 2004

Catalog Number: Scott 3871

Colors: black, cyan, magenta, yellow, yellow (PMS 129)

First-Day Cancel: New York, New York

First-Day Cancellations: 72,110

Format: Panes of 20, horizontal, 4 across, 5 down. Offset printing plates printing 180 stamps per revolution (15 across, 12 around).

Gum Type: self-adhesive

Microprinting: "USPS" on handrail to left of Baldwin's head

Overall Stamp Size: 1.56 by 0.99 inches; 39.625 by 25.146mm

Pane Size: 7.135 by 5.9 inches; 181.229 by 149.86mm

Perforations: 10¾ (die-cut simulated perforations) (IDC two-station die cutter)

Selvage Markings: "©2003/USPS" ".37/x20/$7.40" "PLATE/POSITION" and diagram.

Back Markings: Universal Product Code (UPC) "456600" in 4 locations

Artist: Thomas Blackshear of Colorado Springs, Colorado

Designer, Art Director and Typographer: Phil Jordan of Falls Church, Virginia

Modeler: Joseph Sheeran of Ashton-Potter (USA) Ltd., Williamsville, New York

Stamp Manufacturing: Stamps printed by Ashton-Potter on offset portion of Stevens Variable Size Security Documents A76 modified webfed 6-color offset, 3-color intaglio press. Stamps processed by Ashton-Potter.

Quantity Ordered: 50,000,000

Plate Number Detail: 1 set of 5 plate numbers preceded by the letter P in selvage above or below each corner stamp

Plate Number Combination Reported: P11111

Paper Supplier: Paper Corporation of the United States/Glatfelter

Tagging: phosphored paper

The Stamp

On July 23, the Postal Service issued a stamp in its Literary Arts series honoring American novelist, essayist, playwright and poet James Baldwin. The stamp was dedicated in New York City's Harlem, where Baldwin was born August 22, 1924.

Baldwin was the 20th person to be depicted in the series, which began with a John Steinbeck stamp in 1979, and the first black American male to be so recognized. In 2003, Literary Arts featured its first black writer, Zora Neale Hurston.

The Citizens' Stamp Advisory Committee earlier had placed Baldwin on its approved list for stamp honors, but had considered him for inclusion in the Black Heritage series. Two years earlier the Black Heritage subject had been poet and author Langston Hughes. "I said, 'We need to get more diversity in our Literary Arts series, and Baldwin is a natural,' " said Terrence McCaffrey, manager of stamp development.

Ashton-Potter (USA) Ltd. printed the Baldwin stamp by the offset process and distributed it in panes of 20. The print order, 50 million stamps, is comparable to those for the stamp's recent predecessors in the series: Hurston (70 million), Ogden Nash (75 million), Thomas Wolfe (53 million) and Ayn Rand (42.5 million).

The design was unveiled October 31, 2003, at Chicago State University in Chicago, Illinois, in conjunction with the institution's 13th annual Gwendolyn Brooks Writers' Conference for Black Literature and Creative Writing.

Baldwin, born James Arthur, spent his earliest years in abject poverty. His father abandoned the family, and when James was 3, his mother married a factory worker and storefront preacher named David Baldwin, who gave his surname to her son. The marriage produced eight half-brothers and half-sisters for James.

The boy was a dreamy, bookish child who read everything he could find. At age 12, he published his first story in a church newspaper. By the time he had graduated from high school, he had written articles, plays, fiction and poetry for his school literary magazine, and he knew he wanted to be a writer.

The small Pentecostal church in his community played an important role in Baldwin's early life. He underwent a religious conversion experience at 14, after which he served the church as its preacher for three years. His youthful intimacy with the King James Bible remained among his greatest stylistic influences, and his work has been praised for its moral sense.

During World War II, Baldwin worked at a New Jersey defense plant, quitting in 1943 to write full time. Although he received numerous rejection slips for his fiction, his book reviews and essays began appearing in mainstream periodicals such as *Commentary*, *The Nation*, *New Leader* and *Partisan Review*. With the support of black American writer Richard

Wright, he won a Rosenwald Fellowship in 1948.

Family and personal conflicts and his hatred of American racism combined to send him abroad. He lived at various times in England, Turkey, Switzerland and France, returning occasionally to New York to support the growing civil rights movement. During this time, his fiction began to find publishers, beginning with his semi-autobiographical first novel, *Go Tell It on the Mountain*, completed in Switzerland and published in 1953, which he based on his experience as a boy preacher and his stormy relationship with his parents.

Baldwin's essay collection, *Notes of a Native Son* (1955), became one of the early literary milestones of the black experience in America. In it he wrote of his experiences growing up in Harlem, family relations and the Harlem race riot of 1943. In *Giovanni's Room*, his second novel, published in 1956, the author dealt with his own homosexuality. The protagonist is a young black American who feels trapped by the love of the woman who wants to marry him.

Baldwin's work eloquently articulated the complexities of race relations in the years when the struggle for civil rights was at its height. *The Fire Next Time*, published in 1963, warned that violence was the only possible result if white Americans did not learn to accept and live with their black countrymen (although Baldwin personally advocated pacifism and non-violence). The book landed its author on the cover of *Time* magazine and established his reputation as a prophetic voice of the civil rights movement.

His novels include *Another Country* (1962), *Tell Me How Long the Train's Been Gone* (1968), *If Beale Street Could Talk* (1974) and *Just Above My Head* (1979). His plays are *Blues for Mister Charlie* (1964) and *The Amen Corner* (1968). A collection of short stories, *Going to Meet the Man*, was published in 1965. Other works are the poetry collection *Jimmy's Blues* (1985); essays and nonfiction such as *Nobody Knows My Name* (1961), *No Name in the Street* (1972), *The Devil Finds Work* (1976), *Evidence of Things Not Seen* (1985), and the essay collection *The Price of a Ticket* (1985); and the screenplay *One Day When I Was Lost* (1972).

France awarded Baldwin its highest civilian award, commander of the Legion of Honor, presented by President Francois Mitterrand in 1986. He lived his later years at St. Paul de Vence on the French Riviera, where he died of stomach cancer November 30, 1987, at the age of 63.

The Design

The current design style of the Literary Arts series was established by artist Michael Deas in 1995 with the Tennessee Williams stamp. It is commemorative size, horizontally arranged, depicting a head-and-shoulders portrait of the subject against a background evocative of one of his or her major works, with the person's name superimposed on the portrait across the top in a variant of the Times New Roman typeface developed by USPS art director Richard Sheaff called Times a-Changin'.

James Blackshear's first pencil sketch for the Baldwin stamp showed the author on a Paris balcony with the skyline of the French capital behind him. CSAC asked that the background be changed to a scene in Harlem, where Baldwin grew up.

Since then, all Literary Arts stamps except one (Ayn Rand, 1999) have been in that style, although some of the subjects have been painted by artists other than Deas. The James Baldwin assignment went to Thomas Blackshear, a black American illustrator who has created numerous portraits for U.S. commemoratives beginning with the Jean Baptiste Pointe du Sable stamp of 1987 and including several other Black Heritage stamps, the Classic Films block of four of 1990 and the Classic Movie Monsters block of 1997.

Blackshear has virtually retired from commercial illustrating to devote his time to his popular series of religious prints and his best-selling collection of figurines, but he had made a commitment to Terrence McCaffrey to continue to do stamp art when possible. When he learned that the subject was James Baldwin, he agreed to undertake it. "He made all the deadlines, and it went smoothly from Day One," said Phil Jordan, the art director assigned to the project.

Blackshear based his acrylic painting of the writer on a black-and-white photograph that the Postal Service says was made around 1960, probably in New York. It shows a solemn-faced Baldwin with his head turned to the right to face the viewer. The artist's original pencil sketch included a Paris background, reflecting Baldwin's expatriate days and based on a photo showing him standing on a balcony with rooftops and a church tower

behind him. However, CSAC members felt that a foreign setting was inappropriate for this profoundly American writer, and asked for a background scene in Harlem that would evoke his novel *Go Tell It on the Mountain*.

PhotoAssist, the Postal Service's research firm, obtained a number of Harlem photographs from the Museum of the City of New York and other sources. The photo on which

Blackshear based his portrait of Baldwin on this black-and-white photograph, which USPS says was made around 1960, probably in New York.

144

Blackshear based his background painting on this photograph made by Berenice Abbott June 14, 1938, in the 420 block of Lenox Avenue in Harlem. Visible are a church, a barbershop, a beauty school and salon, an auto school and photo studio, and a delicatessen. In the painting, some of the lettering on the signs is obscured, and Baldwin's portrait hides the woman pedestrian, the barber pole and sign, and the windows of the church.

Blackshear based his stamp art was taken by Berenice Abbott June 14, 1938, in the 420 block of Lenox Avenue in Harlem. The buildings, from left to right, are a church, a ground-floor barber shop with a barber pole and a sign reading "Shave 15¢," May's & Johnson Beauty School and Mae's Beauty Salon, the A.B.C. Auto School, a photo studio, and a delicatessen with produce on a sidewalk table. In the photo, a woman holding a purse walks along the sidewalk, a man stands next to the steps to the church entrance on the left, two people sit at the top of the steps, and another man is seated beside the produce table on the right.

In Blackshear's painting, Baldwin's head hides the woman pedestrian and the signs and windows behind her, as well as one of the persons seated at the church door. The artist purposely obscured some of the lettering on the signs that are visible, in the unlikely event that some of the businesses might still be functioning. He also muted the colors of the background to provide a contrast with the bold hues of the portrait.

The author's name at the top of the stamp and the "USA 37" in two lines beneath it on the right are in a yellow self-color. The rest of the design is in the standard four process colors. Because the stamp is offset-printed, it includes a microtype component for added security: the letters "USPS," on the handrail of the steps to the left of Baldwin's head.

First-Day Facts

Henry Pankey, the Postal Service's vice president for emergency preparedness, dedicated the stamp in the Langston Hughes Auditorium of

The microprinted letters "USPS" can be found on the handrail of the steps to the left of Baldwin's head.

Harlem's Schomburg Center for Research in Black Culture.

Author and actor Maya Angelou and poet and author Amiri Baraka delivered tributes to Baldwin. Other participants were the husband-and-wife actor team of Ossie Davis and Ruby Dee; Howard Dodson, chief of the Schomburg Center; and Samuel Joubert Sr., pastor emeritus of Community Baptist Church in Bayside, New York. Actor Avery Brooks was master of ceremonies. George Baldwin, a brother of the writer, was a guest. Musical selections were provided by folk musician Odetta, singer Jerry Dixon and the Boys Choir of Harlem.

For a limited time, Stamp Fulfillment Services sold uncacheted first-day covers for 75¢.

37¢ MARTIN JOHNSON HEADE
DOUBLE-SIDED CONVERTIBLE BOOKLET OF 20
AMERICAN TREASURES SERIES

Date of Issue: August 12, 2004

Catalog Number: Scott 3872, stamp; 3872a, convertible booklet of 20

Colors: magenta, yellow, cyan, black

First-Day Cancel: Sacramento, California

First-Day Cancellations: 45,653

Format: Convertible booklet pane of 20, horizontal, arranged vertically. Stamps on both sides, 8 (2 across by 4 down) plus label (booklet cover) on one side, 12 (2 across by 6 down) on other side, with horizontal peel-off strips between blocks of 4 on each side. Gravure printing cylinders printing 432 stamps per revolution (18 across, 24 around) manufactured by Southern Graphics Corporation.

Gum Type: self-adhesive

Overall Stamp Size: 1.56 by 0.99 inches; 39.62 by 25.14mm

Pane Size: 3.125 by 6.2083 inches; 79.37 by 157.69mm

Perforations: 10¾ (die-cut simulated perforations) (Comco custom rotary die-cutter). Backing paper rouletted behind peel-off strips.

Selvage Markings: "©2003 USPS" and cylinder numbers on one peel-off strip on all-stamp side

Back Markings: "AMERICAN TREASURES/MARTIN JOHNSON HEADE/ Giant Magnolias on a Blue Velvet Cloth, circa 1890/Twenty 37¢/Self- adhesive/Stamps/$7.40/Fourth in a Series" and Universal Product Code (UPC) "0 673100 3" on booklet cover

Designer, Art Director and Typographer: Derry Noyes of Washington, D.C.

Modeler: Donald H. Woo, Sennett Security Products, Chantilly, Virginia

Stamp Manufacturing: Stamps printed for Sennett Security Products by American Packaging Corporation, Columbus, Wisconsin, on Cerutti 950 gravure press. Stamps finished by Unique Binders of Fredericksburg, Virginia.

Quantity Ordered: 794,000,000 stamps

Cylinder Number Detail: 1 set of 4 cylinder numbers preceded by the letter S on 1 peel-off strip

Cylinder Number Combination Reported: S1111

Paper Supplier: Mactac

Tagging: phosphored paper with phosphor blocker on cover

The Stamp

On August 12, the Postal Service issued a stamp reproducing American artist Martin Johnson Heade's painting *Giant Magnolias on a Blue Velvet Cloth*. Self-adhesive and commemorative-size, it was distributed in double-sided convertible booklets of 20, 12 on one side and eight on the other.

The oil-on-canvas painting was made circa 1890 and hangs in the National Gallery of Art in Washington, D.C. It was the work of a versatile and prolific 19th-century romantic artist from whose palette came seascapes and landscapes, tropical scenes, hummingbirds, butterflies and flowers.

The stamp was issued one day after the 185th anniversary of Heade's birth; the year, 2004, was the 100th anniversary year of his death. It was

the fourth entry in a series called American Treasures, which Terrence McCaffrey, manager of stamp development for USPS, promised at the outset would feature "existing art masterpieces [in] a series of attractive, colorful images that people would be prone to use on their mail."

However, the first two American

Treasures issues, four Amish Quilts (2001) and a John James Audubon single (2002), saw no greater use than other commemoratives. For the third issue, a block of four stamps depicting paintings by Mary Cassatt (2003), USPS switched to the convertible booklet format, which is popular with postal patrons and convenient for clerks to stock. The Cassatt stamps had a gratifyingly wide circulation, and officials said that future American Treasures stamps would be produced in convertible booklets.

The Postal Service ordered 794 million Martin Johnson Heade stamps, slightly more than the 778 million Mary Cassatts of the year before. American Packaging Corporation printed them for Sennett Security Products using the gravure process.

Three blocks of four are on one side of the pane, while on the other side are two blocks of four plus a non-stamp label that serves as a cover for the booklet when the pane is folded. The blocks are separated from each other on both sides by peel-off strips. Each stamp has a straight edge on either the left or right side, and the stamps at the top and bottom of the pane have an additional straight edge.

The label/cover bears an enlarged reproduction of the Heade painting shown on the stamp. It is printed on phosphored paper, like the stamps, but is coated with a phosphor-blocking varnish to prevent users from substituting it for stamps on mail. Sennett had failed to take that precaution in printing the Mary Cassatt convertible booklet, which allowed an envelope bearing a Cassatt label, in at least one instance, to successfully pass through a post office facer-canceler machine.

Martin Joseph Heade, wrote Bennett Schiff in *Smithsonian* magazine, produced perhaps the most varied body of work by any 19th-century American painter in "a career that stretched for 65 years, during which the artist seems never to have put down his brush."

After his death in 1904, however, Heade and his works fell into obscurity. "It was as if Heade had never painted a picture," Schiff wrote. "Except, that is, in hundreds of homes and antique stores, where there was evidence, though seldom seen and rarely recognized, of his particular genius."

His resurrection began with a 1944 exhibition, "Romantic Painting in America," at the Museum of Modern Art in New York City. Here art dealer Robert G. McIntyre came upon a canvas by Heade, an artist unknown to him, and was stunned by the visual drama of the scene. The work was Heade's *Thunder Storm on Narragansett Bay* (1868), which had been discovered in an antiques store only a short time earlier.

The experience prompted McIntyre to learn all he could about Heade and, in 1948, to publish the first biography of him. Some two decades later, Theodore E. Stebbins, a graduate art student at Harvard, purchased a Heade painting at a Boston gallery and was similarly hooked. Stebbins went on to become curator of American painting at the Boston Museum of Fine Arts, wrote a definitive work on Heade in 1975, and organized major retrospective exhibits of his work in 1969 and 1999.

Martin Johnson Heade, shown in an 1860 photograph.

Heade's revival has been amply confirmed in the marketplace. In 1999, the Museum of Fine Arts in Houston, Texas, paid $1.25 million for a painting similar to the one on the stamp, a portrait of magnolias on a bed of golden velvet. For years it had been used to cover a hole in the wall of a house in Indiana.

"Recent critics and collectors have found [Heade's] work compelling in its originality," Stebbins wrote in a 2000 monograph. "We are fascinated by the ways it relates to yet differs from the paintings of his contemporaries. ... Today we admire the subtlety of his atmospheric effects, the glory of his light, the sumptuous warmth of the orchids and tropical scenes, and the inexplicable sensuality of so many of his works in every genre. Above all, to our eyes Heade's work seems wonderfully rich in its handling, its iconography, its originality, and its meaning."

Heade was born August 11, 1819, in Bucks County, Pennsylvania. The family name was spelled "Heed," but Martin changed it to Heade as a young man. He took art lessons from a neighbor, folk artist Edward Hicks, who is known today for the numerous variations he painted of *The Peaceable Kingdom*.

In 1843, Heade left the family farm and moved to New York City. For the next 15 years he traveled in America and abroad, painting portraits, genre scenes and copies of pictures in galleries and museums. In the mid-1850s, he came under the influence of the celebrity landscape painter Frederic Edwin Church and other leaders of the so-called Hudson River School, and gave up portraits and genre studies for landscapes and still lifes.

As he began to develop his own individual style, Heade painted coastal and inland views and tropical landscapes, based on three trips to Central and South America. Hummingbirds, with their iridescent feathers, were a favorite subject. His nautical paintings — including the Narragansett Bay scene that so captivated Robert McIntyre — and no fewer than 120 depictions of Northeastern salt marshes effectively illustrate his mastery of mood, atmosphere and design.

In 1883, Heade married and settled in St. Augustine, Florida, where his last series of works — sensuous still lifes of magnolias and roses — were painted. In *Giant Magnolias on a Blue Velvet Cloth*, a horizontal composition, $24^3/_{16}$ inches wide by $15^1/_8$ inches deep, "the voluptuous white flowers seem almost to glow against the soft, dark velvet, as the glossy leaves reflect the light," says the National Gallery Web site. "Heade's haunting painting seems to have more to do with the painter's memory and imagination than with fact." The canvas was a 1996 gift from The Circle of the National Gallery of Art on the program's 10th anniversary.

The Design

Derry Noyes, the USPS art director who conceived the American Treasures series and designs its stamps, had searched for a usable print of *Giant Magnolias* for a long time. "All the reproductions in books were dingy and dark," Noyes said. "I finally went online and found a copy from the National Gallery of Art that was good enough to present to the [Citizens' Stamp Advisory] Committee.

"They approved it, and PhotoAssist [the Postal Service's research firm] got a transparency from the National Gallery. It went swimmingly from then on. I think it's one of the more successful stamps in the series. The printer held the detail in it well, it was very popular, and I was happy with it."

Because the proportions of the painting are similar to those of the horizontally arranged commemorative-size stamp, there was no need for cropping. Noyes placed the words "MARTIN JOHNSON HEADE" in small dropped-out capitals across the bottom left portion of the stamp and "USA 37" in the lower right corner. The sans-serif font is Cronos. To complement the yellowish tinge of the flower's white petals, she gave the lettering an off-white tint, which the printer reproduced by using a faint magenta screen. She inserted a subtle vertical line in blue between the typographic elements to echo the blue velvet on which the magnolias rest.

On the label/booklet cover is the series logo, "AMERICAN TREASURES" in Minion type, and the name "MARTIN JOHNSON HEADE" in black Cronos letters.

Varieties

The discovery of two convertible booklets of Heade stamps, each with a single die-cut-missing error pair, was reported by stamp dealer Arnold Selengut of Temple Terrace, Florida. Selengut told *Linn's Stamp News* that he bought one of the panes October 24, 2004, from a person who purchased it at a South Carolina post office several weeks earlier.

"A thorough search of that post office's stock by the finder resulted in one additional similar pane being found," Selengut added. "The second pane was offered for sale to a New York dealer in U.S. errors."

The error was the result of a significant misregistration between the continuous roll of printed stamp paper and the die-cutting mat during the finishing process. As illustrated here, the error pair is the bottom pair on the eight-stamp side, just above the label.

In this pane of Martin Johnson Heade stamps, the bottom pair is a die-cut-missing error caused by a misregistration between the web of printed stamp paper and the die-cutting mat during the finishing process. The die cuts are shifted upward, resulting in what normally would be the horizontal "perfs" and selvage strips cutting through the stamps in the top three rows.

A shift of approximately 1½ inches of the die cutting between the stamps left the bottom two stamps with no die cutting and the stamps in the top three rows bisected by either a single or double row of horizontal die cuts. The double rows of die cuts across the stamps in rows one and three were meant to define the pane's pull-off strips.

The 12 stamps on the other side of the pane (not shown) exhibit normal die cutting, although the design images are shifted somewhat to the left in relation to the die cuts.

Scott Publishing Company assigned the error pair the number 3872b in its 2006 stamp catalogs.

First-Day Facts

Robert Rider, a member of the USPS Board of Governors, dedicated the stamp at the American Philatelic Society's Stampshow 2004, held at the Sacramento, California, Convention Center. Others participating were Janet Klug, president of the APS; Elizabeth C. Pope, president of the American Stamp Dealers Association; John M. Hotchner, a member of CSAC; and Rosemarie Fernandez, acting manager of the USPS Sacramento District.

For a limited time, Stamp Fulfillment Services sold uncacheted first-day covers of the Heade stamp for 75¢.

152

37¢ ART OF THE AMERICAN INDIAN (10 DESIGNS)

ART OF THE AMERICAN INDIAN

Mimbres bowl USA37 | Kutenai parfleche USA37 | Tlingit sculptures USA37 | Ho-Chunk bag USA37 | Seminole doll USA37

Mississippian effigy USA37 | Acoma pot USA37 | Navajo weaving USA37 | Seneca carving USA37 | Luiseño basket USA37

Date of Issue: August 21, 2004

Catalog Numbers: Scott 3873a-j, stamps; 3873, pane of 10

Colors: yellow, magenta, cyan, black, beige (PMS 452)

First-Day Cancel: Santa Fe, New Mexico

First-Day Cancellations: 486,737 (includes Art of the American Indian postal cards)

Format: Pane of 10, vertical, 5 across, 2 down. Gravure printing cylinders printing 80 stamps per revolution (2 panes across, 4 panes around) manufactured by Keating Gravure.

Gum Type: self-adhesive

Stamp Size: 1.41 by 1.96 inches; 35.814 by 49.784mm

Pane Size: 8.0 by 5.8125 inches; 203.2 by 147.6375mm

Perforations: 10¾ by 11 (die-cut simulated perforations) (Comco Commander rotary die cutter)

Selvage Inscription: "ART OF THE AMERICAN INDIAN"

Selvage Markings: none

Back Markings: On selvage liner: "These ten stamps offer a sampling of the diverse ways in which Native Americans, in the context of their everyday lives,/created utilitarian, social, spiritual, and commercial objects that were also extraordinary expressions of beauty. Executed in a/variety of media, these artifacts—which date from around the 11th century A.D. to circa 1969—illustrate the talent, ingenuity,/and artistic skills of America's first peoples./Creative expression continues to flourish among American Indian artists today. Some still create traditional forms; others are/expanding their artistic endeavors in new directions in the fields of painting, sculpture, photography, printmaking, video, and/performance art. "© 2003 USPS." Universal Product Code (UPC) "457300." On stamp liners: "During the early decades of/the 20th century, Miccosukee-/Seminole women in Florida/developed a unique style of/patchwork clothing. They/used hand-operated sewing/machines to piece together/brightly colored cotton shirts/and dresses, and they outfitted/dolls made for the tourist/trade in miniature versions of/these traditional garments./This male doll, made circa/1935, wears a man's foksikco.bi,/or big shirt./National Museum of the American Indian/Washington, D.C." "Using ingenious twining/techniques, women of the/Great Lakes and Central Plains/tribes wove beautiful storage/bags of bison hair, plant fibers,/and wool yarn, often/incorporating stylized/depictions of mythological/beings into their designs. The/thunderbird, which embodies/the sky realm, was a favorite/motif; this one is a detail from/an 1840-1860 Ho-Chunk/(Winnebago) bag collected/in Nebraska./Cranbrook Institute of Science/Bloomfield Hills, Michigan." "Wood sculpture was a/fundamental form of artistic/expression among the men of/the Northwest Coast tribes,/and objects carved and/painted in their distinctive/style were eagerly sought by/tourists and collectors. These/two Tlingit sculptures, dated/circa 1890, likely illustrate the/story of Salmon Boy, a youth/who lived for a time with the/Salmon People in their/supernatural realm beneath/the sea./Phoebe A. Hearst Museum of Anthropology/University of California, Berkeley." "Containers of folded or/sewn rawhide, known as/parfleches, were traditionally/used by Plains and Plateau/tribal groups to store and/transport food and material/possessions. These utilitarian/objects were painted with/colorful and distinctive/geometric patterns that had/both aesthetic appeal and/spiritual significance. This/Kutenai parfleche was collected/in 1900, probably in Idaho./American Museum of Natural History/New York, New York." "The Mimbres people of south-/western New Mexico/produced a unique style of/black-on-white pottery/featuring representations of/wildlife, humans, or mythic/beings combined with/geometric motifs. Most bowls/of the Classic Mimbres period/(circa A.D. 1000-1150)/probably served as eating/vessels. This striking example/depicts two stylized bighorn/sheep, animals that were once/common in the Mimbres area./Maxwell Museum of Anthropology/The University of New Mexico, Albuquerque." "Renowned for the exquisite/beauty and technical/excellence of their basket-/work, California Indians—who/used basketry items for every/conceivable utilitarian, social,/and ritual purpose—elevated/a practical craft into fine art./This superb Luiseno coiled/basket, made of split sumac/and natural and black-dyed/juncus rush on a grass/foundation, probably dates/to the 1890s./Riverside Municipal Museum/Riverside, California." "Among the Iroquois, carving/was traditionally men's work,/and they were adept at trans-/forming wooden utensils into/works of art—a skill particu-/larly evident in the diverse/human and animal effigies that/adorn the handles of ladles./This elaborately carved handle/finial, depicting a dog watching/a human eating, ornaments a/mid-19th-century Seneca ladle/from the

Tonawanda/Reservation in New York./New York State/Museum, Albany, New York, on loan to/Akwesasne Museum, Hogansburg, New York." "Weaving is the art form/for which the Navajo are/best known, and the finely/woven textiles from the/Two Grey Hills region in/New Mexico—characterized by/geometric designs executed in/natural shades of hand-spun wool/yarns with wide or multiple/borders—are highly esteemed./Daisy Taugelchee (1911-1990),/who set unprecedented/standards of fine spinning and/weaving, made this stellar/tapestry in the late 1940s./Denver Art Museum/Denver, Colorado." "Acoma Pueblo in New Mexico/is known for exceptionally/thin-walled pottery decorated/with complex geometric/designs carefully painted on a/white slip background. Master/potter Lucy Martin Lewis/(circa 1895-1992) helped revive/the black-on-white style by/adapting 800-year-old Puebloan/pottery designs to modern/Acoma ceramics. The lightning/pattern on this jar, which she/made about 1969, derives from/ancestral traditions./National Museum of the American Indian/Washington, D.C." "This sandstone male effigy is/an outstanding example of the/art of the late Mississippian/culture (A.D. 1300-1550) in/Tennessee. A strikingly/naturalistic portrait, the/statue provides a valuable/glimpse into a complex/prehistoric society. It was/found with a female figurine/that was carved in less/detail; together they may/represent the ancestors of/a founding lineage./Frank H. McClung Museum/The University of Tennessee, Knoxville."

Designer, Art Director and Typographer: Richard Sheaff of Scottsdale, Arizona

Selvage Typography: John Stevens of Winston-Salem, North Carolina

Stamp Manufacturing: Stamps printed by Avery Dennison Security Printing Division, Clinton, South Carolina, on 8-color Dia Nippon Kiko webfed gravure press. Stamps processed by Avery Dennison.

Quantity Ordered: 87,000,000

Cylinder Number Detail: none

Paper Supplier: Fasson Division of Avery Dennison

Tagging: block tagging over stamps

The Stamps

On August 21, the Postal Service issued a pane of 10 stamps depicting examples of Native American art created for utilitarian, spiritual or commercial purposes over a period of nearly a millennium. They were accompanied by a companion set of 10 picture postal cards (see separate chapter).

Although the Postal Service had planned the release of the stamps and cards to coincide with the opening of the National Museum of the American Indian in Washington, D.C., September 21, museum officials found no spot in their week-long schedule of dedication events for a stamp ceremony. Instead, USPS issued the items in Santa Fe, New Mexico, during the Santa Fe Indian Market, an annual arts festival.

Mimbres bowl   USA37

Kutenai parfleche USA37

Tlingit sculptures USA37

The self-adhesive stamps are in the size that USPS calls jumbo, vertically arranged, and are laid out on the pane in two horizontal rows of five stamps each. The jumbo size, 1.41 by 1.96 inches, had been used in recent years for certain airmail, Express Mail and Priority Mail stamps, but not commemoratives.

A header, or wide top selvage, bears the words "ART OF THE AMERICAN INDIAN." There is no other type in the pane selvage and no plate numbers. Text on the back of the liner paper of each stamp describes the artifact in its design; text behind the header gives an overview of the Native American art that is shown. The panes were printed by the gravure process by Avery Dennison Security Printing Division.

The project began in the late 1990s, when USPS was periodically issuing panes of 20 different semijumbo-size commemoratives in a series it called Classic Collections. Richard Sheaff, a USPS art director, proposed 20 stamps featuring "Native American Art and Design," and made a dummy pane using illustrations from books and other sources to show the Citizens' Stamp Advisory Committee what he had in mind.

CSAC liked the concept, but suggested that the number of stamps be reduced to 10. In that way, members said, the designs could be made even

Ho-Chunk bag   USA37

larger than semijumbo and could more effectively showcase the beauty and workmanship of the objects. To justify the cost of producing jumbo stamps, CSAC's design subcommittee proposed that they be issued in a format with special appeal for collectors. Accordingly, USPS referred to the pane as a "souvenir sheet" in its publicity and marketing.

Selecting the images required much more than an eye for aesthetics, however. The pane had to include a variety of art forms and time periods and represent all major U.S. geographic regions. There was also the ticklish issue of Native Amer-

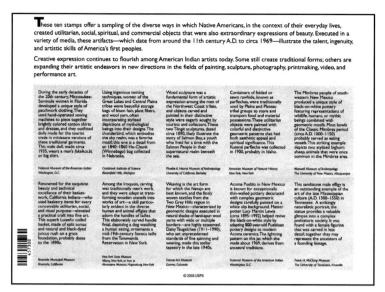

These ten stamps offer a sampling of the diverse ways in which Native Americans, in the context of their everyday lives, created utilitarian, social, spiritual, and commercial objects that were also extraordinary expressions of beauty. Executed in a variety of media, these artifacts—which date from around the 11th century A.D. to circa 1969—illustrate the talent, ingenuity, and artistic skills of America's first peoples.

Creative expression continues to flourish among American Indian artists today. Some still create traditional forms; others are expanding their artistic endeavors in new directions in the fields of painting, sculpture, photography, printmaking, video, and performance art.

Text on the back of the liner paper for each stamp describes the artifact in its design; text behind the header gives an overview of the Native American art that is shown.

ican sensibilities. For example, funerary objects — items related to death ceremonies or graves — could not be shown. Tribal representatives and museum officials had no objection to depicting replicas of such artifacts, but Sheaff wanted to use only photos of original items.

PhotoAssist, the Postal Service's research firm, enlisted the help of officials of the National Museum of the American Indian, then in the development stage. Bruce Bernstein, the museum's assistant director for cultural resources, worked with Sheaff to pare the list of subjects to 10 items, dating from around the 11th century A.D. to circa 1969. W. Richard "Rick" West Jr., the director, and George Horse Capture, a special

Seminole doll USA37

Mississippian effigy USA37

Acoma pot USA37

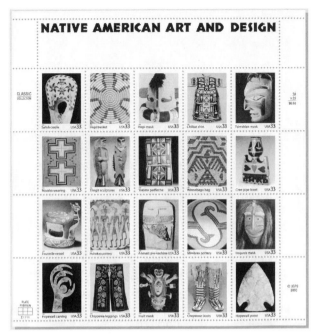

Shown here is Richard Sheaff's original demonstration pane layout of 20 semi-jumbo stamps with pictures of American Indian art that Sheaff borrowed from books and other sources. Three of the examples survive on the issued pane of 10 jumbo stamps: the Tlingit sculptures, Winnebago bag (renamed the Ho-Chung bag) and Mimbres pottery (Mimbres bowl).

assistant to Bernstein, reviewed the stamps' verso text, which Victoria Cooper of PhotoAssist had written after consulting with curators, cultural preservation officers (or equivalent) for each tribe and other experts. The text also was checked by Gaylord Torrance, an expert on parfleche (rawhide containers) and curator of American Indian art at the Nelson-Atkins Museum of Art in Kansas City, Missouri.

Several months before the issue date, Terrence McCaffrey, manager of stamp development for USPS, sent courtesy letters to the leaders of each tribe whose artifacts were represented on the pane. At one point, McCaffrey said, he was

Consultants considered the Iroquois comb, with facing bears in silhouette, to be a possible funerary object and as such inappropriate for stamp use. Accordingly, the design was dropped.

158

Navajo weaving   USA37

Seneca carving   USA37

Luiseño basket   USA37

prepared to travel to Wisconsin at the invitation of the Ho-Chunk Nation to explain to tribal elders why they should allow the depiction of a thunderbird, one of the tribe's most important symbols, on a commercial item such as a postage stamp. Later, however, the Ho-Chunk leaders agreed to approve the design without the need for a meeting.

Previous U.S. stamps have celebrated a variety of Indian arts and rituals.

A 6¢ stamp, issued in 1970 in a block of four marking the 100th anniversary of the American Museum of Natural History, shows a Tlingit chief in a Haida ceremonial canoe (Scott 1389).

Four sets of stamps in the American Folk Art series feature Indian art forms. They are: a block of four 13¢ stamps in 1977 depicting Pueblo Indian pottery (Scott 1706-1709); four 15¢ stamps in 1980 showing Pacific Northwest Indian masks (Scott 1834-1837); four 22¢ stamps in 1986 on the theme of Navajo weaving (Scott 2235-2238); and headdresses of Plains Indian tribes, pictured on five 25¢ booklet stamps of 1990 (Scott 2501-2505).

Two pre-Columbian Indian sculptures are pictured on 1989 stamps that are part of a multi-nation America series. A 25¢ stamp shows a painted wooden figure of a human male from the Mimbres culture (Scott 2426), and a 45¢ airmail stamp features a small wooden sculpture of a human body with the head of a cat found on Key Marco island on Florida's Gulf coast more than a century ago (Scott C121).

One of the 20 29¢ stamps in the Legends of the West pane of 1994 commemorated Native American Culture and showed a Minnetaree warrior performing the "Dog Dance" (Scott 2869e, 2870e). In 1996, the Postal Service issued five additional 32¢ stamps featuring American Indian dances, se-tenant in a pane of 20 (Scott 3072-3076). And just two days before the Art of the American Indian pane was issued, USPS issued a 2¢ definitive in the American Design series showing a Navajo necklace (see separate chapter).

This image of a mound carving was replaced on the issued pane by another crouching figurine, the Mississippian effigy.

Mound carving   USA34

The Designs

In his designs, Richard Sheaff made maximum use of the larger area the jumbo size made available. The rectangular photographs of the objects occupy all but a narrow white strip at the bottom of the vertically arranged stamps. The strip contains a two-word descriptive title and "USA 37," in black Optima characters.

"I didn't want the stamp pane to resemble a museum catalog," Sheaff said, "which is why we made an effort to vary the ways that we showed the objects. On some of these stamps, the nature of each object is pretty clear: the Seminole doll, the Acoma pot and the Tlingit sculptures are easily identifiable. In other cases, such as the Mimbres bowl or the Ho-Chunk bag, we've zoomed in very closely, and what the stamp shows is an almost abstract detail that communicates the artistry of the object.

"The Seneca carving is actually just the top of the handle of a wooden ladle. I wanted to have some figural carving on the pane — realistic things to go with the abstract things — and this was a nice little example.

"This variation makes for a visually striking stamp pane, and I think it helps convey a broad span of time and the differences between the various cultures."

For the stamp showing Navajo weaving, Sheaff admitted he would have preferred a characteristically bold red-and-black blanket of the kind displayed on the Navajo Art block of four of 1986. In the end, however, Daisy Taugelchee's brown tapestry from the 1940s was chosen to give the pane another example of more modern craftsmanship.

Most of the photographs chosen by Sheaff were pre-existing. Photo credits are:

Mimbres bowl: Existing photo provided by the Maxwell Museum of Anthropology.

Kutenai parfleche: Existing photo by Mark Tade.

Hohokan pottery USA33

Only one piece of pottery from the Southwest, circa A.D. 1000-1500, could be shown on the pane. This detail from a Hohokan artifact was replaced on the issued pane by a detail from a Mimbres bowl.

160

Salish cradle USA33

Chilkat shirt USA33

Yakima parfleche USA33

The Salish cradle, Chilkat shirt and Yakima parfleche all originated with Northwest tribes. In the end, only one artifact from the region could be used on the pane: the Tlingit sculptures.

Tlingit sculptures: Photo by Hearst Museum photographer Therese Babineau, made especially for the stamp.

Ho-Chunk bag: Existing photo by Robert Hensleigh, provided by the Detroit Institute of Arts, Detroit, Michigan.

Seminole doll: Existing photo by David Heald, provided by the National Museum of the American Indian.

Mississippian effigy: Existing photo by Dirk Bakker, provided by the Detroit Institute of Arts.

Acoma pot: Existing photo by David Heald, provided by the National Museum of the American Indian.

Navajo weaving: Existing photo provided by the Denver Art Museum.

Seneca carving: Photo by New York State Museum photographer Thaddeus Beblowski, made especially for the stamp.

Luiseno basket: Existing photo by the late Chris L. Moser, then curator of anthropology at the Riverside Municipal Museum, and provided by Moser.

Pima basket tray USA33

The "Man in the Maze" design displayed on this basket tray has been adopted as a sort of logo by the Pima tribe of southern Arizona. However, Sheaff wanted to use a basket from a California tribe, the acknowledged masters of the craft, and developed two stamp designs depicting California baskets, one of which was the Luiseno basket that ultimately was used on the pane.

Sheaff electronically altered the background colors of several of the images to provide more visual variety on the pane. Each stamp has white margins, but the block of 10 is surrounded by solid beige color that extends to the edges of the selvage.

To design the header, Sheaff commissioned John Stevens, a calligrapher from Winston-Salem, North Carolina, whose work he admired. Stevens used watercolors to create the multicolored words "ART OF THE AMERICAN INDIAN" in several variations. "I borrowed some letters from one set and put them in another and sort of pieced it together," Sheaff said.

First-Day Facts

The Santa Fe Indian Market, where the first-day ceremony was held, is sponsored each year by the Southwestern Association for Indian Arts (SWAIA). Anita Bizzotto, USPS senior vice president and chief marketing officer, dedicated the stamps in a ceremony on the Plaza Stage in Santa Fe.

Speakers were Jai Lakshman, executive director of SWAIA; U.S. Senator Jeff Bingaman, Democrat of New Mexico; and Richard Sheaff, designer of the stamps. David Martin, USPS Albuquerque District manager, was master of ceremonies. Santa Fe Postmaster Ruben J. Romero Jr. introduced the participants, and Santa Fe Mayor Larry A. Delgado gave the welcome.

The honored guests included individuals with connections to two of the Indian art items shown on the stamps. They were Chester Taugelchee, a relative of the late Daisy Taugelchee, who created the Navajo weaving, and Delores Lewis Garcia and Emma Lewis Mitchell, daughters of the late Lucy Martin Lewis, master potter and designer of the Acoma pot.

The Santa Fe Indian Market annually draws some 1,200 Indian artists who market their creations to some 100,000 visitors.

For a limited time, Stamp Fulfillment Services sold uncacheted first-day covers of the full pane for $6.20.

37¢ JOHN WAYNE
LEGENDS OF HOLLYWOOD SERIES

Date of Issue: September 9, 2004

Catalog Number: Scott 3876

Colors: magenta, yellow, cyan, black, gray (PMS 5435), dark blue (PMS 7463)

First-Day Cancel: Los Angeles, California

First-Day Cancellations: 112,490

Format: Pane of 20, vertical, 5 across, 4 down. Gravure printing cylinders printing 120 stamps per revolution (10 across, 12 around) manufactured by Armotek Industries. Also sold in uncut press sheets of 6 panes (2 across by 3 down).

Gum Type: self-adhesive

Overall Stamp Size: 0.99 by 1.56 inches; 25.15 by 39.62mm

Pane Size: 8.57 by 7.208 inches; 217.68 by 183.08mm

Uncut Press Sheet Size: 17¼ by 22¼ inches

Perforations: 10¾ (die-cut simulated perforations) (Comco rotary die cutter)

Selvage Inscription: "LEGENDS OF HOLLYWOOD/John Wayne (1907-1979) played many memorable roles/during his 50-year career, but he is perhaps best known/for characters exhibiting the rugged individualism/ associated with the American cowboy. He won an/Academy Award for his role/as Rooster Cogburn, the/one-eyed marshal in/*True Grit* (1969)./ In an effort to/continue John Wayne's/fight against cancer,/the John Wayne/Foundation was/established in/his memory." "THE SEARCHERS © Warner Bros./Entertainment Inc. All Rights Reserved." *"The Man Who Shot Liberty Valance* © Paramount Pictures. All Rights Reserved./Name, image and likeness of John Wayne licensed by Wayne Enterprises, Newport Beach CA. All Rights Reserved."

Selvage Markings: "© 2004 USPS/All Rights Reserved." ".37 x 20 = $7.40." "PLATE/POSITION" and diagram.

Back Markings: Universal Product Code (UPC) "455700" in 4 locations on back of liner paper.

Illustrator: Drew Struzan of Pasadena, California

Designer, Art Director and Typographer: Derry Noyes of Washington, D.C.

Modeler: Donald H. Woo of Sennett Security Products, Chantilly, Virginia

Stamp Manufacturing: Stamps printed for Sennett Security Products by American Packaging Corporation, Columbus, Wisconsin, on Rotomec 3000 gravure press. Stamps finished by Unique Binders of Fredericksburg, Virginia.

Quantity Ordered: 100,000,000

Cylinder Number Detail: 1 set of 6 cylinder numbers preceded by the letter S in selvage beside each corner stamp

Cylinder Number Combination Reported: S111111

Paper Supplier: Mactac

Tagging: block tagging over stamps

The Stamp

On September 9, in Los Angeles, California, the Postal Service issued a stamp honoring actor John Wayne, who specialized in rugged macho roles such as cowboy and soldier in a career spanning 50 years and more than 200 films.

The stamp was the 10th in the annual Legends of Hollywood series, which was launched in 1995 with a commemorative depicting Marilyn Monroe. She was followed by James Dean, Humphrey Bogart, Alfred Hitchcock, James Cagney, Edward G. Robinson, Lucille Ball, Cary Grant and Audrey Hepburn.

Wayne's stamp had been moved both forward and backward on the Postal Service's commemorative stamp schedule. It would have been issued earlier in the series, but a delay in obtaining permission from the actor's family pushed it back to 2005. Then, after plans to honor Spencer Tracy on the 2004 Legends stamp foundered on a dispute over rights to use his name and image, the Wayne stamp was advanced into the 2004 slot.

Like all the previous Legends of Hollywood stamps, it is vertically arranged, was issued in panes of 20 with a wide pictorial selvage on the right side, and was made available to collectors in uncut press sheets at face value — in the case of the six-pane Wayne sheet, $44.40. The Scott *Specialized Catalogue of U.S. Stamps & Covers* lists four position pieces from the uncut sheet: a cross-gutter block of eight, a block of eight with vertical gutter, and horizontal and vertical pairs with gutters.

The stamp is a self-adhesive and was printed by the gravure process by American Packaging Corporation for Sennett Security Products. Sennett or its predecessor, Stamp Venturers, has been the contractor for all the Legends of Hollywood stamps except the Lucille Ball, which was offset-printed by Banknote Corporation of America.

The pattern of the pane's die-cut simulated perfs is similar to that of conventional or die-cut perfs on the previous Legends of Hollywood stamps. A second row of die cuts around the outer edges of the block of 20 stamps creates a narrow inner selvage, which is blank except for a set of cylinder numbers in each corner. The seven horizontal rows of die cuts extend to the edge of the pane on the left side and penetrate the liner paper, enabling postal clerks to detach and sell singles or blocks.

John Wayne had been pictured on one of the four 25¢ stamps in the Classic Films block of four of 1990 as the star of the western movie *Stagecoach*. Afterward, the actor's oldest son, Michael Wayne, complained to USPS officials that the stamp had been issued without his permission as controller of the rights to his father's image. As a result, the Postal Service agreed not to license any commercial products displaying the *Stagecoach* stamp design.

"After that, Michael had a bad taste in his mouth as far as the Postal Service was concerned," said Terrence McCaffrey, manager of stamp development. "As the [Citizens' Stamp Advisory Committee] developed the Legends of Hollywood series and wanted to include John Wayne, we

John Wayne first appeared on a U.S. stamp on the 25¢ Stagecoach commemorative of 1990 that was part of the Classic Films block of four (Scott 2448). In that movie, Wayne starred as the Ringo Kid.

said, 'I don't think Michael is going to let us do it.' "

Wayne "reluctantly" agreed to a meeting, McCaffrey said, and one day in 1999 he flew to Hollywood with Kelly Spinks, the USPS lawyer then handling licensing matters, and James Tolbert, then head of stamp development. After an initially cold reception, the actor's son mellowed over lunch at the Grill in the Alley restaurant in Beverly Hills. "Before you knew it," McCaffrey said, "the three of us were back in his office and trying on John Wayne's cowboy hat, the old stained hat, and his six-gun holster and bandanna. We ended up bonding pretty well, and Michael said, 'OK, I'm willing to talk about' approving a stamp."

When they returned to Washington, the officials sent Louis Plummer of PhotoAssist, the Postal Service's research firm, and Derry Noyes, the art director assigned to the project, to Hollywood to review the wealth of John Wayne images in the son's electronic database. Pictures were selected, artist Drew Struzan was commissioned to make the illustrations, and Michael Wayne monitored the design development process and made suggestions with apparent enthusiasm.

After the artwork was completed in July 2000, however, postal officials were unable to get him to sign off on the finished design. "We kept putting the agreement in front of him, saying, 'Michael, you've got to sign this,' " said McCaffrey. "He said, 'I'll look at it, I'll look at it.' He loved the art, but he never would get back to us.

"Then he stopped communicating with us, totally. Kelly would call and couldn't get through. She would be told, 'He's not in the office today.' We actually went there a couple of times when we were in Hollywood but couldn't make contact. We e-mailed him, telling him that we couldn't go forward until we got the signed agreement.

"Finally, we returned to the committee and said, 'We need to move John Wayne out of the schedule and put somebody else in his place.' "

Meanwhile, the CSAC-approved design of the John Wayne stamp had reached the public. In November 2001, collector Jay Bigalke found the image (with a 34¢ denomination) on a USPS Web site and put it on another online site. *Linn's Stamp News* then published it. USPS spokesman Don Smeraldi denied that Wayne, or anyone else, had been chosen for the 2002 Legends of Hollywood stamp at that point. The picture on the Web site "is not an official USPS stamp design image," he told *Linn's*. "It is an old preliminary image that never was approved for release." In February 2002, the Postal Service announced that Cary Grant would be on that year's Legends stamp.

In April 2003, McCaffrey was notified of the death of Michael Wayne at the age of 68. "It shocked us all," he said. A few weeks later, he received a telephone call from another John Wayne son, Ethan Wayne, who had found McCaffrey's business card in his brother's file. On the back of the card, Michael Wayne's assistant had noted McCaffrey's suggestion that a John Wayne stamp could be issued in 2007, the 100th anniversary year of the actor's birth. Ethan Wayne told McCaffrey he now was controlling the estate as general partner of Wayne Enterprises and was extremely interested in the stamp proposal.

McCaffrey flew to California, showed the stamp design to Ethan Wayne, and left a copy of the necessary release. "Then I went to the committee and told them, 'We're back on track,' " McCaffrey said. "I told them I didn't want to wait until 2007; John Wayne was one of the Hollywood biggies, and every year we would get asked, 'When are you going to do him?' The committee approved Wayne for the 2005 stamp program, and Ethan Wayne signed the papers.

Officials planned to honor Spencer Tracy with the 2004 Legends of Hollywood stamp. They announced the plan in August 2003, and the stamp and pane designs were shown privately to philatelic press representatives. Then a rights issue developed.

"Tracy's daughter Susie had said she controlled the estate, and she wants a stamp for her father very much," McCaffrey said. "But his grandson, Joseph Tracy, said that on behalf of his father, Spencer's son John, he represented half the estate, and so his permission was required. They turned the issue over to the estate representative, who has made demands that we refused to meet."

On January 8, 2004, USPS announced that Tracy would not be on the 2004 Legends stamp. "Issues related to negotiations with the Tracy estate" made it necessary to remove the stamp from the 2004 program, USPS spokeswoman Rita Peer told *Linn's*. A replacement Legends personality would be found for 2004 "if at all possible," she added.

The first public notice that Wayne would be that personality came at the first-day ceremony for the Snowy Egret booklet stamp in Norfolk, Virginia, January 30, 2004. Reading a speech prepared by USPS headquarters, Norfolk postmaster Robert Bennett Jr. surprised listeners by including Wayne in a list of people who would be depicted on stamps in the coming months.

A week later, on February 6, USPS made it official with an announcement and released the design, which turned out to be the same one (with the denomination changed) that had turned up online in November 2001, only to be officially dismissed as "an old preliminary image." The design of the full pane, including selvage, was unveiled by USPS Chief Financial Officer Richard J. Strasser April 3 at the Odyssey Ball at the Beverly Hilton Hotel in Beverly Hills, California, a fund-raiser for the John Wayne Cancer Institute.

John Wayne was born in Winterset, Iowa, May 26, 1907, to Clyde Morrison, a pharmacist, and his wife Mary. He was named Marion Morrison for his grandfather, a Civil War veteran. In 1913, the family moved to California in hopes of improving the father's health, eventually settling in Glendale. Somewhere along the line, the boy acquired the nickname "Duke," a sobriquet that had belonged to the family's pet Airedale.

Young Marion was an honor student and standout football player at Glendale High School. He attended the University of Southern California on a football scholarship, but dropped out during his sophomore year after breaking an ankle on the field.

He worked as a prop boy at Fox studios, where he met Irish-emigrant director John Ford. From 1925 to 1929, Ford used him in uncredited bit parts. His first credited role, in which he was billed as Duke Morrison, was in the romantic comedy *Words and Music*, which was released twice in 1929, first as a silent film and then as a talkie.

His first big break and a new screen name came in 1930 when Ford recommended him to director Raoul Walsh for the lead role in the frontier drama *The Big Trail*. Walsh thought that the young actor needed a more masculine-sounding name to go with his six-foot-four, 225-pound body. At the time, Walsh was reading a biography of General Anthony Wayne of the Indian wars and suggested that name to the studio. Studio officials liked the surname, but changed the first name to John, and Marion Morrison became John Wayne.

Wayne continued in bit parts and later in featured roles in serials and B pictures for another nine years. Then his old friend, John Ford, decided to make an A-movie, big-budget Western that would appeal to adult audiences. He cast Wayne as the Ringo Kid in *Stagecoach*, a role that made the actor a star.

During World War II, Wayne appeared in 13 films, many of them patriotic war movies, but despite the fact that he was draft-eligible the studio intervened with the Selective Service System, and he was deferred. After the war, his popularity with moviegoers climbed as he starred in films directed by Ford and others.

In 1949 he was nominated for a best-actor Academy Award for his role as a Marine drill instructor in *Sands of Iwo Jima*. Other highly regarded Wayne movies were *Red River* (1948), *The Quiet Man* (1952), *Hondo* (1953), *The High and the Mighty* (1954), *The Searchers* (1956), *The Alamo* (1960), *The Man Who Shot Liberty Valance* (1962), *Hatari!* (1962), *The Longest Day* (1962), *How The West Was Won* (1963) and *El Dorado* (1967). His performance as Rooster Cogburn, the whiskey-swilling, disreputable, one-eyed marshal in *True Grit* (1969) won him the Oscar for best actor in his second nomination. His quip on receiving the award could have come straight from one of his laconic screen characters: "If I'd known this was all it would take, I'd have put that eye patch on 40 years ago."

Wayne co-starred with numerous actresses, but he shared a special chemistry with Irish-born Maureen O'Hara, with whom he made five movies between 1950 and 1971. He was married three times, fathering four children with his first wife, Josephine Alicia Saenz, and three with his third wife, Pilar Palette.

Conservatives who criticized the Postal Service for honoring leftists such as Frida Kahlo and Paul Robeson on stamps should have been pleased with the Wayne stamp, for, unlike many Hollywood personalities, Wayne was an outspoken conservative, anti-Communist and Cold War hawk. He supported the Vietnam War, and his 1968 movie *The Green Berets*, which he produced and co-directed, was the only film from a major studio to be made about the conflict while it was going on. On the other hand, he angered some on the right by backing President Jimmy Carter's initiative to turn the Panama Canal over to Panama.

Wayne survived the removal of cancerous tumors from his chest and lung in 1964, but cancer returned 15 years later. His last public appearance was at the 1979 Academy Awards, where he presented the Oscar for best picture. He died two months later, on June 11, of lung and stomach cancer. Appropriately, his last screen role, in *The Shootist* (1976), was as an aging gunfighter dying of cancer. In 1981 his son Michael established what would become the John Wayne Cancer Institute.

He was the number one box-office draw for four years in Quigley's Annual Top Ten Money Makers Poll, and from 1949 through 1974 he was in the top 10 every year except one, 1958. Since 1993, Wayne has placed among the top 10 in the Harris Poll for America's favorite movie star, the only deceased celebrity to achieve such a ranking. A 2001 Gallup Poll identified him as Americans' favorite movie star of all time.

Shortly before his death, Congress authorized a special gold medal in his honor. The medal, presented posthumously to his family, is inscribed "John Wayne, American."

In addition to the U.S. *Stagecoach* stamp of 1990 (Scott 2448), previous stamps depicting Wayne were issued by Antigua (Scott 1046), Barbuda (Scott 921), Grenada (Scott 2470g) and Mali (Scott 723f).

The Design

To illustrate the John Wayne stamp and pane, art director Derry Noyes chose Drew Struzan, an entertainment artist whose work has been prominently featured on film posters. Struzan's stamp credits include the Edward G. Robinson and Lucille Ball stamps in the Legends of Hollywood series, the Zora Neale Hurston commemorative in the Literary Arts series and the 15 Celebrate the Century stamps for the decade of the 1990s.

Drew Struzan based his stamp portrait of John Wayne on this black-and-white publicity photo for the 1962 film The Man Who Shot Liberty Valance, *directed by John Ford and co-starring James Stewart.*

He typically draws his pictures with a carbon pencil on a gessoed illustration board, then airbrushes the colors in acrylic paint and adds the details with colored pencils, which gives the finished work an informal, almost improvised appearance. "I thought Drew's style was appropriate for the rugged cowboy look that was needed," Noyes said.

Among the photographs Noyes chose as reference for the stamp portrait were some showing Wayne as a younger actor, but in these, "he didn't really look like the John Wayne that we all remembered," she said. The image that ultimately was chosen was borrowed from a black-and-white publicity photo for the 1962 film *The Man Who Shot Liberty Valance*, directed by John Ford and co-starring James Stewart. In the photo and in Struzan's interpretation, Wayne's face is appropriately weathered.

As a guide in colorizing the picture, the design team was able to refer to actual outfits worn by the actor in his films. Struzan's finished illustration shows Wayne in what Noyes calls a "salmony and dark blue combination" of bandanna and shirt. The artist made Wayne's eyes a penetrating blue in color. The picture is tightly cropped, with the crown and part of the brim of the hat cut off.

She placed the words "JOHN WAYNE" in black across the top, and "37 USA" in light blue in the lower left corner. "I wanted to keep the type from being overpowering, yet make it masculine," she said. "The font is Universe condensed, and keeping it all capitals seemed to give it some presence but without dominating the portrait."

Struzan's first color sketch for the selvage was based on a scene from *Hondo*, the 1953 film in which Wayne plays cavalry dispatch rider Hondo Lane. It showed the character trudging across a barren landscape, rifle in

his right hand, saddlebag in his left, with his collie dog at his heels. However, Ethan Wayne informed postal officials that the film "was caught in some legal issues, and we wouldn't be able to get permission to use the scene," Terrence McCaffrey said. "Ethan said, 'Let's pick something else.' I said, 'How about my favorite film, *The Searchers*? He said, 'It's my favorite, too.'"

Struzan's first color sketch for the selvage was based on a scene from Hondo (1953), *showing Wayne as Hondo Lane trudging across a barren landscape, carrying rifle and saddlebag, with his dog at his heels. Because of legal problems, rights to the source image weren't easily obtainable, and a different movie was chosen.*

170

Struzan made pencil sketches for two alternative selvage pictures based on publicity stills from **The Searchers.** *In this one, not used, Wayne, as Ethan Edwards, stands sideways with a rifle over his shoulder.*

Working with black-and-white publicity stills from *The Searchers*, Struzan sketched two versions of Wayne as Ethan Edwards, one in which he stands sideways with a rifle over his shoulder, the other showing him facing the viewer with the rifle held across his body at hip level. To the background, Struzan added a red-rock butte resembling the well-known East Mitten in Monument Valley Navajo Tribal Park, where portions of the movie were filmed. The artist created a painting that would fit the full stamp pane, but left empty landscape in the area that was to be covered by the white rectangle containing the 20 stamps. The portions of the artwork that are visible above, below and to the left of the stamps bleed off the sides of the pane.

The Searchers is set during the Comanche wars of the 1860s and 1870s. A *Linn's* reader, J. Richard Rees of Utah, commented in a letter that the selvage art and the still on which it is based show Wayne carrying a model 1892 Winchester carbine, although the weapon wasn't available until some two decades after the period of the film.

First-Day Facts

Richard J. Strasser, chief financial officer and executive vice president of the Postal Service, dedicated the stamp in a ceremony at Grauman's Chinese Theatre in Hollywood.

Speakers were actor Andrew Prine, who co-starred with Wayne in the movie *Chisum*; Ethan Wayne, representing the Wayne family; and Drew Struzan, the stamp's illustrator. David Failor, USPS manager of stamp services, was master of ceremonies, and Al Iniguez, USPS Pacific Area vice president of operations, also took part. Honored guests were the other surviving Wayne children, Patrick, Aissa and Marisa Wayne and Melinda Wayne Munoz and their families; the families of the late Michael Wayne and Toni Wayne La Cava; and two CSAC members, Jean Picker Firstenberg, chief executive officer of the American Film Institute, and Michael R. Brock of Michael Brock Design.

Grauman's, the site of the ceremony, was opened in 1927 and has hosted more Hollywood premieres than any other theater. Generations of

Shown at the first-day ceremony for the John Wayne stamp with an enlargement of the design are, left to right: Aissa Wayne, Melinda Wayne Munoz, stamp illustrator Drew Struzan, actor Andrew Prine, Patrick Wayne, Marisa Wayne, Ethan Wayne and the Postal Service's Richard J. Strasser and Al Iniguez.

actors and actresses have been asked to put their handprints and footprints in wet cement at Grauman's. Wayne imprints — one fist and his cowboy boots — were added to the display January 25, 1950. The plot of a 1955 episode of the television series *I Love Lucy*, in which Wayne appeared, revolves around 2001 Legends of Hollywood subject Lucille Ball's zany housewife character's attempt to steal Wayne's footprints from Grauman's forecourt.

For a limited time, Stamp Fulfillment Services sold uncacheted first-day covers bearing a full pane of Wayne stamps for $9.90 and a single stamp for 75¢.

37¢ SICKLE CELL DISEASE AWARENESS

Date of Issue: September 29, 2004

Catalog Number: Scott 3877

Colors: yellow, magenta, cyan, black, reddish brown (PMS 7532), cool gray 9

First-Day Cancel: Atlanta, Georgia

First-Day Cancellations: 70,632

Format: Pane of 20, vertical, 5 across, 4 down. Gravure printing cylinders printing 200 stamps per revolution (2 panes across, 5 panes around) manufactured by Keating Gravure.

Gum Type: self-adhesive

Stamp Size: 0.99 by 1.56 inches; 25.146 by 39.624mm

Pane Size: 5.85 by 7.25 inches; 148.59 by 184.15mm

Perforations: 11 (die-cut simulated perforations) (Comco Commander rotary die cutter)

Selvage Markings: "©2003/USPS". ".37/x20/$7.40". "PLATE/POSITION" and diagram.

Back Markings: Universal Product Code (UPC) "456900" in 4 locations on back of liner paper

Illustrator: James Gurney of Rhinebeck, New York

Art Director: Howard Paine of Delaplane, Virginia

Typographer: John Boyd of New York, New York

Stamp Manufacturing: Stamps printed by Avery Dennison Security Printing Division, Clinton, South Carolina, on 8-color Dia Nippon Kiko webfed gravure press. Stamps processed by Avery Dennison.

Quantity Ordered: 96,400,000

Cylinder Number Detail: 1 set of 6 cylinder numbers preceded by the letter V in selvage above or below each lower corner stamp

Cylinder Number Combination Reported: V111111

Paper Supplier: Fasson Division of Avery Dennison

Tagging: block tagging over stamps

The Stamp

On September 29, the Postal Service issued the latest in a long line of commemorative stamps aimed at increasing the public's awareness of diseases, their detection and treatment. This one bore the message, "Test Early for Sickle Cell," an inherited condition that is characterized by red blood cells of a curved or sickle shape and that affects one in 12 black Americans.

A sickle cell stamp had been under consideration by the Citizens' Stamp Advisory Committee, and it received approval after LeGree Daniels, a long-time member of the USPS Board of Governors, went to bat for it with Postmaster General John C. Potter. Among Daniels' previous successful stamp lobbying efforts was her advocacy in 1995 of a Great Americans definitive to honor a fellow Pennsylvanian, Milton Hershey.

"We took the proposal to the committee at Mr. Potter's request," said Terrence McCaffrey, manager of stamp development for USPS. "The committee said, 'We don't have a social awareness stamp for 2004, so let's do it.'"

The self-adhesive stamp was printed by the gravure process by Avery Dennison Security Printing Division and distributed in panes of 20. Its design was unveiled September 25, 2003, at the convention of the Sickle Cell Disease Association of America in Beverly Hills, California.

Sickle cell disease is caused by a form of hemoglobin, a protein that enables the red cells to carry oxygen from the lungs via the bloodstream to all parts of the body. Red blood cells with normal hemoglobin are smooth and round and glide easily through the blood vessels. In sickle cell disease, after the carrier cells release their oxygen they assume an abnormal configuration and become hard and sticky, blocking blood flow and causing organ damage. Other complications include periods of intense pain, swelling, fatigue, jaundice and stroke, as well as anemia.

More than 80,000 Americans are estimated to have sickle cell disease and more than two million have the sickle cell trait, meaning that they carry one copy of the gene for the disease. There is no universal cure. Treatments include antibiotic therapy, supplemental oxygen, transfusions and bone marrow transplantation, a technique most successful in younger people. The drug hydroxyurea has been found to mitigate the principal symptoms, apparently by activating a gene that triggers the body's production of fetal hemoglobin. Researchers continue to search for more effective treatments and, ultimately, a cure.

174

"Like diabetes, sickle cell can be monitored and controlled," said Howard Paine, the USPS art director who was assigned the task of designing the stamp. "If two high-risk people marry, and one knows that he or she already has sickle cell, it is important to test the other partner. Two parents, both of them carriers, almost certainly will produce a sickle-cell child, and the earlier that the child can be treated, the better.

"In fact, CSAC made it imperative to add the word 'early' to our stamp caption, 'Test Early for Sickle Cell.'"

However, the message does not specify who should be tested. One doctor, Ken Zierer of Upper Saddle River, New Jersey, felt that its thrust should have been in another direction.

The fact that neonatal screening is standard practice means that "early identification of babies with sickle cell is not the major problem in the United States," Zierer wrote to *Linn's Stamp News*. "The real problem, as with many diseases, is lack of effective treatment.

"While hydroxurea has helped a little, many patients, especially children, suffer greatly from the disease. Therefore, the caption on the stamp should have emphasized finding a cure or effective treatment.

"These goals can only be achieved with further research and greater funding — a message that might be missed with the design of the Sickle Cell Disease stamp."

Among the numerous other diseases and afflictions that have been publicized on U.S. commemorative stamps in recent years are diabetes, prostate cancer, breast cancer, AIDS, malaria, alcoholism and drug abuse.

The Design

"My first idea was to show a photomicrograph with both kinds of blood cells, normal and sickle cell, with a headline saying 'Test for Sickle Cell,'" recalled art director Paine.

"Like a sickle cell myself, I got stuck on the idea that the photomicrograph, with the headline running through it, or stacked beside it, was the way to go. I even tried to play on the word 'sickle' by placing it at an angle, or in a curve, or with the C falling over, a la Charlie Chaplin." (On the Chaplin stamp of the 1994 Silent Screen Stars block of 10, for which Paine was art director, the comedian's elbow is knocking the P in his name out of line.)

"I never found the perfect photo, and I used horrible colors in the

Art director Howard Paine's first idea was to show a photomicrograph of normal and sickle blood cells, and to play on the word "sickle" by tilting the C in the word. The photo is red against a blue background. CSAC found the approach too "clinical."

Howard Paine sent these rough sketches to James Gurney as a guide to the approach he wanted the artist to take. "I have a weakness for the torn-paper urgency I've sketched" for the captions, Paine wrote, "but we may not stay with it." (They didn't.) Also abandoned was the idea of including a microscope and a microscopic image of sickle cells in the design.

design — blood red for the photo, slate blue for the background — and I got lots of resistance to the whole approach," Paine said.

"It wasn't really ugly; it was just too abstract," said Terrence McCaffrey. "We said, 'Howard, this is something that affects humans, and you're making it a very clinical stamp.' "

Paine continued, "After all those years at *National Geographic* [where he had been art director], I should have known better! We decided, let's show a happy mother holding her newborn up high, or in her arms, with or without a microscope or photomicrograph in the background.

"We went to James Gurney, who found the right models and painted the perfect picture you see on the stamp. Jim did the 15 The World of Dinosaurs stamps for us in 1997; he had created *Dinotopia*, a series of children's books about a fantasy land where humans and dinosaurs live together. He also is able to paint in the style of Norman Rockwell, generous with detail, lovingly executed.

"So Jim Gurney saved the day, and we have an appealing, attractive stamp."

For Gurney's preliminary color sketches, he used his wife Jeanette as the model for the mother. "The most successful version showed the mother holding up her year-old child in profile and giving him a kiss," the artist said. "The committee approved the design — sans microscope slide — and gave me the go-ahead.

"Normally, I use friends and neighbors as models, but I didn't know

176

Gurney first photographed model Danica Riddick holding a stuffed bear. After it became clear that the model for the baby, Alexia Velazquez, would not be frightened by being in unfamiliar hands, Danica held Alexia herself for a series of photos on which Gurney based his finished painting.

anyone who had the right look for a young African-American woman, or, for that matter, a baby of the right age."

Gurney found the right individuals through Model Management of Goshen, New York, not far from his home in Rhinebeck. Margo George, the firm's owner, held a casting call and chose Danica Riddick, then 15 years old and a sophomore at Goshen High School, to pose as the mother. Through a friend, George obtained the services of the baby, 1-year-old Alexia Velazquez of Middletown, New York.

The fact that the two subjects were unrelated "meant the modeling session might be risky, since babies of that age often are terrified to be held by strangers," Gurney said. "And, in this case, the woman posing as the mother was a young dancer who didn't yet have children of her own. If the baby started crying, the session would be a disaster.

"To be safe, I scheduled the modeling sessions back to back. The 'mother' posed first, holding a stuffed bear as a stand-in for the baby. Then I photographed the baby being held by a favorite aunt. Finally, we put the baby in the 'mother's' arms. After a moment of wide-eyed consternation, the baby broke into a wide smile, and the two got along wonderfully. The resulting photos provided a beginning basis for the final oil painting."

The fact that Danica Riddick was able to hold the actual child was important, Gurney said, because "the weight of the baby was so different from the weight of the stuffed animal that the pose was ever so slightly different, with the shoulders brought forward to sustain the weight. Hopefully, it made it more convincing by having them actually posing together."

Gurney painted the baby as a boy in his finished artwork. "Every element of the picture is put to work in communicating a parent's tender love for her child," he wrote in a letter to Paine. "The colors are kept in the

James Gurney submitted these three color sketches based on Paine's instructions, retaining in two of them the microscope view of sickle cells. He was told to develop the sketch of the mother kissing the baby into finished art.

golden-hued range, with a warm, sunny background. The white clothes suggest purity and help set off the honey-colored skin tones of the figures. A graceful sinuous line moves down the back of the woman's head, neck, back and waist."

Typographer John Boyd set the type in a font called American Typewriter, medium and bold, condensed. "TEST EARLY FOR SICKLE CELL" is printed in reddish brown and "USA 37" in a shade called cool gray.

First-Day Facts

Henry Pankey, vice president for emergency preparedness, dedicated the stamp at the 32nd annual convention of the Sickle Cell Disease Association of America (SCDAA) at the Renaissance Waverly Hotel in Atlanta, Georgia. Pankey also had presided at the design's unveiling at the previous convention of the SCDAA.

Joseph Phillips, an actor who has appeared on television's *The Cosby Show* and *General Hospital,* was master of ceremonies. Others participating were Atlanta Mayor Shirley Franklin; SCDAA president and chief operating officer Willarda V. Edwards; SCDAA board chairman Kwaku Ohene-Frempong; Priaona Davis, the organization's 2003-2005 National Poster Child; gospel recording artist and evangelist Dorothy Norwood; Tatiana McConnico, recording artist and actress; the Rev. Darrell Elligan, president of Concerned Black Clergy; and Marjorie Brown, Atlanta postmaster.

For a limited time, Stamp Fulfillment Services offered uncacheted first-day covers for 75¢.

37¢ CLOUDSCAPES (15 DESIGNS)

Date of Issue: October 4, 2004

Catalog Numbers: 3878a-o, stamps; 3878, pane of 15

Colors: yellow, magenta, cyan, black, green (PMS 322), blue (PMS 295)

First-Day Cancel: Milton, Massachusetts

First-Day Cancellations: 459,355 (includes Cloudscapes postal cards)

Format: Pane of 15, square, 5 across, 3 down. Gravure printing cylinders printing 180 stamps per revolution (2 panes across, 6 panes around) manufactured by Keating Gravure.

Gum Type: self-adhesive

Stamp Size: 1.225 by 1.225 inches; 31.75 by 31.75mm

Pane Size: 7.15 by 5.4375 inches; 181.61 by 138.1125mm

Perforations: 11 (die-cut simulated perforations) (Comco Commander rotary die cutter)

Selvage Inscription: "CLOUDSCAPES"

Selvage Markings: "© 2003/USPS." ".37/x15/$5.55."

Back Markings: On selvage liner: "Clouds develop when moist air cools to its dew point by rising to a higher altitude or by moving over a cooler surface. Water vapor in the air then condenses in liquid or frozen/form around minute particles such as pollen or dust. The shapes and altitudes of clouds, as well as the sequences in which they develop, help people forecast the weather./In the early 19th century, Englishman Luke

179

Howard — chemist by trade and meteorologist by avocation — created a system for classifying clouds using Latin names. He/described the three most common shapes as *cirrus* (curl of hair), *stratus* (layer), and *cumulus* (heap); he also defined four compound cloud forms that derive from the three/primary shapes, including *nimbus* (rain). Later scientists added terms such as *humilis* (small) and *incus* (anvil) to designate other cloud properties./The *International Cloud-Atlas*, first published in 1896, is based on this classification system./Nine of the ten basic cloud genera are pictured on this stamp pane and arranged according to altitude. The prefixes 'cirro' and 'alto' distinguish high- and middle-altitude/clouds, respectively. Nimbostratus, a dark, featureless cloud marked by falling rain or snow, is not shown." Universal Product Code (UPC) "456800." On stamp liners: "Cumulonimbus incus, or/thunderstorm clouds, form when/rapid updrafts within cumulus/congestus clouds rise into the/upper atmosphere and spread/out into mushroom-shaped/anvils. Thunderstorms always/produce lightning; severe storms/may produce heavy rain, large/hailstones, or tornadoes." "Pouch-like cumulonimbus/mammatus develop when/pockets of air chilled by/evaporating droplets or ice/crystals sink into dry/surroundings under the anvil./They usually indicate the/approach or departure of a/potentially severe thunderstorm."

"Cirrocumulus undulatus/are patches or layers/of small puffy clouds/arranged in patterns. They/have a rippled appearance/due to wind shear and/usually cover only a small/portion of the sky.' "Relatively transparent/cirrostratus fibratus clouds/occur mostly in winter/and often produce a halo/effect around the sun or moon./Thickening cirrostratus/frequently indicate the/approach of a frontal system." "Composed of windblown ice/crystals, cirrus are fibrous,/often wispy clouds that appear/in isolated patches or cover/large areas of the sky./Cirrus radiatus appear to/emerge from the horizon/in parallel bands." "Smooth, almost motionless/altocumulus lenticularis/clouds resemble lenses and/may be iridescent. They often/look like UFOs and form in the/crests of waves that occur when/strong winds cross over a/mountain peak or ridge." "Named for the turret-like/protuberances in their top/portions, altocumulus/castellanus clouds signify/unstable air in the vicinity/and often indicate the/potential for thunderstorms/later in the day." "Resembling ripples on/water, altocumulus/undulatus clouds result/from wind shear — wind/speed or direction that/changes sharply with height./They may appear as patches/or cover the sky." "Altostratus translucidus,/cloud sheets formed by the/rising and cooling of large/air masses, often precede/advancing storm systems./A 'watery' sun (or moon) may/shine dimly through the thinner/sections of the cloud sheet." "Small heaps arranged in layers/or sheets, altocumulus/stratiformis clouds are/primarily composed of water/droplets and, as depicted/here, reflect glorious colors/at sunset. If they become thicker/during the day, a storm may/be approaching." "Among nature's most destructive/phenomena, tornadoes/are rapidly spinning columns of/rising air extending between the/base of a cumulonimbus/cloud and the ground. In/extreme cases, tornado winds/may exceed 250 miles an hour." "Strong, buoyant updrafts/of warm, moist air in an/unstable atmosphere cause/cumulus clouds to develop into/cumulus congestus./These lowering clouds can/produce moderate rain or/snow showers and may grow/into cumulonimbus clouds." "Cumulus humilis — the/smallest of the cumulus/clouds — have flat bases and/rounded tops. Usually wider/than they are tall, these/fair-weather clouds very rarely/produce precipitation and often/evaporate as the sun sets." "Gray, featureless cloud/layers that can spread/over hundreds of square/miles, stratus opacus, like/ stratocumulus, are generally/composed of water droplets./Stratus clouds occasionally/produce drizzle or light snow." "Stratocumulus undulatus/ occur when weak updrafts/spread horizontally, creating a/layer of shallow, puffy clouds/that is blown by strong winds/into wave-like formations/that lie at right angles to the/wind. These clouds seldom/produce precipita-tion."

Photographers: David Rosenfeld, Arjen and Jerrine Verkaik, Richard A. Keen, David Hoadley, T. Smith, H. Michael Mogil, Carlye Calvin, David Gedzelman, John Day, Edi Ann Otto

Designer and Art Director: Howard Paine of Delaplane, Virginia

Typographer: John Boyd of New York, New York

Stamp Manufacturing: Stamps printed by Avery Dennison Security Print-ing Division, Clinton, South Carolina, on 8-color Dia Nippon Kiko webfed gravure press. Stamps processed by Avery Dennison.

Quantity Ordered: 125,040,000

Cylinder Number Detail: 1 set of 6 cylinder numbers preceded by the letter V in selvage below each lower corner stamp

Cylinder Number Combination Reported: V111111

Paper Supplier: Fasson Division of Avery Dennison

Tagging: block tagging over stamps

The Stamps

On October 4, the Postal Service launched its annual National Stamp Collecting Month activities by issuing a pane of 15 self-adhesive stamps and a companion set of picture postal cards reproducing photographs of various types of clouds.

The theme for the observance, which ran through the month of October, was "Reach for the Sky and Collect Stamps!" Joining USPS in the pro-motion were The Weather Channel, the American Meteorological Soci-ety (AMS) and the National Oceanic and Atmospheric Administration's National Weather Service. Many of the nation's television weather report-ers, as AMS members, used the stamps to publicize the atmospheric sci-ences during their forecasting segments.

Avery Dennison Security Printing Division printed the pane by the gravure process. A large top selvage, or header, bears the set's title, "CLOUDSCAPES." Text on the back of the liner paper for the header and each stamp conveys information about clouds and the depicted forma-tions, making the stamps what USPS called "unique educational 'flash cards.' "

The back of the Cloudscapes pane's liner paper contains text describing the clouds shown on the front of the pane.

The stamps had been a dozen years in the making. Howard Paine, one of the Postal Service's art directors and the originator of the idea, recalled how inspiration struck him.

"In 1992, I was walking in the woods of Camp Susquehannock in Pennsylvania, where my wife and I had taken our two young twin sons for a few weeks of boating and swimming," he said. "I saw a poster tacked up on the porch of a cabin. It turned out to be a chart of 35 cloud types, but from a distance it looked like a pane of stamps.

"It gave me the idea that it would be neat to do a stamp pane showing different clouds."

"Howard is incredible in that respect," said Terrence McCaffrey, manager of stamp design. "He likes to come up with new ideas for educational and informative things. When he told me this one, I gave him a funny look and said, 'Clouds?' He said 'Clouds. Go with me here!' I said, 'OK. Develop something.'"

In the following months, Paine collected photographs from books, magazines and other sources, with which Tom Mann, a typographer

Cirrus radiatus

Cirrostratus fibratus

Cirrocumulus undulatus

182

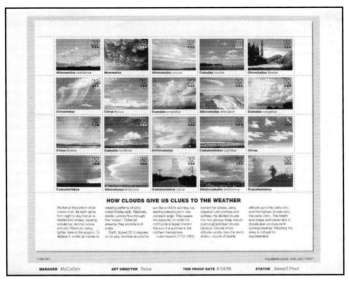

HOW CLOUDS GIVE US CLUES TO THE WEATHER

This is Howard Paine's original demonstration pane of 20 cloud stamps that he constructed in 1995 to show how such a pane might look. The stamps are horizontal semijumbos, while the stamps that were issued nine years later are square. None of the images, which Paine collected from books and magazines, survive in the finished product. The selvage contains Paine's educational text; on the issued pane the text, much revised, is on the back of the liner paper.

and computer graphics specialist, created a demonstration layout of 20 stamps, with explanatory text in the selvage. In August 1995, Paine sent it to McCaffrey with this pitch for what he called the proposal's "many strong features":

"Educational. Straightforward information, with added data printed on the gummed side. Teachers will love it, especially science teachers.

"Environmental. Helps people to look up and take notice of the dynamic world around us.

"Noncontroversial. No politics, sex, race or religion involved! These are really acceptable by all.

"Collectible. Like learning the batting averages on the backs of baseball cards, these informative stamps look alike, but are uniquely different.

Cumulonimbus mammatus

Cumulonimbus incus

Altocumulus stratiformis

Altostratus translucidus

Altocumulus undulatus

Altocumulus castellanus

"Unique and original idea. No other country has done this. Let's beat the U.K. for once!

"Appealing to all ages. What part of the evening news does everyone watch?

"Promotable. Send sheets to every TV weatherman across the country and get instant, enthusiastic news coverage …

"Produceable. Whether from photographs or artwork, this set could be researched and under way immediately!"

Paine's last talking point turned out to be far too optimistic. Nevertheless, McCaffrey and the Citizens' Stamp Advisory Committee were intrigued and told him to proceed.

Paine visualized the stamp art as dramatic paintings, and asked an artist to make some preliminary sketches. However, the results were disappointing, and he turned to photographs as the most accurate and flexible way to depict the clouds. A corollary decision was to rely on existing photos, rather than commission new ones that would take months to obtain.

The text on the back of the selvage credits Englishman Luke Howard (1772-1863), a chemist by trade and meteorologist by avocation, with devising the system for classifying clouds using Latin names. Howard's aim was to create a classification system that would be universally recognized, like the taxonomic method developed by the Swedish botanist Linnaeus.

Paine had credited Luke Howard in his first draft of the text for the pane, and successfully made the case for leaving him in. His inclusion

Altocumulus lenticularis

Stratocumulus undulatus

Stratus opacus

184

Cumulus humilis   **Cumulus congestus**   **Cumulonimbus** with tornado

"puts a 'face' on the subject, lending human interest to all those Latin names and prefixes," Paine argued in a memo to McCaffrey. "Also, it wasn't a board or convention of scientists who named the clouds; it was one man. Why not honor him? It salutes an individual in small type on the verso, not in a major way on the face of the pane. [And] it just might enhance sales of the pane in the U.K."

Howard's classification system did not receive critical recognition for many years, and part of the reason lay in the nature of clouds themselves.

Meteorologist Keith Heidorn told *Linn's Stamp News*: "Prior to the beginning of the 19th century, most weather observers believed that clouds were too transient, too changeable, too short-lived, to be classified or even analyzed. With few exceptions, no cloud types were even named. They were just described by their color and form as each individual saw them."

The Glossary of Meteorology of the American Meteorological Society states that clouds can be distinguished by one of three methods. The first method, according to the glossary, categorizes clouds "according to their appearance and, where possible, to their process of formation." A given cloud name comprises a genera, what the AMS glossary calls "the main characteristic forms of clouds," and a species, which are "the peculiarities in shape and differences in internal structure of clouds." The AMS identifies 10 cloud genera and 14 cloud species.

Clouds also are classified according to their typical altitudes, high, middle and low. High clouds, for example, include cirrus, cirrocumulus, cirrostratus, sometimes altostratus and the tops of cumulonimbus. Particulate composition is the third means of classifying clouds. Here the AMS glossary recognizes water clouds, ice-crystal clouds and mixed clouds.

The Designs

PhotoAssist, the Postal Service's research firm, hired H. Michael Mogil of Rockville, Maryland, as principal consultant for the project. Mogil is a certified consulting meteorologist, photographer and co-author of several books about weather. Also providing expertise were Richard A. Keen of Golden, Colorado, a free-lance writer and photographer on weather and a former "tornado chaser" for the National Center for Atmospheric Research, and John Day of McMinnville, Oregon, author of *The Book of Clouds,* who has called the sky "the greatest free show on earth."

Working from their suggestions, PhotoAssist assembled scores of cloud pictures from stock houses and photographers, including several made by the consultants themselves. On November 25, 1997, Paine and Mogil met with Louis Plummer and Paula Mashore of PhotoAssist at the company's offices and began the process of choosing the images.

It was Paine's idea to arrange the stamps on the pane in horizontal rows according to the altitude of the clouds thereon, with the top row of five depicting clouds that are farthest from the earth's surface and the bottom row featuring low-lying varieties. The art director also specified that each picture have a horizon to provide scale and context for the sky scene.

"With Mike Mogil's guidance, we selected 20 images and gave them proper names, and I began tacking them up on the wall in a giant-sized version of my little sheet," Paine said. "We had rows A, B, C and D and positions 1 through 5, so I didn't have to use the name of the clouds when I moved them around; I would just say, 'C-3, shouldn't that move to the left or right so the color balance is better?'

"They had to be in the correct rows, but I didn't want all the orangey ones to be on the left and I didn't want the sky to be beautiful in the top row and not so good-looking in the others. I wanted to break up the design so it looked lively, not routine. I didn't want two images side by side that

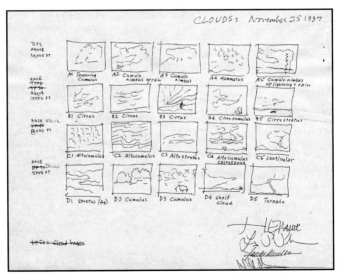

In November 1997, Paine, cloud expert H. Michael Mogil and PhotoAssist staffers held what Paine called a "crucial" meeting and created a preliminary layout for a pane of 20 by tacking photographs on the wall and moving them to find the right arrangement based on the clouds' altitude and the interaction of their shapes and colors. Paine then made a quick sketch of the result, shown here.

After the November 1997 meeting, Paine assembled another layout of 20 semi-jumbo stamps. Several of them incorporated photographs that would remain in the pane of 15 square stamps that eventually was issued. Shown here are some that were dropped or replaced, including a picture of a rainbow that Paine's associates convinced him would be out of place in a cloud collection.

looked identical. It was a matter of filling in the spaces and keeping everyone happy as far as accuracy and attractiveness were concerned.

"When we were finished, it was balanced and colorful and workable. There may have been one or two photos where they said, 'Well, we'll leave that one in B-2 for now, and it's OK, but we can get a better one.' And they did. That meeting was crucial to the whole process."

In the end, none of the pictures Paine had brought together in his demonstration layout of two years earlier remained in the running.

Later, Paine said, "I asked Tom Mann to cut a stair-step path through the pane of 20 and slide the left side over the right side, arbitrarily obscuring four stamps, just to see how the pane would look with only 16 stamps. The purpose was to reduce the overall size of the pane to reduce printing costs. The problem was that with 16 stamps, counter clerks would have to make change in pennies, which we wanted to avoid."

For that reason, it was decided to trim the pane to 15 stamps, which would require no pennies in change.

In his preliminary layouts, Paine had included a photograph of a rainbow, but his associates convinced him that it was not a cloud and would be out of place. The 15th stamp on the issued pane is somewhat of an anomaly, however, because it pictures a tornado, a destructive weather phenomenon that contrasts sharply with the relatively serene images on the other stamps. "It gave the pane a little excitement," the art director said.

As late as 2003, when press time was near, the design team was replacing individual photos with new ones, because the consultants recommended changes or because USPS was having trouble securing the rights to reproduce the pictures. One of the last decisions involved two competing images of cumulus congestus, stamp number 14 on the pane. In a note to Victoria Cooper of PhotoAssist, Paine made clear his preference. "It seems to me that cloud 4110 [the photograph number] hovers sullenly, like cold, leftover mashed potatoes," he wrote, "while cloud 5894 bursts proudly upward out of its neighboring cloud bank, proclaiming, 'Look at me! I'm a cumulus congestus!'" Paine's choice won out.

The 15 images that made the final cut span almost three decades. The oldest photograph was made in 1971 and the most recent in 2000. The precise dates of some of the photos are not known.

Cirrus radiatus: David Rosenfeld/Photo Researchers Inc., New York, New York. Rosenfeld, who died in 1994, lived most of his life in The Bronx, New York. The picture probably was taken at Blue Hill Bay, Maine, in July 1981.

Cirrostratus fibratus: This is the first of four photos credited to Arjen and Jerrine Verkaik/SKYART, Elmwood, Ontario, Canada. The picture with its halo effect was taken June 26, 1988, northeast of Duluth, Minnesota.

Cirrocumulus undulatus: Richard A. Keen, a project consultant. The photo was made September 16, 1992, in Coal Creek Canyon, Colorado.

Cumulonimbus mammatus: David Hoadley, Falls Church, Virginia. This golden sky was captured on film June 6, 1971, near Barnes, Kansas. It is the oldest photograph of the 15.

Cumulonimbus incus: Arjen and Jerrine Verkaik/SKYART. It was made April 22, 1994, west of Amarillo, Texas.

Altocumulus stratoformis: Scott T. Smith, Logan, Utah. This multicolored sky was shot in December 1988 near Las Cruces, New Mexico.

Altostratus translucidus: Richard A. Keen. The sun behind these cloud bands is reflected in the Atlantic Ocean off Cape May, New Jersey, December 26, 1988.

Altocumulus undulatus: H. Michael Mogil, the project's chief consultant. The photo was taken in Rockville, Maryland, probably in May in the mid-1990s.

Altocumulus castellanus: Arjen and Jerrine Verkaik/SKYART. The photo was made July 3, 1992, east-southeast of Wichita, Kansas.

Altocumulus lenticularis: Carlye Calvin, Nederland, Colorado. This deep orange lens-shaped cloud formation was shot near Nederland in September 1988.

Stratocumulus undulatus: Another Richard A. Keen photo, taken October 5, 1977, at Muddy Bay, Labrador, Canada.

Stratus opacus: Stanley David Gedzelman, Upper Saddle River, New Jersey. This misty scene was photographed October 3, 1987, at Chittenden Reservoir, Vermont.

The composition of the photograph that is reproduced on the cumulus humilis stamp, with its blue sky, white clouds, red barn and field of grain, recalls the similar composition on the photo shown on the 32¢ Wisconsin Statehood commemorative of 1998.

Cumulus humilis: John Day, the third of the project's consultants. The picture was taken in McMinnville, Oregon, in August, year unknown. Its red barn and grain field, beneath a blue sky filled with white clouds, recalls the 32¢ Wisconsin Statehood commemorative of 1998, which reproduced Zane Williams' photo of a similar barn and field in Door County, Wisconsin.

Cumulus congestus: Arjen and Jerrine Verkaik/SKYART. The towering, billowy cloud structure was photographed August 28, 2000, north of Douglas, Arizona.

Cumulonimbus with tornado: Edi Ann Otto, Osnabrock, North Dakota. This ominous looking twister was photographed near Osnabrock July 25, 1978.

The stamps are square, a Paine trademark. "I made some layouts in which the stamps are semijumbos," he said, "but at one point, just to get everything condensed a little better, I said, 'Let's try square,' and every one of those photos cropped well in that shape."

Early on, Paine created a header with a cloud-filled blue sky and a title, "Clouds and the weather." "I was looking at that blue title panel," he said, "and I thought, it's competing with the clouds on the stamps, so let's

Paine felt that this header with its cloud-filled blue sky was competing with the stamps, so he settled for a single word, "CLOUDSCAPES," on a white panel.

189

just go with one word, Cloudscapes, on a white panel." The printer used a special green ink for the word and a special blue for the typography on the stamps. Paine chose a Helvetica font for what he called its "crisp, clean, scientific look."

Paine's original draft of the descriptive text underwent numerous changes and insertions by PhotoAssist and the consultants, "so I've lost track of whose copy it really is," he said. To preserve the simple, uncluttered appearance of the pane, it was decided to move all the explanatory material to the back of the liner paper.

First-Day Facts

William Johnstone, secretary to the USPS Board of Governors, dedicated the Cloudscapes stamps at the Blue Hill Observatory in East Milton, Massachusetts, home of the oldest continuous weather record-keeping in North America.

Participants in the ceremony included Jim Cantore and Nick Walker, on-camera meteorologists for The Weather Channel; Susan K. Avery, president of the American Meteorological Society; David L. Johnson, director of the National Oceanic and Atmospheric Administration's National Weather Service; Mark Castle of the Massachusetts Department of Conservation and Recreation; and Charles Lynch, manager of the Postal Service's Boston District.

The observatory, a National Historic Landmark founded in 1885, offered five cacheted first-day covers, each depicting a different weather phenomenon and including an informative insert about clouds. For a limited time, Stamp Fulfillment Services offered a set of uncacheted first-day covers together with a mint pane for $13.60.

37¢ MOSS HART

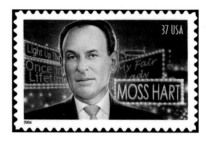

Date of Issue: October 24, 2004

Catalog Number: Scott 3882

Colors: light blue (PMS 2706), yellow, magenta, cyan, black

First-Day Cancel: New York, New York

First-Day Cancellations: 67,786

Format: Pane of 20, horizontal, 4 across, 5 down. Gravure printing cylinders printing 200 stamps per revolution (2 panes across, 5 panes around) manufactured by Keating Gravure.

Gum Type: self-adhesive

Stamp Size: l.56 by 0.99 inches; 39.624 by 25.146mm

Pane Size: 7.25 by 5.85 inches; 184.15 by 148.59mm

Perforations: 11 (die-cut simulated perforations) (Comco Commander rotary die cutter)

Selvage Markings: "© 2003/USPS". ".37/x20/$7.40". "PLATE/POSITION" and diagram.

Back Markings: Universal Product Code (UPC) "457000" in 4 locations on back of liner paper

Illustrator: Tim O'Brien of Brooklyn, New York

Designer, Art Director and Typographer: Ethel Kessler of Bethesda, Maryland

Stamp Manufacturing: Stamps printed by Avery Dennison Security Printing Division, Clinton, South Carolina, on 8-color Dia Nippon Kiko webfed gravure press. Stamps processed by Avery Dennison.

Quantity Ordered: 45,000,000

Cylinder Number Detail: 1 set of 5 cylinder numbers preceded by the letter V in selvage above or below each lower corner stamp

Cylinder Number Combination Reported: V1111

Paper Supplier: Fasson Division of Avery Dennison

Tagging: block tagging over stamps

The Stamp

On October 24, the 100th anniversary of Moss Hart's birth, the Postal Service issued a commemorative stamp honoring the prolific playwright, director and producer.

Hart, who collaborated with George S. Kaufman to write a series of classic stage comedies in the 1930s and later directed the landmark musical *My Fair Lady,* was "one of the legends of the golden age of Broadway," as John Walsh, vice chairman of the USPS Board of Governors, said at the first-day ceremony in New York City. Nevertheless, it took the determined efforts of his widow, actress and singer Kitty Carlisle Hart, to get the stamp issued.

"She, like Ginny Mancini [widow of Henry Mancini], is a mover and shaker, but on the East Coast," recalled Terrence McCaffrey, manager of stamp development for USPS. "She's 94 years old now, and still going strong, still performing.

"She's a friend of a former postmaster general, Preston Tisch. A couple of years ago she called up Tisch, and he wrote to us and said, 'You need to do a Moss Hart stamp,' with Hart's 100th birthday coming up.

"The [Citizens' Stamp Advisory] Committee never really did anything about it. Then Tisch called John Nolan, our deputy postmaster general, and said, 'You need to get that committee moving. Kitty Hart's on my case, and she wants this stamp.'

"So John Nolan contacted David Failor [executive director of Stamp Services] and me and said, 'Can you please put this on the committee's agenda?' I said, 'It's under consideration.' He said, 'I know, but you never do anything with those. Put it at the front of the agenda.' So we put it forward."

CSAC agreed to place Hart on the commemorative stamp program for 2004.

Kitty Carlisle Hart herself said it was her friendship with actor and CSAC member Karl Malden that closed the sale. "I found his name on the committee, and I called him," she told the online Virtual Stamp Club. "I said, 'Would you help me get a stamp for Moss?' And he said, 'I've never done this before for anybody, but I'll do it for him, because I admired him a great deal.'

"I am dazzled and delighted and thrilled that I could get such an honor for my husband and I did it single-handedly. I did it all by myself."

The self-adhesive stamp was printed by the gravure process by Avery Dennison Security Products Division and distributed in panes of 20.

Hart was born October 24, 1904, in New York's Bronx, the son of Jewish immigrants from Great Britain. He grew up in poverty with an ambition to make his mark in the theater. At age 14, he quit school to help support his family. He worked several years in the garment industry before getting his foot in the door of show business as office boy for a theatrical producer.

Later, he worked as an actor, a social director at summer camps and a director of amateur theatrical groups, while writing plays and hoping for a break. As he once stated, "My feet were embedded in the Upper Bronx, but my eyes were set firmly toward Broadway."

His breakthrough came in 1930 with *Once in a Lifetime,* a spoof of Hollywood, written with George S. Kaufman. After its success, Kaufman and Hart would write seven other plays, including *Merrily We Roll Along* (1934); *You Can't Take It With You* (1936), which won the Pulitzer Prize for drama; and *The Man Who Came to Dinner* (1939). Among the plays he wrote alone was *Light Up the Sky* (1948), a backstage comedy.

Hart also wrote librettos for musical comedies by some of Broadway's most illustrious songwriters: Irving Berlin, Cole Porter, Richard Rodgers and Lorenz Hart (no relation), and Kurt Weill and Ira Gershwin. His greatest success as a director came in 1956 with *My Fair Lady*, an adaptation of George Bernard Shaw's *Pygmalion*, with libretto and lyrics by Alan Jay Lerner and music by Frederick Loewe. The show won nine Tony awards, including one to Hart for best direction. He also directed Lerner and Loewe's last musical, *Camelot* (1960), but suffered a heart attack and turned over the direction to Lerner before it arrived on Broadway.

Films for which Hart wrote screenplays included *Gentlemen's Agreement* (1947), which won the Academy Award for best picture; *Hans Christian Andersen* (1952); and *A Star is Born* (1954), starring Judy Garland.

In 1959, Hart's autobiography *Act One* became a best seller. The book covers the early years of his life, up to his first big success in 1930. Though the title and scope of the book invited a sequel, none was written.

Hart married Kitty Carlisle in 1946, and the couple had two children. The family moved in 1961 to Palm Springs, California, where he died of heart failure December 20, 1961, at the age of 57. Only a few months earlier, he had delivered the eulogy at the funeral of his friend and theatrical mentor, George S. Kaufman.

The Design

Searching for an appropriate portrait of Hart for use on the stamp, art director Ethel Kessler and Mike Owens of PhotoAssist, the Postal Service's research firm, visited Kitty Carlisle Hart in her New York apartment. Here they saw a framed photograph by Cecil Beaton, the costume

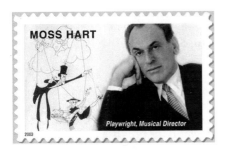

This preliminary design by Ethel Kessler combined a photograph of Moss Hart by Cecil Beaton and the well-known Al Hirschfeld promotional drawing for the Hart-directed musical **My Fair Lady.**

designer for *My Fair Lady*, that seemed just right. Kitty Hart was "so excited with the idea of the stamp, that it was moving forward, that she said, 'Just take it!' " Kessler recalled. "She removed it from the frame, and we took it with us."

Kessler made a mockup of a horizontal commemorative-size stamp with the Beaton photograph on the right. On the left, she placed the late Al Hirschfeld's well-known drawing used on posters and the original-cast record album for *My Fair Lady*, showing playwright George Bernard Shaw as a heavenly puppetmaster manipulating the strings of the musical's stars, Rex Harrison as Professor Henry Higgins and Julie Andrews as Eliza Doolittle.

However, the rights to use the photograph turned out to be unavailable. "Unfortunately, the Beaton estate wanted far too much money," said the Postal Service's Terrence McCaffrey. So Kessler resumed her search. In a selection of photos furnished by PhotoAssist, she found a black-and-white picture of Hart, holding a pipe, leaning on a lamppost in Times Square with the lights of Broadway behind him. The photo was made in 1959 by Alfred Eisenstaedt. To the combination of confident pose and a background that evoked Hart's theater career, Kessler's reaction, she said, was: "Of course!"

"It didn't seem as if we should just use the photo," she added. "It seemed as if we ought to have it painted." Working on another stamp assignment for her at the time was Tim O'Brien of Brooklyn, New York, a magazine and book illustrator (and amateur boxer) who prides himself on executing his realistic images on tight deadlines. Kessler thought the Hart stamp would be "right up his alley," and O'Brien put the other job aside to create an oil painting of Hart, with marquees in the background bearing the illuminated titles of some of the playwright-director's best-known theatrical productions.

O'Brien began the new assignment by scanning the source photograph into his computer and electronically adding color tones and other details. "What he has then looks like a drawing-painting instead of a photo," Kessler said of the artist's method. "He'll send that back to me and say, 'Is this what you mean?' He hasn't painted anything yet — he has only exercised his creative ability in a computer-driven way.

This is the 1959 Alfred Eisenstaedt photo on which Tim O'Brien based his painting of Hart. It shows the playwright-director leaning against a lamppost in Times Square with the lights of Broadway behind him.

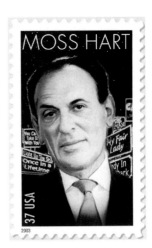

This vertical layout combined Tim O'Brien's preliminary computer sketch of Moss Hart, based on the Eisenstaedt photo, with theatrical marquees bearing the titles of seven productions that Hart authored, co-authored or directed.

"Once we say, 'Yes, that's the mood, that's the approach, give him a little more hair, fill in the blanks there a little bit,' and so forth, he'll start his painting."

Kessler originally decided to make the stamp a vertical to distinguish it from the Literary Arts series commemoratives, which are horizontal, and O'Brien created his preliminary sketches with that plan in mind. However, when Kessler presented them at a meeting of her fellow USPS art directors, Carl Herrman complained that the background was cramped and small and he couldn't "see Broadway." If she made the design horizontal, he said, she could get "more of Broadway in."

"I looked at him and said, 'Absolutely right,' " Kessler said. "Sometimes we get myopic in wanting to solve a problem but not infringe on another kind of design. Of course it had to be a horizontal.

"With a little help from my friends, all of them, researchers and art directors, I think we got to the essence of Moss Hart."

After trying different combinations of marquees behind the playwright, Kessler and O'Brien settled on three with the titles *Light Up the Sky, Once in a Lifetime* and *My Fair Lady,* and a fourth, the most prominent, with the subject's name: "Moss Hart."

In the upper right corner of the design, Kessler placed "37 USA" in small characters in a font called Romeo.

"We called Kitty and said, 'We'd like to show you the finished art,' " said Terrence McCaffrey. "Ethel and I and Bill Gicker [creative director of stamp design for USPS] took it to Kitty's apartment. Tim had just finished it, and the oil paint hadn't dried yet. We had it in a box with a lid.

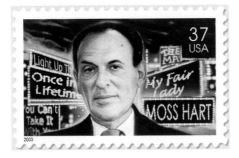

The design team came closer to the finished composition with this horizontal layout that incorporated the Tim O'Brien computer portrait and presented Moss Hart's name in lights. The six marquees were deemed too many and were reduced to four in the final painting.

195

"She came out in a little Givenchy suit with a little hat and purse to meet us in her apartment. She sat down, makeup on, everything in place. Ethel opened the box, and she sat and stared at the painting. She opened her purse and took out her hanky and dabbed her eyes. She cried for five minutes — she was just so touched.

"I said, 'Would he have worn a tie of this color? Are the eye colors right?' She said, 'Don't touch it, my dear, it's perfect!'

"We stayed for a while, and she told us stories about Moss and herself and the people they knew in show business. She even sang for us. It was one of the most exciting hours of my career."

First-Day Facts

John Walsh, vice chairman of the USPS Board of Governors, dedicated the stamp in a ceremony at the Rosenthal Pavilion of New York University's Kimmel Center.

John Sexton, president of NYU, gave the welcome. Speakers were Hart's wife, Kitty Carlisle Hart; their son, Christopher Hart; and playwright John Guare. Others on hand were Moss Hart's daughter, Catherine Hart, and Anne Kaufman, daughter of Hart's writing partner, George S. Kaufman. David L. Solomon, New York Metropolitan Area vice president of USPS, was master of ceremonies.

For a limited time Stamp Fulfillment Services sold uncacheted first-day covers of the stamp for 75¢.

196

37¢ LOVE CANDY HEARTS
CONVERTIBLE BOOKLET OF 20

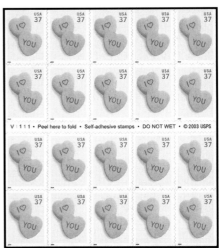

Date of Issue: January 14, 2004

Catalog Number: Scott 3833, single stamp; 3833a or BC198, convertible booklet of 20

Colors: yellow, magenta, cyan, black

First-Day Cancel: Revere, Massachusetts

First-Day Cancellations: 82,157

Format: Convertible booklet of 20, vertical, 5 across, 4 down, with horizontal peel-off strip between horizontal rows 2 and 3. Gravure printing cylinders printing 210 stamps per revolution (3 panes across, 7 panes around) manufactured by Keating Gravure.

Gum Type: self-adhesive

Overall Stamp Size: 0.91 by 1.19 inches; 23.114 by 30.226mm

Pane Size: 4.55 by 5 inches; 115.57 by 127mm

Perforations: 10¾ (die-cut simulated perforations) (Comco Commander rotary die cutter). Backing paper rouletted behind peel-off strip.

Selvage Markings: Plate numbers and "• Peel here to fold • Self-adhesive stamps • DO NOT WET • ©2003 USPS."

Back Markings: "LOVE/Twenty/37-cent/First-Class/self-adhesive/stamps/ $7.40." Promotion for The Postal Store Web site. USPS logo. "©2003 USPS." Universal Product Code (UPC) "0 672800 9."

Designer and Typographer: Michael Osborne of San Francisco, California

Art Director: Ethel Kessler of Bethesda, Maryland

Stamp Manufacturing: Stamps printed by Avery Dennison Security Printing Division, Clinton, South Carolina, on Dia Nippon Kiko gravure press. Stamps finished by Avery Dennison.

Quantity Ordered: 750,000,000

Plate Number Detail: 1 set of 4 plate numbers preceded by the letter V on peel-off strip

Plate Number Combination Reported: V1111

Paper Supplier: Fasson Division of Avery Dennison

Tagging: phosphored paper

The Stamp

On January 14, the Postal Service issued a 37¢ Love stamp depicting two overlapping candy hearts, one imprinted with "I [heart]" and the other with the word "YOU." The first-day ceremony was held at the New England Confectionery Company (Necco) in Revere, Massachusetts, which manufactures the popular Sweethearts Conversation Hearts that inspired the design.

The self-adhesive stamp was distributed in convertible booklets of 20. It was printed by the gravure process by Avery Dennison Security Printing Division.

Although Necco offers Sweetheart candies with a variety of sentiments, the company previously had no "I [heart] YOU" in its inventory. To celebrate the stamp's issuance, however, Necco made a special batch of hearts for the first-day ceremony with that message in full — an example of life imitating art. The new candies were included in boxes along with perennial favorites such as "BE MINE," "HUG ME," and "CUTIE PIE."

The concept of the Sweethearts Conversation Heart dates to the 19th century, when printed sayings on colored paper were placed in "Cockles," small crisp candies formed in the shape of a scalloped shell. In 1866, Daniel Chase invented the process whereby the sayings could be printed directly on the candy.

Chase's brother Oliver R. Chase had founded Chase and Co., predecessor of Necco, in 1847. In 1901 the company joined with two other firms, Forbes, Hayward and Co. and Wright and Moody, to form the New England Confectionery Company. Its signature product, the Necco wafer, became a fixture in candy stores across the country.

Sweethearts Conversation Hearts originally were called Motto Hearts. In 1990 Necco obtained the brand from the Stark Candy Company. The Sweethearts recipe has been the same since the candy first was made.

To meet the Valentine's Day demand for Sweethearts, Necco produces some 8 billion hearts per year at three U.S. manufacturing plants. The entire production — roughly 100,000 pounds a day — sells out in just six weeks.

According to the Necco Web site, "We do produce custom conversation hearts (hearts with your own sayings). However, in order to purchase custom hearts, you must purchase a full production run of 3,500 pounds."

In recent years, USPS had issued the Love stamps every other year, in pairs covering the current one-ounce and two-ounce first-class rates. The two-ounce-rate stamp, with a design similar in theme to its companion but not identical, was intended primarily for use in mailing wedding invitations or announcements that are accompanied by RSVP cards and return envelopes.

However, brides and their mothers were dissatisfied with many of the designs, considering them too whimsical or graphic to be appropriate for wedding invitations. To meet their needs, the Citizens' Stamp Advisory Committee changed its approach. Beginning in 2004, the one-ounce and two-ounce special stamps that are issued in alternate years would be designed with weddings in mind, CSAC decided, and a separate Love stamp at the one-ounce rate would be issued every year. The 37¢ Candy Hearts stamp became the first in the latter category.

The Design

The Love Candy Hearts stamp was designed by Michael Osborne under the art direction of Ethel Kessler. Osborne heads his own design firm in San Francisco, California, and owns a letterpress business, One Heart Press, at which he designs and prints valentines each year that he sends to

These two designs were among 14 sets of Love stamp concept sketches submitted to USPS by Michael Osborne in 2001. Two of the designs became the 37¢ and 60¢ graphic Love stamps of 2002, and the 34¢ design shown here became the basis for Osborne's 37¢ Love Candy Hearts stamp of 2004. The script word "love" was considered redundant and was omitted.

clients. He also is a stamp collector who considers stamps a fascinating artistic medium.

The Candy Hearts design was included among 14 pairs of colorful Love stamp treatments that Osborne sent to USPS at Kessler's invitation in 2001. Her fellow Postal Service art directors were delighted with Osborne's work, but the flood of designs from a single source created "sensory overload," said Terrence McCaffrey, director of stamp development for USPS.

"They didn't know what to do with them," McCaffrey recalled. "They said, 'It's just too much! Let's use them all!' " Later, the directors narrowed the group of concepts to three or four to be shown to CSAC's design subcommittee for a final selection. The subcommittee, in turn, chose one pair featuring graphic treatments of the word LOVE that became the 2002 Love stamps — and approved the Candy Hearts set for future issuance.

The concept of a Love stamp depicting Sweethearts-like candies wasn't new. In the mid-1990s, photographer Pete McArthur sent USPS art director Richard Sheaff some sketches incorporating the concept, and a few years later Sheaff developed a proposed design featuring five candies, each with a different message. But the idea didn't click with CSAC until the members saw Osborne's designs.

When the time came to use them, however, the committee had changed its Love stamp policy and only one stamp was needed. Osborne set about transforming his original design sketch into finished stamp art, working with a computer graphics specialist in his firm.

"We bought a bag of Sweethearts candies and found a handful of them in various colors with shapes that were close to perfect," Osborne said. "We used a fingernail file and a little bit of extra-fine sandpaper to sand off the messages and sand down the hearts until they were as smooth and even as we could make them.

"Then we stacked them in some different arrangements on a white background and took digital photographs. One of the compositions worked really well in the stamp dimensions, so we made a digital com-

A few years earlier, USPS art director Richard Sheaff developed this proposed Love stamp design featuring five candies, each with a different message. But the idea of a Candy Hearts stamp didn't click with CSAC until the members saw Michael Osborne's design treatment.

200

puter file of it. Using Photoshop [software], we touched up the shapes, applied a shadow behind the hearts, fine-tuned the colors to make them as close to the originals as possible, and applied the wording."

The type font, for both the messages on the candy and the stamp itself, is called Trade Gothic. "We modified it on the candy to make it a little bit distressed, and rough and uneven, for a realistic look," Osborne said.

The candies are pink, for the foreground heart, and orange, for the one behind, and are shown against a soft yellow background framed by a white border. The inscriptions on both candies and the "USA 37" on the stamp are red. Avery Dennison used the four standard process colors, yellow, magenta, cyan and black, to print the stamp.

Osborne's original design had included the word "love" in red script, but it was felt to be redundant, given the nature of the design, and was omitted in the final version, allowing the image of the candies to be somewhat larger.

"One of Michael's fortes is to eliminate everything that is unnecessary in a design and get it down to its essence," said Ethel Kessler. "I give him tremendous credit for the simplicity of this design. It couldn't be sweeter!"

First-Day Facts

Alan Kessler, a member of the Postal Service Board of Governors, dedicated the stamp at the Necco plant. Domenic M. Antonellis, president and chief executive officer of the company, welcomed the guests. The principal speaker was Wayne Levy, director of community relations for the Boston Celtics professional basketball team and a member of the Make-a-Wish Foundation. Also participating in the ceremony were stamp designer Michael Osborne; Marsha Cannon, postmaster of Boston; and Megan J. Brennan, manager of operations for the USPS Northeast Area.

37¢ GARDEN BOUQUET
CONVERTIBLE BOOKLET OF 20

Date of Issue: March 4, 2004

Catalog Number: Scott 3836, single stamp; 3836a or BC199, convertible booklet of 20

Colors: black, cyan, magenta, yellow, green (PMS 563C)

First-Day Cancel: New York, New York

First-Day Cancellations: 86,657 (includes 60¢ Garden Botanical)

Format: Convertible booklet of 20, vertical, 5 across, 4 down, with horizontal peel-off strip between horizontal rows 2 and 3. Offset printing plates printing 500 stamps per revolution (25 across, 20 around).

Gum Type: self-adhesive

Microprinting: none

Overall Stamp Size: 0.91 by 1.19 inches; 23.114 by 30.226mm

Pane Size: 4.55 by 5 inches; 115.57 by 127mm

Perforations: 10¾ (die-cut simulated perforations) (IDC custom rotary die cutter). Backing paper rouletted behind peel-off strip.

Selvage Markings: Plate numbers and "Peel here to fold" "© 2003 USPS"

Back Markings: "Garden Bouquet/Twenty 37-cent First-Class/Self-adhesive Stamps/$7.40." Promotion for The Postal Store Web site. "© 2003 USPS." USPS logo. Universal Product Code (UPC) "0 673500 9."

Designer, Art Director and Typographer: Richard Sheaff of Scottsdale, Arizona

Modeler: Joseph Sheeran of Ashton-Potter (USA) Ltd., Williamsville, New York

Stamp Manufacturing: Stamps printed by Ashton-Potter on a Mueller Martini A76 modified offset press. Stamps finished by Ashton-Potter.

Quantity Ordered: 750,000,000

Plate Number Detail: 1 set of 5 plate numbers preceded by the letter P on peel-off strip

Plate Number Combinations Reported: P11111, P22222, P33333, P44444, P55555, P66666, P77777, P88888

Paper Supplier: Flexcon/Glatfelter

Tagging: phosphored paper

60¢ GARDEN BOTANICAL

Date of Issue: March 4, 2004

Catalog Number: Scott 3837

Colors: magenta, yellow, cyan, black, turquoise (PMS 563)

First-Day Cancel: New York, New York

First-Day Cancellations: 86,657 (includes 37¢ Garden Bouquet)

Format: Pane of 20, vertical, 5 across, 4 down. Gravure printing cylinders printing 320 stamps per revolution, manufactured by Southern Graphics Systems.

Gum Type: self-adhesive

Overall Stamp Size: 0.91 by 1.19 inches; 23.11 by 30.22mm

Pane Size: 5.46 by 5.8125 inches; 138.68 by 131.63mm

Perforations: 11½ by 11 (die-cut simulated perforations) (Comco rotary die cutter)

Selvage Markings: "©2003/USPS." "60/x 20/$12.00." "PLATE/POSITION" and diagram.

Back Markings: Universal Product Code (UPC) "566200" in 4 locations.

Designer, Art Director and Typographer: Richard Sheaff of Scottsdale, Arizona

Modeler: Donald H. Woo of Sennett Security Products, Chantilly, Virginia

Stamp Manufacturing: Stamps printed for Sennett Security Products by American Packaging Corporation, Columbus, Wisconsin, on Rotomec 5 3000 gravure press. Stamps finished by Unique Binders of Fredericksburg, Virginia.

Quantity Ordered: 150,000,000

Cylinder Number Detail: 1 set of 5 cylinder numbers preceded by the letter S in selvage above or below each corner stamp

Cylinder Number Combination Reported: S11111

Paper Supplier: Mactac

Tagging: phosphored paper

The Stamps

Beginning in 1994, USPS issued all its Love stamps in pairs with similar designs and denominations covering the one-ounce and two-ounce first-class rate. The double-rate stamps were intended primarily for use in mailing wedding invitations or announcements that are accompanied by RSVP cards and response envelopes. However, the policy of using one design theme for both stamps led to unanticipated sales resistance from the public.

The problem was that brides and their mothers didn't consider some of the designs suitable for wedding correspondence. The first of the Love stamps to meet a cool reception from potential users was the 1995 pair reproducing the two Cupidlike figures from Raphael's painting *Sistine Madonna*. Because the figures actually were angels whose role was related to mortal death rather than love, some bridal families refused to use them for fear they would invite bad luck on the forthcoming marriage.

Even more resistance was generated by Michael Osborne's designs for the 37¢ and 60¢ Love stamps of 2002. These strongly graphic images with their bold flat colors delighted the design professionals on the Citizens' Stamp Advisory Committee, but mothers of brides were another story. "They weren't the pretty and soft stamps they wanted to see," said Terrence McCaffrey, manager of stamp development for USPS. "They didn't match the bridesmaids' dresses or flowers, and the mothers or daughters would call and say, 'Don't you have another Love stamp? Can I have the old Love stamp? I don't want this one.'

"I took the problem to the committee at one of our retreats. I said, 'I think we're hindering ourselves by trying to make the Love stamp a wedding stamp as well. We want the stamps to sell, but we don't want to cede control of the designs to the wedding side and let it dictate what we do.

" 'We know now that the wedding stamp should be pretty and feminine and in pastel colors. So why don't we continue to do Love stamps, but just one at a time — for the one-ounce rate — instead of two, and also do what we'll call wedding stamps, one for the extra-weight envelope and one for the reply envelope, to give the brides and their mothers what they want?' "

CSAC approved the policy and decided that a new pair of wedding stamps would be issued every other year. The first set was issued March 4 and depicted clusters of flowers from 19th-century chromolithographs.

205

The Postal Service called the 37¢ stamp, showing a bouquet of white lilacs and pink roses, "Garden Bouquet," and its 60¢ companion, reproducing an illustration of five varieties of simple pink roses, "Garden Botanical."

The stamps bear no wording other than "USA," the denomination and the year date. This meant that they are appropriate not only for wedding correspondence but also for general use by the Postal Service's many customers who regularly ask window clerks for "pretty flower stamps," McCaffrey said. The 60¢ stamp, in addition to covering the two-ounce first-class rate, also satisfies the one-ounce rate for a letter to Canada or Mexico.

Both stamps are of the special size used by USPS for Love and Holiday stamps. The 37¢ Garden Bouquet stamp was printed by the offset process by Ashton-Potter (USA) Ltd. and distributed in convertible booklets of 20, five across by four down, with a horizontal peel-off strip between horizontal rows two and three. Each of the 14 outer stamps on the pane has a straight edge on one side and/or the top or bottom; the six interior stamps have die-cut simulated perfs on all four edges. The 60¢ Garden Blossoms stamp was printed by the gravure process by American Packaging Corporation for Sennett Security Products and distributed in panes of 20, five across by four down, with selvage all around. None of the stamps has a straight edge.

Postal clerks were permitted to break panes of the 60¢ stamp and sell individual stamps, but they were required to sell the 37¢ convertible booklets intact.

The Postal Service intended to accompany the stamps with an imprinted letter sheet bearing the image of the 37¢ stamp, to be sold in packs of 12 for $14.95. The item, described as "stamped stationery," was listed for sale, with no prior announcement, in the Fall 2004 issue of *USA Philatelic*, the catalog of Stamp Fulfillment Services.

However, postal officials deemed the letter sheet not ready for distribution after similar letter sheets issued June 23 bearing reproductions of The Art of Disney commemorative stamps suffered frequent damage during mail processing. USPS postponed the issue date of the Garden Bouquet letter sheet until 2005.

The Designs

Richard Sheaff, one of the Postal Service's part-time art directors, is a collector of ephemera — antique printed paper products — and has designed numerous holiday and Love stamps for USPS reproducing pictures from such sources. One of the advantages postal officials find in using images from ephemera is that most copyrights, if any, have long since expired.

For the 2004 wedding stamps, Sheaff once again turned to his collection and came up with a pair of chromolithographs depicting flowers. Chromolithography is a color printing process that was developed in the early 19th century and became more efficient and very popular as the century progressed.

The 37¢ art, a bouquet of white lilacs and pink roses, reproduces a chromolithograph probably printed in Germany circa 1880-1900. The artist and engraver are unknown. "It's from a die-cut piece of scrap," Sheaff said. "It's an example of something that was very popular at that time. People would collect them and glue them into scrapbooks in various patterns. They came in all sizes, some of them quite large."

The 60¢ stamp art, a botanical illustration of five varieties of simple pink roses, is a chromolithograph created from a drawing by English artist Anne Pratt. The drawing was one of hundreds appearing in a five-volume book of Pratt's illustrations published in England between 1850 and 1866 and reprinted in England and New York between 1889 and 1900. "The book was full of flower illustrations, but this one turned out to be a nice match for the other artwork," Sheaff said. "Even though they come from different sources, they really look as if they belong together."

Both stamps show their floral images against a plain white background with no borders. On the Garden Bouquet stamp, Sheaff found a convenient corner space in which he could tuck "37 USA" in two lines of Frutiger Light type. The flowers on the Garden Botanical stamp filled the stamp more fully, and he had to separate the typography, with "60" in the upper left corner and "USA" diagonally opposite it. Both sets of typography are printed in similar self-colors that one printer called turquoise and the other green.

Although USPS policy calls for offset-printed, single-design stamps to contain microprinting as a security measure, Ashton-Potter did not include microtype in the 37¢ stamp's design.

First-Day Facts

Charles E. Bravo, USPS senior vice president for intelligent mail and address quality, dedicated the stamps at the Postage Stamp Mega-Event Show in the Expo Center of New York City's Madison Square Garden. The show was sponsored by the American Stamp Dealers Association, the American Philatelic Society and the Postal Service.

Carley Roney, co-founder and editor-in-chief of *The Knot*, a wedding publication, who was billed as "America's Favorite Wedding Expert," participated in the ceremony. Elizabeth C. Pope, president of the ASDA, gave the welcome, and David E. Failor, executive director of stamp services for USPS, was master of ceremonies. Joe Savarese, executive vice president of the ASDA, and Robert E. Lamb, executive director of the APS, were honored guests.

Stamp Fulfillment Services sold uncacheted first-day covers of the 37¢ and 60¢ Garden stamps for 75¢ and 98¢ respectively.

37¢ CHRISTMAS MADONNA AND CHILD
DOUBLE-SIDED CONVERTIBLE BOOKLET OF 20

Date of Issue: October 14, 2004

Catalog Number: Scott 3879, stamp; 3879a, convertible booklet of 20

Colors: black, cyan, magenta, yellow

First-Day Cancel: New York, New York

First-Day Cancellations: 43,269

Format: Convertible booklet pane of 20, vertical, arranged horizontally. Stamps on both sides, 8 (4 across by 2 down) plus label (booklet cover) on one side, 12 (6 across by 2 down) on other side, with vertical peel-off strips between blocks of 4 on each side. Offset printing plates printing 528 stamps per revolution (24 across, 22 around), all-stamp side; 432 stamps per revolution (24 across, 18 around), cover side.

Gum Type: self-adhesive

Microprinting: "USPS" on inside of cloak below Mary's left hand

Overall Stamp Size: 0.91 by 1.19 inches; 23.114 by 30.226mm

Pane Size: 5.76 by 2.38 inches; 146.304 by 60.452mm

Perforations: 10¾ by 11 (die-cut simulated perforations), IDC custom rotary die-cutter. Backing paper rouletted behind peel-off strips.

Selvage Markings: "Peel here to fold" and plate numbers on 2 peel-off strips and "©2003 USPS" "Peel here to fold" on other 2 peel-off strips

Back Markings: "Twenty 37-cent First-Class/Self-adhesive stamps/$7.40" and Universal Product Code (UPC) "0 673400 0" on booklet cover

Designer, Typographer and Art Director: Richard Sheaff of Scottsdale, Arizona

Modeler: Joseph Sheeran of Ashton-Potter USA (Ltd.), Williamsville, New York

Stamp Manufacturing: Stamps printed by Ashton-Potter on Mueller Martini A74 offset press. Stamps finished by Ashton-Potter.

Quantity Ordered: 776,400,000

Cylinder Number Detail: 1 set of 4 plate numbers preceded by the letter P on 2 peel-off strips

Cylinder Number Combination Reported: P1111

Paper Supplier: Flexcon/Glatfelter

Tagging: phosphored paper with phosphor block on cover

The Stamp

The Postal Service presently observes two policies of timing adopted by the Citizens' Stamp Advisory Committee regarding the "traditional" Christmas stamp that features artwork of Mary and the infant Jesus. It changes the stamp's design only every other year, unless a rate increase intervenes. And instead of depicting a preponderance of paintings from the National Gallery of Art in Washington, D.C., as it had done in the past, USPS now alternates the designs between works in the National Gallery and those from other U.S. museums.

In 2002, USPS issued a traditional Christmas stamp depicting the Renaissance painting *Virgin and Child* by Jan Gossaert that hangs in the Art Institute of Chicago, Illinois. A new design — from the National Gallery — was due in 2004, and on October 14, USPS placed on sale a stamp showing a detail of a tempera-on-panel *Madonna and Child* by the medieval artist Lorenzo Monaco.

The self-adhesive stamp was produced in double-sided panes of 20, or convertible booklets, with 12 stamps on one side and eight plus a label that serves as a booklet cover on the other. All 20 stamps have straight edges at the top or bottom and six have straight edges on the left or right side as well. The stamps were printed by the offset process by Ashton-Potter (USA) Ltd.

Lorenzo Monaco was born Piero di Giovanni around 1370, probably in Siena, Italy. In 1391, he professed vows as a monk of the Camaldolese Congregation of the Order of Saint Benedict at the monastery of Santa Maria degli Angeli in Florence. He also assumed a monastic name (Lorenzo Monaco means "Lorenzo the Monk"). Over the next few years, Lorenzo became known as an artist of exceptional talent and skill, whose output included exquisite illuminated manuscripts, miniatures in choir

Shown here is Lorenzo Monaco's tempera-on-panel painting **Madonna and Child** *(1413), a detail of which appears on the 2004 traditional Christmas stamp.*

books and paintings on panels.

By the turn of the century, Lorenzo was one of the leading artists in Florence. Today his works — notable for their graceful lines, decorative details and rich colors — are considered some of the finest examples of late medieval European art. He died in or after 1422 and was buried at Santa Maria degli Angeli.

The panel excerpted on the stamp dates from 1413. Measuring 46 inches high by 21¾ inches across, it bears a full-length image of the Virgin Mary in a floor-length dark purple hooded cloak against a gold background. The infant Jesus, with curly blond hair and wearing a flowing red gown, sits on Mary's left forearm, his right arm resting on her shoulder, his hand holding a scroll in which a Latin phrase can be partially seen: EGO SUM LUX MUNDI (I am the light of the world, from John 8:12). Across the bottom of the panel is the date: ANO MCCCCXIII.

The panel was purchased by the Samuel H. Kress Foundation in 1940 and was given to the National Gallery in 1943. It is part of the gallery's Samuel H. Kress Collection.

The Design

The design of the stamp is one of a number of Madonna and Child designs that were developed by USPS art director Richard Sheaff in 1995 and approved as a group by CSAC.

The Monaco stamp, like all traditional Christmas stamps since 1988, is in what USPS calls its special size, slightly larger than a definitive, and vertically arranged. The vignette is rectangular and set within four white borders; the denomination is in an upper corner, in black. Across the top, in black Garamond capitals, is the word "CHRISTMAS"; across the bottom, in uppercase and lowercase Garamond, appear the name of the artist and the location of the artwork — in this case, "Lorenzo Monaco" and "National Gallery of Art."

Sheaff cropped a reproduction of the original artwork below the infant Jesus' red gown, so that the infant's feet, Mary's feet and the lower part of her cloak are excluded. The gold background of the painting is lightened

210

Lorenzo Monaco   National Gallery

This is Richard Sheaff's original design for the Loren-zo Monaco traditional Christmas stamp, which he created in 1995. He later redesigned it to allow insertion of the word "CHRISTMAS" across the top.

to yellow on the stamp for maximum contrast.

When Sheaff designed the group of traditional Christmas stamps in 1995, at CSAC's direction he omitted the word "Christmas," which had been part of the design of previous stamps in the series. The omission on the 1995 stamp was criticized, and USPS promised that "Christmas" would appear on future stamps. This required Sheaff to redesign the Monaco stamp and others, shrinking the image slightly and cropping it more closely at the bottom so the word could be inserted at the top.

The microprinting, which is a standard feature of offset-printed single-design stamps, consists of the letters "USPS" in black on the inside of Mary's cloak below her left hand.

First-Day Facts

The Lorenzo Monaco stamp was dedicated by Robert Rider, a member of the USPS Board of Governors, at noon October 14 at the Postage Stamp Mega Show at New York City's Jacob K. Javits Convention Center.

For a limited time, Stamp Fulfillment Services sold uncacheted first-day covers of the Monaco stamp for 75¢.

The microprinting on the stamp consists of the letters "USPS" in black on the inside of Mary's cloak below her left hand.

37¢ HANUKKAH
HOLIDAY CELEBRATIONS SERIES

Date of Issue: October 15, 2004

Catalog Number: Scott 3881

Colors: black, cyan, magenta, yellow

First-Day Cancel: New York, New York

First-Day Cancellations: 66,182

Format: Pane of 20, vertical, 5 across, 4 down. Offset printing plates printing 300 stamps per revolution (5 panes across, 3 panes around).

Gum Type: self-adhesive

Microprinting: "USPS" along right side of dreidel

Stamp Size: 0.91 by 1.19 inches; 23.11 by 30.23mm

Pane Size: 5.55 by 5.76 inches; 140.97 by 146.3mm

Perforations: 10¾ (die-cut simulated perforations) (Heidelberg rotary die cutter)

Selvage Markings: "©2003/USPS". ".37/x20/$7.40". "PLATE/POSITION" and diagram.

Back Markings: On selvage liner: Universal Product Code (UPC) "566600" in 4 locations.

Photographer: Elise Moore of Bethesda, Maryland

Designer and Art Director: Ethel Kessler of Bethesda, Maryland

Typographer: Greg Berger of Bethesda, Maryland

Modeler: Donald Woo of Sennett Security Products

Stamp Manufacturing: Stamps printed by Banknote Corporation of America/ Sennett Security Products, Browns Summit, North Carolina, on MAN Roland 300 offset press. Stamps processed by Unique Binders, Fredericksburg, Virginia.

Quantity Ordered: 60,000,000

Plate Number Detail: 1 set of 4 plate numbers preceded by the letter S in selvage above or below each lower corner stamp

Plate Number Combination Reported: S1111

Paper Supplier: Mactac

Tagging: block tagging over stamps

The Stamp

In 1996, the Postal Service issued its first stamp designed specifically for use in mailing greetings and gifts for Hanukkah, the Jewish Festival of Lights. The 32¢ stamp, a joint issue with Israel, depicted a stylized menorah with nine colored candles.

Such an issue had been advocated for years by many people, but the Citizens' Stamp Advisory Committee consistently had said no. The committee feared that to produce such a stamp would be to invite pressure for a new design each year, like the Christmas stamps that had been issued annually since 1962. "We didn't want to open Pandora's box," one member said.

In the end, however, CSAC agreed to a Hanukkah stamp with the encouragement of Postal Service management, which had been placing increasing emphasis on reflecting the diversity of the American people in the U.S. stamp program. The stamp would inaugurate a Holiday Celebrations series that would honor a different cultural or religious holiday annually. In this way, officials hoped to head off requests for new Hanukkah designs in the future.

CSAC was able to maintain that position through the next three rate changes. As the first-class rate rose to 33¢, then 34¢ and finally 37¢, the Hanukkah stamp was reissued with new denominations while retaining the old design. And in 2001, when a Holiday Celebrations stamp was issued to honor Thanksgiving, USPS announced that it would be the last new design in the series.

Consistency is not a strong point of U.S. stamp policymakers, however, so it is likely that few were surprised when on October 15, 2004, there appeared a 37¢ Hanukkah stamp with a brand-new design featuring a dreidel, a four-sided top that children spin as part of the Hanukkah tradition.

Terrence McCaffrey, manager of stamp development, explained that the Postal Service had gotten "real pressure" to produce new designs not only for Hanukkah but also Kwanzaa (another Holiday Celebrations stamp for which the design had been recycled three times with new denominations). "People were getting tired of the designs," he said, "and we were getting tired of the designs, so we thought perhaps we should rethink our position.

"The committee said, fine, go ahead and design new ones."

The new Hanukkah stamp, a self-adhesive, was printed by the offset process by Ashton-Potter (USA) Ltd. and distributed in panes of 20. It is special size, as all Holiday Celebrations stamps have been since the first Hanukkah stamp, which was commemorative size as part of the joint-issue agreement with the Israel Postal Authority.

The joyous yearly festival of Hanukkah commemorates a miracle that occurred after Judah the Maccabee led a successful Jewish revolt against the oppressive government of Antiochus IV in 165 B.C. As the Maccabees prepared to rededicate the temple in Jerusalem, they were unable to find enough undefiled olive oil to light the lamps. In one chamber, however, a small jar of oil was discovered. Its contents kept the temple illuminated for eight days, long enough to locate more oil and have it consecrated for use in the temple.

Thus, Jews celebrate the holiday for eight days, beginning at sundown on the 25th of the Hebrew month Kislev, which in 2004 was December 7. Each night, families gather around the menorah, exchange gifts, chant blessings and light candles — one the first night, two the second night, and so on, until eight candles are lit the final night. The ninth candle in the menorah is called the Shamash, meaning "helper," and is used to light the other candles.

Dreidels commonly bear a Hebrew letter on each side, the first letters of a phrase meaning "a great miracle happened there." The letters indicate the outcome of every spin, and children typically use chocolate gelt (coins) as betting currency. Like Hanukkah lamps, dreidels were made from a variety of materials, with most surviving examples from Eastern European communities carved from wood. Another common type was of lead, cast by hand in a wooden mold.

The Design

"My family has celebrated Hanukkah since long before I was born," said Ethel Kessler, the USPS art director assigned to design the stamp. "It's a holiday with joyous memories for me, so I wanted to do something that was worthy."

First, she said, she had to answer the question, "Should the stamp represent the ancient story or be a contemporary interpretation?" She commissioned Avraham Cohen, an artist and calligrapher who specializes in Jewish themes, to develop a design with the ancient-story approach.

Cohen created some sketches with multiple subjects: a menorah, oil lamps and tablets bearing Hebrew text, all enclosed in elaborately patterned borders. But the complex sketches didn't "read" well when reduced to stamp size, even after Kessler had simplified them to the point that the artist protested that the changes were unacceptable.

It was during this process, in August 2003, that Terrence McCaffrey met with stamp journalists at the American Philatelic Stampshow in Columbus, Ohio, and displayed preliminary designs of some 2004 stamps, including one of Cohen's Hanukkah designs. Soon afterward, however,

Shown here are a pen-and-ink drawing and two color sketches by Avraham Cohen, including one that was shown to journalists as the preliminary design of the Hanukkah stamp. Later, officials decided to take a different approach.

CSAC advised Kessler to abandon the direction represented by those efforts and try something different.

The deadline was approaching. After considering several other ways to use a menorah as the principal subject, possibly accompanied by a quotation about religious freedom, Kessler decided to make a dreidel the centerpiece. "I had rejected the idea early on as frivolous, or not serious enough, even though Hanukkah is a fun holiday," she said.

She experimented with a sketch and a silhouette. Because neither clearly said "dreidel" at stamp size, it was decided to use a photograph. PhotoAssist, the Postal Service's research firm, found an attractive painted wooden dreidel in the Judaica collection of Rabbi Lennard R. Thal, a leader in Reform Judaism in America, and his wife Linda Thal. The Thals had bought the artifact from a street vendor in Jerusalem. Elise Moore of PhotoAssist photographed it for the Postal Service.

After the design team decided to use a dreidel as the central design subject, Ethel Kessler developed these two essays, one with a colorful free-form dreidel sketched by her associate, Greg Berger, and the other showing the toy as a silhouette amid the letters of the word HANUKKAH, all in different colors.

To ensure that the dreidel could readily be identified, a photograph was used. These two essays represent experiments with the size of the dreidel and the typography.

"Ultimately, this little dreidel captured a lot of the things I wanted to be on the stamp," Kessler said. "It has a lot of spirit. It captured the idea of craft because it's hand-painted. The holiday takes place in an ancient city, so certainly the artwork on the sides is representative of that."

It was Kessler's inspiration to make the word "HANUKKAH" a co-equal part of the design with the dreidel. She and Greg Berger, an associate with whom she had previously worked on stamp-design projects, broke the word into three segments and set the dreidel against it on a plain white background.

The letters are in an Adobe Originals font called Trajan, which is patterned after the carved inscription on the base of the Trajan Column in Rome. They shade from light blue at the top to pale yellow at the bottom. Inside two legs of the first K is "37 USA" in Frutiger characters, arranged vertically, in a red that mimics the color of the dreidel's base.

"Trajan is a very elegant typeface, but we varied the size and height of the letters to suggest a little playfulness," Kessler said.

As a single-design offset-printed issue, the stamp contains microprinting as a security measure. The letters "USPS" can be found along the right side of the dreidel.

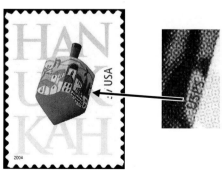

The microprinting on the Hanukkah stamp consists of the letters "USPS" along the right side of the dreidel.

216

First-Day Facts

S. David Fineman, chairman of the Postal Service Board of Governors, dedicated the Hanukkah stamp during the Postage Stamp Mega Show at the Jacob K. Javits Convention Center in New York City.

Speakers were Janet Klug, president of the American Philatelic Society, and Daniel Hadar, intellectual property attorney for USPS. Elizabeth Pope, president of the American Stamp Dealers Association, gave the welcome. The master of ceremonies was Rabbi Morton Howard Pomerantz of the New York State Office of Mental Retardation and Developmental Disabilities.

For a limited time, Stamp Fulfillment Services offered uncacheted first-day covers of the stamp for 75¢.

37¢ KWANZAA
HOLIDAY CELEBRATIONS SERIES

Date of Issue: October 16, 2004

Catalog Number: Scott 3881

Colors: black, hexachrome cyan, red (PMS 1788), yellow (PMS 109), orange (PMS 143), green (PMS 355)

First-Day Cancel: Chicago, Illinois

First-Day Cancellations: 61,650

Format: Pane of 20, horizontal, 4 across, 5 down. Offset printing plates printing 320 stamps per revolution (20 across, 16 around).

Gum Type: self-adhesive

Microprinting: "USPS" in bottom left corner

Overall Stamp Size: 1.19 by 0.91 inches; 30.226 by 23.114mm

Pane Size: 5.76 by 5.5 inches; 146.304 by 139.7mm

Perforations: 10¾ (die-cut simulated perforations) (IDC custom two-station rotary die cutter).

Selvage Markings: "© 2003/USPS" ".37/x20/$7.40" "PLATE/POSITION" and diagram.

Back Markings: Universal Product Code (UPC) "566500" in 4 locations.

Illustrator: Daniel Minter of Portland, Maine

Designer, Art Director and Typographer: Derry Noyes of Washington, D.C.

Modeler: Joseph Sheeran of Ashton-Potter (USA) Ltd., Williamsville, New York

Stamp Manufacturing: Stamps printed by Ashton-Potter on a Mueller Martini A74 offset press. Stamps finished by Ashton-Potter.

Quantity Ordered: 60,000,000

Plate Number Detail: 1 set of 6 plate numbers preceded by the letter P above or below each corner stamp

Plate Number Combination Reported: P111111

Paper Supplier: Paper Corporation of the United States/Glatfelter

The Stamp

On October 16, the Postal Service issued the fifth U.S. stamp since 1997 to honor the African-American festival of Kwanzaa.

The first four had a common design but different denominations, ranging from 32¢ to 37¢, to cover periodic increases in the first-class postage rate. The new one did not accompany a rate change and offered a completely new design.

Officials previously had said they would not revise the stamp's design and, in fact, that there would be no new designs in the Holiday Celebrations series, of which the Kwanzaa stamp was a part. Nevertheless, the new-look Kwanzaa was added to the series, one day after USPS introduced a new design for Hanukkah, another Holiday Celebrations stamp.

"People were getting tired of the designs," explained Terrence McCaffrey, manager of stamp development, "and we were getting tired of the designs, so we thought perhaps we should rethink our position.

"The [Citizens' Stamp Advisory] committee said, fine, go ahead and design new ones."

The new Kwanzaa stamp, like its predecessors, is self-adhesive and special size, horizontally arranged. It was printed by the offset process by Ashton-Potter (USA) Ltd. and distributed in panes of 20. The design was shown to stamp journalists at the American Philatelic Society Stampshow in Columbus, Ohio, in August 2003.

Kwanzaa is an "invented" non-religious holiday. Created in 1966 by Maulana Karenga, chairman of the Department of Black Studies at California State University-Long Beach, it is a seven-day cultural celebration beginning December 26 and ending January 1. It derives its name from the Swahili phrase "matunda ya kwanza," meaning "first fruits," and honors

These two essays feature Daniel Minter sketches of a mother and seven Kwanzaa candles. In one, Minter wrote, she is "initiating the holiday by pouring the libation to the ancestors," representing "the source of all life and nurturing."

Of this illustration, Minter wrote: "The seven gourds of Kwanzaa can be used to represent gifts for each day of the celebration, and the vessels holding the spirits of the ancestors and the libations poured in their honor."

the African tradition of celebrating the harvest.

The holiday is a celebration of seven principles, called the Nguzo Saba — unity, self-determination, collective work and responsibility, cooperative economics, purpose, creativity and faith — based on values prevalent in African culture.

The Design

USPS art director Derry Noyes asked Daniel Minter of Portland, Maine, to produce a new Kwanzaa stamp image on the recommendation of CSAC member Sylvia Harris, a graphic designer. Harris was familiar with Minter's work, particularly the distinctive linoleum-block prints he created to illustrate *Seven Spools of Thread*, a children's book about Kwanzaa by Angela Shelf Medearis published in 2000.

"His illustrations for the book were very refreshing, and the fact he was familiar with the subject of Kwanzaa made it seem too good to be true," Noyes said. "Then he turned out to be a delightful person to work with. He came up with a lot of great ideas and was very receptive to suggestions. If something wasn't working, he was willing to go back and change it."

Noyes asked Minter to make the stamp image "African in feeling." The artist produced several design concepts incorporating the number seven, to represent the seven days of Kwanzaa and the seven principles they signify: a mother in African garb with seven candles; seven colorfully painted gourds; seven birds perched in a tree. The illustration that ultimately was chosen for the stamp depicts seven black silhouetted figures in robes of red, green, orange, blue and yellow that wave to the left like festive flags

In this image, Minter symbolized the seven principles of Kwanzaa with seven birds perched in a tree. The dominant colors of this essay are red, green and black, the colors of African unity.

220

This is Minter's initial sketch for what would become the stamp design, in which the robed figures' arms and legs are visible. The seven people represent the seven principles of Kwanzaa.

and overlap across the width of the stamp.

For the final design, "I started off by creating a black-and-white linoleum-block print," Minter told the Postal Service. "I scanned that and used two different computer programs to add color. The result is half digital art, half old-fashioned print art."

Noyes inserted the word "KWANZAA," in gray block Universe letters, across the top of the stamp, just behind and slightly above the figures' heads. The denomination, "37 USA," in black Myriad type, is at the upper left.

Because the stamp was printed by the offset process, it includes security microprinting in the design, consisting of the letters "USPS" in the bottom left corner just above the 2004 year date.

A microprinted "USPS" is at the lower left, just above the 2004 year date.

First-Day Facts

Akinyinka Akinyele, USPS Chicago District manager, dedicated the stamp in a ceremony in the Illinois Black Legislature Auditorium of the DuSable Museum of African-American History in Chicago.

Others participating were Antoinette Wright, president and chief executive officer of the DuSable Museum; Melody Spann-Cooper, president and CEO, WVON Radio, who served as master of ceremonies; stamp illustrator Daniel Minter; D. Kucha Brown Lee, storyteller; and Chicago Postmaster Kelvin Mack.

For a limited time, Stamp Fulfillment Services offered uncacheted first-day covers for 75¢.

37¢ HOLIDAY ORNAMENTS (4 DESIGNS)
PANE OF 20

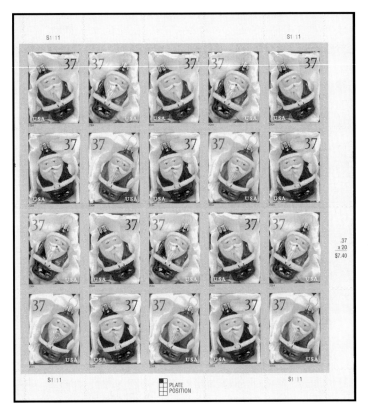

Date of Issue: November 16, 2004

Catalog Numbers: Scott 3883-3886, stamps; 3883a, block or strip of 4

Colors: magenta, yellow, cyan, black

First-Day Cancel: New York, New York

First-Day Cancellations: 112,483 (includes all formats)

Format: Pane of 20, vertical, 5 across, 4 down. Gravure printing cylinders printing 320 stamps per revolution, manufactured by Southern Graphics Systems.

Gum Type: self-adhesive

Overall Stamp Size: 0.91 by 1.19 inches; 23.11 by 30.22mm

Pane Size: 5.46 by 5.8125 inches; 136.68 by 131.63mm

Perforations: 11½ by 11 (die-cut simulated perforations) (Comco custom rotary die cutter)

Selvage Markings: "© 2003/USPS." ".37/x 20/$7.40." "PLATE/POSITION" and diagram.

Back Markings: Universal Product Code (UPC) "566400" in 4 locations on back of liner paper

Photographer: Sally Andersen-Bruce of New Milford, Connecticut

Designer, Art Director and Photographer: Derry Noyes of Washington, D.C.

Modeler: Donald H. Woo, Sennett Security Products

Stamp Manufacturing: Stamps printed for Sennett Security Products by American Packaging Corporation, Columbus, Wisconsin, on Rotomec 5 3000 gravure press. Stamps finished by Unique Binders of Fredericksburg, Virginia.

Quantity Ordered: 125,000,000 stamps

Cylinder Number Detail: 1 set of 4 cylinder numbers preceded by the letter S above or below each corner stamp

Cylinder Number Combination Reported: S1111

Paper Supplier: Mactac

Tagging: phosphored paper

37¢ HOLIDAY ORNAMENTS (4 DESIGNS)
DOUBLE-SIDED CONVERTIBLE BOOKLET OF 20

 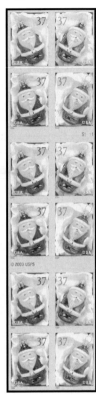

Date of Issue: November 16, 2004

Catalog Numbers: Scott 3883-3886, stamps; 3886a, block of 4; 3886b, convertible booklet of 20

Colors: magenta, yellow, cyan, black, stamps; same plus red (PMS 193), booklet cover

First-Day Cancel: New York, New York

First-Day Cancellations: 112,483 (includes all formats)

Format: Convertible booklet pane of 20, vertical, arranged vertically. Stamps on both sides, 8 (2 across by 4 down) plus label (booklet cover) on one side, 12 (2 across by 6 down) on other side, with horizontal peel-off strips between blocks of 4 on each side. Gravure printing cylinders printing 288 stamps per revolution (12 across, 24 around), all-stamp side; 192 stamps per revolution (8 across, 24 around), cover side.

Gum Type: self-adhesive

Overall Stamp Size: 0.91 by 1.19 inches; 23.11 by 30.22mm

Pane Size: 1.823 by 7.5 inches; 46.3 by 190.5mm

Perforations: 11½ by 11 (die-cut simulated perforations) (Comco custom rotary die-cutter). Backing paper rouletted behind peel-off strips.

Selvage Markings: "© 2003 USPS" on one peel-off strip on all-stamp side, cylinder numbers on the other peel-off strip on all-stamp side

Back Markings: "Holiday Ornaments/4 different designs/Twenty 37c/Self-adhesive/Stamps $7.40" and Universal Product Code (UPC) "0 673200 2" on booklet cover

Photographer: Sally Andersen-Bruce of New Milford, Connecticut

Designer, Art Director and Typographer: Derry Noyes of Washington, D.C.

Modeler: Donald H. Woo, Sennett Security Products

Stamp Manufacturing: Stamps printed for Sennett Security Products by American Packaging Corporation, Columbus, Wisconsin, on Rotomec 3000 gravure press. Stamps finished by Unique Binders of Fredericksburg, Virginia.

Quantity Ordered: 1,670,000,000 stamps

Cylinder Number Detail: 1 set of 4 cylinder numbers preceded by the letter S on 1 peel-off strip

Cylinder Number Combinations Reported: S1111, S2222

Paper Supplier: Mactac

Tagging: phosphored paper with phosphor blocker on cover

37¢ HOLIDAY ORNAMENTS (4 DESIGNS)
VENDING BOOKLET OF 20

Date of Issue: November 16, 2004

Catalog Numbers: Scott 3887-3890, stamps; 3890a, block of 4; 3890b, booklet pane of 4; 3890c, booklet pane of 6, 2 each 3887 and 3888; 3890d, booklet pane of 6, 2 each 3889 and 3890; BK298, complete booklet

Colors: magenta, yellow, cyan, black, stamps; same plus red (PMS 193), booklet cover

First-Day Cancel: New York, New York

First-Day Cancellations: 112,483 (includes all formats)

Format: Vending booklet of 20, vertical, arranged vertically, 2 across by 10 down, in 2 4-stamp segments (2 by 2) and 2 6-stamp segments (2 by 3). Gravure printing cylinders printing 480 stamps per revolution (24 across, 20 around) manufactured by Southern Graphics Systems.

Gum Type: self-adhesive

Overall Stamp Size: 0.87 by 0.982 inches; 22.09 by 24.94mm

Pane Size: 1.74 by 10.375 inches; 44.19 by 263.52mm

Perforations: 10¼ by 10¾ (die-cut simulated perforations) (Comco custom rotary die cutter). Cover scored for folding.

Selvage Markings: none

Back Markings: "Holiday/Ornaments/4 different designs/Twenty 37c/Self-adhesive/Stamps/$7.40" on front of cover. Promotion for Postal Store Web site, USPS logo, "© 2003 USPS," cylinder numbers and Universal Product Code (UPC) "0 673300 1" on back cover.

Photographer: Sally Andersen-Bruce of New Milford, Connecticut

Designer, Art Director and Typographer: Derry Noyes of Washington, D.C.

Modeler: Donald H. Woo, Sennett Security Products

Stamp Manufacturing: Stamps printed for Sennett Security Products by American Packaging Corporation, Columbus, Wisconsin, on Rotomec 5 3000 gravure press. Stamps finished by Unique Binders of Fredericksburg, Virginia.

Quantity Ordered: 200,990,000 stamps

Cylinder Number Detail: 1 set of 5 cylinder numbers preceded by the letter S on back cover

Cylinder Number Combination Reported: S11111

Paper Supplier: Mactac

Tagging: phosphored paper

37¢ HOLIDAY ORNAMENTS
PANE OF 18, ATM-VENDED

 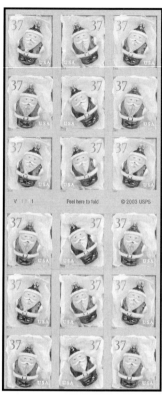

Date of Issue: November 16, 2004

Catalog Numbers: Scott 3891-3894, single stamps; 3894a, block of 4; 3894b, pane of 18

Colors: yellow, magenta, cyan, tan (PMS 4665), black, stamps; same colors plus red (PMS 193), back

First-Day Cancel: New York, New York

First-Day Cancellations: 112,483 (includes all formats)

Format: Pane of 18, vertical, arranged vertically 3 across by 6 down, with horizontal peel-off strip between horizontal rows 3 and 4. Gravure printing cylinders printing 30 panes per revolution (5 across, 6 around), manufactured by Southern Graphics Systems.

Gum Type: self-adhesive

Overall Stamp Size: 0.87 by .982 inches; 22.098 by 24.942mm

Pane Size: 2.61 by 6.125 inches; 66.29 by 155.58mm

Perforations: 8 (die-cut simulated perforations) (Comco Commander rotary die cutter)

Selvage Markings: on peel-off strip: "Peel here to fold • © 2003 USPS" and cylinder numbers

Back Markings: "Holiday Ornaments/4 different designs/Eighteen 37c/Self-adhesive/Stamps/$6.66." Promotion for Postal Store Web site, USPS logo and Universal Product Code (UPC) "0 566900 0."

Photographer: Sally Andersen-Bruce of New Milford, Connecticut

Designer, Art Director and Typographer: Derry Noyes of Washington, D.C.

Stamp Manufacturing: Stamps printed by Avery Dennison Security Printing Division, Clinton, South Carolina, on a Dia Nippon Kiko 8-station gravure press. Stamps lacquer coated, front and back, die cut, processed and shipped by Avery Dennison.

Quantity Ordered: 270,000,000

Cylinder Number Detail: 1 group of 5 gravure cylinder numbers preceded by the letter V on peel-off strip

Cylinder Number Combination Reported: V11111

Paper Supplier: Fasson Division of Avery Dennison

Tagging: Unphosphored paper. Phosphor added to lacquer coating applied to front of pane.

The Stamps

On November 16, the Postal Service issued a block of four contemporary Christmas stamps, each featuring a photograph of a Santa Claus ornament in a costume of purple, green, blue or red. The design of the block, and of the larger formats in which it is reproduced, suggests a wooden storage box in which the ornaments nestle in tissue paper in individual compartments.

The stamps were dedicated at the Lord & Taylor department store at 39th Street and Fifth Avenue in New York City in conjunction with the store's unveiling of its annual window Christmas display.

Gravure-printed and self-adhesive, the stamps were produced in four formats and two different sets of design variations. They are:

• A pane of 20, five across by four down, with purple and green Santas alternating in the first and third horizontal rows and blue and red Santas alternating in the second and fourth rows (Scott 3883-3885). The stamps are what

USPS calls its special size, which is slightly larger than the definitive size and used principally for Holiday and Love stamps. The pane has selvage on all four sides, and the stamps have die-cut simulated perforations all around, gauging 11½ by 11. The printer was American Packaging Corporation for Sennett Security Products.

• A double-sided convertible booklet of 20, with 12 stamps on one side and eight stamps plus a nonstamp label that doubles as a booklet cover on the other side (Scott 3883-3885). The stamps are grouped in blocks of four separated by horizontal pull-off strips, with purple and green Santas above and blue and red Santas beneath. Like their counterparts on the pane of 20, the stamps are special size with 11½ by 11 die cuts. They differ from the pane stamps only in that they have straight edges at the top or bottom and/or along one edge. The printer was American Packaging/Sennett.

• A vending booklet of 20, with the stamps grouped in two blocks of four and two blocks of six separated by narrow spaces where horizontal pull-off strips were removed during processing (Scott 3887-3890). The arrangement of Santas on the blocks of four is the same as on the convertible-booklet blocks. The stamps are definitive size. The design of each stamp differs somewhat from its larger counterpart on the pane or convertible booklet to fit the smaller design area. The gauge of the simulated perfs is 10¼ by 10¾. All 20 stamps have at least one straight edge. American Packaging/Sennett produced the booklet.

• A pane of 18, three across by six down, laid out as two blocks of nine separated by a pull-off strip, created for sale in automated teller machines (Scott 3891-3894). The stamps are definitive size, with simulated perforations gauging 8, and are of the same design as the vending-booklet stamps. The layout of the horizontal rows alternates between green-purple-green and red-blue-red, resulting in a pane with six each of the green and red Santas in the outer vertical rows and three each of the purple and blue Santas in the middle vertical row. Each stamp has at least one straight edge except the four stamps — two purple and two blue — in the center of the pane. The stamps are printed on thin paper, which, together with the liner, matches the thickness and shape of the U.S. currency dispensed by ATMs. Avery Dennison Security Printing Division was the printer; the same firm, or its predecessor, Avery International, has produced all ATM-vended U.S. stamps since the first one appeared in 1990.

Scott catalog editor James E. Kloetzel, writing in *Scott Stamp Monthly* for May 2005, noted that there are three distinct design varieties of each stamp on the ATM pane, for a total of 12 such varieties. The variations are

in the tan-colored borders that bleed off the edges and into the adjacent stamps, and stem from the construction of the box in which the ornaments were placed to be photographed.

"While the varieties are subtle, once identified they are clearly evident and consistent throughout all panes," Kloetzel wrote. "... It was not immediately evident that the pieces of wood making up the box were not just a continuous wood-grain color, but were actually a more detailed design simulating distinct and separate wood pieces arranged as they would be in the construction of an actual box ...

"There is one piece running all the way across the top of the pane, from edge to edge, and this pattern is duplicated at the bottom of the pane and at the wider central horizontal divider piece. Vertical pieces of wood then run between these three horizontal pieces. Finally, short connecting wood pieces join the vertical pieces to complete the box construction. There are dividing lines defining the wood pieces, and these lines cause the stamp varieties."

The three types of each stamp are shown in a nearby illustration. Kloetzel's descriptions follow:

"Type 1 stamps are from the top row of each block of nine, and these are characterized by a single piece of wood across the entire top of the stamp, vertical wood pieces at each side connecting to the top piece and extending off the stamp at bottom, and a short horizontal connecting piece at bottom between the vertical side pieces.

"Type 2 stamps are from the center row of each block of nine, and these

The three types of each Santa stamp on the ATM-vended pane are characterized by the arrangement of the wood pieces making up the box in which the ornaments were stored to be photographed. Shown here are the green Santas. From left to right are: type 1, from the top row of each block of nine; type 2, from the center row of each block; and type 3, from the bottom row of each block.

stamps are characterized by wood pieces at the sides running vertically from the top of each stamp to the bottom, with short horizontal connecting wood pieces at both top and bottom between the vertical side pieces.

"Type 3 stamps are from the bottom rows of each block of nine, and these stamps are characterized by a single piece of wood across the entire bottom of the stamp, vertical wood pieces at each side connecting to the bottom piece and extending off the stamp at top, and a short horizontal connecting piece at top between the vertical side pieces."

The pane of 18 contains two each of Scott 3891 type 1 (green Santa), 3891 type 2, 3891 type 3, Scott 3893 type 1 (red Santa), 3893 type 2 and 3893 type 3. There are one each of Scott 3892 type 1 (purple Santa), 3892 type 2, 3892 type 3, Scott 3894 type 1 (blue Santa), 3894 type 2 and 3894 type 3.

The same characteristics don't apply to the Holiday Ornaments convertible booklet or vending booklet, Kloetzel noted. "The designs of these booklets were not planned or executed with anything like the detail and care of the [ATM] pane of 18," he wrote. On the other booklets, he explained, "the designs were laid down in identical blocks of four ... but since each block of four has the same characteristics, there is only one variety of each stamp."

After "careful reflection," the editor wrote, Scott decided not to assign separate minor-number listings to the ATM design varieties. Instead, he continued, the editors would add a detailed footnote to the catalog "to explain that dedicated specialists will want to consider the varieties that appear on this pane.

"We hope this decision will be satisfactory to all concerned, including general collectors who are frustrated by the many minor varieties that seem to emanate from [USPS] these days, as well as the specialists who delight in all these new-issue varieties.

"General collectors will benefit from the more straightforward Scott catalog listings that require the collecting of only the four basic stamps, while the specialists will have all the information they need to collect the issue as they see fit."

The ATM pane was a late addition to the 2004 stamp program, with Stamp Services officials getting the request from a postal management source in June, barely five months before the issue date. It was the first ATM stamp issue to have a distinctive holiday or winter theme since the 32¢ Skaters stamp of 1996 (Scott 3117). Between 1992 and 1996, USPS had produced a new ATM-vended stamp for Christmas seasonal mail each year.

However, the ornaments pane was unpopular with some postal customers, who complained that they didn't want Christmas-related stamps but that the ATM gave them no choice. Terrence McCaffrey, manager of stamp development for USPS, told *The Yearbook* it was unlikely that future Christmas stamps would be issued in that format.

Several previous U.S. Christmas stamps have depicted ornament-bedecked Christmas trees, but only one specifically features an ornament. The 22¢ stamp of 1987 (Scott 2368) depicts a round red glass ball hanging from a branch in the foreground. Blue and gold ornaments are partially pictured on the right side of the design.

The Designs

The Holiday Ornaments stamps were designed by USPS art director Derry Noyes, using photographs made by Sally Andersen-Bruce. The same design team had created the 15 32¢ American Dolls commemoratives of 1997 and, in 2002, the four 37¢ Antique Toys definitives, the 37¢ Neuter and Spay se-tenant pair and the four 37¢ Snowmen stamps and picture postal cards.

For several years, Noyes and Andersen-Bruce had discussed the idea of a pane of stamps depicting vintage Christmas ornaments. Andersen-Bruce, a meticulous researcher, explored the subject through her local library, museums, the Internet and Golden Glow of Christmas Past, a national club for collectors of antique Christmas ornaments and other artifacts.

"Derry's idea was that the page of stamps would be a box of ornaments, the type that you pass from generation to generation, and each Christmas you would open the box and it would remind you of past Christmases and relatives," she said. "Removing a stamp would be like taking an ornament from the box.

"The problem was that I could find one or two or three wonderful ornaments, but they were different sizes, and they wouldn't work in the same template. I would find something like a ball with a Santa painted on the side, and a great little golden trumpet with a red ribbon, but the scale would be altogether different. I couldn't find four ornaments of the same scale."

These Christmas ornaments were found and individually photographed by Sally Andersen-Bruce as she and Derry Noyes attempted to develop a pane of ornament stamps so arranged as to resemble a compartmented box. Because the ornaments differed in size and shape, they concluded that the plan would work best with similar ornaments in different colors.

This is a cardboard box of six Santa ornaments, just as Andersen-Bruce found them at D. Blumchen & Company. At the photographer's request, Diane Boyce, the company's creative director, repainted a set of the ornaments for her to shoot for the stamps.

During her search, however, she turned up numerous snowman figurines made of cotton felt, wood, Styrofoam and other materials. These serendipitous acquisitions were so attractive that she took a break from the ornaments project to photograph the snowmen, and the pictures became the basis for the contemporary Christmas stamps and postal cards of 2002.

Several collectors referred Andersen-Bruce to D. Blumchen & Company of Ridgewood, New Jersey, which sells reproductions of old Christmas ornaments and other items. After finding a sketch in a Blumchen catalog of a blown-glass "happy Santa" that looked promising, she visited the company's atelier in Ridgewood.

The Santas came boxed in sets of six. Approximately two inches long, they were a frosted white color with costumes of purple, red, blue, green, orange and red-violet, with coats and caps trimmed in a kind of ground glass called diamond dust. Tiny black dots for eyes and a red dot for a mouth completed the decorations.

"I thought they were stunning," Andersen-Bruce said. "I realized that the scale problem would be resolved if I could work with four of these."

She asked Diane Boyce, the company's president and creative director, whether the Santas could be touched up to make them "happier, jollier, and with a better definition." Boyce quickly repainted the face on one of the ornaments in a way that assured the photographer that what she wanted could be done.

Andersen-Bruce returned to her studio with a box of the unaltered Santas, made a quick 35-millimeter photograph of them in the box and sent it to Derry Noyes, who agreed that the ornaments would fill the bill. The photographer then commissioned Boyce to custom-paint faces on all six Santas. "At this point, I still couldn't tell her that we wanted them for stamps," she said. "I just said, 'I'm going to make a very large photo, so

I'll need the best quality painting work you can give me.' "

The ornaments had been made in Lauscha, Germany, a town in the Thuringian Mountains in the former East German Democratic Republic with a glass-manufacturing tradition that dates to 1597. Lauscha glassblowers began making Christmas tree ornaments in 1848 in designs that eventually would include bells, trumpets, stars, angels, food items and Santa Claus figures, known as Klausmaun, with rounded bases in place of legs.

Boyce found the Santas when she and her mother, Beatrice, were in Lauscha on a winter buying trip. "We were headed on foot up a steep hill to a factory where we had an appointment, and we stopped to catch our breath," she said. "We saw a little sign on a house that said 'Christmas Ornaments' in German, and knocked on the door. The woman who answered took us in to a showroom that had been a garage, with ornaments hanging on pegboards around the wall. It was so cold you could see your breath.

"The ornament we selected that day was the happy Santa. We chose the colors of lacquer to be used on the costumes, and asked that diamond dust be added to the trim, which is quite traditional. We ordered 200 sets of six to be sent to us."

Because old-fashioned glass ornaments have become popular in recent years, glassblowers in Germany use antique molds to create new ornaments with traditional designs. The Santa ornaments chosen by Boyce were made in 1999 from a mold that probably dates to the years immediately before or after World War II.

For Andersen-Bruce's set of six, Boyce said, "I scratched off all the lacquer and repainted them, using a tiny paintbrush, and then painted the little faces and hands in flesh color and the beards and mustaches and eyebrows in white. I put on layers and layers and layers of paint so they wouldn't look flat and the flesh would have a little translucence. I gave them tiny blue eyes. I took off the diamond-dust trim and glued chenille roping in its place. I made the belt buckles out of embossed gold foil that's called Dresden paper.

"It took me hours of meticulous painting to achieve just the right happy look for each Santa. When I saw the stamps blown up to huge size at Lord & Taylor, I was very glad I had been so careful!"

Andersen-Bruce chose four of the six ornaments, leaving out the orange and red-violet Santas, and replaced their silver-colored hanger caps with gold ones. Her husband, Gordon Bruce, an industrial designer, built a wooden box containing four compartments with the same length-to-width ratio as that of a special size postage stamp. She tried several materials on which to lay the Santas, including straw and shredded red and green paper, before deciding on a special tissue paper provided by Diane Boyce. She then placed the ornaments in the compartments and photographed the box, using a view camera and four- by five-inch film.

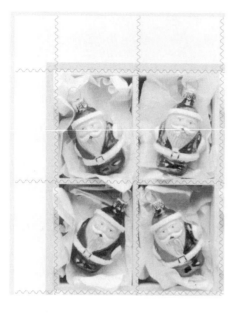

This represents Noyes' first attempt to create a pane of 20 stamps from Andersen-Bruce's photograph of the ornaments in the four-section wooden box her husband made for the project. Because some of the tissue paper spilled over onto adjoining stamps, Andersen-Bruce rephotographed the box with the paper packed more closely around the ornaments.

"I wanted the ornaments to look askew, as if they had been tossed into the box somewhat haphazardly to be packed away," she said. "In reality, though, I used a knitting needle with a padded tip to tap them a fraction of an inch at a time to line them up and fill the frame and leave enough room at the top for the denomination. Of course, I was scared to death that they might break.

"When I shoot for a stamp, I draw the template on the back of my camera to make sure the image is going to fit. I usually shoot one sheet of film for each stamp, but this time I shot one sheet for the entire box — four stamps.

"I had a little bit of tissue paper hanging over one of the compartments. It created a problem with the perfs because it crossed into another stamp, so I had to reshoot it. Then we found that Gordon's box had shifted one-sixty-fourth of an inch when it was clamped to let the glue dry, which would have been enough to create another problem with the perfs. So he rebuilt the box."

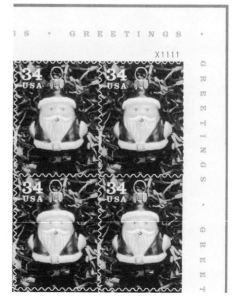

As an alternative to the ornament-box design treatment, Noyes mocked up a single-design pane of 20 stamps showing only the red Santa ornament, hanging on a Christmas tree. A block from the pane is shown here.

These are might-have-beens that were designed by Noyes but not issued by USPS: a coil version of the stamps, without the tan borders to suggest a compartmented wooden box, and a picture postal card, based on an Andersen-Bruce photograph of all six custom-painted ornaments hanging on a Christmas tree.

Because the vending-booklet and ATM-vended stamps had to be definitive size, smaller and squarer than the stamps for the pane and convertible booklet, Gordon Bruce built still another box for a new set of photographs. On these stamps, the Santas lie at different angles in their compartments and fill more of the space. The green ornament's circular hanger actually hangs over the compartment edge that serves as the stamp's top border.

Noyes chose a font called Seria for the typography. On each stamp, the "37" denomination is printed in the same color as the Santa, purple, green, blue or red, while the "USA" is in dropout white in a lower corner. To make the numbers and letters clearly legible against their tissue-paper background, the background was electronically lightened or darkened as necessary during the stamps' prepress stage.

Noyes also designed the stamps in two formats that USPS had used for contemporary Christmas stamps in the past but decided not to use this time. One was a coil strip, for which she dropped the simulated-box treatment and left the stamp borders white. The other was a picture postal card, using on the picture side an Andersen-Bruce photograph showing all six of the Blumchen & Company happy Santas hanging from a Christmas tree branch with falling snow in the background.

First-Day Facts

Deputy Postmaster General John Nolan dedicated the Holiday Ornaments stamps in a 5 p.m. ceremony at the Lord & Taylor store, which unveils its Christmas windows each year on the third Tuesday of November. Also participating was Jane Elfers, president and chief executive officer of Lord & Taylor.

The theme of the store's 2004 exhibit was "Deliver the Joy." When the windows were illuminated, six scenes with animated figures were revealed, depicting methods of delivering the U.S. mail: horse, steamboat, stagecoach, steam locomotive, airplane and truck. Enlarged stamp images were shown on the right side of each window, making each scene appear to be a giant holiday postcard.

After the ceremony and until closing time, Lord & Taylor customers were given a first-day cover of a Holiday Ornaments stamp with any purchase. For a limited time, Stamp Fulfillment Services offered sets of four uncacheted first-day covers in each of the stamps' formats except the vending booklet for $3 per set.

37¢ SNOWY EGRET CONVERTIBLE BOOKLET OF 20

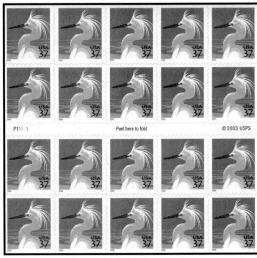

Date of Issue: January 30, 2004

Catalog Number: Scott 3830, single stamp; 3830a or BC197, convertible booklet of 20

Colors: black, cyan, magenta, yellow, special blue (match color)

First-Day Cancel: Norfolk, Virginia

First-Day Cancellations: 12,996

Format: Convertible booklet of 20, vertical, 5 across, 4 down, with horizontal peel-off strip between horizontal rows 2 and 3. Offset printing plates printing 400 stamps per revolution (20 across, 20 around).

Gum Type: self-adhesive

Microprinting: none

Overall Stamp Size: 0.87 by 0.98 inches; 22.098 by 24.892mm

Pane Size: 4.125 by 4.35 inches; 104.775 by 110.49mm

Perforations: 11½ by 11 (die-cut simulated perforations) (IDC custom rotary die cutter). Backing paper rouletted behind peel-off strip.

Selvage Markings: Plate numbers and "Peel here to fold" "© 2003 USPS"

Back Markings: "Snowy/Egret/Twenty 37-cent First-Class/self-adhesive stamps/$7.40." Promotion for The Postal Store web site. USPS logo. Universal Product Code (UPC) "0 672600 1."

Illustrator: Nancy Stahl of New York, New York

Designer, Art Director and Typographer: Carl Herrman of Carlsbad, California

Modeler: Joseph Sheeran of Ashton-Potter (USA) Ltd., Williamsville, New York

Stamp Manufacturing: Stamps printed by Ashton-Potter on offset portion of Stevens Variable Size Security Documents webfed 6-color offset, 3-color intaglio press. Stamps finished by Ashton-Potter.

Quantity Ordered: 1,500,000,000

Plate Number Detail: 1 set of 5 plate numbers preceded by the letter P on peel-off strip

Plate Number Combinations Reported: P11111, P22222, P33333, P44444, P55555

Paper Supplier: Glatfelter/Flexcon

Tagging: phosphored paper

37¢ SNOWY EGRET, 2004 YEAR DATE
COIL OF 100

Date of Issue: March 2004

Catalog Number: Scott 3829A

Colors: black, cyan, magenta, yellow, special match blue

First-Day Cancel: none

Format: Coil of 100 stamps, vertical. Offset printing plates printing 744 stamps per revolution (24 across, 31 around)

Gum Type: self-adhesive

Microprinting: "USPS" at base of bird's neck

Overall Stamp Size: 0.87 by 0.98 inches; 22.098 by 24.892mm

Perforations: 9½ (die-cut simulated perforations) (IDC custom die cutter)

Illustrator: Nancy Stahl of New York, New York

Designer, Art Director and Typographer: Carl Herrman of Carlsbad, California

Modeler: Joseph Sheeran, Ashton-Potter (USA) Ltd., Williamsville, New York

Stamp Manufacturing: Stamps printed by Ashton-Potter on Mueller Martini A76 offset press. Stamps finished by Ashton-Potter.

Quantity Ordered: 1,500,000,000

Plate Number Detail: 5 plate numbers preceded by the letter P on every 31st stamp

Plate Number Combinations Reported: P11111, P22222, P33333, P55555

Paper Supplier: Glatfelter/Spinnaker

Tagging: phosphored paper

The Stamps

In 2004, the Postal Service issued two new varieties of its 37¢ Snowy Egret definitive stamp.

The original variety, which made its debut October 24, 2003, and bears a 2003 year date, was a self-adhesive coil stamp in rolls of 100, gravure-printed by Avery Dennison Security Products Division.

The new varieties, also self-adhesives, were:

• A pane of 20 in convertible booklet format, dedicated January 30. The stamp was printed by the offset process by Ashton-Potter (USA) Ltd. Although issued in 2004, it also bears a 2003 year date.

• A coil stamp in rolls of 100, issued without previous announcement sometime in March. This variety also was offset-printed by Ashton-Potter. Its printed year date is 2004. It was available from Stamp Fulfillment Services only in full rolls.

The Designs

The 2004 stamps incorporate the same basic design as their predecessor. The design features Nancy Stahl's computer rendering of a left-facing snowy egret with long, recurved plumes against a blue background. Stylized ripples of water suggest the bird's wetlands habitat. There is no gradation of tone anywhere in the design. "USA 37," in two lines of black type, is at the lower right, and the year dates are black.

Minor differences between the vignettes of the Avery-Dennison coil stamp of 2003 and that of the two Ashton-Potter stamps of 2004 can be seen with a magnifying glass. These result from the different printing methods and combinations of colors used by the two printers. The Avery-Dennison stamp was gravure-printed, using yellow (for the bird's eye and lores), two different blues and black. The Ashton-Potter stamps were offset-printed with the four standard process colors — black, cyan, magenta and yellow — plus a special blue.

The two Ashton-Potter stamps differ in appearance from each other in two respects. As noted above, their year dates are different. Also, the convertible booklet stamp has no microprinting, whereas the coil stamp has a tiny black "USPS" on the blue shaded portion at the base of the bird's neck.

The microprinted letters "USPS" can be found at the base of the bird's neck on the Snowy Egret coil stamp printed by Ashton-Potter (USA) Ltd.

First-Day Facts

The convertible booklet stamp was dedicated in a ceremony at the American Philatelic Society's Ameristamp Expo show at the Scope Exhibition Hall in Norfolk, Virginia.

For a brief period, Stamp Fulfillment Services offered uncacheted first-day covers for sale for 75¢.

The convertible booklet was sold in at least one location long before its scheduled release date. *Linn's Stamp News* reported that it purchased a pane from a post office November 25, 2003, more than two months early.

No first-day cancellation was available for the Ashton-Potter coil version of the stamp.

37¢ FLAG COIL (2004 YEAR DATE)

Date of Issue: late January 2004

Catalog Number: Scott 3632C, single stamp, solid tagging; 3632Cd, single stamp, mottled tagging

Colors: magenta, yellow, cyan, black

First-Day Cancel: none

Format: Coils of 3,000 and 10,000, vertical. Gravure printing cylinders printing 400 stamps per revolution, manufactured by Armotek Industries, Palmyra, New Jersey.

Gum Type: self-adhesive

Overall Stamp Size: 0.87 by 0.982 inches; 22.1 by 24.94mm

Perforations: 11¾ (die-cut simulated perforations)

Designer, Art Director and Typographer: Terrence McCaffrey, USPS

Photograph: from Pictor International

Stamp Manufacturing: Stamps printed by American Packaging Corporation, Columbus, Wisconsin, for Sennett Security Products, Chantilly, Virginia, on a Rotomec 3000 gravure press. Stamps processed by Unique Binders, Fredericksburg, Virginia.

Quantity Ordered: 60,000,000 in rolls of 3,000; 150,000,000 in rolls of 10,000

Cylinder Number Detail: 1 set of 4 cylinder numbers preceded by the letter S on every 20th stamp

Cylinder Number Combination Reported: S1111

Counting Number Detail: 1 5-digit counting number in magenta on back of liner paper behind every 10th stamp

Tagging: phosphored paper

37¢ FLAG CONVERTIBLE BOOKLET OF 20
2004 YEAR DATE

Date of Issue: late July 2004

Catalog Number: Scott 3636D, single stamp; 3636De, booklet pane of 20

Colors: yellow, magenta, cyan, black, stamps; yellow, magenta, cyan, black, blue (PMS 294), cover

First-Day Cancel: none

Format: Convertible booklet pane of 20, vertical. Stamps on both sides, 8 (2 across by 4 down) plus label (booklet cover) on one side, 12 (2 across by 6 down) on other side, with horizontal peel-off strips between blocks of 4 on each side.

Gum Type: self-adhesive

Overall Stamp Size: 0.87 by 0.98 inches; 22.098 by 24.892mm

Pane Size: 1.74 by 6.167 inches; 44.196 by 155.58mm

Perforations: 11¼ by 11 (die-cut simulated perforations)

Selvage Markings: "© 2002 USPS • Peel here to fold • Self-adhesive stamps

• DO NOT WET" on first peel-off strip on all-stamp side; "• Peel here to fold • Self-adhesive stamps • © 2002 USPS" plus cylinder numbers on second peel-off strip on all-stamp side.

Back Markings: "$7.40/© 2002 USPS/U.S. Flag/Twenty 37-cent First-Class/ self-adhesive stamps" and Universal Product Code (UPC) "670800" on label (booklet cover).

Designer, Art Director and Typographer: Terrence McCaffrey, USPS

Photograph: from Pictor International

Stamp Manufacturing: Stamps printed by Avery Dennison Security Division, Clinton, South Carolina, on an 8-color Dia Nippon Kiko webfed gravure press. Stamps processed by Avery Dennison.

Quantity Ordered: 900,960,000 stamps

Cylinder Number Detail: 1 set of 4 cylinder numbers preceded by the letter V on second peel-off strip on all-stamp side

Cylinder Number Combinations: V1111, V1112

Paper Supplier: Fasson Division of Avery Dennison

Tagging: phosphored paper

The Stamps

In 2004, the Postal Service recycled its familiar American Flag design on two new collectible varieties, a coil stamp and a convertible booklet stamp. Each has a 2004 year date.

The stamps — issued without announcement or first-day cancellations — brought the total number of varieties bearing the Flag design to 20 since it made its debut in 2002. All have a postage value of 37¢, although the first seven were printed without denominations.

Both the 2004 stamps are self-adhesive and were gravure-printed.

The first is a coil stamp in rolls of 3,000 and 10,000, printed by American Packaging Corporation for Sennett Security Products. The stamp replaced a variety distributed in those two size rolls in 2002 and printed by Guilford Gravure for Banknote Corporation of America, which lost its contract to produce stamps in 2003. The new variety's existence was first reported by philatelic clerk Donna Rajotte of the Providence, Rhode Island, post office, who began selling the stamp January 30.

The backing paper is deeper than the stamps, which are spaced 3½mm apart. The die-cut "teeth" at the corners are rounded. Four-digit cylinder numbers preceded by the letter S are found on every 20th stamp, and magenta counting numbers are on the back of the backing paper on every 10th stamp.

In March 2004, collector Gregg Greenwald discovered that the stamp existed on two types of phospored paper. This was confirmed by the Scott Publishing Company, which listed the stamps as having solid tagging (Scott 3632C) and mottled tagging (3632Cd).

246

The second American Flag stamp of the year was produced in double-sided convertible booklets of 20. This variety was first reported July 21, again by Providence postal clerk Donna Rajotte. The stamp was printed by Avery Dennison Security Printing Division. Its Scott catalog number is 3636D. A similar convertible-booklet stamp, printed by American Packaging Corporation for Sennett Security Products, was issued June 7, 2002, and bears a 2002 year date (Scott 3636).

The Design

In the design common to all varieties, the frame is filled by a portion of a waving American flag, from an unattributed photograph. A corner of the starry blue field occupies the upper left quadrant, and seven red-and-white stripes, crossed diagonally by two dramatic ripples, occupy the rest of the space. The typography — "37," in black, and "USA," in dropout white — is at the bottom.

As usual, a close comparison of the 2004 varieties with each other and with the earlier stamps discloses subtle differences, most noticeable in the stars in the upper left corner. On the Sennett coil stamp, the points of two stars can be seen descending from the top frameline; on the Avery Dennison convertible-booklet variety, only a hint of one point is visible.

First-Day Facts

The Postal Service held no first-day ceremony for either of the 2004 Flag varieties. In 2003, writer-dealer Stephen G. Esrati quoted David Failor, director of Stamp Services for USPS, as saying: "If there is a change in the design, the denomination or the format [of a stamp], there will be a first-day-of-issue cancellation and possibly a ceremony. If it is simply a reprint with a different printer, there will not be a first-day ceremony or postmark." "Apparently, Failor did not view a change of the date on the stamp as a design change," Esrati commented.

4¢ CHIPPENDALE CHAIR
AMERICAN DESIGN SERIES

Date of Issue: March 5, 2004

Catalog Number: Scott 3750

Colors: brown (PMS 476), brown (PMS 477), tan (PMS 7407), orange (PMS 172)

First-Day Cancel: New York, New York

First-Day Cancellations: 12,922

Format: pane of 20, vertical, 5 across, 4 down. Offset printing plates printing 240 stamps per revolution (15 across, 16 around).

Gum Type: self-adhesive

Overall Stamp Size: 0.87 by 0.98 inches; 22.098 by 24.892mm

Pane Size: 5.35 by 4.93 inches; 135.89 by 125.222mm

Perforations: 10¾ by 10¼ (die-cut simulated perforations) (IDC two-station die cutter)

Selvage Markings: "©2003/USPS." ".04/x20/$0.80." "PLATE/POSITION" and diagram.

Back Markings: Universal Product Code (UPC) "100400" in 4 locations on back of liner paper

Illustrator: Lou Nolan of McLean, Virginia

Designer, Art Director and Typographer: Derry Noyes of Washington, D.C.

Modeler: Joseph Sheeran of Ashton-Potter (USA) Ltd., Williamsville, New York

Stamp Manufacturing: Stamps printed by Ashton-Potter on offset portion of Stevens Variable Size Security Documents webfed 6-color offset, 3-color intaglio press. Stamps processed by Ashton-Potter.

Quantity Ordered: 100,000,000 stamps

Plate Number Detail: 1 set of 4 plate numbers preceded by the letter P in selvage above or below each corner stamp.

248

Plate Number Combination Reported: P1111

Paper Supplier: Flexcon/International Paper

Tagging: untagged

The Stamp

On March 5, the Postal Service issued a 4¢ definitive stamp depicting a portion of an American chair built in the style named for the English cabinetmaker Thomas Chippendale.

A self-adhesive, the stamp was printed by the offset process by Ashton-Potter (USA) Ltd. and distributed in panes of 20. It had its first-day sale at the Postage Stamp Mega-Event in New York City, sponsored by the American Stamp Dealers Association, the American Philatelic Society and USPS.

The stamp was the fourth entry in the USPS American Design series, which the Postal Service says was created to "reflect the rich diversity of American design, showcasing objects from various eras, regions and ethnic cultures that combine utility with beauty and function with form."

The series will consist of pane and coil stamps ranging in denomination from 1¢ to 10¢. It was launched in 2002 with a 5¢ coil stamp with water-activated gum depicting a toleware coffeepot. A 10¢ American Clock pane stamp and a 1¢ Tiffany Lamp coil followed in 2003. All are untagged, in keeping with the Postal Service's policy of not tagging low-denomination stamps.

The last 4¢ stamp produced by USPS before this one was a nondenominated makeup-rate stamp issued in January 1991 (Scott 2521) to enable postal customers to use their leftover 25¢ stamps when the first-class rate jumped to 29¢ the following month.

Collectors of used stamps discovered that the Chippendale Chair stamp was a problem soaker of the kind that turns up periodically among the Postal Service's output. One reader of J.A. Watercutter's "Stamp Soaker" column in *Linn's Stamp News* reported that he soaked a specimen for 36 hours and even then had to "peel away (very slowly) the adhesive and paper remnants from the back of the stamp." Watercutter had better luck by using water at near-boiling temperature, but even then, he wrote, "the adhesive layer ... did not let go so easily. The goo stuck to the edges of the stamp before letting go and adhering to the envelope paper."

News that the Chippendale Chair stamp would be issued, and a picture, first appeared on the ASDA's Web site in late February. Joseph B. Savarese, the organization's executive vice president, told *Linn's Stamp News* that the Postal Service wanted to dedicate the stamp at the spring mega-event show.

Some questioned the use of a piece of furniture with such a strong British ancestry on a series called American Design. Patricia A. Du-Chene, associate editor of *Antique Trader* magazine, told *Stamp Collector*:

"Though the influence of ... Thomas Chippendale on American furniture makers and designers cannot be denied, there are truly American styles — such as the beautifully simple designs of Shaker furniture — that might have been a better choice for the series."

Terrence McCaffrey, manager of stamp development for USPS, explained how the selection was made:

"The chair used as reference for the art dates to 1760-1765 and was made in Philadelphia. The chair is considered an excellent example of the American Chippendale style and is in the collection [of decorative arts in the diplomatic reception rooms] at the U.S. Department of State.

"The Postal Service consulted with Harry Schnable, curator for the U.S. Department of State, and Jeremy Adamson, assistant curator for the Renwick Museum, in 1994. Both felt that while the Chippendale chair was not distinctly American because of its English origin and style, they indicated that it is part of the American visual design iconography and, as such, appropriate for inclusion in the series."

McCaffrey pointed out that the Postal Service had "defined the series very broadly" from the outset.

Thomas Chippendale (1718-1779) was the author of *The Gentleman and Cabinet-Maker's Director*, a book that influenced furniture design on both sides of the Atlantic Ocean. His works were known for their carved decorations and elaborate chair backs. In America, the style varied by region, with Philadelphia artisans producing the most extensively ornamented furniture.

The Design

As conceived in the early 1990s by USPS art director Derry Noyes and illustrator Lou Nolan, the American Design series consists of definitive-sized stamps featuring simplified renderings that are so tightly cropped

that portions of the artifact are omitted from the picture. The background is a solid color, and the stamp border also is a solid color that complements the background. "USA" and the denomination, with the letter c standing for "cents," are in the upper left corner, while the name of the featured object, in Garamond type, is arranged vertically along the left side.

This is Lou Nolan's painting of the Chippendale chair that was cropped for use on the stamp. It shows the chair's full cabriole, or curved legs, and claw-and-ball feet.

250

Nolan created the illustrations for five stamps, using water-soluble designer colors on illustration board. For several years, the designs sat in the Stamp Services section's "bank," until it was decided to use them on low-denomination definitives.

The Chippendale chair shown on the stamp is a side chair, or chair without arms. Its intricately patterned back features spiral ornaments called scrolls as well as carvings of a tassel and a shell. Another shell decorates the front of the seat. The chair has a graceful cabriole, or curved legs. Not shown are the claw-and-ball feet, which resemble the claws of an animal grasping a sphere.

"In this interpretation," said antiques expert Leigh Keno, one of the speakers at the first-day ceremony, "the artist has captured the essence of the chair — the graceful ears of the crest rail, the pierced splat and the projecting knees of the cabriole legs. Certainly, chairs such as this one were made to sit in, but they were also made to be admired."

The stamp was printed in four PMS colors: tan for the chair (the original chair is mahogany), orange for the seat, chocolate brown for the background and dark brown for the border

There is no microprinting on the stamp, although single-design offset-printed stamps normally include microprinting for security purposes.

First-Day Facts

Vinnie Malloy, New York District manager/postmaster for USPS, dedicated the Chippendale Chair stamp in a ceremony at the Expo Center at Madison Square Garden in New York City, site of the ASDA mega-event show.

The featured speakers were Leigh and Leslie Keno, antiques experts and co-hosts of *Find!*, a weekly home design and collectibles series on the Public Broadcasting System. Elizabeth C. Pope, president of the American Stamp Dealers Association, gave the welcome. Raschelle A. Miley, manager of marketing for the USPS New York District, was master of ceremonies. Honored guests were Joseph B. Savarese, ASDA executive vice president, and Robert E. Lamb, executive director of the American Philatelic Society.

For a limited time, Stamp Fulfillment Services sold uncacheted first-day covers bearing a Chippendale Chair stamp and a 37¢ first-class-rate stamp for 79¢.

NONDENOMINATED (5¢) SEA COAST
2003 YEAR DATE
NONPROFIT-RATE COIL (DIE CUTS ALL AROUND)
AMERICAN SCENES SERIES

Date of Issue: April 6, 2004

Catalog Numbers: Scott 3785a, untagged; 3785b, phosphored paper

Colors: cyan, magenta, yellow, black

First-Day Cancel: Washington, D.C.

First-Day Cancellations: 6,943

Format: Coil rolls of 3,000 and 10,000, vertical. Gravure printing cylinders printing 567 stamps per revolution (21 across, 27 around).

Gum Type: self-adhesive

Overall Stamp Size: 0.87 by 0.98 inches; 22.098 by 24.892mm

Perforations: 9¼ by 10 (die-cut simulated perforations) (Champlain Model 29 die cutter)

Illustrator: Tom Engeman of Brunswick, Maryland

Art Director and Typographer: Phil Jordan of Falls Church, Virginia

Modeler: Joseph Sheeran of Ashton-Potter (USA) Ltd., Williamsville, New York

Stamp Manufacturing: Stamps printed for Ashton-Potter by J.W. Fergusson and Sons, Richmond, Virginia, on a gravure press. Stamps processed by Ashton-Potter.

Quantity Ordered: 105,000,000 stamps in rolls of 3,000

Cylinder Number Detail: 1 set of 4 cylinder numbers preceded by the letter P on every 27th stamp

Cylinder Number Combination Reported: P2222

Counting Number Detail: 1 2-, 3- or 4-digit counting number printed in blue on backing paper behind every 10th stamp

Paper Supplier: Flexcon/Glatfelter

Tagging: untagged or phosphored paper

NONDENOMINATED (5¢) SEA COAST
2004 YEAR DATE
NONPROFIT-RATE COIL (WATER-ACTIVATED GUM)
AMERICAN SCENES SERIES

Date of Issue: June 11, 2004

Catalog Number: Scott 3864

Colors: magenta, yellow, cyan, black

First-Day Cancel: Washington, D.C.

First-Day Cancellations: 7,279

Format: Coil rolls of 3,000 and 10,000, vertical. Gravure printing cylinders printing 616 stamps per revolution (22 across, 28 around) manufactured by Southern Graphics.

Gum Type: water-activated

Overall Stamp Size: 0.87 by 0.96 inches; 22.09 by 24.38mm

Perforations: 9¾ (APS custom rotary perforator)

Illustrator: Tom Engeman of Brunswick, Maryland

Art Director and Typographer: Phil Jordan of Falls Church, Virginia

Modeler: Donald H. Woo of Sennett Security Products, Chantilly, Virginia

Stamp Manufacturing: Stamps printed for Sennett Security Products by American Packaging Corporation, Columbus, Wisconsin, on a Rotomec 3000 gravure press. Stamps processed by Unique Binders, Fredericksburg, Virginia.

Quantity Ordered: 60,000,000 in rolls of 3,000

Cylinder Number Detail: 1 set of 4 cylinder numbers preceded by the letter S on every 14th stamp

Cylinder Number Combination Reported: S1111

Counting Number Detail: counting number printed in magenta on back of every 10th stamp

Paper Supplier: Tullis Russell

Tagging: untagged

NONDENOMINATED (5¢) SEA COAST
2003 YEAR DATE
NONPROFIT-RATE COIL
AMERICAN SCENES SERIES

Date of Issue: August 2004

Catalog Number: Scott 3874, large year date

Colors: cyan, magenta, yellow, black

First-Day Cancel: none

Format: Coil rolls of 10,000, vertical. Gravure printing cylinders printing 567 stamps per revolution (21 across, 27 around)

Gum Type: self-adhesive

Overall Stamp Size: 0.87 by 0.98 inches; 22.098 by 24.392mm

Perforations: 10 (die-cut simulated perforations)

Illustrator: Tom Engeman of Brunswick, Maryland

Art Director and Typographer: Phil Jordan of Falls Church, Virginia

Modeler: Joseph Sheeran of Ashton-Potter (USA) Ltd., Williamsville, New York

Stamp Manufacturing: Stamps printed for Ashton-Potter by J.W. Fergusson and Sons, Richmond, Virginia, on a Champlain 29 gravure press. Stamps processed by Ashton-Potter.

Quantity Ordered: 1,200,000,000

Cylinder Number Detail: 1 set of 4 cylinder numbers preceded by the letter P on every 27th stamp

Cylinder Number Combination Reported: P2222

Counting Number Detail: counting number printed in blue on backing paper behind every 10th stamp

Paper Supplier: Flexcon/Glatfelter

Tagging: untagged

NONDENOMINATED (5¢) SEA COAST
2004 YEAR DATE
NONPROFIT-RATE COIL
AMERICAN SCENES SERIES

Date of Issue: August 2004

Catalog Number: Scott 3875, untagged

Colors: magenta, yellow, cyan, black

First-Day Cancel: none

Format: Coils of 10,000, vertical. Gravure printing cylinders printing 400 stamps per revolution.

Gum Type: self-adhesive

Overall Stamp Size: 0.87 by 0.982 inches; 22.09 by 24.74mm

Perforations: 11½ (die-cut simulated perforations)

Illustrator: Tom Engeman of Brunswick, Maryland

Art Director and Typographer: Phil Jordan of Falls Church, Virginia

Modeler: Donald H. Woo of Sennett Security Products, Chantilly, Virginia

Stamp Manufacturing: Stamps printed for Sennett Security Products by American Packaging Corporation, Columbus, Wisconsin, on a Rotomec 3000 gravure press. Stamps processed by Unique Binders, Fredericksburg, Virginia.

Quantity Ordered: 400,000,000

Cylinder Number Detail: 1 set of 4 cylinder numbers preceded by the letter S on every 20th stamp

Cylinder Number Combination Reported: S1111

Counting Number Detail: 1 5-digit counting number in magenta on backing paper behind every 10th stamp

Tagging: untagged or phosphored paper

The Stamps

In 2004, the Postal Service issued seven new collectible varieties of its nondenominated Sea Coast coil stamp. Five of the seven were unannounced and came to the attention of collectors only after they had been distributed to post offices. The latter include two that were not discovered until February 2005 but are listed here as part of the 2004 group.

The seven varieties were in addition to three previous varieties produced by three different printers, and were a major factor in creating what *Scott Stamp Monthly* called "a whirlpool of confusion" over the look-alike stamps.

Like their predecessors, the Sea Coast stamps of 2004 sold for 5¢ and were intended for use by nonprofit organizations on presorted bulk mail. Bulk-mail users of the Sea Coast stamp with appropriate permits are required to pay the difference between its 5¢ cost and the actual mailing cost for each piece at the time the items are brought to the post office. The "NONPROFIT ORG." service inscription that is part of the stamp's design is considered a precancel. Mail bearing stamps with service inscriptions bypasses post office canceling machines, and for that reason, the stamps are not intended to be tagged.

All 10 Sea Coast varieties issued to date have been printed by the gravure process. The three varieties that were in existence when 2004 began were:

• The 2002 prototype, a self-adhesive printed by Guilford Gravure for Banknote Corporation of America and distributed in rolls of 10,000 (Scott 3693). It bears a blue 2002 year date. It was printed on phosphored paper, a mistake for which USPS acknowledged responsibility.

• A 2003 version with water-activated gum and conventional perforations, also printed by Guilford Gravure for BCA (Scott 3775). It was produced in rolls of 500 and 10,000 and has a blue 2003 year date. It is untagged.

• A self-adhesive version in rolls of 10,000, issued in 2003 and bearing a black 2003 year date (Scott 3785). Unlike any previous modern U.S. coil stamp, it has no straight edges, but has die-cut simulated perforations on all four sides. It was printed by J.W. Fergusson & Sons for Ashton-Potter (USA) Ltd. after USPS terminated its stamp printing contract with BCA. It is untagged.

The first Sea Coast variety of 2004 was a new printing of the above-mentioned Ashton-Potter stamp in rolls of 3,000 and 10,000, untagged. It was formally announced in advance by the Postal Service and was given an official first-day cancellation on April 6 in Washington, D.C.

The provision for first-day covers was puzzling, because Scott 3785 — to which the new stamp at first was thought to be identical, down to its 2003 year date — had been issued without a first-day cancellation. *Linn's Stamp News* editor Michael Schreiber speculated that "this is a make-nice for the oversight to FDC collectors in 2003, but it turns history on end."

Scott Publishing Company said it would not give the stamp a separate catalog listing because it was, essentially, the same stamp that had been issued in 2003. Later, however, Scott concluded that there are collectible differences between the 2003 and 2004 Ashton-Potter stamps, and assigned it a new minor number.

"The original Scott 3785 is serpentine die cut 9½ by 10, while the new Scott 3785a is serpentine die cut 9¼ by 10," Scott catalog editor James E. Kloetzel explained in *Scott Stamp Monthly* for March 2005. "Scott 3785, issued in June 2003, is from plate P1111 and has more scarlet, or even a fuchsia shade, in the sky. Scott 3785a was issued in March 2004 in coil rolls of 10,000 and again on June 11, 2004, in coil rolls of 3,000, is from plate P2222, and has a sky that is more carmine-rose in shade."

Others pointed out a tiny design difference between the two stamps, with Scott 3785 showing slightly more of the pine tree on the extreme left of the design than Scott 3785a. Also, when plate-number coil specimens are compared, the numbers "P1111" on Scott 3785 are taller than "P2222" on Scott 3785a.

The second Sea Coast variety of 2004 is identical in appearance to the preceding stamp — the Ashton-Potter printing with die cuts all around — but is on phosphored paper. No explanation was given for this anomaly. Scott's editors originally assigned the 3785a minor catalog number to this stamp, but later reassigned it to the variety with the different gauge of die cuts, and designated the tagged stamp 3785b.

The next Sea Coast variety to appear (Scott 3864) has water-activated gum, conventional perforations and no tagging. In these respects, it resembles Scott 3775, which was printed by Guilford Gravure for BCA and issued in 2003. This one, however, was printed by American Packaging Corporation for Sennett Security Products. It is the first Sea Coast stamp to bear a 2004 year date, which is in black. Produced in rolls of 3,000 and 10,000, the stamp was issued June 11, 2004, in Washington, D.C.

When USPS announced that the Sennett stamp was forthcoming, it said only that the item would be distributed in rolls of 3,000. Collectors did not learn of the 10,000-stamp rolls until they received the Fall issue of *USA Philatelic*, the mail-order catalog of Stamp Fulfillment Services. According to *USA Philatelic*, the 10,000-stamp rolls were printed in March. Yet it was the stamp from a roll of 3,000 that received the official issue date of June 11.

"This odd discrepancy might explain why *Linn's* received numerous reports from readers who received a mailing franked with a 2004 Sea Coast water-activated coil several weeks or more before the June 11 official first day," Charles Snee wrote in *Linn's Stamp News*. "Most of these covers did not bear a postmark date, which is the rule for a letter franked with a service-inscribed stamp intended for use on bulk mail."

The remaining four Sea Coast stamps that will be described in this chapter are self-adhesives distributed in rolls of 10,000. With them, USPS returned to its old practice of issuing collectible varieties without prior announcement or official first-day dates.

The first of the four appeared some time in August and is similar to the Ashton-Potter 2003-year-date variety of the previous April 6, but instead of having die-cut simulated perforations on all four sides, it has conventional coil-stamp straight edges at top and bottom. Like the April 6 stamp, it has a P2222 cylinder-number combination. "It appears that [Ashton-Potter] is either experimenting with different die-cutting mats or has sets of both mat types that it will continue to use interchangeably," wrote Robert Rabinowitz in *Linn's*. Scott assigned the variety the catalog number 3874.

In mid-February 2005, Donna Rajotte, a postal employee in Providence, Rhode Island, reported receiving what appeared to be Scott 3874, but with a distinctly smaller 2003 year date and with the cylinder-number combination P3333. The smaller date is printed by black cylinder 3. Scott's James Kloetzel told *Linn's Stamp News* that this year-date variety probably would receive a minor catalog number in the 2006 Scott *Specialized Catalogue of United States Stamps & Covers*.

In late August 2004, another Sea Coast variety printed for Sennett by American Packaging Corporation turned up. The stamp has a black 2004 year date. It is untagged, and the die cutting on its vertical sides gauges 11½ — the highest gauge for perfs, whether real or simulated, on any of the Sea Coast stamps. Its catalog number is Scott 3875.

In late February 2005, modern U.S. specialist Doug Iams told *Linn's* of finding a tagged version of the Sennett stamp described in the preceding paragraph. Kloetzel said that this tagging variety, too, probably would receive a minor catalog number in the 2006 Scott U.S. specialized catalog.

Shown here are the two Sea Coast "year date" varieties printed by Ashton-Potter. On the left is a single of Scott 3874, a variety that appeared some time in August 2004, with a black 2003 year date. The stamp is a PNC (plate-number coil) single with cylinder number combination P2222. Next to it is a non-PNC single with a distinctly smaller 2003 year date. This variety came to light in February 2005 and is expected to receive a minor catalog number in the 2006 Scott U.S. specialized catalog.

The Design

The basic design of the 2004 Sea Coast stamps is the same as its predecessors. It incorporates artist Tom Engeman's acrylic painting, which is an invented scene, based on no actual geographic location. In it, pine trees atop a dark blue cliff are silhouetted against a red sky. Between the cliff and a rugged coastline in the foreground, surf crashes on a rock in a cloud of white spray.

The Scott catalog listing for the June 11 Sennett stamp includes a paragraph pointing out differences in the appearance of the two water-activated Sea Coasts. "No. 3864 [the 2004 stamp] has 2004 year date in black, rows of distinctly separated dots in surf area, and the small orange cloud is indistinct," Scott says. "No. 3775 [the earlier BCA/Guilford version] has 2003 year date in blue, dots that run together in surf area, and a distinct small orange cloud." Only three colors, cyan, magenta and yellow, were used to print the BCA/Guilford stamp; for the 2004 variety, Sennett/American Packaging added a fourth process color, black.

First-Day Facts

No first-day ceremonies were held for any of the 2004 varieties, and first-day cancellations (Washington, D.C.) were offered for only the April 6 and June 11 stamps. Collectors were given 60 days to submit self-addressed envelopes bearing the April 6 stamp and 90 days to submit envelopes bearing the June 11 stamp to the Washington postmaster for canceling. An additional 37¢ in denominated postage was required to prepay the first-class mailing cost.

For a limited time, Stamp Fulfillment Services offered uncacheted first-day covers of the stamp from rolls of 3,000 for 80¢. The covers also bear a 37¢ Flag stamp.

The earliest recorded pre-first-day use of a 2004 Sea Coast stamp was of a cover bearing a June 11 stamp with a hand cancellation from Mountainside, New Jersey, dated May 6, more than five weeks before the official June 11 release date. It was submitted to *Linn's Stamp News* by Murlin Ehrgott, a New Jersey collector.

The Sea Coast stamp on the cover was soaked off a political mailing Ehrgott had received in mid-April, he said. "I had no previous notice of this stamp, and in the usual course of events, I clipped it from the [original] cover and soaked it off," Ehrgott said. "On seeing the issue date of June 11 for this stamp, I prepared this cover."

NONDENOMINATED (25¢) AMERICAN EAGLE (10 DESIGNS) WATER-ACTIVATED GUM PRESORTED FIRST-CLASS RATE COIL

Date of Issue: May 12, 2004

Catalog Numbers: Scott 3844-3853, stamps; 3853a, strip of 11

Colors: yellow (PMS 135), red (PMS 186), green (PMS 348), blue (PMS 7461), dark blue (PMS 646), gray (PMS 431), black

First-Day Cancel: Washington, D.C.

First-Day Cancellations: 36,434

Format: Coil of 3,000, vertical. Gravure printing cylinders printing 660 stamps per revolution (22 across, 30 around) manufactured by Southern Graphics Systems.

Gum Type: water-activated

Overall Stamp Size: 0.87 by 0.96 inches; 22.09 by 24.38mm

Perforations: 9¾ (Comco custom rotary perforator)

Designer and Typographer: Tom Engeman of Brunswick, Maryland

Art Director: Ethel Kessler of Bethesda, Maryland

Modeler: Donald H. Woo of Sennett Security Products, Chantilly, Virginia

Stamp Manufacturing: Stamps printed for Sennett Security Products by American Packinging Corporation, Columbus, Wisconsin, on Rotomec 3000 gravure press. Stamps processed by Unique Binders, Fredericksburg, Virginia.

Quantity Ordered and Distributed: 75,000,000

Cylinder Number Detail: 1 group of 7 cylinder numbers preceded by the letter S on every 10th stamp

Cylinder Number Combination Reported: S1111111

Counting Number Detail: 1 4-digit counting number in magenta on back of every 10th stamp

Paper Supplier: Mactac

Tagging: untagged

The Stamps

On May 12, the Postal Service issued 10 nondenominated stamps with water-activated gum, arranged se-tenant in coil rolls of 3,000. Their common design is simple and graphic, depicting a portion of the eagle that is on the Great Shield of the United States. The stamps differ in appearance only in color.

The design and color combinations are the same as those displayed on a set of 10 self-adhesive stamps issued in 2003 in coil rolls of 10,000, except that the year date is 2004 rather than 2003.

Both self-adhesive and lick-and-stick versions were printed by the gravure process by American Packaging Corporation for Sennett Security Products. However, the printer changed the sequence of colors in the second version.

On the new roll, the sequence is gold eagle on dark blue background, followed by red eagle on gold background, gold on gray, green on gold, gold on red, dark blue on gold, gold on blue, gray on gold, gold on green, blue on gold. With the self-adhesive stamps, the sequence is gold on dark blue, blue on gold, gold on green, gray on gold, gold on blue, dark blue on gold, gold on red, green on gold, gold on gray, red on gold.

The price of each stamp, 25¢, represents a credit for mailers of first-class bulk mail against the actual cost of mailing their pieces. The service inscription in the design, "PRESORTED FIRST-CLASS," is considered a precancel, and the untagged stamps bypass the canceling machines in post offices.

The new version of the American Eagle coil proved to be much more collector-friendly than the self-adhesive version.

On the self-adhesive coil, the cylinder number combination is found on every other gold-on-green stamp, or every 20th stamp on the roll. That made it necessary for collectors to save a strip of 21 stamps in order to have the collectible ideal: a symmetrical strip with the PNC (plate-number coil) single centered and an example of every color variety, including the gold-on-green stamp with and without cylinder numbers. Such a strip is too large to be displayed on a standard album page.

With the water-activated gum version, however, the cylinder number combination is printed on every gray-on-gold stamp, which is every 10th stamp on the roll. No gray-on-gold stamps exist without cylinder numbers. Thus, a strip of stamps with the PNC centered and all color varieties represented comprises only 11 stamps, with duplicates of only the gold-on-green variety, one

261

on each end. This can be mounted diagonally on a standard album page. The Scott *Specialized Catalogue of U.S. Stamps & Covers* recognizes the 11-stamp strip as a collectible multiple.

The water-activated American Eagle has a four-digit magenta counting number, marking 10-stamp intervals, printed on the back of every gold-on-blue stamp.

Although the cylinder numbers also come at 10-stamp intervals, Stamp Fulfillment Services required collectors to purchase a strip of 25 stamps at $6.25 to obtain a PNC. Stamp Fulfillment Services also sold strips of five for $1.25. Collectors wishing to use surplus stamps for postage were required to obtain a precancel permit from USPS and present it with each mailing.

The Designs

Tom Engeman of Brunswick, Maryland, created the illustration used for the 2003 and 2004 American Eagle se-tenant coil stamps. The detail of the Great Seal shown on the stamps consists of the head and outstretched right wing of the eagle, a portion of the shield on its breast, and the tip of the olive branch held in its right talon.

The stamps are printed in nonmetallic gold and five supplemental colors. Each bicolored stamp has a counterpart on which the colors of the background and design are reversed. Backgrounds of a graduated gold tone alternate on the roll with gold eagles. The seventh color used by the printer, black, was used for the year date.

"USA" is in the upper right corner of each stamp, and the words "PRE-SORTED FIRST-CLASS" are across the bottom. The typeface is a modified Copperplate Gothic.

First-Day Facts

The first-day city for the water-activated American Eagle coils was Washington, D.C., but no ceremony was held. Collectors were given 90 days to submit self-addressed envelopes franked with one or more of the stamps to the postmaster in Washington for first-day cancellations. If only one American Eagle stamp was affixed, additional postage sufficient to cover the 37¢ first-class rate was required. For a limited time, Stamp Fulfillment Services offered uncacheted first-day covers bearing two American Eagle stamps chosen at random for 88¢.

5¢ AMERICAN TOLEWARE
AMERICAN DESIGN SERIES

Date of Issue: June 25, 2004

Catalog Number: Scott 3750A

Colors: dark gray (PMS 7536), light gray (PMS 454), light brown (PMS 7504), magenta, yellow, cyan, black

First-Day Cancel: Santa Clara, California

First-Day Cancellations: 8,093

Format: pane of 20, vertical, 5 across, 4 down. Gravure printing cylinders printing 320 stamps per revolution (20 across by 16 around) manufactured by Armotek Industries.

Gum Type: self-adhesive

Overall Stamp Size: 0.87 by 0.98 inches; 22.09 by 24.89mm

Pane Size: 5.38 by 4.969 inches; 136.65 by 126.21mm

Perforations: 11¼ by 11 (die-cut simulated perforations) (APS custom rotary die cutter)

Selvage Markings: "©2001/USPS." ".05/x20/$1.00." "PLATE/POSITION" and diagram.

Back Markings: Universal Product Code (UPC) "100500" in 4 locations on liner paper

Illustrator: Lou Nolan of McLean, Virginia

Designer, Art Director and Typographer: Derry Noyes of Washington, D.C.

Modeler: Donald H. Woo of Sennett Security Products, Chantilly, Virginia

Stamp Manufacturing: Stamps printed for Sennett Security Products of Chantilly, Virginia, by American Packaging Corporation, Columbus, Wisconsin, on Rotomec 3000 gravure press. Stamps processed by Unique Binders, Fredericksburg, Virginia.

Quantity Ordered: 100,000,000

Cylinder Number Detail: 1 set of 7 numbers preceded by the letter S in selvage above or below each corner stamp

Cylinder Number Combination Reported: S1111111

Paper Supplier: Mactac

Tagging: untagged

The Stamp

On June 25, the Postal Service issued a new variety of the 5¢ American Toleware definitive stamp it first had issued in 2002 in 10,000-stamp coil rolls with water-activated gum.

The new stamp is self-adhesive and was distributed in panes of 20. It had its first-day sale at the American Stamp Dealers Association Summer Postage Stamp Show in Santa Clara, California.

It was the fifth stamp in the Postal Service's American Design series — which began with the American Toleware coil — and the second in the series to be issued in 2004. On March 5, USPS dedicated a 4¢ pane stamp depicting a Chippendale chair.

The American Design series, when completed, will consist of pane and coil stamps ranging in denomination from 1¢ to 10¢. They are untagged, in keeping with the Postal Service's policy of not tagging low-denomination stamps.

The American Toleware stamp in panes was gravure-printed by American Packaging Corporation for Sennett Security Products. The same process and printer had produced the coil version.

Toleware is japanned (varnished) or painted tinware fashioned into a variety of household objects, including coffeepots, teapots, cups, trays and candlesticks, which are decorated with motifs such as fruits and flowers. Typically, these designs, in deep red, green, pumpkin yellow and other colors, are either hand-painted or stenciled onto a black background of asphaltum — a naturally occurring tarlike substance — mixed with varnish. Produced primarily in New England and Pennsylvania, American toleware was popular during the 19th century.

The Design

The new variety features the same illustration of a Toleware coffeepot that is shown on the coil version of 2002. Lou Nolan's painting, in water-soluble designer colors on illustration board, depicts a pot decorated with red flowers, a purple forget-me-not and yellow, green and orange leaves. Curators at the Winterthur Museum in Delaware, which owns the utensil, believe it was manufactured in Philadelphia between 1850 and 1875.

To fit the artwork on the stamp, designer and art director Derry Noyes cropped it slightly. The frame of the stamp cuts off the bottom of the coffeepot and part of the handle. As with all stamps in the American Design series, the border between the vignette and the tips of the die-cut simulated perforations is a solid color, in this case dark gray.

The coil and pane stamps were printed in the same combination of seven colors on the same Rotomec 3000 gravure press and are virtually identical in appearance. Only the black year date differs: 2002 on the coil stamp, 2004 on the pane version. The coil stamp has perforations on the sides and straight edges at top and bottom, while the pane stamp has die-cuts on all four sides.

First-Day Facts

David Failor, executive director of Stamp Services for USPS, dedicated the stamp in a ceremony at the Santa Clara Convention Center. Others taking part were Joe Savarese and Edward Hines, executive vice president and treasurer, respectively, of the American Stamp Dealers Association, and Santa Clara Postmaster Catherine Shearer.

For a limited time, Stamp Fulfillment Services offered uncacheted first-day covers bearing one American Toleware stamp and one 37¢ Flag stamp for 80¢.

23¢ WILMA RUDOLPH, PANE OF 20
DISTINGUISHED AMERICANS SERIES

Date of Issue: July 14, 2004

Catalog Number: Scott 3422

Colors: black, warm red (offset); black (intaglio)

First-Day Cancel: Sacramento, California

First-Day Cancellations: 21,473 (includes all formats of Wilma Rudolph stamp)

Format: Pane of 20, vertical, 5 across, 4 down. Offset and intaglio printing plates printing 240 stamps per revolution (15 across, 16 around).

Gum: self-adhesive

Overall Stamp Size: 0.87 by 0.98 inches; 22.098 by 24.892mm

Pane Size: 5.35 by 4.93 inches; 135.89 by 125.22mm

Perforations: 11¼ by 10¾ (die-cut simulated perforations) (IDC two-station die cutter)

Selvage Markings: "©2003/USPS." ".23/x20/$4.60." "PLATE/POSITION" and diagram.

Back Markings: Universal Product Code (UPC) "108400"

Illustrator: Mark Summers of Waterdown, Ontario, Canada

Designer, Art Director and Typographer: Richard Sheaff of Scottsdale, Arizona

Modeler: Joseph Sheeran of Ashton-Potter (USA) Ltd., Williamsville, New York

Engraver: Chemically engraved by Ashton-Potter

Stamp Manufacturing: Stamps printed by Ashton-Potter on Stevens Variable Size Security Documents webfed 6-color offset, 3-color intaglio press. Stamps finished by Ashton-Potter.

Quantity Ordered and Distributed: 100,000,000

Plate Number Detail: 2 offset plate numbers preceded by the letter P and 1 intaglio plate number in selvage above or below each corner stamp

Plate Number Combinations Reported: P11-1, P22-1

Tagging: phosphored paper

23¢ WILMA RUDOLPH CONVERTIBLE BOOKLET OF 10
DISTINGUISHED AMERICANS SERIES

Date of Issue: July 14, 2004

Catalog Number: Scott 3436, single stamp; 3436a, booklet pane of 4; 3436b, booklet pane of 6; 3436c, booklet pane of 10

Colors: black, warm red, stamps; black, special match pink, cover

First-Day Cancel: Sacramento, California

First-Day Cancellations: 21,473 (includes all formats of Wilma Rudolph stamp)

Format: Convertible booklet pane of 10, vertical, 2 across, 5 down, with horizontal peel-off strip covering roulettes between second and third horizontal row. Offset printing plates of 390 subjects (15 across, 26 around).

Gum: self-adhesive

Microprinting: "USPS" in stripe on left side of tank top

268

Overall Stamp Size: 0.87 by 0.982 inches; 22.098 by 24.942mm

Pane Size: 1.74 by 6.5 inches; 44.196 by 165.1mm

Perforations: 11¼ by 10¾ (die-cut simulated perforations) (IDC custom rotary die cutter). Two bull's-eye die cuts in top selvage.

Selvage Markings: USPS logo in top selvage. "Peel here to fold," "©2003 USPS" and plate numbers on peel-off strip.

Back Markings: "Wilma Rudolph/Ten 23¢ self-adhesive stamps/$2.30" on front cover. Promotion for The Postal Store Web site, "©2003 USPS" and Universal Product Code (UPC) "673000" on back cover.

Illustrator: Mark Summers of Waterdown, Ontario, Canada

Designer, Art Director and Typographer: Richard Sheaff of Scottsdale, Arizona

Modeler: Joseph Sheeran of Ashton-Potter (USA) Ltd., Williamsville, New York

Stamp Manufacturing: Stamps printed by Ashton-Potter on Muller A76 modified offset press. Stamps finished by Ashton-Potter.

Quantity Ordered and Distributed: 300,000,000

Plate Number Detail: 2 offset plate numbers preceded by the letter P on peel-off strip.

Plate Number Combination Reported: P11, P22

Tagging: phosphored paper

23¢ WILMA RUDOLPH VENDING BOOKLET OF 10
DISTINGUISHED AMERICANS SERIES

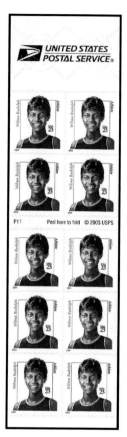

Date of Issue: July 14, 2004

Catalog Number: Scott 3436, single stamp; 3436a, booklet pane of 4; 3436b, booklet pane of 6; 3436c, booklet pane of 10; BK 279A, complete booklet

Colors: black, warm red, stamps; black, special match pink, cover

First-Day Cancel: Sacramento, California

First-Day Cancellations: 21,473 (includes all formats of Wilma Rudolph stamp)

Format: Vending booklet pane of 10, vertical, 2 across, 5 down, with rouletted horizontal gap between second and third horizontal row. Offset printing plates of 390 subjects (15 across, 26 around).

Gum: self-adhesive

Microprinting: "USPS" in stripe on left side of tank top

Overall Stamp Size: 0.87 by 0.982 inches; 22.098 by 24.942mm

Pane Size: 1.74 by 6.5 inches; 44.196 by 165.1mm

Perforations: 11¼ by 10¾ (die-cut simulated perforations) (IDC custom rotary die cutter). Two bull's-eye die cuts in top selvage.

Selvage Markings: USPS logo in top selvage.

Back Markings: "Wilma Rudolph/Ten 23¢ self-adhesive stamps/$2.30" on front cover. Promotion for The Postal Store web site, "©2003 USPS" and Universal Product Code (UPC) "672900" on back cover.

Illustrator: Mark Summers of Waterdown, Ontario, Canada

Designer, Art Director and Typographer: Richard Sheaff of Scottsdale, Arizona

Modeler: Joseph Sheeran of Ashton-Potter (USA) Ltd., Williamsville, New York

Stamp Manufacturing: Stamps printed by Ashton-Potter on Muller A76 modified offset press. Stamps finished by Ashton-Potter.

Quantity Ordered and Distributed: 40,495,000

Plate Number Detail: none

Tagging: phosphored paper

The Stamps

On July 14, the Postal Service issued a definitive stamp honoring Wilma Rudolph, a sprinter who overcame polio to win three gold medals in the 1960 Summer Olympic Games.

The stamp was the fifth face-different entry in the Distinguished Americans series. Its 23¢ denomination covered the domestic postcard rate and the first-class letter rate for the second ounce and each additional ounce.

A self-adhesive, the Rudolph stamp was the first in the series to be issued in multiple formats — in this case, three. All three were produced by Ashton-Potter (USA) Ltd. They were:

• Pane of 20 (Scott 3422). Like the previous Distinguished Americans stamps, this variety was printed by a combination of intaglio and offset. Stamps from a pane have die-cut simulated perforations on all four edges.

• Convertible booklet of 10 (Scott 3436), printed by offset only. The pane of stamps is sold flat, and a horizontal peel-off strip permits it to be folded into a booklet. The strip contains the plate number. All stamps have a straight edge on the left or right side.

• Vending booklet of 10 (Scott 3436), also offset printed. The stamps and booklet are iden-

271

tical to those of the convertible booklet except that the vending booklet comes prefolded, the horizontal peel-off strip with the plate number has been removed and its Universal Product Code (UPC) on the cover is different.

As of this writing, there have been no reports of die-cut gauge varieties such as those that have complicated the collecting of previous 10-stamp booklets printed by Ashton-Potter: the 20¢ George Washington and 21¢ Bison of 2001 and the 23¢ Washington of 2002. These varieties were caused by inconsistencies in the die-cutting mats used by the printer, and USPS apparently was unaware they existed until collectors discovered and reported them.

The multiple formats of the Rudolph stamp, plus its large initial press run, meant that it eventually would take the place of the aforementioned 23¢ George Washington stamp, USPS said.

Rudolph is the first black American to be pictured on a Distinguished Americans stamp. "The [Citizens' Stamp Advisory] Committee decided that we needed diversity in the series," said Terrence McCaffrey, manager of stamp development for USPS. "They said, 'Let's put her in there, as opposed to the Black Heritage series or a stand-alone stamp. At 23 cents, the stamp will get good mail-use coverage."

Wilma Glodean Rudolph was born June 23, 1940, in St. Bethlehem, Tennessee, to Ed Rudolph, a railroad porter, and Blanche Rudolph, who worked as a maid. The family was a large one, but accounts differ as to its size: One summary places her as the 17th of 19 children, while another says she was the 20th of 22.

The family moved to nearby Clarksville, Tennessee, the town that would be her home for most of her life. Numerous illnesses — chicken pox, measles, mumps, scarlet fever and double pneumonia — plagued Rudolph during her childhood. When she was diagnosed with polio that affected her leg and foot, the local doctor told Mrs. Rudolph that her daughter would never walk.

Unwilling to accept that verdict, Wilma's mother eventually sought treatment for her at Meharry Hospital, part of the Fisk University Medical College in nearby Nashville. Two years of intense physical therapy, which involved twice-a-week trips to the hospital, eventually enabled the child to walk with a metal leg brace.

The therapy continued at home, with her mother and siblings taking turns administering leg massages and other treatments. "From that day on," Rudolph wrote in her 1977 autobiography *Wilma*, "people were going to start separating me from that brace, start thinking about me differently, start saying that Wilma is a healthy kid, just like the rest of them.

"I went from being a sickly kid the other kids teased to a normal person accepted by my peer group, and that was the most important thing that could have happened to me at that point in my life."

Rudolph eventually was able to walk using just a corrective shoe. When she was 12, she put the shoe aside and could walk normally.

She first gravitated to basketball, playing pickup games in the back yard. During her sophomore year in high school, Ed Temple, coach of the women's track team at Tennessee State University, saw her potential as a runner and invited her to college for a summer sports camp.

The training there paid off when Rudolph helped the United States win a bronze medal in the 400-meter relay at the 1956 Olympic Games in Melbourne, Australia. She enrolled at Tennessee State in 1957 with a full scholarship.

In 1960, at Rome, Italy, she became the first American woman to win three gold medals in the Olympics, bringing home first places in the 100-meter and 200-meter dashes and anchoring the winning 400-meter relay team. Her 200-meter performance set an Olympic record, and the relay team set a world record.

Rudolph was the United Press Athlete of the Year for 1960 and the Associated Press Woman Athlete of the Year for 1960 and 1961, and received the 1961 James E. Sullivan award for sportsmanship. She took a one-year break from college to compete in international meets and make appearances, and in 1963 was a goodwill ambassador for the U.S. State Department at the Games of Friendship in Senegal.

In the same year, she received her bachelor's degree in education and married Robert Eldridge, her high school sweetheart. Together they had four children. She taught second grade at Clarksville's Cobb Elementary School and coached track at Burt High School, both of which she had attended.

She founded the Wilma Rudolph Foundation in 1982 to support athletic programs for underprivileged youth.

Wilma Rudolph died November 12, 1994, of brain cancer at the age of 54. (The Postal Service says that its rule requiring a 10-year interval between a person's death and stamp honors for that person applies to the year of death, not the exact date.) In 1997, Tennessee Governor Don Sundquist declared her birthday, June 23, Wilma Rudolph Day in that state.

The Design

The design style developed for the Distinguished Americans series by USPS art director

Mark Summers based his scratchboard stamp portrait of Wilma Rudolph on this uncredited photograph of the sprinter taken after she had won her three medals at the Rome Olympics. For the stamp, Summers omitted the medal ribbon around Rudolph's neck and changed her white shirt to a dark tank top.

On the booklet version of the stamp, a microprinted "USPS" is in the white stripe of Wilma Rudolph's tank top on the left side.

Richard Sheaff calls for printing in two colors, red and black, and a portrait executed by a technique known as scratchboard. In scratchboard, the craftsman begins with a black surface and scratches away the unwanted areas, leaving the remaining lines and shapes to form a picture that is reminiscent of classic line engraving or a fine woodcut.

Mark Summers of Waterdown, Ontario, Canada, a master of the technique, has created all the portraits for the series. For Wilma Rudolph, he worked from an uncredited photograph furnished by PhotoAssist, the Postal Service's research firm, that shows the smiling sprinter after she had won her three medals at the Rome Olympics. In the photo, Rudolph is wearing a white shirt with a collar, and the ribbon of one of the medals is around her neck. The artist deleted the ribbon and changed the shirt to a dark tank top.

In the pane version of the stamp, all the black portions of the stamp are printed in intaglio: the portrait, the thin three-sided frameline behind it, the word "Athlete" down the right side, "USA 23" inside the frameline at the right, and the "2004" year date. The red portion, consisting of the name "Wilma Rudolph" up the left side, is offset-printed. The only black offset printing on the pane is the selvage information: number of the black offset plate, pane-position diagram, copyright notice, face-value arithmetic and, on the back of the liner paper, the bar code.

The booklet version of the stamp is entirely printed in offset. Compared side by side, the pane and booklet versions look quite similar, but if the pane stamp is viewed at an angle, its raised intaglio ink is easily distinguished. The booklet stamp also includes microprinting for added security against photocopying: It consists of the letters "USPS" in the stripe of Rudolph's tank top on the left side.

First-Day Facts

The first-day ceremony for the Rudolph stamp coincided with the U.S. Olympic team track-and-field trials at the Alex G. Spanos Sports Complex on the campus of California State University in Sacramento. The trials for spots on the 2004 team began July 9 and concluded July 18.

The initial ceremony was a 9 a.m. press conference for media attendees only and took place in the grand ballroom of the Sacramento Convention Center. Henry A. Pankey, vice president of emergency preparedness for USPS, dedicated the stamp. Among track-and-field athletes who attended were U.S. Olympic medalists Bob Beamon, Michael Johnson, Jackie Joyner-Kersee, Bob Mathias and Bill Mills, and the Tennessee State Tigerbelle Olympians. A public stamp dedication event was held at noon on the west steps of the Capitol in Sacramento.

For a limited time, Stamp Fulfillment Services sold uncacheted first-day covers of the pane and booklet versions for 84¢. Each cover bore two stamps.

2¢ NAVAJO JEWELRY
AMERICAN DESIGN SERIES

Date of Issue: August 20, 2004

Catalog Number: Scott 3749

Colors: greenish blue (PMS 309), yellow, magenta, cyan, black

First-Day Cancel: Indianapolis, Indiana

First-Day Cancellations: 13,305

Format: pane of 20, vertical, 5 across, 4 down. Gravure printing cylinders printing 280 stamps per revolution (8 across, 35 around).

Gum Type: self-adhesive

Overall Stamp Size: 0.87 by 0.98 inches; 22.098 by 24.943mm

Pane Size: 5.25 by 4.921 inches; 133.35 by 124.9934mm

Perforations: 11 (die-cut simulated perforations) (Comco Commander rotary die cutter)

Selvage Markings: "© 2004/USPS." ".02/x20/$0.40." "PLATE/POSITION" and diagram.

Back Markings: Universal Product Code (UPC) "107200" in 4 locations on back of liner paper

Illustrator: Lou Nolan of McLean, Virginia

Designer, Art Director and Typographer: Derry Noyes of Washington, D.C.

Stamp Manufacturing: Stamps printed by Avery Dennison Security Printing Division, Clinton, South Carolina, on an 8-color Dia Nippon Kiko webfed gravure press. Stamps processed by Avery Dennison.

Quantity Ordered: 100,000,000 stamps

Cylinder Number Detail: 1 set of 5 cylinder numbers preceded by the letter V in selvage above or below each corner stamp.

Cylinder Number Combination Reported: V11111

Paper Supplier: Fasson Division of Avery Dennison

Tagging: untagged

The Stamp

On August 20, the Postal Service issued a 2¢ self-adhesive stamp in the American Design definitive series depicting a portion of a Navajo silver-and-turquoise "squash blossom" necklace. The stamp, printed by the gravure process by Avery Dennison Security Printing Division, was distributed in panes of 20.

USPS announced the stamp and made public its design January 29, 2004.

The American Design series ranges in denomination from 1¢ to 10¢ and showcases distinguished examples of the utilitarian art of the United States. It was inaugurated in 2002 with a 5¢ coil stamp picturing a toleware coffeepot.

The Navajo Jewelry stamp was the fifth face-different stamp in the series, the sixth overall, and the third to be issued in 2004. All the stamps issued to date were designed in the early 1990s by veteran stamp artist Lou Nolan of McLean, Virginia.

In the 19th century, Navajos learned to work silver from traveling Mexican plateros, or silversmiths. Jewelry making, along with the older tradition of weaving, became an important aspect of Navajo material culture.

Early Navajo silversmiths were known for their bracelets, concha belts and necklaces. Today's craftsmen use silver, gold and a variety of semiprecious and precious stones to create traditional and contemporary designs.

The squash blossom necklace remains popular in the Southwest. It is typically composed of silver beads resembling stylized blossoms, with a single crescent-shaped pendant in the center. Some squash blossom necklaces, particularly older examples, are made entirely of silver, while others combine silver and turquoise or silver and coral.

The design is based on a Spanish-Mexican trouser ornament that actually was a stylized version of the pomegranate blossom. The Navajo name for this type of necklace, squash blossom, has nothing to do with either squash or pomegranate blossoms, however. It simply means "round beads that spread out."

The Navajo word for the pendant is "nazhah," meaning "curve," but such pendants usually are referred to simply as "najas." Initially, the crescent-shaped naja pendants probably were based on Spanish colonial bridle ornaments, which, in turn, were derived from a Moorish crescent design.

Around 1880, Navajo silversmiths began setting stones — especially large, rough-cut nuggets of turquoise — into silver. Turquoise was, and remains, highly regarded and appreciated in the Southwest. To many Southwest tribes, turquoise is a sacred stone. The Navajos, who use it lavishly in their jewelry, believe that wearing turquoise brings good fortune.

The Design

The design for the Navajo Jewelry stamp is the last of five prepared for the American Design stamps by Lou Nolan before his retirement from

The illustration of an Amish quilt on this stamp is one of Lou Nolan's original paintings for the American Design series. However, the design was shelved after CSAC decided to launch the American Treasures commemorative series with four Amish Quilt stamps in 2001.

freelance artwork in 1995. Nolan also created a design depicting an Amish quilt, but it was withdrawn from consideration when USPS launched its American Treasures commemorative series with a block of four Amish Quilt stamps in 1991. Future American Design stamps will be the work of other artists.

Nolan's final painting for the series, in water-soluble designer colors on illustration board, shows the naja pendant of a Navajo necklace and 14 silver squash blossom beads set with polished blue turquoise nuggets. He based the painting on a photograph by Peter T. Furst of a necklace that is believed to have been made in the 1940s or 1950s and now is in a private collection. Derry Noyes, who conceived the series and is its art director, cropped the illustration to focus on the pendant and three beads on each side.

The squash blossoms are sand-cast, a process that involves carving a design into two complementary pieces of rock that then are joined together to form a mold. Molten metal, in this case silver, is poured into

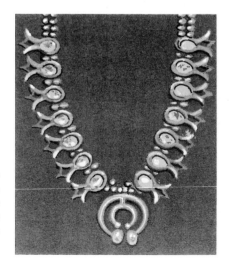

Lou Nolan's painting of the Navajo necklace that was cropped for use on the stamp shows 14 silver squash blossom beads set with turquoise nuggets and a portion of the chain. Only six squash blossoms are seen on the stamp.

the mold and allowed to cool. The mold is carefully broken away, and the hardened metal is filed to remove small spurs and other blemishes before being polished.

As is standard with the American Design series, the descriptive words, in this case "Navajo Jewelry," in Garamond type, run up the left side. "USA" and "2c" are in the lower left corner. The denomination is in turquoise blue, echoing the color of the beads on the necklace.

The background color is black, chosen to make the silhouette of the necklace "pop out," Noyes said. The stamp border is a greenish blue (PMS 309).

First-Day Facts

David Failor, executive director of stamp services for USPS, dedicated the Navajo Jewelry stamp in a ceremony at Americover 2004, the American First Day Cover Society show, at the Indianapolis Marriott East in Indianapolis, Indiana. Also participating was Tom Foust, president of the society.

For a limited time, Stamp Fulfillment Services sold uncacheted first-day covers for 77¢. The covers bore one Navajo Jewelry stamp and one 37¢ first-class rate stamp.

REVISED DEFINITIVES

Nondenominated (10¢) Lion Statue, 2003 year date

In early October 2004, collectors discovered that the nondenominated (10¢) Lion Statue self-adhesive coil stamp printed from the cylinder number combination S55555 bears a "2003" year date.

Specimens of the stamp printed from combinations S11111, S22222, S33333 and S44444 bear a "2000" date.

The stamp, displaying a stylized image of one of the two stone lions at the New York Public Library in New York City, is intended for a class of presorted quantity mail called standard that formerly was known as third-class bulk mail. It was gravure-printed in rolls of 10,000 by American Packaging Corporation for Sennett Security Products and made its debut November 9, 2000.

On February 4, 2003, a version of the stamp with water-activated gum was issued. Also produced by American Packaging for Sennett, it was distributed in rolls of 500 and 3,000. This version bore a "2003" year date.

The Postal Service told *Linn's Stamp News* that the "2003" year date on the self-adhesive stamps printed from cylinders S55555 resulted when the manufacturer mistakenly used an electronic file for black cylinder 5 that had been made for the water-activated stamp.

Once the mistake was brought to its attention, the Postal Service said it would instruct Sennett to restore the "2000" year date on future printings of the self-adhesive stamp.

On January 25, 2005, a dealer reported to *Linn's* that stamps from cylinder number combination S77777 had the original "2000" year date.

Scott Publishing Company assigned the minor number 3447a to the "2003" variety. Scott 3447 is the number of the original self-adhesive Lion Statue stamp issued in 2000.

The nondenominated (10¢) Lion Statue self-adhesive coil stamp issued in October 2004 and printed from the cylinder number combination S55555 bears a "2003" year date.

Nondenominated (10¢) Atlas Statue, coil of 3,000

On September 13, the Postal Service issued a version of its nondenominated Atlas Statue self-adhesive coil stamp in rolls of 3,000. It sold for 10¢ and, like the Lion Statue stamp described above, is intended for use on presorted standard mail. USPS offered first-day cancellations, of which a total of 5,922 were applied. For a limited time, Stamp Fulfillment Services offered uncacheted first-day covers for sale for 78¢.

The basic stamp is the same one USPS had issued in October 2003 in rolls of 10,000 without announcement or first-day cancellations (Scott 3770). Both were printed by Avery Dennison Security Printing Division by the gravure process in five colors and bear a 2003 year date. Scott Publishing Company did not give the 2004 version a separate catalog listing.

The rolls of 3,000 have a five-digit cylinder number preceded by the letter V on every 10th stamp. The rolls of 10,000 issued in 2003 have the five-digit number on every 20th stamp.

The Atlas Statue design first was used on a coil stamp printed by Banknote Corporation of America and issued in 2001 (Scott 3520).

A nondenominated Atlas Statue self-adhesive coil stamp was issued September 13 in rolls of 3,000. Scott Publishing Company did not assign this 2004 version a separate catalog listing.

$15 MIGRATORY BIRD HUNTING (DUCK) STAMP 2004-2005

Date of Issue: July 1, 2004

Catalog Number: Scott RW71

Colors: Face: yellow, magenta, cyan, black (offset); black (intaglio). Back: black.

First-Day Cancel: Washington, D.C.

Format: Panes of 20, horizontal, 5 across, 4 down. Printing plates printing 80 stamps per repeat (2 panes across, 2 panes around).

Gum Type: water-activated

Microprinting: "FWS" along right edge of design below female's beak

Overall Stamp Size: 1.98 by 1.42 inches; 50.29 by 36.07mm

Pane Size: 11.32 by 7.08 inches; 287.53 by 179.83mm

Perforations: 11 (Wista BPA 9700 stroke perforator)

Selvage Markings: "ARTIST:/SCOT STORM" in 4 locations. "DEPARTMENT OF THE INTERIOR/20 x $15.00" in 4 locations. "PLATE/POSITION" and diagram. 5 duck-shaped color bars in 2 locations.

Back Inscription (printed on top of gum): On stamp: "INVEST IN AMERICA'S FUTURE/BUY DUCK STAMPS AND/SAVE WETLANDS/SEND IN OR REPORT ALL/BIRD BANDS TO/1-800-327-BAND/IT IS UNLAWFUL TO HUNT WATERFOWL OR USE THIS STAMP/AS A PASS TO A NATIONAL WILDLIFE REFUGE UNLESS/YOU SIGN YOUR NAME IN INK ON THE FACE OF THIS STAMP." On selvage: Universal Product Code (UPC) "332900" in 4 locations.

Artist: Scot Storm of Sartell, Minnesota

Art Director, Designer and Typographer: Phil Jordan of Falls Church, Virginia

Modeler: Donald Woo of Sennett Security Products, Chantilly, Virginia

Engraver: photochemically engraved

Stamp Manufacturing: Stamps printed by Banknote Corporation of America, Browns Summit, North Carolina, for Sennett Security Products on Heidelberg Speedmaster 40 offset and intaglio press. Stamps finished by BCA.

Quantity Ordered: 1,000,000 stamps

Plate Number: 1 4-digit offset plate number preceded by the letter S and 1 intaglio plate number in selvage above or below each corner stamp

Plate Number Reported: S1111 1

Paper Supplier: Tullis Russell Coatings

Tagging: untagged

$15 MIGRATORY BIRD HUNTING (DUCK) STAMP 2004-2005 (SELF-ADHESIVE)

Date of Issue: July 1, 2004

Catalog Number: Scott RW71A

Colors: yellow, magenta, cyan, black (offset); black (intaglio)

City of Issue: Washington, D.C.

Format: Sold in single-stamp panes. Printing plates printing 18 stamps per repeat (3 across, 6 around).

Gum Type: self-adhesive

Microprinting: "FWS" along right edge of design below female's beak

Overall Stamp Size: 1.98 by 1.42 inches; 50.29 by 36.07mm

Pane Size: 6.13 by 2.63 inches; 155.7 by 66.8mm

Perforations: 11 by 10¾ (die-cut simulated perforations)

Selvage and Back Markings: see illustrations above

Artist: Scot Storm of Sartell, Minnesota

Art Director, Designer and Typographer: Phil Jordan of Falls Church, Virginia

Modeler: Donald Woo of Sennett Security Products, Chantilly, Virginia

Engraver: photochemically engraved

Stamp Manufacturing: Stamps printed by Banknote Corporation of America for Sennett Security Products on Komori Lithrone 40 offset and intaglio press. Stamps finished by BCA.

Quantity Ordered: 3,000,000 stamps

Plate Number: none

Paper Supplier: Paper Corporation of the United States/Spinnaker Coatings

Tagging: untagged

The Stamps

A pair of redheads in flight is featured on the federal migratory bird hunting and conservation (duck) stamp that was issued July 1 for use by duck hunters during the 2004-2005 hunting season.

The image was adapted from an acrylic painting by wildlife artist Scot Storm of Sartell, Minnesota, that won the annual U.S. Fish and Wildlife Service duck stamp design competition November 6, 2003. It was Storm's first victory in 12 attempts.

The duck stamp competition is the U.S. government's only art contest. First place carries no cash award, but the winners earn substantial returns from the sale of limited-edition prints of the artwork and other ancillary products.

A victory also carries great prestige that can pay off in painting commissions, as well as contracts to design the various wildlife stamps produced by state fish and game agencies.

This is Scot Storm's winning acrylic painting of two redheads coming in for a landing on Hay Bale Slough in North Dakota. It is reproduced on the 2004-2005 federal duck stamp.

The 2004 duck stamp, like its recent predecessors, was issued in two formats, conventionally perforated with water-activated gum and die-cut with pressure-sensitive gum. Banknote Corporation of America produced both versions for Sennett Security Products by a combination of intaglio and offset lithography printing. BCA printed the self-adhesive version in-house on a Komori Lithrone press, and subcontracted the water-activated version, which was produced on a Heidelberg Speedmaster 40 press. The U.S. Postal Service's stamps section handled design and production details for the Fish and Wildlife Service.

The self-adhesive, the version most commonly used by hunters, is issued in single-stamp panes the size of a dollar bill for convenient storage in cash drawers at post offices and the chain and sporting-goods stores that sell duck stamps on consignment. The conventionally gummed and perfed version is distributed in panes of 20.

The 214 artists who paid the $100 entry fee for the 2003 competition for the 2004 stamp were required to choose their subjects from among five species: redhead, Ross' goose, northern shoveler, ruddy duck and brant. The judges for the two-day competition were Adele Earnshaw, an award-winning wildlife artist; William Horn, chairman of the National Wildlife Refuge Centennial Committee; Allen Kane, director of the National Postal Museum; Dennis Schroeder, a well-known decoy carver; and William R. Stott Jr., ornithologist and artist.

Second place in the 2003 competition went to Jim Hautman of Chaska, Minnesota, for an acrylic painting of a pair of swimming redheads. Hautman is one of three brothers who have dominated duck stamp contests in recent years, amassing a total of seven first-place awards between

Jim Hautman of Chaska, Minnesota, placed second in the competition with this acrylic rendering of a pair of redheads swimming.

This acrylic portrait of a Ross' goose against a backdrop of flying geese won third place for Sherrie Russell-Meline of Mount Shasta, California.

1989 and 2001 and finishing in the top five numerous times. Third place was won by Sherrie Russell-Meline of Mount Shasta, California, for her acrylic depiction of the head and neck of a Ross' goose.

The duck stamp program was established by the Migratory Bird Hunting Stamp Act of 1934, which requires all waterfowl hunters 16 years of age and older to annually buy and carry a federal duck stamp. Other purchasers include stamp collectors, art lovers and conservationists.

Proceeds from the sale of duck stamps — approximately 98 cents of each dollar raised — are used to purchase and conserve migratory bird habitat. Over the years, as the face value of the stamp has increased incrementally from the original $1 to the present $15, some $600 million has been collected and more than six million acres of habitat conserved.

In 2002, the first year the duck stamps were produced by a private contractor, the version with water-activated gum was plagued by poor centering. The 2003 stamp was even worse, and also manifested inconsistent coloring, according to Bob Dumaine, a leading duck stamp dealer, columnist, author and former contest judge. However, the production quality of the 2004 stamp was "way above" its two predecessors, Dumaine said.

The redhead is a medium-sized diving duck resembling the canvasback, but distinguishable by its darker gray plumage, rounder head-shape, and yellow eye in the drake. Redheads are the only diving ducks to breed primarily in the prairies and prairie parklands. They winter in great concentrations from the Chesapeake Bay southward throughout the Gulf coast of the United States and Mexico, and in Idaho and California in the west. Redheads feed in a variety of water depths, consuming seeds of marsh plants and shoalgrass.

The species had made three previous appearances in the federal duck stamp series. The 1946 stamp displayed Robert W. Hines' picture of a redhead coming in for a water landing. The 1960 edition reproduced John A. Ruthven's gouache drawing of a swimming drake and hen with four ducklings in tow. Arthur G. Anderson's painting of a flight of three redheads sweeping across a backwater marsh adorned the 1987 duck stamp.

The Design

As a boy, Scot Storm showed a talent for drawing, sketching and design. He earned a degree in architecture at North Dakota State University, but while he was working in this field his love of hunting and the outdoors inspired him to try his hand at wildlife art. In 1987, as a self-taught artist, he entered the Minnesota duck stamp contest and placed second. He entered the federal duck stamp competition for the first time in 1990, and the following year won his first top state award in the Indiana pheasant stamp contest.

In 1999, Storm decided to give up his architectural career and devote his full time to painting. Since then, he has provided the artwork for the 2000 Minnesota pheasant habitat stamp and the 2004 Minnesota and Oklahoma duck stamps, in addition to winning the contest for the 2004 federal duck stamp.

His first-place painting shows a male and female redhead, wings spread, webbed feet hanging, preparing to land on a watery surface on which four swimming ducks can be seen. Overhead is a cloudy, pastel evening sky that is strikingly reflected in the water below. A distant shoreline stretches from one side of the painting to the other.

"The redhead is one of my favorite ducks, and I had that scenery in mind for several years that I wanted to show in a painting," Storm said. "The two seemed to click together in my mind." He based the setting on two different photographs he had made earlier: one of the cloud cover, the other of Hay Bale Slough near York, North Dakota, a favorite hunting spot some 300 miles from Storm's home.

To depict the birds, Storm referred to photos of live redheads, along with specimens in the workshops of some taxidermist friends. He found the mounted ducks to be particularly useful for studying the play of light on the feathers. In his painting, sunlight coming from the left illuminates the belly of the hen and outlines the drake's back and head and the trailing edges of both birds' wings.

The task of turning the winning artwork into a stamp design again went to USPS art director Phil Jordan, who also had designed the 2002 and 2003 duck stamps. Jordan's toughest problem, as before, was to find a place for all the wording that must be included: "Migratory Bird Hunting and Conservation Stamp," "U.S. Department of the Interior," the denomination, the name of the species shown and the stamp's void date.

Jordan inserted the words "Migratory Bird Hunting and Conservation

Stamp" in three lines of Akzidenz Grotesk condensed bold type in the upper right corner. The denomination, "$15," in Helvetica Neue, is just beneath. He tucked the word "Redheads," in dropped-out Caflish script, between the drake's right wing and right foot on the left side of the stamp, and "Void after June 30, 2005," in black Caflish, below the foot. "U.S. Department of the Interior," in a line of dropped-out Akzidenz Grotesk condensed italic, is across the bottom, with the drake's left wingtip wedging between the last two words.

Duck stamps are produced by a combination of offset lithography and photochemical engraving. On the 2004 stamp, the engraved component is minimal, consisting only of a patch of black feathers on the drake's breast and the "Void after June 30, 2005" inscription.

Although microprinting is not required on a duck stamp because the intaglio component of the stamp provides the needed security, the printer included the microprinted initials "FWS" (for Fish and Wildlife Service) in the design. They can be found along the right edge, just below the female bird's beak.

First-Day Facts

The first-day ceremony for the 2004 duck stamp was held July 1 at the National Postal Museum in Washington, D.C. Speakers were Steve Williams, director of the Fish and Wildlife Service; Allen Kane, director of the museum, who gave the welcome; Scot Storm; and Adam Nisbett, the 2004-2005 Junior Duck Stamp artist.

Those taking part in the ceremonial signing of the first sheet of stamps included Williams; Kane; Storm; Chris Tollefson, chief of the Federal Duck Stamp Office; Delores Killette, District of Columbia postmaster; the judges of the 2003 contest; and Donald Woo, representing Sennett Security Products, the stamps' contractor.

The microprinted letters "FWS" (for Fish and Wildlife Service) can be found along the right edge of the design, just below the female redhead's beak.

37¢ THE ART OF DISNEY: FRIENDSHIP STAMPED STATIONERY (4 DESIGNS)

Date of Issue: June 23, 2004

Price: $14.95 for a pad of 12 sheets

Catalog Numbers: Scott U653-U656, single letter sheets; U656a, booklet of 12 letter sheets, 3 each

Colors: cyan, magenta, yellow, black

First-Day Cancel: Anaheim, California

First-Day Cancellations: 340,448 (includes Disney stamps and postal cards)

Format: letter sheets of 4 different designs, vertical, with three grooves for folding the sheet and the gummed tab, printed in press sheets of 8 letter sheets each.

Size: 6.25 by 14.31 inches; 158.75 by 363.47mm

Markings: "©DISNEY" on letter side, "AFFIX HERE" on outside

Cover Markings: Card Markings: On address side of each card: "Disney Materials ©Disney," "©2003 USPS."

On individual cards: Cover Markings: On front: "The Art of Disney/FRIEND-SHIP/Stamp is Pre-Printed — No Postage Required!"/"WRITE/TO/FRIENDS"/"12 Self-Mailers/4 Designs". On back: "THE ART OF DISNEY: FRIENDSHIP/Every good story has heroes and villains, but friends play a part, too./From the friendships in Disney films, we've learned how to share, trust, laugh in spite of difficulties, and sometimes, just have fun." "Mickey Mouse and Friends/Mickey first appeared in *Steamboat Willie*/in 1928, while Goofy started playing for/laughs in 1932, and Donald added fuel to/the fun in 1934. Since then, the pals have/shared adventures and misadventures while/always keeping their friendship intact." "Bambi and Thumper/Irrepressible Thumper isn't awed by Bambi's/status as the 'young prince of the forest' but/simply sees a new playmate. Genera-tions/have treasured this coming-of-age story for/its natural beauty and gentle, laughter-filled/depiction of childhood friendships." "Mufasa and Simba/When we grow up we make new friends/who share different parts of our lives. But if/we are fortunate like the lion cub Simba,/who idolizes his father Mufasa, our parents/are our first 'best' friends who anchor us/with friendship that grows from love no one/else can match." "Pinocchio and Jiminy Cricket/Sometimes a friend has to play the role of/'Official Conscience' for us. Although/Pinocchio doesn't always want to hear what/Jiminy Cricket has to say, the chipper little/fellow is a steady, stalwart mentor when/Pinocchio/needs him most." "Fold and Seal for Mailing." USPS logo and Stamp Products Web site. "©U.S. Postal Service/Disney Materials ©DISNEY." "The Art of Disney:/Friendship/12 Stamped Statio-nery/Item No. 566794/Price" $14.95/AIC 092/Package Not Suitable for/ Philatelic Archiving." Universal Product Code (UPS) "0 566794 3."

Designer of Letter Sheets: Tanenbaum Graphic Design & Advertising, Bethesda, Maryland

Designer of Imprinted Stamps: David Pacheco, Burbank, California

Illustrator of Imprinted Stamps: Peter Emmerich, New York, New York

Art Director: Terrence McCaffrey

Modeler: Donald Woo of Sennett Security Products, Chantilly, Virginia

Stamp Manufacturing: Printed by Banknote Corporation of America/Sennett Security Products, Browns Summit, North Carolina, on Komori Lithrone 6-color offset press. Sheets processed by Banknote Corporation of America.

Quantity Ordered: 480,000 (40,000 sets)

Paper Type: opaque text, white, 100 weight

Tagging: phosphor tagging on imprinted stamps

The Letter Sheets

On June 23, when the Postal Service issued a block of four stamps honoring the art of the Walt Disney Studios, it issued two companion sets of postal stationery: four postpaid letter sheets bearing reproductions of the 37¢ stamps and four 23¢ picture postal cards that also reproduced the stamp designs.

The postal cards, a familiar format, stirred no controversy. The novel letter sheets, however, drew strong criticism.

What the critics deplored was the price. The letter sheets were sold in packets of 12 — three specimens of each variety — for $14.95, nearly 340 percent of the total face value of $4.44.

Michael Schreiber, editor of *Linn's Stamp News*, called the surcharge a "rip-off" in his Open Album column. It was "so high that Scrooge McDuck could not be happier," Schreiber wrote. "This is an unconscionable amount for a congressionally overseen quasi-governmental institution that is charged with providing universal mail service." He urged Postmaster General John E. Potter to cancel the extra charge.

Wayne Youngblood, editor/publisher of *Stamp Collector*, called the markup an example of "a stamp-issuing policy I'd expect only from goat-infested atolls and sand-dune nations of the 1970s." In his opinion, the letter sheets weren't intended to be used, but were issued primarily "to exploit the collector." "Don't buy them, don't use them, don't catalog or collect them, and the Postal Service will most likely stop making them," Youngblood wrote.

And postal activist Douglas F. Carlson, a lawyer and assistant dean at the University of California/Santa Cruz who had fought other postal policies on previous occasions, filed a formal complaint with the Postal Rate Commission June 24, 2004, arguing that the price of the letter sheets was excessive.

The commission should have been asked to approve the product and set its price under the same standards it applies to postal stationery items, Carlson contended. He asked the panel to establish a new category of "stamped stationery" and to require such products to be sold at a "fair and consistent price."

"The fee for stamped stationery unduly and unreasonably discriminates against stamp collectors, who are users of the mail and who may feel compelled to purchase The Art of Disney: Friendship stamped stationery to avoid a gap or omission in their stamp collections," Carlson added.

USPS rejected these arguments in a nine-page answer signed by Daniel J. Foucheaux Jr., chief counsel for ratemaking, and attorney Scott L. Reiter. "The stationery at issue is a philatelic item and mailing product which has much more in common with similar items over which the com-

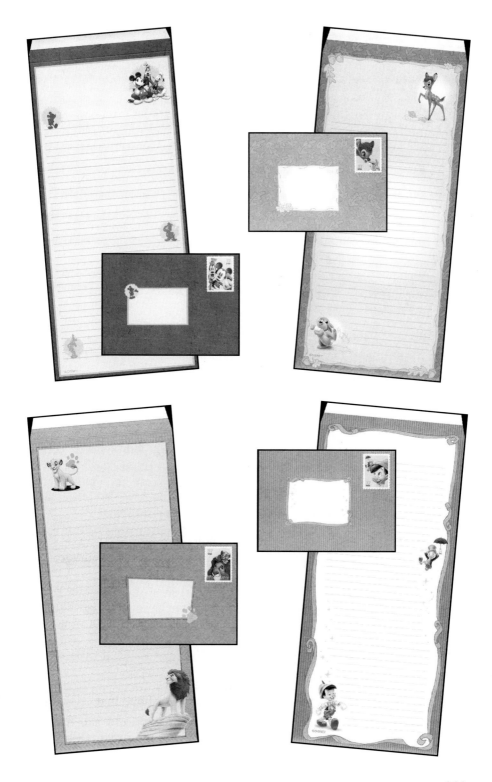

mission does not assert jurisdiction than the utilitarian stamp envelope," the Postal Service said.

The statement denied Carlson's contention that the Disney letter sheets were essentially the equivalent of Postal Service aerograms, which are the cheapest way to send overseas mail and traditionally have carried no markup. "The only similarity to aerograms is superficial: that both are tri-fold one-piece stationery," it said. "Unlike the Disney stamped stationery, however, aerograms are a utilitarian product printed on lightweight paper and having little artistic value.

"The Disney stationery is printed on superior paper stock and displays high-quality graphics and designs, including the Disney characters featured on the postage stamps issued as part of this product line."

No customer need purchase the letter sheets in order to use the mail, USPS said. It added that once a letter sheet is mailed, it is handled no differently from other first-class mail letters.

David Failor, USPS executive director of stamp services, also defended the price markup in an interview with Jay Bigalke published in *Stamp Collector* May 24, 2004.

"For many years now we've been selling the stamped postal cards, like Southeastern Lighthouses, that have the stamp image preprinted on them ... and we sell them for $9.95 [for a package of 20]. I've never received a complaint from anybody about those," Failor said.

"We do take into consideration the feelings and the understanding of the collecting community. The Disney prestamped stationery is not targeted to the collecting community."

Failor said the Postal Service's "sole intent behind this was to develop a product that would be easy and convenient for people to use ...

"Whether it's sending Johnny off to camp, or a son and daughter off to school, you can give them a prepaid piece of stationery, they can write a note on there, they can fold it up and drop it in the mail ... They don't have to worry about going and buying stamps or anything like that.

"What we hope to accomplish with this stationery is that people get a feeling that it's easy to send somebody a note or a message. That's what the Postal Service is all about. That's what we're trying to encourage, and maintain and strengthen the relevancy of the mail.

"I went into a card store the other day, and I looked at stationery that had envelopes with it, that had nice designs on it, some licensed images, and it was $10. If you take that same $10, and add $4.44 in postage, it's pretty close to $14.95, which is what we're charging.

"Again, we don't think it's out of line with what the marketplace currently has out there ...

"Those who say we're doing this to gouge the stamp collector are wrong. We hope that people find them attractive, we hope that people use them, we hope that stamp collectors would maybe want to add them to their collection. That's fine ... but if they don't, we won't be disappointed because that's not why we're doing it …

"We think the stationery is going to be popular. And we'll see. The marketplace will tell us if it is, or if it isn't."

The letter sheets were sold in pads of 12, three of each variety. The sheets are elongated (6.25 inches wide by 14.31 inches deep), and are horizontally grooved in three places to facilitate folding. Each variety has a distinctive design and color scheme, with decorations and characters related to the subject of its imprinted stamp.

The message side of each sheet is lined to help keep the writer's penmanship from wandering. On the other side is the imprinted stamp, plus a rectangular-shaped address space in a lighter color, and a printed strip marked "Affix Here" to indicate where the gummed flap should be stuck after it is moistened.

The resulting stationery is like an envelope with no sides, and *Linn's* reported that the letter sheets did not fare well in the Postal Service's automated, high-speed mail-processing equipment. "The heavy paper stock

Shown here are postally used examples of each of the four The Art of Disney: Friendship letter sheets (addresses are graphically obscured) that had a rough ride through the Postal Service's automated, high-speed mail-processing equipment. The sheets are arranged according to the relative amount of mangling that each received, from fairly light damage to the Pinocchio-Jiminy Cricket sheet, top left, to significant scraping and tearing on the Bambi and Thumper sheet, bottom right.

likely is the culprit, because when a given sheet is first folded and sealed, it bows out at the middle, instead of lying flat," *Linn's* said. "This bowing significantly increases the probability that the leading edge of the folded sheet will be bent, scraped, torn or otherwise mutilated as the sheet moves through a facer-canceler machine."

The letter sheets were offset-printed, eight to a press sheet, by Banknote Corporation of America for Sennett Security Products.

Only twice before, in the 19th century, had the United States issued letter sheets for domestic mail. In 1861, during the Civil War, a 3¢ sheet was issued bearing George Washington's portrait (Scott U36), and in 1886, a 2¢ sheet was produced depicting Ulysses S. Grant (Scott U293).

The Designs

Like the stamps, the imprinted stamps on the letter sheets depict close-ups of familiar Disney characters: Mickey Mouse, Donald Duck and Goofy; Bambi and Thumper; Mustafa and Simba; and Pinocchio and Jiminy Cricket. The designs are the work of two veterans of Disney's animation section, art director David Pacheco and illustrator Peter Emmerich.

The imprinted stamps are of the same design and size as their stamp counterparts, but the images are slightly less sharp and the background colors vary somewhat from the beige on the stamps. The depicted die-cut simulated perforations on the imprinted stamps have the same number and shape as the actual die-cuts.

First-Day Facts

Information on the first-day ceremony at Disneyland in Anaheim, California, can be found in the chapter on The Art of Disney: Friendship stamps.

23¢ COLUMBIA UNIVERSITY POSTAL CARD
HISTORIC PRESERVATION SERIES

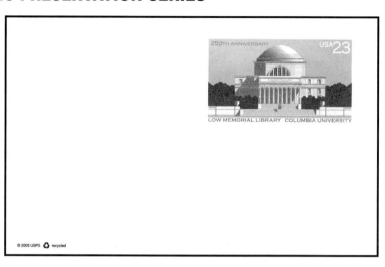

Date of Issue: March 25, 2004

Catalog Number: Scott UX405

Colors: yellow, magenta, cyan, black

First-Day Cancel: New York, New York

First-Day Cancellations: 7,975

Format: Cards available only as single-cut cards. Offset printing plates of 80 subjects (8 across, 10 down).

Size: 5.5 by 3.5 inches; 139.59 by 88.83mm

Marking: "© 2003 USPS." Recycled logo followed by "recycled."

Illustrator, Designer and Typographer: Tom Engeman of Brunswick, Maryland

Art Director: Derry Noyes of Washington, D.C.

Card Manufacturing: Cards printed by the Government Printing Office in Washington, D.C., on a 5-color MAN Roland sheetfed offset press. Cards processed and shipped by GPO.

Quantity Ordered: 6,000,000

Paper Type: 22-pound bright white

Tagging: vertical bar to right of stamp

The Card

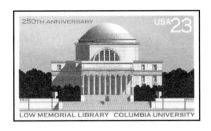

On March 25, the Postal Service issued a 23¢ postal card in the Historic Preservation series to mark the 250th anniversary of the founding of Columbia University in New York City. Its stamped image depicts the university's Low Memorial Library.

The card was the 56th, by the Postal Service's count, in the Historic Preservation series, which began in 1977 with a 9¢ card depicting the Galveston, Texas, Court House. Twenty-nine previous cards had marked the anniversaries of colleges and universities; the most recent, in 2001, was a 23¢ card for the 200th anniversary of the founding of Ohio University.

The latter was the first to be issued under a revised criterion adopted in 2001 by the Citizens' Stamp Advisory Committee that reads: "Requests for commemoration of universities and other institutions of higher education shall be considered only for stamped cards and only in connection with the 200th anniversaries of their founding." Taken literally, that would mean that the Columbia University card, for the 250th anniversary, was a violation of the rule.

CSAC's intention was that "the minimum is 200 years," said Terrence McCaffrey, manager of stamp development. "It starts with 200 and then it goes up in 50-year increments," he said. The committee made the change after discovering that a growing number of colleges and universities would be eligible for postal cards under the old criterion. "In one year, 14 colleges would have been eligible," McCaffrey said. "It had the potential for crippling the program."

The Columbia University card was a regional issue, like the nine other postal cards issued since 1999 in honor of colleges or universities. Only six million were printed, and they were sold only at New York post offices, as well as at philatelic counters nationwide and by mail from Stamp Fulfillment Services in Kansas City, Missouri. The Postal Service charges a 2¢ premium over the 23¢ face value for its non-picture postal cards.

The card was the second U.S. postal issue to mark Columbia's founding. The U.S. Post Office Department issued a 3¢ blue intaglio-printed stamp for the 200th anniversary (Scott 1029) on January 4, 1954, which

This 3¢ blue intaglio-printed stamp (Scott 1029) was issued January 4, 1954, to commemorate the 200th anniversary of Columbia University's founding. It presents a similar view of Low Memorial Library's south façade to the one on the 2004 postal card.

298

was before the creation of CSAC and its rule restricting commemoration of colleges to postal cards. The stamp, like the 2004 postal card, depicted Low Memorial Library's south facade.

Columbia University is the fifth oldest institution of higher education in the United States. It was established as King's College by King George II of England in 1754, and its first class of eight students met in a schoolhouse adjoining Trinity Church in lower Manhattan. Its name was changed to Columbia College after the American Revolution, and today it is officially known as Columbia University in the City of New York.

In 1897, the university moved from midtown Manhattan to a campus in Morningside Heights. In the same year, Low Memorial Library was finished. The limestone edifice was designed in the Roman classical style by Charles McKim of the architectural firm of McKim, Mead and White and was named for the father of Seth Low, who became president of Columbia in 1890. With its monumental colonnaded temple front and the largest all-granite dome in the country, it was intended to be the centerpiece of the campus. It served as the university's main library until 1934; today, it contains administrative offices and a visitors' center and houses archives and memorabilia of the history of Columbia. The rotunda, once the library's main reading room, now is used for major events, including the Pulitzer Prize award ceremony. The library was designated a historic landmark by the city of New York in 1967.

The university, a member of the informal grouping of distinguished Eastern institutions known as the Ivy League, has a tradition of outstanding instruction and research. Among other distinctions, it administers the annual Pulitzer Prizes under the will of benefactor Joseph Pulitzer. Currently, it enrolls more than 20,000 students.

Many faculty and alumni of Columbia and its professional schools have appeared on U.S. postage stamps, including Virginia Apgar, Ruth Benedict, John Dewey, Enrico Fermi, Lou Gehrig, Alexander Hamilton, Oscar Hammerstein II, Lorenz Hart, Charles Evans Hughes, Langston Hughes, Zora Neale Hurston, John Jay, Robert R. Livingston, Margaret Mead, Paul Robeson, Richard Rodgers, Franklin D. Roosevelt, Theodore Roosevelt and Harlan F. Stone. Dwight D. Eisenhower was president of the university between his retirement from the U.S. Army and his election as president of the United States.

The Design

Art director Derry Noyes commissioned veteran stamp illustrator Tom Engeman to create the artwork for the postal card. PhotoAssist, the Postal Service's research firm, obtained architectural drawings of Low Library, which Engeman scanned into his computer to begin the process.

A characteristic Engeman image, such as that of the Ohio University card of 2003 and the World War II Memorial stamp issued later in 2004, simplifies its subject, omits detail and features blocks of contrasting light

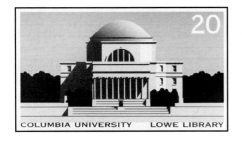

This is Tom Engeman's original computer-generated artwork for the Low Library postal card (note misspelling of the library's name), with the building simplified in the way that is characteristic of Engeman's illustrations. The anniversary committee at Columbia wanted more detail added.

and shadow. However, that kind of treatment of their signature building was not what the Columbia University anniversary committee had in mind.

"Tom created this beautiful design in a bright, graphic, contemporary approach," said Terrence McCaffrey. "Columbia rejected it. They thought it was too contemporary and didn't dignify the library enough. They demanded numerous changes and more details. We pushed back and said 'The beauty of this design is its simplicy; it conveys the essence of the building.' They didn't buy it.

An early alternative Engeman design showed the library at twilight with light shining through the windows and the colonnade.

"So we sent the art back to Tom and had him add line work, windows, shadows, steps, even simulated lettering over the colonnade. [CSAC] was very concerned and wondered if the detail would hold up at the size of the postal card image, given the quality of the paper and the print process we use."

In fact, although much of the detail and the lettering did not translate to the printed card, the overall effect was satisfactory — although it was definitely not a typical Engeman illustration. "I guess they are just more literal than we are," McCaffrey said of the Columbia representatives. "I still think Tom's original was superior."

Engeman experimented with several color combinations, including one

After Columbia rejected the simplified design, Engeman revised it with additional detail, including simulated lettering above the colonnade. As postal officials suspected, much of the detail was lost on the finished postal card because of the paper and printing process used.

of a darkened building, with light shining through its windows, and a twilight sky that shaded from deep mauve to orange. CSAC felt the latter was too garish and voted for a daytime scene with a peach-colored sky.

Noyes placed the words "LOW MEMORIAL LIBRARY COLUMBIA UNIVERSITY," in blue Copperplate Gothic letters, beneath the picture. "USA 23" is dropped out of the upper right corner of the vignette, and "250TH ANNIVERSARY," in blue letters, is in the upper left corner.

First-Day Facts

Donna Peak, USPS controller and vice president for finance, dedicated the card in a ceremony at the Low Memorial Library. Peak is an alumna of the university's Senior Executive Program. Lee C. Bollinger, president of Columbia, gave the welcome. The master of ceremonies was former New York City Mayor David Dinkins, a professor in the practice of public affairs at Columbia's School of International and Public Affairs.

For a limited time, Stamp Fulfillment Services sold the card with a first-day cancellation for 35¢.

23¢ HARRITON HOUSE
HISTORIC PRESERVATION SERIES

HARRITON HOUSE, BRYN MAWR, PENNSYLVANIA

© 2003 USPS ♲ recycled

Date of Issue: June 10, 2004

Catalog Number: Scott UX406

Colors: yellow, magenta, cyan, black

First-Day Cancel: Bryn Mawr, Pennsylvania

First-Day Cancellations: 2,904

Format: Cards available only as single-cut cards. Offset printing plates of 80 subjects (8 across, 10 down).

Size: 5.5 by 3.5 inches; 139.59 by 88.83mm

Marking: "©2003 USPS." Recycled logo followed by "recycled."

Designer and Art Director: Carl Herrman of Carlsbad, California

Typographer: John Boyd of New York, New York

Card Manufacturing: Cards printed by the Government Printing Office in Washington, D.C., on a 5-color MAN Roland sheetfed offset press. Cards processed and shipped by GPO.

Quantity Ordered: 5,000,000

Paper Type: 22-pound bright white

Tagging: vertical bar to right of stamp

The Card

On June 10, the Postal Service issued a 23¢ postal card in the Historic Preservation series to commemorate the 300th anniversary of Harriton House in Bryn Mawr, Pennsylvania.

302

By the Postal Service's count, the card was the 57th in the series, which began in 1977 with a 9¢ card depicting the Galveston, Texas, Court House. Twenty-nine cards, or more than half, have marked the anniversaries of colleges and universities; the most recent, on March 25, 2004, was for the 250th anniversary of Columbia University.

HARRITON HOUSE, BRYN MAWR, PENNSYLVANIA

Harriton House, an outstanding example of a colonial-era Pennsylvania home, was at one time the residence of Charles Thomson, who served as secretary to the Continental Congress from 1774 to 1789. In 1975, Thomson himself was pictured on a 7¢ postal card in the lengthy Patriots series issued during the Bicentennial period (Scott UX68).

The card was a regional issue, like all recent Historic Preservation cards. Only 5 million were printed, and they were sold only at Pennsylvania post offices, philatelic counters nationwide and, by mail, from Stamp Fulfillment Services in Kansas City, Missouri. USPS charged 25¢ for the card, including the standard 2¢ premium.

The Harriton House anniversary was brought to the attention of the Citizens' Stamp Advisory Committee by CSAC member David Eynon, a marketing consultant, writer and stamp collector who lives in Bryn Mawr. Eynon, in turn, had been enlisted by Bruce Gill, executive director and curator of the Harriton Association, which administers the house and the surrounding 16.5-acre grounds for the owner, the Township of Lower Merion.

Gill told *Linn's Stamp News* that a committee that began restoring Harriton House to its 18th-century appearance in 1970 had sought a stamp for the anniversary. "I went to high school with a fellow who became my representative in Washington, but I had no success with him," he said. "Finally, over the years, someone observed that I was approaching the wrong people.

"I was told to talk to the short man with the big camera who attended many of our events. He turned out to be David Eynon."

Eynon convinced CSAC that Harriton House would be a worthy subject for a Historic Preservation postal card. "I had asked the committee to

Harriton House's most famous resident, Charles Thomson, was pictured on this 7¢ postal card in the Patriots series issued during the Bicentennial period (Scott UX68).

come up with historic subjects for cards, other than colleges and universities," said Terrence McCaffrey, manager of stamp development for USPS. "This is a great little house, representative of the colonial era, with a lot of history behind it, and the committee bought into it."

Originally called Bryn Mawr, which is Welsh for "high hill," Harriton House is a three-story, T-shaped stone house with ornate features, including flaring eaves and tall brick chimneys. It was completed in 1704 for Rowland Ellis, a Welsh Quaker, on what is believed to have been the northernmost plantation in the slave economy, with tobacco as its crop.

The house received its name from Richard Harrison, a Maryland tobacco farmer who purchased the building and nearly 700 acres of surrounding farmland in 1719. The term "Harriton" was probably meant to imitate "Norriton," the name of nearby land owned by the family of Harrison's wife, Hannah Norris.

From 1774 until 1824, Harriton House was owned by its most famous resident, Charles Thomson, who married Harrison's daughter in 1774. The first public reading of the Declaration of Independence has sometimes been attributed to Thomson. Some early historical sources suggest that his final official act as secretary to the Continental Congress was to travel to Mount Vernon in 1789 to inform George Washington that he had been elected president. A design by Thomson is believed to have inspired the Great Seal of the United States.

Thomson continued to reside at Harriton House after his retirement from public life in 1789 until his death in 1824. An ardent abolitionist, he ended slavery on the Harrison farmstead. He also experimented with agriculture and indulged a love of the classics, writing what is believed to be the first published North American translation of the Bible from Greek into English.

Today, the restored house is open to the public and furnished to reflect the period when Charles Thomson occupied it.

The Design

The stamped portion of the card is unusually large, measuring $1^{13}/_{16}$ by $1^{7}/_{16}$ inches, and reproduces a circa 1828 watercolor of Harriton House by William L. Breton. A white picket fence crosses the scene in front of the house, and a weeping willow frames the building on the right. Art director and designer Carl Herrman did minimal cropping to fit the painting to the shape of the imprinted stamp.

Breton is known for creating several watercolor views of the Philadelphia area during the 1820s and 1830s. The Harriton House painting, in the collection of the Athenaeum of Philadelphia, shows the building without certain reconstructed architectural features that were not present in 1828, such as a small balcony and lower eaves across the front.

PhotoAssist, the Postal Service's research firm, found the painting. "I thought it was too good for us not to use," Herrman said. The decision eliminated the need to commission an artist to produce a new painting that then would have had to be checked by consultants for accuracy, and Herrman called it "the easiest postal card I've ever done."

Herrman placed the words "HARRITON HOUSE, BRYN MAWR, PENNSYLVANIA" in black Trajan capitals beneath the bottom frameline of the image area, dropped the year dates "1704-2004" out of the green grass in the lower right corner of the picture, and put "23 USA" in black against the sky in the upper left corner.

First-Day Facts

S. David Fineman, chairman of the USPS Board of Governors, dedicated the postal card in a ceremony at the Harriton House. Other participants included Bruce Gill of the Harriton Association; Jordan Small, district manager/lead executive of the Postal Service's Philadelphia Metro Performance Cluster; and Dennis Carr, officer-in-charge of the Bryn Mawr post office. Among the honored guests were CSAC member David Eynon and Philadelphia Postmaster Henry Dix.

The 7¢ Charles Thomson postal card mentioned earlier also had its first-day sale in Bryn Mawr, on September 14, 1975.

For a limited time, Stamp Fulfillment Services sold uncacheted first-day covers of the Harriton House card for 35¢.

37¢ THE ART OF DISNEY: FRIENDSHIP PICTURE POSTAL CARDS (4 DESIGNS)

Date of Issue: June 23, 2004

Price: $9.75 for book of 20 cards

Catalog Numbers: Scott UX407-UX410, single cards; UX410a, book of 20 cards

Colors: cyan, magenta, yellow, black. Aqueous coating added to picture sides and book covers.

First-Day Cancel: Anaheim, California

First-Day Cancellations: 340,448 (includes Disney stamps and stamped stationery)

Format: Book containing 20 cards, 5 of each design, with microperforations to permit removal of individual cards. Cards offset-printed in 12-subject sheets.

Size of Card: 6 by 4.25 inches; 152.4 by 107.95mm

Size of Book: 6.75 by 4.25 inches; 171.45 by 107.95mm

Card Markings: On address side of each card: "Disney Materials © Disney," "© 2003 USPS." On individual cards: "Bambi and Thumper/Irrepressible Thumper isn't awed by Bambi's status as the 'young prince/of the forest' but simply sees a new playmate. Generations have treasured/this coming-of-age story for its natural beauty and gentle, laughter-filled/depiction of childhood friendships." "Mufasa and Simba/When we grow up we make new friends who share different parts of our/lives. But if we are fortunate like the lion cub Simba, who idolizes his father/Mufasa, our parents are our first 'best' friends who anchor us with/friendship that grows from love no one else can match." "Mickey Mouse and Friends/Mickey first appeared in *Steamboat Willie* in 1928, while Goofy started/playing for laughs in 1932, and Donald added fuel to the fun in 1934./Since then, the pals have shared adventures and misadventures while/always keeping their friendship intact." "Pinocchio and Jiminy Cricket/Sometimes a friend has to play the role of 'Official Conscience' for us./Although Pinocchio doesn't always want to hear what Jiminy Cricket has to/say, the chipper little fellow is a steady, stalwart mentor when Pinocchio/needs him most."

Cover Markings: On outside front: "The Art of Disney/FRIENDSHIP/TWENTY STAMPED POSTAL CARDS • FOUR DESIGNS • $9.75." On outside back: "THE ART OF DISNEY: FRIENDSHIP/Every good story has heroes and villains, but friends play a part, too./From the friendships in Disney films, we've learned how to share,/trust, laugh in spite of difficulties, and sometimes, just have fun." Promotion for the Postal Store Web site. "Disney Materials © Disney."/ "© 2003 USPS."/ "The Art of Disney: Friendship/20 Stamped Postal Cards/Item No. 885100/Price" $9.75/AIC 092/Package Not Suitable for Philatelic Archiving." USPS logo. Universal Product Code (UPS) "0 885100 2."

Designer: David Pacheco, Burbank, California

Illustrator: Peter Emmerich, New York, New York

Art Director: Terrence McCaffrey

Modeler: Donald Woo of Sennett Security Products, Chantilly, Virginia

Card Manufacturing: Cards printed by Banknote Corporation of America/Sennett Security Products, Browns Summit, North Carolina, on Komori Lithrone 6-color offset press. Cards processed by BCA.

Quantity Ordered: 68,000 books (1,360,000 cards)

Paper Type: Carolina 10 PT, C1S

Tagging: vertical bar to right of stamp

The Cards

On June 23, the Postal Service issued a set of four 23¢ picture postal cards illustrating The Art of Disney: Friendship. The cards were companion pieces to a block of four 37¢ self-adhesive stamps and four 37¢ letter sheets on the same theme that were issued the same day (see separate chapters).

The postal cards are bound in a book of 20 cards, five of each variety. USPS sold the book for $9.75, or 48.75¢ per card.

On the address side of each postal card is an imprinted stamp reproducing the design of one of the four Disney postage stamps. In the upper left corner is a paragraph of descriptive text, identical to the text on the back of the liner behind the corresponding stamp. An enlargement of the stamp design, without typography, fills the picture side of the card.

The cards were produced by offset lithography by Banknote Corporation of America for Sennett Security Products. The picture sides and the book covers were printed in the four process colors, cyan, magenta, yellow and black. An aqueous coating for protection against scuffing was applied to the picture sides and the covers.

The Designs

The imprinted stamp on the address side of each postal card is slightly smaller than its postage-stamp counterpart, but otherwise is identical, except that the denomination is 23¢ rather than 37¢ and there is no tiny 2004 year date beneath the frameline. The images are less crisp than those on the stamps because of the 150-line screening, which was coarser than that used on the stamps, and the difference in quality between postal-card stock and stamp paper.

However, the images on the picture sides, printed with a 200-line screen, are large and clear, and do full justice to the detail and texture of Peter Emmerich's acrylic paintings. Because the postal cards are slightly deeper and narrower than the stamp designs, there is more of each design at top and/or bottom of the cards and less on the sides. For example, on the stamp showing Mickey and his friends, Goofy's hat is cropped at the top, but the full hat is shown on the picture side of the postal card.

The cover of the postal-card book bears reproductions of each of the four designs, minus typography, against a light blue background that reproduces the inscription, Tinker Bell image and stars from the header of the stamp pane.

First-Day Facts

Information on the first-day ceremony at Disneyland in Anaheim, California, can be found in the chapter on The Art of Disney: Friendship stamps.

23¢ ART OF THE AMERICAN INDIAN
PICTURE POSTAL CARDS (10 DESIGNS)

Date of Issue: August 21, 2004

Price: $9.75 for book of 20 cards

Catalog Numbers: Scott UX411-UX420, single cards; UX420a, book of 20 cards

Colors: cyan, magenta, yellow, black. Aqueous coating added to picture sides and book covers.

First-Day Cancel: Santa Fe, New Mexico

First-Day Cancellations: 486,737 (includes Art of the American Indian stamps)

Format: Book containing 20 cards, 2 of each variety, with microperforations to permit removal of individual cards. Cards offset-printed in 18-subject sheets.

Size of Card: 6 by 4.25 inches; 152.4 by 107.95mm

Size of Book: 6.75 by 4.25 inches; 171.45 by 107.95mm

Card Markings: On address side of each card: "© 2004 USPS." On individual cards:

"The Mimbres people of southwestern New Mexico produced a unique style of black-on-/white pottery featuring representations of wildlife, humans, or mythic beings combined/with geometric motifs. Most bowls of the Classic Mimbres period (circa A.D. 1000-1150)/probably served as eating vessels. This striking example depicts two stylized bighorn sheep,/animals that were once common in the Mimbres area./Maxwell Museum of Anthropology, The University of New Mexico, Albuquerque."

"Containers of folded or sewn rawhide, known as parfleches, were traditionally used by/Plains and Plateau tribal groups to store and transport food and material possessions./These utilitarian objects were painted with colorful and distinctive geometric patterns that/had both aesthetic appeal and spiritual significance. This Kutenai parfleche was collected/in 1900, probably in Idaho./American Museum of Natural History, New York, New York."

"Wood sculpture was a fundamental form of artistic expression among the men of the/Northwest Coast tribes, and objects carved and painted in their distinctive style were/eagerly sought by tourists and collectors. These two Tlingit sculptures, dated circa 1890,/likely illustrate the story of Salmon Boy, a youth who lived for a time with the Salmon/People in their supernatural realm beneath the sea./Phoebe A. Hearst Museum of Anthropology, University of California, Berkeley."

"Using ingenious twining techniques, women of the Great Lakes and Central Plains tribes/wove beautiful storage bags of bison hair, plant fibers, and wool yarn, often incorporating/stylized depictions of mythological beings into their designs. The thunderbird, which/embodies the sky realm, was a favorite motif; this one is a detail from an 1840-1860/Ho-Chunk (Winnebago) bag collected in Nebraska./Cranbrook Institute of Science, Bloomfield Hills, Michigan."

"During the early decades of the 20th century, Miccosukee-Seminole women in Florida/developed a unique style of patchwork clothing. They used hand-operated sewing machines/to piece together brightly colored cotton shirts and dresses, and they outfitted dolls made/for the tourist trade in miniature versions of these traditional garments. This male doll, made/circa 1935, wears a man's *foksikco.bi,* or big shirt./National Museum of the American Indian, Washington, D.C."

"This sandstone male effigy is an outstanding example of the art of the late Mississippian/culture (A.D. 1300-1550) in Tennessee. A strikingly naturalistic portrait, the statue provides a/valuable glimpse into a complex prehistoric society. It was found with a female figurine that/was carved in less detail; together they may represent the ancestors of a founding lineage./Frank H. McClung Museum, The University of Tennessee, Knoxville."

"Acoma Pueblo in New Mexico is known for exceptionally thin-walled pottery decorated/with complex geometric designs carefully painted on a white slip background. Master potter/Lucy Martin Lewis (circa 1895-1992) helped revive the black-on-white style by adapting/800-year-old Puebloan pottery designs to modern Acoma ceramics. The lightning pattern on/ this jar, which she made about 1969, derives from ancestral traditions./ National Museum of the American Indian, Washington, D.C."

"Weaving is the art form for which the Navajo are best known, and the finely woven textiles/from the Two Grey Hills region in New Mexico — characterized by geometric designs/executed in natural shades of hand-spun wool yarns with wide or multiple borders — are/highly esteemed. Daisy Taugelchee (1911-1990), who set unprecedented standards of fine/spinning and weaving, made this stellar tapestry in the late 1940s./Denver Art Museum, Denver, Colorado."

"Among the Iroquois, carving was traditionally men's work, and they were adept at trans-/forming wooden utensils into works of art — a skill particularly evident in the diverse human/and animal effigies that adorn the handles of ladles. This elaborately carved handle finial,/depicting a dog watching a human eating, ornaments a mid-19th-century Seneca ladle from/the Tonawanda Reservation in New York./New York State Museum, Albany, New York, on loan to/Akwesasne Museum, Hogansburg, New York."

"Renowned for the exquisite beauty and technical excellence of their basket-work, California/Indians — who used basketry items for every conceivable utilitarian, social, and ritual/purpose — elevated a practical craft into fine art. This superb Luiseno coiled basket, made of/split sumac and natural and black-dyed juncus rush on a grass foundation, probably dates/to the 1890s./Riverside Municipal Museum, Riverside, California."

Cover Markings: On outside front: "ART OF THE AMERICAN INDIAN/Twenty Stamped Postal Cards • Ten Designs • $9.75." On inside front: "These ten stamped postal cards offer a sampling of the diverse/ways in which Native Americans, in the context of their everyday/lives, created utilitarian, social, spiritual, and commercial objects/that were also extraordinary expressions of beauty. Executed in a/variety of media, these artifacts — which date from around the 11th/century A.D. to circa 1969 — illustrate the talent, ingenuity, and/artistic skills of America's first peoples./Creative expression continues to flourish among American/Indian artists today. Some still create traditional forms; others are/expanding their artistic endeavors in new directions in the fields/of painting, sculpture, photography, printmaking, video, and performance/art." On inside back: "Front cover:/Kutenai parfleche (detail)/American Museum of Natural History/ Photo © Mark Tade/Back cover:/Navajo weaving by Daisy Taugelchee (detail)/Denver Art Museum/Photo © Denver Art Museum." On outside back: Promotion for The Postal Store Web site. "© 2004 USPS"/USPS logo/"The Art of the American Indian/20 Stamped Postal Cards/Item No. 884500/Price: $9.75/AIC 092/Package Not Suitable for/Philatelic Archiving." Universal Product Code (UPC) "0 884500 1."

Designer, Art Director and Typographer: Richard Sheaff of Scottsdale, Arizona

Calligrapher: John Stevens of Winston-Salem, North Carolina

Modeler: Donald Woo of Sennett Security Products, Chantilly, Virginia

Card Manufacturing: Cards printed by Banknote Corporation of America/ Sennett Security Products, Browns Summit, North Carolina, on MAN Roland 300 offset press. Cards processed by BCA.

Quantity Ordered: 35,000 books (700,000 cards)

Paper Type: Carolina 10 PT, C1S

Tagging: vertical bar to right of stamp

The Cards

On August 21, the Postal Service issued a set of 10 23¢ picture postal cards reproducing photographs of examples of Native American art. The cards were companion pieces to a pane of 10 37¢ self-adhesive stamps on the same theme, Art of the American Indian (see separate chapter). Both cards and stamps had their first day sale in Santa Fe, New Mexico.

The postal cards are bound in a book of 20, with two of each variety. USPS sold the book for $9.75, or 48.75¢ per card.

On the address side of each card is an imprinted stamp reproducing the design of one of the 10 stamps. In the upper left corner is a paragraph of descriptive text, identical to the text on the back of the liner behind the matching stamp. An enlargement of the stamp design, without typography, fills the picture side of the card.

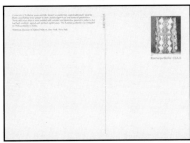

313

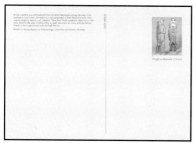

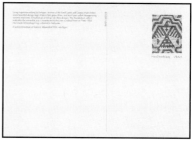

314

The cards were produced by offset lithography by Banknote Corporation of America for Sennett Security Products, whereas the stamps were printed by Avery Dennison Security Products Division.

The Designs

The imprinted stamps on the postal cards are miniature versions of the jumbo-size postage stamps, which are approximately one-third wider and deeper. Except for their denomination, 23¢ instead of 37¢, their designs are the same, including the 2004 year date beneath the image area on the left, so small that most purchasers will require a magnifying glass to make it out.

The cards' picture sides, being much larger than the stamps and printed on coated paper, show the color photographs of the artifacts to great advantage. The cards are deeper and narrower than the design portions of the stamps, meaning that the cropping of the images is tighter on the sides and looser at top and bottom. Three of the pictures, the Mimbres bowl, Ho-Chunk bag and Luiseno basket, lose details on the right and left that are on the stamps. On the other hand, the Seminole doll on the card is complete, head to feet, while on the stamp her feet are cut off by the bottom frameline.

The book cover illustration shows the central portion of the Kutenai parfleche. "I liked that one especially," said Richard Sheaff, the designer of the stamps and cards. "It looks like an abstract painting. Putting it on the cover was an opportunity to blow up the image so people would notice it."

Across the top of the cover are the words "ART OF THE AMERICAN INDIAN," which calligrapher John Stevens created in watercolor for the header of the stamp pane.

BCA printed the picture sides and the book covers in the four standard process colors, cyan, magenta, yellow and black.

When a card is removed from its book, a narrow strip at the top of the picture-side image remains on the book stub.

First-Day Facts

Information on the first-day ceremony at the Santa Fe Indian Market can be found in the chapter on the Art of the American Indian stamps.

23¢ CLOUDSCAPES
PICTURE POSTAL CARDS (15 DESIGNS)

CLOUDSCAPES

20 STAMPED POSTAL CARDS, 15 DESIGNS $9.75

Clouds develop when moist air cools to its dew point by rising to a higher altitude or by moving over a cooler surface. Water vapor in the air then condenses in liquid or frozen form around minute particles such as pollen or dust. The shapes and altitudes of clouds, as well as the sequences in which they develop, help people forecast the weather.

In the early 19th century, Englishman Luke Howard—chemist by trade and meteorologist by avocation—created a system for classifying clouds using Latin names. He described the three most common shapes as *cirrus* (curl of hair), *stratus* (layer), and *cumulus* (heap); he also defined four compound cloud forms that derive from the three primary shapes, including *nimbus* (rain). Later scientists added terms such as *humilis* (small) and *incus* (anvil) to designate other cloud properties. The *International Cloud-Atlas*, first published in 1896, is based on this classification system.

Nine of the ten basic cloud genera are pictured on these stamped postal cards. Nimbostratus, a dark, featureless cloud marked by falling rain or snow, is not included.

Have you visited our Web site lately?
If you want to see what's new in stamps and stamp products, or get the latest information on stamps issued throughout the year, visit The Postal Store at **www.usps.com**.

© 2004 USPS

UNITED STATES
POSTAL SERVICE®

0 884600 0

Cloudscapes
20 Stamped Postal Cards
Item No. 884600
Price: $9.75
AIC 092
Package Not Suitable for Philatelic Archiving

Date of Issue: October 4, 2004

Price: $9.75 for book of 20 cards

Catalog Numbers: Scott UX421-UX435, single cards; UX435a, book of 20 cards

Colors: cyan, magenta, yellow, black, blue (PMS 295). Aqueous coating added to picture sides and book covers.

First-Day Cancel: Milton, Massachusetts

First-Day Cancellations: 459,355 (includes Cloudscapes stamps)

Format: Book containing 20 cards, 2 each of Scott UX423, UX424, UX425, UX428 and UX430, 1 each of remaining varieties, with microperforations to permit removal of individual cards. Cards offset-printed in 18-subject sheets.

Size of Card: 6 by 4.25 inches; 152.4 by 107.95mm

Size of Book: 6.75 by 4.25 inches; 171.45 by 107.95mm

Card Markings: On address side of each card: "©2004 USPS." On individual cards: "Composed of windblown ice crystals, cirrus are fibrous, often/wispy clouds that appear in isolated patches or cover large areas/of the sky. **Cirrus radiatus** appear to emerge from the horizon in/parallel bands./Photograph ©David Rosenfeld Photo Researchers, Inc." "Relatively transparent **cirrostratus fibratus** clouds occur mostly/in winter and often produce a halo effect around the sun or moon./Thickening cirrostratus frequently indicate the approach of a/frontal system./Photograph 1988 ©Arjen & Jerrine Verkaik SKYART." "**Cirrocumulus undulatus** are patches or layers of small puffy/clouds arranged in patterns. They have a rippled appearance due/to wind shear and usually cover only a small portion of the sky./Photograph ©Richard A. Keen." "Pouch-like **cumulonimbus mammatus** develop when pockets/of air chilled by evaporating droplets or ice crystals sink into dry/surroundings under the anvil. They usually indicate the approach/or departure of a potentially severe thunderstorm./Photograph ©David Hoadley 1977." "**Cumulonimbus incus,** or thunderstorm clouds, form when rapid/updrafts within cumulus congestus clouds rise into the upper/atmosphere and spread out into mushroom-shaped anvils./Thunderstorms always produce lightning; severe storms may/produce heavy rain, large hailstones, or tornadoes./Photograph 1994 ©Arjen & Jerrine Verkaik SKYART." "Small heaps arranged in layers or sheets, **altocumulus/stratiformis** clouds are primarily composed of water droplets/and, as depicted here, reflect glorious colors at sunset. If they/become thicker during the day, a storm may be approaching./Photograph 1988 ©Scott T. Smith." "**Altostratus translucidus,** cloud sheets formed by the rising and/cooling of large air masses, often precede advancing storm/systems. A 'watery' sun (or moon) may shine dimly through the/thinner sections of the cloud sheet./Photograph ©Richard A. Keen." "Resembling ripples on water, **altocumulus undulatus** clouds/result from wind shear — wind speed or direction that changes/sharply with height. They may appear as patches or cover the sky./Photograph ©H. Michael Mogil." "Named for the turret-like protuberances in their top portions,/**altocumulus castellanus** clouds signify unstable air in the vicinity/and often indicate the potential for thunderstorms later in the day./Photograph ©1992 Arjen & Jerrine Verkaik SKYART." "Smooth, almost motionless **altocumulus lenticularis** clouds/resemble lenses and may be iridescent. They often look like UFOs/and form in the crests of waves that occur when strong winds/cross over a mountain peak or ridge./Photograph ©Carlye Calvin." "**Stratocumulus undulatus** occur when weak updrafts spread/horizontally, creating a layer of shallow, puffy clouds that is blown/by strong winds into wave-like formations that lie at right angles to/the wind. These clouds seldom produce precipitation./Photograph ©Richard A. Keen." "Gray, featureless cloud layers that can spread over hundreds of/square miles, **stratus opacus**, like stratocumulus, are generally/composed of water droplets. Stratus clouds occasionally produce/drizzle or light snow./Photograph ©1987 Stanley David Gedzelman." "**Cumulus humilis** — the smallest of the cumulus clouds — have flat/bases and rounded tops. Usually wider than they are tall, these/fair-weather clouds very rarely produce precipitation and often/evaporate as the sun sets./Photograph by John Day, Oregon Nature Photographer." "Strong, buoyant updrafts of warm, moist air in an unstable/atmosphere cause cumulus clouds to develop into **cumulus/ congestus**. These lowering clouds can produce moderate rain/or snow showers and may grow into cumulonimbus clouds./Photograph ©2000 Arjen & Jerrine Verkaik SKYART." "Among nature's most destructive phenomena, **tornadoes** are/rapidly spinning columns of rising air extending between the base/of a **cumulonimbus** cloud and the ground. In extreme cases,/tornado winds/may exceed 250 miles an hour./Photograph ©Edi Ann Otto."

Cover Markings: On outside front: "CLOUDSCAPES/20 STAMPED POSTAL CARDS, 15 DESIGNS $9.75." On outside back: "Clouds develop when moist air cools to its dew point by rising to a higher altitude or by moving/over a cooler surface. Water vapor in the air then condenses in liquid or frozen form around minute/particles such as pollen or dust. The shapes and altitudes of clouds, as well as the sequences in/which they develop, help people forecast the weather./In the early 19th century, Englishman Luke Howard — chemist by trade and meteorologist by/avocation — created a system for classifying clouds using Latin names. He described the three most/common shapes as cirrus (curl of hair), stratus (layer), and cumulus (heap); he also defined four/compound cloud forms that derive from the three primary shapes, including nimbus (rain). Later/scientists added terms such as humilis (small) and incus (anvil) to designate other cloud properties./The *International Cloud-Atlas,* first published in 1896, is based on this classification system./Nine of the ten basic cloud genera are pictured on these stamped postal cards. Nimbostratus, a/dark, featureless cloud marked by falling rain or snow, is not included." Promotion for the Postal Store website. "©2004 USPS"./"Cloudscapes/20 Stamped Postal Cards/Item No. 884600/Price" $9.75/AIC 092/Package Not Suitable for Philatelic Archiving." USPS logo. Universal Product Code (UPC) "0 884600 0".

Designer and Art Director: Howard Paine of Delaplane, Virginia

Typographer: John Boyd of New York, New York

Modeler: Donald Woo of Sennett Security Products, Chantilly, Virginia

Card Manufacturing: Cards printed by Banknote Corporation of America/ Sennett Security Products, Browns Summit, North Carolina, on MAN Roland 300 offset press. Cards processed by BCA.

Quantity Ordered: 45,000 books (900,000 cards)

Paper Type: Carolina 10 PT, C1S

Tagging: vertical bar to right of stamp

The Cards

On October 4, the Postal Service issued a set of 15 23¢ "Cloudscapes" picture postal cards reproducing photographs of various types of clouds. The cards were companion pieces to a pane of 15 37¢ self-adhesive stamps on the same theme that was issued the same day. The joint debut of the stamps and cards marked the start of USPS' annual National Stamp Collecting Month.

The postal cards are bound in a book of 20, with five of the varieties represented twice. USPS sold the book for $9.75, or 48.75¢ per card.

On the address side of each card is an imprinted stamp reproducing the design of one of the 15 stamps. In the upper left corner is a paragraph of descriptive text, identical to the text on the back of the liner behind the matching stamp. An enlargement of the stamp design, without typography, fills the picture side of the card.

The first 15 cards in the book appear in the same order as the corresponding stamps on the pane, starting with Cirrus radiatus and ending with Cumulonimbus with tornado. The last five are duplicates of Cirrocumulus undulatus, Cumulonimbus mammatus, Altocumulus stratiformis, Altocumulus undulatus and Altocumulus lenticularis.

Howard Paine, the art director and designer for the project, said he couldn't remember the rationale for choosing the cards to be duplicated. "I might have said, 'Just do the prettiest ones twice,' " he said. In fact, the duplicated designs are among the most visually striking and colorful.

The cards were produced by offset lithography by Banknote Corporation of America for Sennett Security Products, unlike the Cloudscapes stamps, which were printed by Avery Dennison Security Products Division.

The Designs

The imprinted stamps on the postal cards are identical in design and size to the postage stamps, with two exceptions. Their denomination is 23¢, not 37¢, and they lack the tiny 2004 year date that is found near the lower left corner of the stamps.

The cards' picture sides, being much larger than the stamps, display the color cloud photographs to maximum advantage. Because the cards are horizontal, 6 inches wide by 4.25 inches deep, Howard Paine was able to restore the portions on the two sides of each photo that he had cropped to fit the photos into the square stamp shape. For example, on the Altostratus translucidus card, a sea bird that is missing on the stamp hovers over the tranquil ocean surface on the right side. On Altocumulus lenticularis, the golden lens-shaped cloud on the left that is only partially visible on the stamp can be seen in full. And the farm scene on Cumulus humilis — a red barn and a second outbuilding on the stamp — also includes a white farmhouse on the postal card.

To illustrate the book cover, Paine chose five of the stamp images,

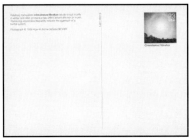

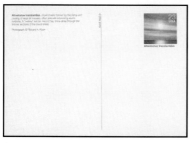

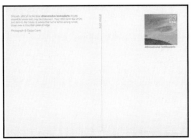

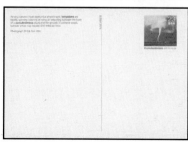

without typography. "I scattered them along like a handful of cards in a poker game," he said.

BCA printed the picture sides and the book covers in the four process colors, cyan, magenta, yellow and black. In addition, a PMS 295 blue was used for the typography on the imprinted stamps. An aqueous coating for protection against scuffing was applied to the picture sides and the covers.

When a card is removed from its book, a narrow strip on the left side of the picture-side image remains on the book stub.

First-Day Facts

Information on the first-day ceremony at Blue Hill Observatory in Milton, Massachusetts, can be found in the chapter on the Cloudscapes stamps.

VARIETIES

Unissued H Postcard-Rate Stamps

As of this writing, the *Linn's Stamp News* tally of unissued 1998 United States H for Hat postcard-rate stamps has risen to 22. All are used, and some are on cover.

The stamp shows a stylized Uncle Sam's hat against a yellow background and has water-activated gum. It was printed by the Bureau of Engraving and Printing for distribution in panes of 20. The Postal Service intended to issue it in November 1998 with other nondenominated H stamps in preparation for the general postal rate increase of January 1999. Shortly before the planned issue date, USPS decided not to raise the domestic postcard rate, so the stamp was not needed. However, some of the stamps reached the public by mistake.

On February 4, 2005, stamp dealer Michael E. Aldrich of Arizona sold a used strip of five of the unissued stamps to an anonymous West Coast collector for $15,750, including a 5 percent buyer's premium. The strip bears two full and two partial strikes of an October 27, 2001, double-outline circular datestamp of Greencastle, Indiana. The five stamps are sound, unlike all but one of the other known specimens of the stamp. Aldrich bought the strip from a collector in November 2004.

The Scott Publishing Company has not assigned a catalog listing to the stamp, citing its long-standing policy against recognition for "unissued items that are not officially distributed or released by the issuing postal authority." "[F]ailing actual evidence that any of these stamps were sold over the counter, the Scott catalog takes the conservative approach of considering these stamps to be unissued," editor James E. Kloetzel wrote in the April 2005 issue of *Scott Stamp Monthly*. However, the Scott *Specialized Catalogue of United States Stamps & Covers* notes the existence "in the marketplace" of the H postcard-rate stamps.

On February 4, 2005, stamp dealer Michael E. Aldrich of Arizona sold a used strip of five of the unissued 1998 United States H for Hat postcard-rate stamps to a West Coast collector for $15,750, including a 5 percent buyer's premium.

2003 duck stamp

In mid-April 2004, Robert Dumaine of the Sam Houston Duck Company reported purchasing an imperforate pane of 20 of the 2003 federal duck stamp with water-activated gum and a plate block of four from a second imperforate pane. "The location of the discovery was not made known to me, as I bought the item through a third party," said Dumaine, a well-known duck stamp dealer and author. "The owner and his location remain anonymous."

Scott Publishing Company lists the error in its catalogs as RW70b for a pair. It is the first known imperforate duck stamp since 1934, when RW1a — which some believe is printer's waste — was found. Pairs of the new discovery have sold for from $3,500 to $7,000, with plate blocks going for about twice that amount, Dumaine said, and the entire pane was sold within days.

"The timing of the error's appearance seems to imply that they were discovered during the inventory/return phase for unsold 2003 stamps," Dumaine said. "After the close of duck-hunting season, post offices reduce their accountable-paper inventory as soon as possible. Only major

An imperforate pane of 20 of the 2003 federal duck stamp with water-activated gum and a plate block of four from a second imperforate pane were purchased by Robert Dumaine of the Sam Houston Duck Company in April 2004.

post offices, distribution centers or private distribution firms had large quantities on hand."

A few weeks later, Dumaine reported the discovery in Kentucky of 12 specimens of the 2003 stamp with full perforations — but without the black inscription normally found printed on the gum. A duck hunter who also was a stamp collector made the find when buying a stamp for hunting. Noticing the lack of backside printing, he returned the next day to find only 12 stamps were left, and bought them. In June 2004, he contacted Dumaine's stamp company and sold the stamps.

Scott lists the printing-omitted error as RW70c. Only three other duck stamps with certified similar errors are known: RW29, RW35 and RW57.

The 2003 Duck Stamp, depicting a pair of snow geese, was the first in the series to be printed by Ashton-Potter (USA) Ltd. Well-centered examples have been difficult to locate, Dumaine said, and about a half-dozen color variations are known.

37¢ Gossaert Madonna and Child

A double-sided convertible booklet of the 37¢ Gossaert Madonna and Child stamp of 2003 without die cuts on one side was discovered and bought from an unsuspecting post office customer by Harold Wave of Maine in late December 2004. The side with eight stamps and the non-stamp label that serves as a booklet cover is the side with no simulated perforations; the other side is die cut normally, and all 12 stamps have been removed.

"I was standing in line at the post office," Wave wrote in a letter to *Linn's Stamp News*, "when an unknown patron was about to return the suspect pane for a refund because he could not separate the stamps on one side ... I asked to look at the pane and eventually purchased it from him. The 12 stamps on the normal side of the pane had been used before I bought it." Scott Publishing Company assigned the variety the catalog number 3820b.

34¢ Love Letters

A miscut convertible booklet of 20 34¢ Love Letters stamps of 2001 containing five vertical pairs with horizontal die cuts missing was sold in a Matthew Bennett auction in January 2004. The imperforate-between pairs comprise rows two and three of the three rows of intact stamps in the pane. The top and bottom rows each bear five partial stamps. The pane realized $3,250 in the auction, including the 15 percent buyer's premium. A Maryland collector told *Linn's Stamp News* he had purchased the pane at his local post office shortly after the stamp was issued February 14, 2001. Scott lists the vertical error pair as 3497b.

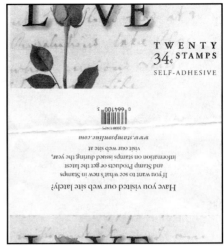

A miscut convertible booklet of 20 34¢ Love Letters stamps of 2001 containing five vertical pairs with horizontal die cuts missing was sold in a Matthew Bennett auction in January 2004.

20¢ Dogs block of four

A pane of 40 of the 1984 20¢ Dogs commemoratives (Scott 2098-2101) with horizontal perforations missing was scheduled to be auctioned by H.R. Harmer in New York City February 22-24, 2005. The owner, a Maryland collector who wishes to remain anonymous, said he purchased the pane as a new issue in 1984 at a post office in Bethesda, Maryland. The error received a certificate of authenticity November 17, 2004, from the Philatelic Foundation.

37¢ Purple Heart

A pane of 20 37¢ Purple Heart definitives (Scott 3784A) printed by Ashton-Potter (USA) Ltd. was found with no die-cut simulated perforations. It was purchased by Kerry Heffner at a post office in Omaha, Nebraska, in mid-October 2004. The pane has two horizontal bends, the result of a postal

The horizontal perforations are missing on this pane of 40 of the 1984 20¢ Dogs commemoratives (Scott 2098-2101).

A pane of 20 37¢ Purple Heart definitives (Scott 3784A) with no die-cut simulated perforations was found at a post office in Omaha, Nebraska.

clerk trying to locate the die cuts between the rows of stamps, Heffner told *Linn's Stamp News.*

39¢ Montgomery Blair aerogram

Four specimens of the 39¢ Montgomery Blair aerogram of 1989 have been found with multiple impressions. Apex, the expertizing service of the American Philatelic Society, has certified that one is a quadruple impression, one is a triple impression and two are double impressions. No other U.S. aerogram has ever been reported with more than a single impression.

Scott lists the double, triple and quadruple impressions as UC62a, UC62b and UC62c, respectively, in its catalogs. The specimen shown in the accompanying illustration is a double impression.

Multiple impressions can be seen on this 39¢ Montgomery Blair aerogram of 1989.

The air-letter sheets were printed by the Bureau of Engraving and Printing on a six-color Goebel Optiforma offset press. The multicolor, multi-image aerogram shows Blair, postmaster general under President Abraham Lincoln, standing beside a seated Lincoln. A second image shows a locomotive and a mailbag, honoring the Railway Mail Service, free city delivery and the money-order system. At the bottom of the sheet is a larger design with a scene commemorating the formation in 1874 of the Universal Postal Union, which was inspired by the 1863 Paris Conference that Blair initiated.

CSAC opposes U.S. personalized stamps

By a vote of 8 to 3, the Citizens' Stamp Advisory Committee recommended that Postmaster General John E. Potter reject a proposal that USPS follow the lead of some other countries' postal agencies and issue so-called personalized stamps. Potter accepted the advice.

The proposal, made in 2003 by the Presidential Commission on the Future of the U.S. Postal Service, was that individuals and companies be allowed to place their own images on stamps as a way to improve the USPS bottom line.

CSAC said personalized stamps, first issued by Australia in 1999 and also issued by Ireland, Canada, the United Nations and other jurisdictions, were a bad idea for several reasons, which committee chair Virginia Noelke listed in a letter to Potter. These were:

"In a society already too divided and fractured, stamps serve as a unifying symbol of American culture and community.

"The right-hand corner of the envelope is a dedicated, legally regulated space and should not be opened to personalized messages.

"The United States is one of the most contentious legal environments in the world, and freedom of speech issues versus regulated and appropriate content on personalized postage would place the Postal Service in a legally difficult situation.

"There is no such thing as personalized currency, and the creation of customized postage blurs the distinction between securities and other nonsecure paper products.

"It will be impossible to prevent individuals from using other people's likenesses and/or copyrighted material without permission, and the potential for abuse is overwhelming.

"It will be increasingly difficult to catch and stop counterfeiters.

"The public does not differentiate between stamps and postage, and customized postage will only further blur the two.

"The U.S. Postal Service is a leader in the global communications market and should not copy what other [postal] administrations have already done.

"... The financial payoff would be small. Neither Australia nor Canada Post touts customized postage as a big revenue generator."

Beginning in September, however, and apparently without Potter's knowledge, USPS allowed a private contractor dealing in computer-generated postage labels, Stamps.com, to conduct a three-month experiment allowing its customers to "create postage with their own designs, images and photographs." Stamps.com called the public response to what it termed "PhotoStamps" "overwhelmingly successful," even though the experiment took an unexpected turn when pranksters at a Web site called thesmoking-

331

gun.com succeeded in obtaining and using on mail PhotoStamps labels bearing the college graduation photo of Unabomber Ted Kaczynski, as well as photos of convicted spies Julius and Ethel Rosenberg, accused war criminal Slobodan Milosevic, missing Teamsters leader Jimmy Hoffa, the late Romanian dictator Nicolae Ceaucescu, former New Jersey Governor James E. McGreevey and his supposed gay lover, and Monica Lewinsky's famous blue Gap dress.

The company then announced it would accept only "color images of children who appear to be age 12 or younger, pets and animals, business and charity logos, landscapes, wildlife and vehicles."

The experiment ended September 30. On April 26, 2005, USPS announced what it called "the second phase of an extensive test of this popular product." This time the test would be allowed to run for one year and would be open to all qualified companies interested in selling the personalized postage.

Marvin T. Runyon dies

Marvin T. Runyon, the nation's 70th postmaster general, died May 3 at his home in Nashville, Tennessee, at the age of 79. Runyon served from 1992 to early 1998, when he retired. On his orders, the Postal Service began selling self-adhesive stamps at face value instead of charging a premium, as it had been doing. His decision is credited with paving the way for nearly universal production and acceptance of self-adhesives by USPS and most other postal authorities.

Collectors will remember Runyon for several other reasons, as well. He vigorously promoted the use of stamps to publicize social causes, beginning with the AIDS

Marvin T. Runyon, (left), the nation's 70th postmaster general, died May 3, 2004 at age 79.

Awareness commemorative of 1993. He pushed the Postal Service to seek cheaper stamp production in the private sector, which included a reduction in the number of engraved stamps so loved by collectors.

Donald M. McDowell dies

Donald M. McDowell, who played a key role in most of the major U.S. stamp policy and production innovations of the late 20th century, died September 14 in Fountain Hills, Arizona, at the age of 65.

McDowell joined USPS in 1973 as manager of the old Stamp Development Branch and 19 years later was forced out of his post as director of the

Office of Stamp and Philatelic Marketing in a headquarters reorganization ordered by Postmaster General Runyon.

Working closely with Assistant Postmaster General Gordon C. Morison, McDowell had been personally responsible for or closely associated with these developments, among others: annual stamp programs consistently topping 100 varieties, the extensive use of private printers for stamp production, significant improvements in multicolor printing quality, the inclusion of plate numbers on coil stamps, the inclusion of text information about stamp subjects on the selvage or reverse side, the use of non-denominated stamps to help smooth rate-change transitions and simplify stamp use in bulk mailings, self-adhesive stamps that are easy to use and have collector-friendly water-soluble adhesives, patch-and-window stamped envelopes to allow the use of multicolor fine-screen printing and holograms, 50-variety commemorative stamp panes, and computer-vended stamps and postal cards.

Lewis and Clark stamp tops Linn's poll

The 37¢ Lewis and Clark commemorative stamp won the title of overall favorite issue in the 2004 U.S. Stamp Popularity Poll conducted by *Linn's Stamp News*. It was the first single-design issue chosen by *Linn's* readers as their overall favorite since the category was established in 1984.

The pane of 15 37¢ Cloudscapes stamps placed second, and the first-place stamp's companion issue, the 37¢ Meriwether Lewis and 37¢ William Clark stamps that were printed in a souvenir-booklet format, finished third. Rounding out the top five were the 37¢ Pacific Coral Reef pane of 10 and the 37¢ John Wayne commemorative.

Following are the top three finishers, in order, in each of the other poll categories:

Commemoratives: Best Design: Lewis and Clark single; Lewis and Clark booklet stamps; Cloudscapes. Worst Design: R. Buckminster Fuller; Summer Olympic Games; Isamu Noguchi. Most Important: National World War II Memorial; Lewis and Clark single; Lewis and Clark booklet stamps. Least Necessary: Art of Disney; Isamu Noguchi; Cloudscapes.

Definitives and Special Stamps: Best Design: Holiday Ornaments; Navajo Necklace; 37¢ Garden Bouquet. Worst Design: Kwanzaa; Love Candy Hearts; Chippendale Chair. Most Important: Christmas Madonna; Wilma Rudolph; Holiday Ornaments. Least Necessary: Chippendale Chair; Love Candy Hearts; Kwanzaa.

Postal Stationery: Best Design: Cloudscapes postal cards; Art of the American Indian postal cards; Harriton House postal card. Worst Design: Art of the American Indian postal cards; Harriton House postal card; Art of Disney letter sheets. Most Important: Art of the American Indian postal cards; Columbia University postal card; Cloudscapes postal cards. Least Necessary: Art of Disney letter sheets; Cloudscapes postal cards; Harriton House postal card.

PLATE NUMBER COILS, SHEET, BOOKLET AND SELF-ADHESIVE STAMPS

Page guide for plate number groups

Changes to the plate number listings that appeared in the 2003 *Linn's U.S. Stamp Yearbook*, as well as all new listings, are shown in bold typeface.

Great Americans sheet stamps

Scott number	Stamp	Plate number	Perf type	Tagging type
1844	1¢ Dix	1 floating	bull's-eye	block
1844c	1¢ Dix	1, 2 floating	L perf	block
2168	1¢ Mitchell	1	bull's-eye	block
1845	2¢ Stravinsky	1, 2, 3, 4, 5, 6	electric-eye	overall
2169	2¢ Lyon	1, 2	bull's-eye	block
2169a	2¢ Lyon	3	bull's-eye	untagged

Scott number	Stamp	Plate number	Perf type	Tagging type
1846	3¢ Clay	1, 2	electric-eye	overall
2170a	3¢ White	4	bull's-eye	untagged[17]
1847	4¢ Schurz	1, 2, 3, 4	electric-eye	overall
2171	4¢ Flanagan	1	bull's-eye	block
2171a	4¢ Flanagan	1, 2	bull's-eye	untagged
1848	5¢ Buck	1, 2, 3, 4	electric-eye	overall
2172	5¢ Black	1, 2	bull's-eye	block
2173	5¢ Munoz	1	bull's-eye	overall
2173a	5¢ Munoz	2	bull's-eye	untagged
1849	6¢ Lippmann	1 floating	L perf	block
1850	7¢ Baldwin	1 floating	L perf	block
1851	8¢ Knox	3, 4, 5, 6	L perf	overall
1852	9¢ Thayer	1 floating	L perf	block
1853	10¢ Russell	1 floating	L perf	block
2175	10¢ Red Cloud	1	bull's-eye	block
2175a	10¢ Red Cloud	1, 2	bull's-eye	overall
2175c	10¢ Red Cloud	2	bull's-eye	prephosphored[17]
2175d	10¢ Red Cloud	2	bull's-eye	prephosphored[18]
1854	11¢ Partridge	2, 3, 4, 5	L perf	overall
1855	13¢ Crazy Horse	1, 2, 3, 4	electric-eye	overall
1856	14¢ Lewis	1 floating	L perf	block
2176	14¢ Howe	1, 2	bull's-eye	block
2177	15¢ Cody	1, 3	bull's-eye	block
2177a	15¢ Cody	2, 3	bull's-eye	overall
2177b	15¢ Cody	1	bull's-eye	prephosphored
1857	17¢ Carson	1, 2, 3, 4, 13, 14, 15, 16	electric-eye	overall
2178	17¢ Lockwood	1, 2	bull's-eye	block
1858	18¢ Mason	1, 2, 3, 4, 5, 6	electric-eye	overall
1859	19¢ Sequoyah	39529, 39530	electric-eye	overall
1860	20¢ Bunche	1, 2, 3, 4, 5, 6, 7, 8, 10, 11, 13	electric-eye	overall
1861	20¢ Gallaudet	1, 2, 5, 6, 8, 9	electric-eye	overall
1862	20¢ Truman	1 floating	L perf	block
1862a	20¢ Truman	2	bull's-eye	block
1862b	20¢ Truman	3	bull's-eye	overall
1862d	20¢ Truman	4	bull's-eye	prephosphored[18]
2179	20¢ Apgar	B1, B2, B3	bull's-eye	prephosphored
2180	21¢ Carlson	1	bull's-eye	block
1863	22¢ Audubon	1 floating	L perf	block
1863d	22¢ Audubon	3	bull's-eye	block

Scott number	Stamp	Plate number	Perf type	Tagging type
2181	23¢ Cassatt	1	bull's-eye	block
2181a	23¢ Cassatt	1, 2	bull's-eye	overall
2181b	23¢ Cassatt	2, 3	bull's-eye	prephosphored[19]
2182	25¢ London	1, 2	bull's-eye	block
2183	28¢ Sitting Bull	1	bull's-eye	block
2184	29¢ Warren	S1, S2 (six positions)	bull's-eye	prephosphored
2185	29¢ Jefferson	S1, S2 (six positions)	bull's-eye	prephosphored
1864	30¢ Laubach	1 floating	L perf	block
1864a	30¢ Laubach	2	bull's-eye	block
1864b	30¢ Laubach	2	bull's-eye	overall
2933	32¢ Hershey	B1, B2	bull's-eye	prephosphored
2934	32¢ Farley	B1	bull's-eye	prephosphored
2935	32¢ Luce	B1	bull's-eye	prephosphored
2936	32¢ Wallaces	P1	bull's-eye	prephosphored
1865	35¢ Drew	1, 2, 3, 4	electric-eye	overall
2186	35¢ Chavez	S1, S2 (six positions)	L perf	prephosphored
1866	37¢ Millikan	1, 2, 3, 4	electric-eye	overall
1867	39¢ Clark	1 floating	L perf	block
1867c	39¢ Clark	2	bull's-eye	block
1868	40¢ Gilbreth	1 floating	L perf	block
1868a	40¢ Gilbreth	2	bull's-eye	block
2187	40¢ Chennault	1	bull's-eye	overall
2187a	40¢ Chennault	2	bull's-eye	prephosphored[17]
2188	45¢ Cushing	1	bull's-eye	block
2188a	45¢ Cushing	1	bull's-eye	overall
2938	46¢ Benedict	1	bull's-eye	prephosphored
1869	50¢ Nimitz	1, 2, 3, 4	L perf	overall[18]
1869a	50¢ Nimitz	1, 2	bull's-eye	block
1869d	50¢ Nimitz	2, 3	bull's-eye	overall
1869e	50¢ Nimitz	3	bull's-eye	prephosphored[17]
2189	52¢ Humphrey	1, 2	bull's-eye	prephosphored[20]
2940	55¢ Hamilton	B1, B2, B3	bull's-eye	prephosphored
2941	55¢ J. Morrill	B1, B2	die-cut	prephosphored
2190	56¢ Harvard	1	bull's-eye	block
2191	65¢ Arnold	1	bull's-eye	block
2192	75¢ Willkie	1	bull's-eye	prephosphored[17]
2942	77¢ Breckinridge	B1, B2	die-cut	prephosphored
2943	78¢ Paul	B1, B2	bull's-eye	prephosphored
2193	$1 Revel	1	bull's-eye	block
2194	$1 Hopkins	1	bull's-eye	block

Scott number	Stamp	Plate number	Perf type	Tagging type
2194b	$1 Hopkins	1	bull's-eye	overall
2194d	$1 Hopkins	2	bull's-eye	prephosphored[17]
2195	$2 Bryan	2	bull's-eye	block
2196	$5 Bret Harte	1	bull's-eye	block
2196b	$5 Bret Harte	2	bull's-eye	prephosphored

Great Americans sheet stamps notes

17 *Shiny gum and dull gum*
18 *Shiny gum*
19 *Plate number 3 shiny gum*
20 *Plate number 1 shiny and dull gum, plate number 2 shiny gum*

General notes

Plate positions: Floating plate number positions are left or right, either blocks of six or strips of 20 (number must be centered in selvage in a block of six). All other plate number positions consist of upper left, upper right, lower left and lower right, with the following exceptions: 29¢ Warren, 29¢ Jefferson and 35¢ Chavez, which have positions of upper left, center upper right, upper right, lower left, center lower right and lower right. (Traditional corners have plate numbers to the side of the stamps; center positions have plate numbers above or below stamps.)

Tagging types

Block: tagging block centered over design of stamp; no tagging in selvage.
Overall: tagging applied to entire pane, often leaving an untagged strip at outer edge of large margin selvage.
Prephosphored: paper that has phosphorescent taggant applied to the paper by the paper supplier prior to printing. On some stamps, under shortwave UV light, the appearance of the phosphorescent tagging is smooth and even (surface taggant), while on others, the taggant appears mottled (embedded taggant). Examples that exhibit both are the 10¢ Red Cloud, 23¢ Cassatt, 40¢ Chennault, 52¢ Humphrey, 75¢ Willkie and $1 Hopkins from the Great Americans and the 23¢ Lunch Wagon, 29¢ Flag Over Mount Rushmore and the variable-denomination coil (Scott 31, 31a, 31b and 31c) from the plate number coils.

Transportation coil stamps

Scott number	Stamp	Plate number	Tagging type
1897	1¢ Omnibus (1983)	1, 2, 3, 5, 6	overall
2225	1¢ Omnibus (1986)	1, 2	block
2225a	1¢ Omnibus (1991)	2, 3	untagged[2]
2225a	1¢ Omnibus (1997)	3	untagged[19]
1897A	2¢ Locomotive (1982)	2, 3, 4, 6, 8, 10	overall
2226	2¢ Locomotive (1987)	1	block
2226a	2¢ Locomotive (1993)	2	untagged
2226a	2¢ Locomotive (1997)	2	untagged[20]
1898	3¢ Handcar (1983)	1, 2, 3, 4	overall
2252	3¢ Conestoga Wagon (1988)	1	block
2252a	3¢ Conestoga Wagon (1992)	2, 3, 5, 6	untagged[15]
2123	3.4¢ School Bus (1985)	1, 2	overall
2123a	3.4¢ School Bus (1985)	1, 2	untagged

Scott number	Stamp	Plate number	Tagging type
1898A	4¢ Stagecoach (1982)	1, 2, 3, 4, 5, 6	overall
1898Ab	4¢ Stagecoach (1982)	3, 4, 5, 6	untagged
2228	4¢ Stagecoach (1986)	1	block
2228a	4¢ Stagecoach (1990)	1	overall
2451	4¢ Steam Carriage (1991)	1	overall
2451b	4¢ Steam Carriage (1991)	1	untagged
2124	4.9¢ Buckboard (1985)	3, 4	overall
2124a	4.9¢ Buckboard (1985)	1, 2, 3, 4, 5, 6	untagged
1899	5¢ Motorcycle (1983)	1, 2, 3, 4	overall
2253	5¢ Milk Wagon (1987)	1	block
2452	5¢ Circus Wagon (1990)	1	overall
2452a	5¢ Circus Wagon (1991)	1, 2	untagged[33]
2452B	5¢ Circus Wagon (gravure) (1992)	A1, A2	untagged
2452Bf	5¢ Circus Wagon (gravure) (1992)	A3	untagged[32]
2452D	5¢ Circus Wagon (gravure) (1995)	S1, S2	untagged[12]
2452Dg	5¢ Circus Wagon (gravure) (1995)	S2, S3	untagged[32]
2453	5¢ Canoe (1991)	1, 2, 3	untagged
2454	5¢ Canoe (gravure) (1991)	S11	untagged
1900	5.2¢ Sleigh (1983)	1, 2, 3, 5	overall
1900a	5.2¢ Sleigh (1983)	1, 2, 3, 4, 5, 6	untagged
2254	5.3¢ Elevator (1988)	1	untagged
2125	5.5¢ Star Route Truck (1986)	1	block
2125a	5.5¢ Star Route Truck (1986)	1, 2	untagged
1901	5.9¢ Bicycle (1982)	3, 4	overall
1901a	5.9¢ Bicycle (1982)	3, 4, 5, 6	untagged
2126	6¢ Tricycle (1985)	1	block
2126a	6¢ Tricycle (1985)	1, 2	untagged
2127	7.1¢ Tractor (1987)	1	block
2127a	7.1¢ Tractor (1987)	1	untagged[3]
2127b	7.1¢ Tractor (1989)	1	untagged[4]
1902	7.4¢ Baby Buggy (1984)	2	block
1902a	7.4¢ Buggy (1984)	2	untagged
2255	7.6¢ Carreta (1988)	1, 2, 3	untagged
2128	8.3¢ Ambulance (1985)	1, 2	overall
2128a	8.3¢ Ambulance (1985)	1, 2, 3, 4	untagged
2231	8.3¢ Ambulance (1986)	1, 2	untagged
2256	8.4¢ Wheel Chair (1988)	1, 2, 3	untagged
2129a	8.5¢ Tow Truck (1987)	1, 2	untagged
2129	8.5¢ Tow Truck (1987)	1	block
1903a	9.3¢ Mail Wagon (1981)	1, 2, 3, 4, 5, 6, 8	untagged

Scott number	Stamp	Plate number	Tagging type
1903	9.3¢ Mail Wagon (1981)	1, 2, 3, 4, 5, 6	overall
2257	10¢ Canal Boat (1987)	1	block
2257a	10¢ Canal Boat (1991)	1, 4	overall
2257b	10¢ Canal Boat (1992)	1, 2, 3, 4	prephosphored[1]
2257c	10¢ Canal Boat (1999)	5	prephosphored[25]
2457	10¢ Tractor Trailer (1991)	1	untagged
2458	10¢ Tractor Trailer (gravure) (1994)	11, 22	untagged
2130	10.1¢ Oil Wagon (1985)	1	block
2130a	10.1¢ Oil Wagon (1985)	1, 2	untagged[5]
2130a	10.1¢ Oil Wagon (1988)	2, 3	untagged[6]
1904a	10.9¢ Hansom Cab (1982)	1, 2, 3, 4	untagged
1904	10.9¢ Hansom Cab (1982)	1, 2	overall
1905	11¢ Caboose (1984)	1	block
1905a	11¢ Caboose (1984)	1	untagged[7]
1905a	11¢ Caboose (1991)	2	untagged
2131	11¢ Stutz Bearcat (1985)	1, 2, 3, 4	overall
2132	12¢ Stanley Steamer (1985)	1, 2	overall
2132a	12¢ Stanley Steamer (1985)	1, 2	untagged
2132b	12¢ Stanley Steamer (1987)	1	untagged
2133a	12.5¢ Pushcart (1985)	1, 2	untagged
2133	12.5¢ Pushcart (1985)	1, 2	block
2258	13¢ Patrol Wagon (1988)	1	untagged
2259	13.2¢ Coal Car (1988)	1, 2	untagged
2134	14¢ Iceboat (1985)	1, 2, 3, 4	overall
2134b	14¢ Iceboat (1986)	2	block
2260	15¢ Tugboat (1988)	1, 2	block
2260a	15¢ Tugboat (1988)	2	overall
2261	16.7¢ Popcorn Wagon (1988)	1, 2	untagged
1906	17¢ Electric Auto (1981)	1, 2, 3, 4, 5, 6, 7	overall
1906a	17¢ Electric Auto (1981)	1, 2, 3, 4, 5, 6, 7	untagged
2135	17¢ Dog Sled (1986)	2	block
2262	17.5¢ Racing Car (1987)	1	block
2262a	17.5¢ Racing Car (1987)	1	untagged
1907	18¢ Surrey (1981)	1, 2, 3, 4, 5, 6, 7, 8, 9, 10, 11, 12, 13, 14, 15, 16, 17, 18	overall
1908	20¢ Fire Pumper (1981)	1, 2, 3, 4, 5, 6, 7, 8, 9, 10, 11, 12, 13, 14, 15, 16	overall
2263	20¢ Cable Car (1988)	1, 2	block
2263b	20¢ Cable Car (1990)	2	overall
2463	20¢ Cog Railway (1995)	1, 2	prephosphored
2264	20.5¢ Fire Engine (1988)	1	untagged

Scott number	Stamp	Plate number	Tagging type
2265	21¢ Railroad Mail Car (1988)	1, 2	untagged
2464	23¢ Lunch Wagon (1991)	2, 3	prephosphored[17]
2464a	23¢ Lunch Wagon (1993)	3, 4, 5	prephosphored[2]
2464b	23¢ Lunch Wagon (1991)	2, 3	prephosphored
2266	24.1¢ Tandem Bicycle (1988)	1	untagged
2136	25¢ Bread Wagon (1986)	1, 2, 3, 4, 5	block
2466	32¢ Ferryboat (1995)	2, 3, 4, 5	prephosphored[13]
2466b	32¢ Ferryboat (1995)	5	prephosphored
2468	$1 Seaplane (1990)	1	overall[28]
2468b	$1 Seaplane (1993)	3	prephosphored[1]
2468c	$1 Seaplane (1998)	3	prephosphored[19]

American Transportation coil stamps

Scott number	Stamp	Plate number	Tagging type
2905	(10¢) Auto (1995)	S111, S222	untagged[12]
2905a	(10¢) Auto (1996)	S333	untagged
2906	(10¢) Auto (1996)	S111	untagged[12]
3229	(10¢) Green Bicycle (1998)	S111	untagged[23, 25]
3228	(10¢) Green Bicycle (1998)	111, 221, 222, 333, 344, 444, 555	untagged[21, 23, 24]
3228a	(10¢) Green Bicycle (1998)	666, 777, 888, 999	untagged

Special services self-adhesive panes

Scott number	Stamp	Denomination	Number of subjects	Total value	Date of issue	Plate numbers	Notes
3261	Shuttle Landing	$3.20	20	$64.00	11/9/98	B1111, B2222, B3333	15
3262	Shuttle Piggyback	$11.75	20	$235.00	11/19/98	B11111, B22222, B33333	15
3472	Capitol Dome	$3.50	20	$70.00	1/29/01	B1111, B2222	
3647	Jefferson Memorial	$3.85	20	$77.00	7/30/02	B1111	
3647A	Jefferson Memorial	$3.85	20	$77.00	12/03	S11111	
3473	Washington Monument	$12.25	20	$245.00	1/29/01	B1111	
3648	Capitol at Dusk	$13.65	20	$273.00	7/30/02	B1111	

National Symbols coil stamps

Scott number	Stamp	Plate number	Tagging type
3615	3¢ Star (2002)	S111	untagged

340

Scott number	Stamp	Plate number	Tagging type
2602	(10¢) Eagle & Shield (1991) "Bulk Rate USA"	A11111, A11112, A12213, A21112, A21113, A22112, A22113, A32333, A33333, A33334, A33335, A34424, A34426, A43324, A43325, A43326, A43334, A43335, A43426, A53335, A54444, A54445, A77777, A88888, A88889, A89999, A99998,	untagged
2602	(10¢) Eagle & Shield (1991) "Bulk Rate USA" (continued)	A99999, A1010101010, A1011101010, A1011101011, A1011101012, A1110101010, A1110101011, A1110111110, A1111101010, A1111111010, A1211101010, A1411101010, A1411101011, A1412111110, A1412111111	
2603	(10¢) Eagle & Shield "USA Bulk Rate" (1993)	11111, 22221, 22222, 33333, 44444	untagged[9]
2603b	(10¢) Eagle & Shield "USA Bulk Rate" (1993)	11111, 22221, 22222	tagged error
2604	(10¢) Eagle & Shield (gold) "USA Bulk Rate" (1993)	S11111, S22222	untagged[16]
2907	(10¢) Eagle & Shield (1996)	S11111	untagged[12]
3270	(10¢) Eagle & Shield "USA Presorted Std" (1998)	11111	untagged
3270a	(10¢) Eagle & Shield "USA Presorted Std" (1998)	22222	untagged
3271	(10¢) Eagle & Shield "USA Presorted Std" (1998)	11111, 22222	untagged[21, 22, 24]
3271a	(10¢) Eagle & Shield "USA Presorted Std" (1998)	33333	untagged[21, 22, 24]
3271b	(10¢) Eagle & Shield "Presorted Std"	11111	tagged error[21, 22, 24]
2149	18¢ Washington (1985)	1112, 3333	block
2149a	18¢ Washington (1985)	11121, 33333, 43444	untagged[10]
3475	21¢ Bison (2001)	V1111, V2222	prephosphored
3263	22¢ Uncle Sam (1998)	1111	prephosphored[21]
3353	22¢ Uncle Sam (1999)	1111	prephosphored[21]
2606	23¢ USA Presort (1992) (dark blue)	A1111, A2222, A2232, A2233, A3333, A4364, A4443, A4444, A4453	untagged
2607	23¢ USA Presort (1992) (light blue)	1111	untagged[2]
2608	23¢ USA Presort (1993) (violet blue)	S111	untagged
3475A	23¢ George Washington (2001)	B11	prephosphored

Scott number	Stamp	Plate number	Tagging type
3617	23¢ George Washington (2002)	V11, V13, V21, V22, V24, V35 , **V36, V45, V46**	prephosphored
3801a	(25¢) American Eagle (2003)	S1111111, S2222222, S3333333	prephosphored
3853a	**(25¢) American Eagle (2004)**	**S1111111**	**prephosphored**
3452	(34¢) Statue of Liberty (2000)	1111	prephosphored
3453	(34¢) Statue of Liberty (2000)	1111	prephosphored
3466	34¢ Statue of Liberty (2001)	1111, 2222	prephosphored
3476	34¢ Statue of Liberty (2001)	1111	prephosphored
3477	34¢ Statue of Liberty (2001)	1111, 2222, 3333, 4444, 5555, 6666, 7777	prephosphored
3550	34¢ United We Stand (2001)	1111, 2222, 3333	prephosphored
3550A	34¢ United We Stand (2001)	1111	prephosphored

National Symbols panes

Scott number	Stamp	Denomi-nation	Number of subjects	Total value	Date of issue	Plate numbers	Notes
3613	Star	3¢	50	$1.50	6/7/02	B111, B222, B333, B444	
3614	Star	3¢	50	$1.50	6/7/02	B111	
3482a	George Washington	20¢	10	$2.00	2/22/01	P1, P2, P3	
3483c/f	George Washington	20¢	10	$2.00	2/22/01	P1, P2, P3	
3484d	Bison	21¢	10	$2.10	2/22/01	P111111, P222222, P333333, P444444, P555555	
3484Ag/j	Bison	21¢	10	$2.10	2/22/01	P111111, P222222, P333333, P444444, P555555	
3467	Bison	21¢	100	$21.00	9/20/01	P111111	
3468	Bison	21¢	20	$4.20	2/22/01	V1111, V1112, V2222	
3259	Uncle Sam	22¢	20	$4.40	11/9/98	S1111	15
3468A	George Washington	23¢	20	$4.60	9/20/01	B111, B222, B333	
3616	George Washington	23¢	100	$23.00	6/7/02	P1	
3618c	George Washington	23¢	10	$2.30	6/7/02	P1, P2, P3, **P4**	
3619e-f	George Washington	23¢	10	$2.30	6/7/02	P1	
3819	George Washington	23¢	20	$4.60	10/03	V11	
2431a	Eagle & Shield	25¢	18	$4.50	11/10/89	A1111	1, 2, 3

Scott number	Stamp	Denomination	Number of subjects	Total value	Date of issue	Plate numbers	Notes
2595a	Eagle & Shield	29¢	17	$4.93	9/25/92	B1111-1, B1111-2, B2222-1, B2222-2, B3333-1, B3333-3, B3434-1, B3434-3, B4344-1, B4344-3, B4444-1, B4444-3	3, 6, 7
2596a	Eagle & Shield	29¢	7	$4.93	19/25/92	D11111, D21221, D22322, D32322, D32332, D32342, D42342, D43352, D43452, D43453, D54561, D54563, D54571, D54573, D54673, D61384, D65784	3, 6, 7
2597a	Eagle & Shield	29¢	17	$4.93	9/25/92	S1111	3, 6, 7
2598a	Eagle	29¢	18	$5.22	2/4/94	M111, M112	5
2599a	Statue of Liberty	29¢	18	$5.22	6/24/94	D1111, D1212	5
3122a	Statue of Liberty	32¢	20	$6.40	2/1/97	V1111, V1211, V1311, V2122, V2222, V2311, V2331, V3233, V3333, V3513, V4532	13, 14, 16
3122E	Statue of Liberty	32¢	20	$6.40	2/1/97	V1111, V1211, V2122, V2222	14, 16, 18
3451a	Statue of Liberty	(34¢)	20	$6.80	12/15/00	V1111, V2222	
3485a	Statue of Liberty	34¢	10	$3.40	2/7/01	V1111, V1221, V2222	
3485b	Statue of Liberty	34¢	20	$6.80	2/7/01	V1111, V1211, V1221, V2111, V2121, V2122, V2212, V2222	
3549a	United We Stand	34¢	20	$6.80	10/24/01	B1111, B2222, B3333, B4444	
3549Be	United We Stand	34¢	20	$6.80	1/?/02	S1111	
3471	Art Deco Eagle	55¢	20	$11.00	2/22/01	S11111	
3471A	Art Deco Eagle	57¢	20	$11.40	9/20/01	S11111	
3646	Coverlet Eagle	60¢	20	$12.00	7/12/02	P1111, P2222, P3333, P4444, **P6666, P7777**	

Flag coil stamps

Scott number	Stamp	Plate number	Tagging type
1891	18¢ Sea to Shining Sea (1981)	1, 2, 3, 4, 5, 6, 7	block
1895	20¢ Flag Over Supreme Court (1981)	1, 2, 3, 4, 5, 6, 8, 9, 10, 12, 13, 14	block
1895e	20¢ Flag Over Supreme Court precanceled (1984)	14	untagged
2115	22¢ Flag Over Capitol Dome (1985)	1, 2, 3, 4, 5, 6, 7, 8, 10, 11, 12, 13, 14, 15, 16, 17, 18, 19, 20, 21, 22	block

Scott number	Stamp	Plate number	Tagging type
2115a	22¢ Flag Over Capitol Dome (1985)	**1, 3, 5, 7, 8, 11, 12, 17 18, 19, 20, 22**	prephosphored
2115b	**22¢ Flag Over Capitol Dome (1985)**	**18, 20, 22**	**block**
2115c	**22¢ Flag Over Capitol Dome (1987)**	**1**	**prephosphored**
2605	23¢ Flag Presort (1991)	A111, A112, A122, A212, A222, A333	untagged
2280	25¢ Flag Over Yosemite (1988)	1, 2, 3, 4, 5, 7, 8, 9	block
2280	25¢ Flag Over Yosemite (1989)	1, 2, 3, 5, 6, 7, 8, 9, 10, 11, 12, 13, 14, 15	prephosphored
2523	29¢ Flag Over Mount Rushmore (1991)	1, 2, 3, 4, 5, 6, 7, 8, 9	prephosphored
2523A	29¢ Flag Over Mount Rushmore (1991) (gravure)	A111111, A222211	prephosphored
2609	29¢ Flag Over White House (1992)	1, 2, 3, 4, 5, 6, 7, 8, 9, 10, 11, 12, 13, 14, 15, 16, 18	prephosphored
2913	32¢ Flag Over Porch (1995)	11111, 22221, 22222, 22322, 33333, 34333, 44444, 45444, 66646, 66666, 77767, 78767, 91161, 99969	prephosphored[14]
2914	32¢ Flag Over Porch (1995)	S11111	prephosphored[12]
2915	32¢ Flag Over Porch (1995)	V11111	prephosphored
2915A	32¢ Flag Over Porch (1996)	11111, 22222, 23222, 33333, 44444, 45444, 55555, 66666, 78777, 87888, 87898, 88888, 88898, 89878, 89888, 89898, 89899, 97898, 99899, 99999, 11111A, 13211A, 13231A, 13311A, 22222A, 33333A, 44444A, 55555A, 66666A, 77777A, 78777A, 88888A	prephosphored[1, 2]
2915B	32¢ Flag Over Porch (1996)	S11111	prephosphored[12]
2915C	32¢ Flag Over Porch (1996)	55555, 66666, 88888	prephosphored
2915D	32¢ Flag Over Porch (1997)	11111	prephosphored
3133	32¢ Flag Over Porch (1997)	M11111	prephosphored
3280	33¢ Flag Over City (1999)	1111, 2222	prephosphored
3280a	33¢ Flag Over City (1999)	3333	prephosphored
3281	33¢ Flag Over City (1999) (large date)	6666, 7777, 8888, 9999, 1111A, 2222A, 3333A, 4444A, 5555A, 6666A, 7777A, 8888A, 1111B, 2222B	prephosphored
3281c	33¢ Flag Over City (1999) (small date)	1111, 2222, 3333, 3433, 4443, 4444, 5555, 9999A	prephosphored
3282	33¢ Flag Over City (1999)	1111, 2222	prephosphored

Scott number	Stamp	Plate number	Tagging type
3622	(37¢) Flag (2002)	1111, 2222	prephosphored
3631	37¢ Flag (2002)	S1111	prephosphored
3632	37¢ Flag (2002)	1111, 2222, 3333, 4444, 5555, 6666, **7777, 8888, 9999, 1111A, 2222A, 3333A, 4444A, 5555A**	prephosphored
3632A	37¢ Flag (2003)	S1111, S2222, S3333, **S4444**	prephosphored
3632Ae	**37¢ Flag (2003)**	**S1111, S3333, S4444**	**prephosphored**
3632C	**37¢ Flag (2004)**	**S1111**	**prephosphored**
3633	37¢ Flag (2002)	B1111	prephosphored
3633A	37¢ Flag (2003)	B1111	prephosphored

Flag panes

Scott number	Stamp	Denomination	Number of subjects	Total value	Date of issue	Plate numbers	Notes
2920a	Flag Over Porch	32¢	20	$6.40	4/18/95	V12211, V12212, V12312, V12321, V12322, V12331, V13322, V13831, V13834, V13836, V22211, V23322, V23422, V23432, V23522, V34743, V34745, V36743, V42556, V45554, V54663, V56663, V56665, V56763, V57663, V65976, V78989	5, 9, 10, 11, 16
2920c	Flag Over Porch	32¢	20	$6.40	4/18/95	V11111	16
2920De	Flag Over Porch	32¢	10	$3.20	1/20/96	V11111, V12111, V23222, V31121, V32111, V32121, V44322, V44333, V44444, V55555, V66666, V66886, V67886, V68886, V68896, V76989, V77666, V77668, V77766, V77776, V78698, V78886, V78896, V78898, V78986, V78989, V89999	10
3278	Flag Over City	33¢	15	$6.60	2/25/99	V1111, V1211, V2222	14, 15
3278d	Flag Over City	33¢	10	$3.30	2/25/99	V1111, V1112, V1113, V2222, V2322, V2324, V3433, V3434, V3545	14
3278e	Flag Over City	33¢	20	$6.60	2/25/99	V1111, V1211, V2122, V2222, V2223, V3333, V4444, V8789	14, 16

Scott number	Stamp	Denomination	Number of subjects	Total value	Date of issue	Plate numbers	Notes
3278Fg	Flag Over City	33¢	20	$6.60	2/25/99	V1111, V1131, V2222, V2223, V2227, V2243, V2323, V2423, V2443, V3333, V4444, V5428, V5445, V5446, V5576, V5578, V6423, V6456, V6546, V6556, V6575, V6576, V7567, V7663, V7667, V7676, V8789	14, 16
3278j	Flag Over City	33¢	10	$3.30	1999	V1111, V1112, V1113, V2222	
3449	Flag Over Farm	33¢	20	$6.60	12/15/00	P1111, P2222, P3333	
3469	Flag Over Farm	34¢	100	$34.00	2/7/01	P1111, P2222	
3470	Flag Over Farm	34¢	20	$6.80	3/6/01	P1111, P2222, P3333, P4444, P5555	
3620	Flag	(37¢)	100	$37.00	6/7/02	P1111	
3621	Flag	(37¢)	20	$7.40	6/7/02	P1111, P2222, P3333	
3623a	Flag	(37¢)	20	$7.40	6/7/02	B1111, B2222, B3333, B4444, B5555	
3624c	Flag	(37¢)	0	$7.40	26/7/02	S1111	
3629F	Flag	37¢	100	$37.00	11/24/03	P1111	
3630	Flag	37¢	20	$7.40	6/7/02	P1111, P2222, P3333, P4444, P5555	
3634a	Flag	37¢	10	$3.70	6/7/02	V1111	
3635a	Flag	37¢	20	$7.40	6/7/02	B1111, B2222, B3333, B4444, B5555, B6666, B7777	
3636c	Flag	37¢	20	$7.40	6/7/02	S1111, S2222, S3333, S44444, S5555	
3636D	**Flag**	**37¢**	**20**	**$7.40**	**7/04**	**V1111**	

Nondenominated rate-change coil stamps

Scott number	Stamp	Plate number	Tagging type
2112	D (22¢) Eagle (1985)	1, 2	block
O139	D (22¢) Official (1985)	1	block
2279	E (25¢) Earth (1988)	1111, 1211, 1222, 2222	block
2518	F (29¢) Flower (1991)	1111, 1211, 1222, 2211, 2222	prephosphored
2893	G (5¢) Old Glory (1995) nonprofit	A11111, A21111	untagged
2888	G (25¢) Old Glory (1994) presort	S11111	prephosphored
2886	G (32¢) Old Glory (1994)	V11111	prephosphored
2889	G (32¢) Old Glory (1994)	1111, 2222	prephosphored

346

Scott number	Stamp	Plate number	Tagging type
2890	G (32¢) Old Glory (1994)	A1111, A1112, A1113, A1211, A1212, A1222, A1311, A1313, A1314, A1324, A1417, A1433, A2211, A2212, A2213, A2214, A2223, A2313, A3113, A3114, A3314, A3315, A3323, A3324, A3423, A3426, A3433, A3435, A3436, A4426, A4427, A4435, A5327, A5417, A5427, A5437	prephosphored
2891	G (32¢) Old Glory (1994)	S1111	prephosphored[11]
2892	G (32¢) Old Glory (1994)	S1111, S2222	prephosphored
3264	H (33¢) Hat (1998)	1111, 3333, 3343, 3344, 3444	prephosphored[25, 26]
3265	H (33¢) Hat (1998)	1111, 1131, 1141, 2222, 3333	prephosphored[21]
3266	H (33¢) Hat (1998)	1111	prephosphored[21, 22, 23, 27]

Nondenominated rate-change panes

Scott number	Stamp	Denomi-nation	Total value	Number of subjects	Date of issue	Plate numbers	Notes
2883a	**G**	**(32¢)**	**$3.20**	**10**	**12/13/94**	**2222**	**5**
2886a	G	(32¢)	$5.76	18	12/13/94	V11111, V22222	5
3268a	H (Hat)	(33¢)	$3.30	10	11/9/98	V1111, V1211, V2211, V2222	
3268b	H (Hat)	(33¢)	$6.60	20	11/9/98	V1111, V1112, V1113, V1122, V1213, V1222, V2113,V2122, V2213, V2222, V2223	16

American Scenes coil stamps

Scott number	Stamp	Plate number	Tagging type
2902	(5¢) Butte (1995)	S111, S222, S333	untagged[12]
2902B	(5¢) Butte (1996)	S111	untagged[12]
2903	(5¢) Mountains (1996)	11111	untagged
2904	(5¢) Mountains (1996)	S111	untagged
2904A	(5¢) Mountains (1996)	V222222, V333323, V333333, V333342, V333343	untagged[12]
2904B	(5¢) Mountains (1997)	1111	untagged[11, 21, 23, 24]
3207	(5¢) Wetlands (1998)	S1111	untagged
3207A	(5¢) Wetlands (1998)	1111, 2222, 3333, 4444, 5555, 6666	untagged[11, 21, 22, 23]
3207Ab	**(5¢) Wetlands (1998)**	**5555, 6666**	**untagged**
3693	(5¢) Sea Coast (2002)	B111	prephosphored
3775	(5¢) Sea Coast (2003)	B111	untagged
3785	(5¢) Sea Coast (2003)	P1111	untagged

Scott number	Stamp	Plate number	Tagging type
3785a	(5¢) Sea Coast (2004)	P2222	untagged
3864	(5¢) Sea Coast (2004)	S1111	untagged
3874	(5¢) Sea Coast (2004)	P2222, P3333	untagged
3874a	(5¢) Sea Coast Small "2003"	P3333	untagged
3875	(5¢) Sea Coast (2004)	S1111	untagged

American Design coil stamps

Scott number	Stamp	Plate number	Tagging type
3757	1¢ Tiffany Lamp	S11111	untagged
3612	5¢ American Toleware	S1111111	untagged

American Design panes

Scott number	Stamp	Denomi-nation	Total value	Number of subjects	Date of issue	Plate number	Notes
3750	Chippendale Chair	4¢	20	$0.80	3/5/04	P1111	
3750A	American Toleware (2004)	5¢	20	$1.00	6/25/04	S1111111	
3751	American Clock	10¢	20	$2.00	1/24/03	P1111, P2222	

American Culture coil stamps

Scott number	Stamp	Plate number	Tagging type
3447	(10¢) Lion Statue (2000)	S11111, S22222 S33333, S44444, S77777	untagged
3447a	(10¢) Lion Statue (2004)	S55555	untagged
3769	(10¢) Lion Statue (2003)	S11111, S22222, S33333, S44444, S55555	untagged
3520	(10¢) Atlas Statue (2001)	B1111	untagged
3770	(10¢) Atlas Statue (2003)	V11111, V11222, V12111, V12222, V21111, V22111, V22222	untagged
2908	(15¢) Tail Fin (1995)	11111	untagged
2909	(15¢) Tail Fin (1995)	S11111	untagged[12]
2910	(15¢) Tail Fin (1996)	S11111	untagged[12]
3522	(15¢) Woody Wagon (2001)	S11111	untagged
2911	(25¢) Jukebox (1995) "Presorted First-Class"	111111, 212222, 222222, 332222	untagged
2912	(25¢) Jukebox (1995) "Presorted First-Class"	S11111, S22222	untagged[12]
2912A	(25¢) Jukebox (1997) "Presorted First-Class"	S11111, S22222	untagged[21, 22, 23, 24, 27]
2912B	(25¢) Jukebox (1997) "Presorted First-Class"	111111, 222222	untagged[21, 22, 23, 24, 27]

348

Scott number	Stamp	Plate number	Tagging type
3132	(25¢) Jukebox (1997)	M11111	untagged
3208	(25¢) Diner (1998) "Presorted First-Class"	S11111	untagged[23, 25]
3208A	(25¢) Diner (1998) "Presorted First-Class"	11111, 22211, 22222, 33333, 44444, 55555	prephosphored untagged[21, 22, 23, 24, 27]

American Culture panes

Scott number	Stamp	Denomination	Number of subjects	Total value	Date of issue	Plate numbers	Notes
3766	Wisdom	$1	20	$20.00	2/28/03	P22222, **P33333**	

Flora and Fauna coil stamps

Scott number	Stamp	Plate number	Tagging type
3044	1¢ Kestrel (1996)	1111	untagged[29]
3044	1¢ Kestrel (1996-99)	1111	untagged[30]
3044a	1¢ Kestrel (1999)	1111, 2222, 3333, 4444	untagged[31]
3045	2¢ Woodpecker	11111, 22222	untagged
3053	20¢ Blue Jay (1996)	S1111	prephosphored
3055	20¢ Pheasant (1998)	1111, 2222	prephosphored[21]
2281	25¢ Honey Bee (1988)	1, 2	block
2525	29¢ Flower (1991)	S1111, S2222	prephosphored
2526	29¢ Flower (1992)	S2222	prephosphored
2491	29¢ Pine Cone (1993)	B1	prephosphored
2598	29¢ Eagle (1994)	111	prephosphored
2599	29¢ Statue of Liberty (1994)	D1111	prephosphored
2492	32¢ Pink Rose (1995)	S111	prephosphored
2495-95A	32¢ Peach/Pear (1995)	V11111	prephosphored
3054	32¢ Yellow Rose (1997)	1111, 1112, 1122, 2222, 2223, 2233, 2333, 3344, 3444, 4455, 5455, 5555, 5556, 5566, 5666, 6666, 6677, 6777, 7777, 8888	prephosphored[1, 2]
3302-05	33¢ Four Fruit Berries (1999)	B1111, B1112, B2211, B2221, B2222	prephosphored[1, 2]
3404-07	33¢ Four Fruit Berries (2000) linerless	G1111	prephosphored
3462-65	(34¢) Four Flowers (2000)	B1111	prephosphored
3478-81	34¢ Four Flowers (2001)	B1111, B2111, B2122, B2211, B2222	prephosphored

Flora and Fauna panes

Scott number	Stamp	Denomination	Number of subjects	Total value	Date of issue	Plate numbers	Notes
3031	Kestrel	1¢	50	$0.50	11/19/99	1111, 2222, 2322, 4444, 5555, 5655, 6666, 6766, 7777, 8888, 9999, 1111A, 2222A, 3222A, 3322A, 4322A, 4333A, 4433A, 5433A, 5544A, 5644A, 6755A, 6766A, 7777A, 8888A, 9999A, 1111B, 2222B, 3333B, 4444B, 5555B, **8888B**, 9999B, 1111C	15
3031A	Kestrel	1¢	50	$0.50	10/2000	B111111, B222222, B333333, B444444, B555555	
3048a	Blue Jay	20¢	10	$2.00	8/2/96	S1111, S2222	10, 14
3050a	Pheasant	20¢	10	$2.00	7/31/98	V1111, V2222, V2232, V2342, V2343, V3232, V3233	14
3050c	Pheasant	20¢	10	$2.00	7/31/98	V2232, V2332, V2333, V2342, V2343, V3232, V3243, V3333	
3051A	Pheasant	20¢	10	$2.00	7/31/98	V1111	
2489a	Red Squirrel	29¢	18	$5.22	6/25/93	D11111, D22211, D22221, D22222, D23133	3
2490a	Red Rose	29¢	18	$5.22	8/19/93	S111	3, 4
2491a	Pine Cone	29¢	18	$5.22	11/5/93	B1, B2, B3, B4, B5, B6, B7, B8, B9, B10, B11, B12, B13, B14, B15, B16	5
2492a	Pink Rose	32¢	20	$6.40	6/2/95	S111, S112, S333, S444, S555	5, 9, 10
2494a	Peach/Pear	32¢	20	$6.40	7/8/95	V11111, V11122, V11131, V11132, V11232, V12131, V12132, V12211, V12221, V12232, V22212, V22221, V22222, V33142, V33143, V33243, V33323, V33333, V33343, V33353, V33363, V33453, V44424, V44434, V44454, V45434, V45464, V54365, V54565, V55365, V55565	5, 9, 10
3127a	Botanical Prints	32¢	20	$6.40	3/3/97	S11111, S22222, S33333	14, 16
3049a	Yellow Rose	32¢	20	$6.40	10/24/96	S1111, S2222	
3052d	Coral Rose	33¢	20	$6.60	8/13/99	S111, S222	14, 16

Scott number	Stamp	Denomination	Number of subjects	Total value	Date of Plate numbers		Notes
3052Ef	Pink Coral Rose	33¢	20	$6.60	4/7/00	S111, S222, S333	14, 16
3297b	Fruit Berries	33¢	20	$6.60	4/10/99	B1111, B1112, B2211, B2222, B3331, B3332, B3333, B4444, B5555	14, 16
3297d	Fruit Berries	33¢	20	$6.60	3/15/00	B1111	
3457e	Four Flowers	(34¢)	20	$6.80	12/15/00	S1111	
3461b	Four Flowers	(34¢)	20	$6.80	12/15/00	S1111	
3461c	Four Flowers	(34¢)	20	$6.80	12/15/00	S1111	
3490e	Four Flowers	34¢	20	$6.80	2/7/01	S1111, S2222	
3492b	Apple & Orange	34¢	20	$6.80	3/6/01	B1111, B2222, B3333, B4444, B5555, B6666, B7777	
3036	Red Fox	$1	20	$20.00	8/14/98	B1111, B3333	15
3036a	Red Fox	$1	20	$20.00	2002	B1111	

Holiday and Love coil stamps

Scott number	Stamp	Plate number	Tagging type
2799a	29¢ Snowman (1993)	V1111111	prephosphored
2813	29¢ Sunrise Love (1994)	B1	prephosphored
2873	29¢ Christmas Santa (1994)	V1111	prephosphored
3014-17	32¢ Santa/Children with Toys (1995)	V1111	prephosphored
3018	32¢ Midnight Angel (1995)	B1111	prephosphored
3683a	37¢ Snowmen (2002)	G1111, G1112	prephosphored

Holiday and Love panes

Scott number	Stamp	Denomination	Number of subjects	Total value	Date of Plate numbers		Notes
2802a	Christmas	29¢	12	$3.48	10/28/93	V111-1111, V222-1222, V222-2112, V222-2122, V222-2221, V222-2222, V333-3333	5
2813a	Sunrise Love	29¢	18	$5.22	1/27/94	B111-1, B111-2, B111-3, B111-4, B111-5, B121-5, B221-5, B222-4, B222-5, B222-6, B333-5, B333-7, B333-8, B333-9, B333-10, B333-11, B333-12, B333-14, B333-17, B334-11, B344-11, B344-12, B344-13, B434-10, B444-7, B444-8, B444-9, B444-10, B444-13, B444-14, B444-15, B444-16, B444-17, B444-18, B444-19, B555-20, B555-21	5

Scott number	Stamp	Denomination	Number of subjects	Total value	Date of Plate numbers		Notes
2873a	Christmas	29¢	12	$3.48	10/20/94	V1111	5
2949a	Love Cherub	(32¢)	20	$6.40	2/1/95	B1111-1, B2222-1, B2222-2, B3333-2	16
3011a	Santa/Children with Toys	32¢	20	$6.40	9/30/95	V1111, V1211, V1212, V3233, V3333, V4444	5, 16
3012a	Midnight Angel	32¢	20	$6.40	10/19/95	B1111, B2222, B33333	5, 10, 16
3030a	Love Cherub	32¢	20	$6.40	1/20/96	B1111-1, B1111-2, B2222-1, B2222-2, B3333-1, B3333-3, B3434-1, B3434-3, B4344-1, B4344-3, B4444-1, B4444-3	16
3112a	Madonna and Child	32¢	20	$6.40	11/1/96	1111-1, 1211-1, 2212-1, 2222-1, 2323-1, 3323-1, 3333-1, 3334-1, 4444-1, 5544-1, 5555-1, 5556-1, 5556-2, 5656-2, 6656-2, 6666-1, 6666-2, 6766-1, 7887-1, 7887-2, 7888-2, 7988-2	16
3116a	Family Scenes	32¢	20	$6.40	10/8/96	B1111, B2222, B3333	16
3118	Hanukkah	32¢	20	$6.40	10/22/96	V11111	15, 17
3123a	Love Swans	32¢	20	$6.40	2/4/97	B1111, B2222, B3333, B4444, B5555, B6666, B7777	16
3175	Kwanzaa	32¢	50	$16.00	10/22/97	V1111	15
3176a	Madonna and Child	32¢	20	$6.40	10/27/97	1111, 2222, 3333	14, 16
3177a	American Holly	32¢	20	$6.40	10/30/97	B1111, B2222, B3333	14, 16
3203	Cinco de Mayo	32¢	20	$6.40	4/16/98	S11111	15
3244a	Madonna and Child	32¢	20	$6.40	10/15/98	11111, 22222, 33333	16
3252c	Wreaths	32¢	20	$6.40	10/15/98	B222222, B333333, B444444, B555555	14, 16
3252e	Wreaths	32¢	20	$6.40	10/15/98	B111111, **B222222**	
3274a	Victorian Love	33¢	20	$6.60	1/28/99	V1111, V1112, V1117, V1118, V1211, V1212, V1213, V1233, V1313, V1314, V1333, V1334, V1335, V2123, V2221, V2222, V2223, V2324, V2424, V2425, V2426, V3123,	15

Scott number	Stamp	Denomi- nation	Number of subjects	Total value	Date of Plate numbers		Notes
3274a	Victorian Love (continued)	33¢	20	$6.60	1/28/99	V3124, V3125, V3133, V3134, V3323, V3327, V3333, V3334, V3336, V4549, V5650	
3309	Cinco de Mayo	33¢	20	$6.60	4/27/99	B111111	15
3352	Hanukkah	33¢	20	$6.60	10/8/99	V11111	15
3355a	Madonna and Child	33¢	20	$6.60	10/20/99	B1111, B2222, B3333	19
3359a	Deer	33¢	20	$6.60	10/20/99	B111111	14, 15
3363a	Deer	33¢	20	$6.60	10/20/99	B111111, B222222, B333333, B444444, B555555, B666666, B777777, B888888, B999999, B000000, BAAAAAA, BBBBBBB	14
3368	Kwanzaa	33¢	20	$6.60	10/29/99	V1111	15
3496a	Rose and Love Letter	(34¢)	20	$6.80	1/19/01	B1111, B2222	
3497a	Rose and Love Letter	34¢	20	$6.80	2/14/01	B1111, B2222, B3333, B4444, B5555	
3532	Eid	34¢	20	$6.80	9/1/01	V111	
3536a	Madonna and Child	34¢	20	$6.80	10/10/01	B1111	
3537-40	Four Santas	34¢	20	$6.80	10/10/01	S1111	
3540d	Four Santas	34¢	20	$6.80	10/10/01	S1111, S3333, S4444	
3540g	Four Santas	34¢	20	$6.80	10/10/01	S1111, S3333, S4444	
3546	We Give Thanks	34¢	20	$6.80	10/19/01	P1111, P2222	
3547	Hanukkah	34¢	20	$6.80	10/21/01	V11111	
3548	Kwanzaa	34¢	20	$6.80	10/21/01	V1111	
3657	Stylized Love	37¢	20	$7.40	8/16/02	B11111, B22222, B33333, B44444, B55555, B66666, B77777	
3658	Stylized Love	60¢	20	$12.00	8/16/02	V11111	
3672	Hanukkah	37¢	20	$7.40	10/10/02	V11111	
3673	Kwanzaa	37¢	20	$7.40	10/10/02	V1111	
3674	Eid	37¢	20	$7.40	10/10/02	V111	
3675a	Madonna and Child	37¢	20	$7.40	10/10/02	B1111, B2222 , **B4444**	
3679a	Snowmen	37¢	20	$7.40	10/28/02	V1111	
3687b	Snowmen	37¢	20	$7.40	10/28/02	S1111, S1113, S2222, S4444	
3695	**Happy Birthday**	**37¢**	**20**	**$7.40**	**10/25/02**	**V1111**	
3820a	Madonna and Child	37¢	20	$7.40	10/23/03	P1111, P2222, P3333, P4444	

Scott number	Stamp	Denomi- nation	Number of subjects	Total value	Date of Plate numbers		Notes
3824b	Music Makers	37¢	20	$7.40	10/23/03	S1111, S2222	
3833a	**Candy Hearts Love**	**37¢**	**20**	**$7.40**	**1/14/04**	**V1111**	
3836	Garden Bouquet	37¢	20	$7.40	3/4/04	**P11111, P22222, P33333 P44444, P55555, P66666, P77777, P88888**	
3879a	Madonna and Child	37¢	20	$7.40	10/14/04	**P1111**	
3880	Hanukkah (Dreidel)	37¢	20	$7.40	10/15/04	**S1111**	
3881	Kwanzaa	37¢	20	$7.40	10/16/04	P111111	
3886a	Holiday Ornaments	37¢	20		11/16/04	S1111	
3886b	Holiday Ornaments	37¢	20		11/16/04	S1111, S2222	
3890b	Holiday Ornaments	37¢	20	$7.30	11/16/04	S11111	
2960a	Love Cherub	55¢	20	$11.00	5/12/95	B1111-1, B2222-1	9, 16
3124a	Love Swans	55¢	20	$11.00	2/4/97	B1111, B2222, B3333, B4444	16
3275	Victorian Love	55¢	20	$11.00	1/28/99	B1111111, B2222222, B3333333	15
3499	Rose and Love Letter	55¢	20	$11.00	2/14/01	B1111	
3551	Rose and Love Letter	57¢	20	$11.40	11/19/01	B11111	
3837	**Garden Blossoms**	**60¢**	**20**	**$12.00**	**3/4/04**	**S11111**	

Distinguished Americans stamps

Scott number	Stamp	Denomi- nation	Total value	Number of subjects	Date of issue	Plate numbers	Notes
3420	Joseph W. Stilwell	10¢	$2.00	20	8/24/00	B11-1	
3422	**Wilma Rudolph**	**23¢**	**$4.60**	**20**	**7/14/04**	**P11-1, P22-1**	
3436c	**Wilma Rudolph**	**23¢**	**$2.30**	**10**	**7/14/04**	**P11, P22**	
3426	Claude Pepper	33¢	$6.60	20	9/7/00	B11-1	
3330	Billy Mitchell	55¢	$11.00	20	7/30/99	B11111, B11211	15
3431	Hattie Caraway	76¢	$15.20	20	2/21/01	B11-1	
3433	Edna Ferber	83¢	$16.60	20	7/29/02	B11-1	
3434	Edna Ferber	83¢	$16.60	20	8/03	P11-1, **P22-1**	

Scenic American Landmarks panes

Scott number	Stamp	Denomination	Number of subjects	Total value	Date of Plate numbers		Notes
C134	Rio Grande	40¢	20	$8.00	7/30/99	V11111	15
C133	Niagara Falls	48¢	20	$9.60	5/12/00	V11111, V22111, V22222	15
C135	Grand Canyon	60¢	20	$12.00	1/20/00	B1111	
C138	Acadia National Park	60¢	20	$12.00	5/30/01	B1111	
C138a	Acadia National Park	60¢	20	$12.00	6/03	B2222	
C136	Nine Mile Prairie	70¢	20	$14.00	3/6/01	P11111, P22222, P33333, **P44444**	
C137	Mount McKinley	80¢	20	$16.00	4/17/01	V11111	

Regular issues 1982-85

Scott number	Stamp	Plate number	Tagging type
2005	20¢ Consumer Education (1982)	1, 2, 3, 4	overall
2150	21.1¢ Letters (1985)	111111, 111121	block
2150a	21.1¢ Letters (1985)	111111, 111121	untagged

Regular issue coil stamps, 1991-94

Scott number	Stamp	Plate number	Tagging type
2529	19¢ Fishing Boat (1991)	A1111, A1112, A1212, A2424	prephosphored
2529a	19¢ Fishing Boat (1993)	A5555, A5556, A6667, A7667, A7679, A7766, A7767, A7779	prephosphored
2529c	19¢ Fishing Boat (1994)	S11	prephosphored

Regular issue coil stamps 2002-04

Scott number	Stamp	Plate number	Tagging type
3640	37¢ Antique Toys (2002)	B11111, B12222	prephosphored
3829	37¢ Snowy Egret (2003)	V1111, V2111, V2222, **V3211, V3212,** V3222	prephosphored
3829A	37¢ Snowy Egret (2004)	P11111, P22222, **P33333, P55555**	prephosphored

Regular issue panes 2002-04

Scott number	Stamp	Denomination	Number of subjects	Total value	Date of Plate numbers		Notes
3629e	Antique Toys	(37¢)	20	$7.40	6/7/02	V1111, V1112, V2222	

Scott number	Stamp	Denomi- nation	Number of subjects	Total value	Date of Plate numbers		Notes
3645e	Antique Toys	37¢	20	$7.40	7/26/02	V1111, V2221, V2222	
3645h	Antique Toys	37¢	20	$7.40	9/3/03	V1111, V1112, V2222	
3784	Purple Heart	37¢	20	$7.40	5/30/03	B1111	
3784A	Purple Heart	37¢	20	$7.40	5/30/03	P1111, P2222, P3333 **P4444, P5555, P7777**	
3830a	**Snowy Egret**	**37¢**	**20**	**$7.40**	**1/30/04**	**P11111, P22222, P33333, P44444, P55555**	

Official coil stamps

Scott number	Stamp	Plate number	Tagging type
O135	20¢ Official (1983)	1	block
O159	37¢ Official (2002)	S111	prephosphored

Variable-denomination coil stamps

Scott number	Stamp	Plate number	Tagging type
CVP31 and CVP31a	variable-denomination coil (1992)	1	prephosphored[8]
CVP31b and CVP31c	variable-denomination coil (1994) (new font)	1	prephosphored[8]
CVP32	variable-denomination (1994)	A11	prephosphored
CVP33	variable-denomination (1996)	11	prephosphored

Test coil stamps

Scott number	Stamp	Plate number	Tagging type
Unassigned	For Testing Purposes Only self-adhesive coil (1996) black on blue printing paper	1111	untagged[12, 18]
Unassigned	For Testing Purposes Only self-adhesive coil (1996) black on white	V1	untagged
Unassigned	For Testing Purposes Only self-adhesive ATM booklet straight-line die cut	V1	untagged
Unassigned	For Testing Purposes Only self-adhesive ATM booklet serpentine die cut gauge 7.8	V1	untagged
Unassigned	For ATM Testing (blue temple) self-adhesive ATM booklet	V1	untagged
Unassigned	Eagle Over Forest sheet (World Stamp Expo 2000)	S1111	untagged
Unassigned	Eagle linerless coil (1997)	1111	untagged

Scott number	Stamp	Plate number	Tagging type
Unassigned	NCR For ATM Testing paper ATM booklet	V1	untagged
Unassigned	For Testing Purposes Only self-adhesive ATM booklet magenta stamps/blue back cover	V1	untagged
Unassigned	29¢ red-rose paper ATM booklet	V1	untagged

Automated teller machine (ATM) panes

Scott number	Stamp	Denomi-nation	Number of subjects	Total value	Date of Plate numbers		Notes
2475a	Stylized Flag	25¢	12	$3.00	5/18/90	—	
2522a	F	(29¢)	12	$3.48	1/22/91	—	
2531Ab	Liberty Torch	29¢	18	$5.22	6/25/91	—	
	(revised back)	29¢	18	$5.22	10/??/92	—	8
2719a	Locomotive	29¢	18	$5.22	1/28/92	V11111	
2803a	Snowman	29¢	18	$5.22	10/28/93	V1111, V2222	
2874a	Cardinal	29¢	18	$5.22	10/20/94	V1111, V2222	
2887a	G	(32¢)	18	$5.76	12/13/97	—	
2919a	Flag Over Field	32¢	18	$5.76	3/17/95	V1111, V1311, V1433, V2111, V2222, V2322	
3013a	Children Sledding	32¢	18	$5.76	10/19/95	V1111	
3117a	Skaters	32¢	18	$5.76	10/8/96	V1111, V2111	
3269a	H	(33¢)	18	$5.94	11/9/98	V1111	
3283a	Flag Over Chalkboard	33¢	18	$5.94	5/13/99	V1111	
3450a	Flag Over Farm	(34¢)	18	$6.12	12/15/00	V1111s	
3495a	Flag Over Farm	34¢	18	$6.12	12/17/01	V1111	
3625a	Flag	(37¢)	18	$6.66	6/7/02	V1111	
3637a	Flag	37¢	18	$6.66	2/4/03	V1111	
3894a	**Holiday Ornaments**	**37¢**	**18**	**$6.66**	**11/16/04**	**V11111**	

Plate number coil notes

1 Shiny gum
2 Plate number 3 shiny and dull gum
3 Service inscribed in black "Nonprofit Org."
4 Service inscribed in black "Nonprofit Org. 5-Digit ZIP+4"
5 Service inscribed in black "Bulk Rate" (between two lines)
6 Service inscribed in red "Bulk Rate Carrier Route Sort"
7 Has two black precancel lines
8 Shiny gum and dull gum
9 22222 shiny and dull gum, 33333 dull gum
10 11121 shiny gum, 33333 and 43444 dull gum
11 Rolls of 3,000 and 10,000 have back numbers
12 Has back numbers
13 2 and 4 shiny gum, 3, 4 and 5 low gloss and shiny gum

14 22221 shiny only and 11111, 22222 shiny and low gloss gum; others low-gloss gum only
15 2 dull gum, 3 dull and shiny gum, 6 shiny gum
16 S22222 has back numbers
17 Plate number 2 dull gum, 3 shiny dull, 4 shiny
18 Tagged paper printed with three layers of opaque white
19 3 low-gloss gum
20 Shiny gum, new white paper on 2¢ Locomotive
21 Die cut, equivalent to perf 10
22 Stamps spaced on backing paper
23 Back numbers, can be both top and bottom
24 Self-adhesive
25 Water-activated gum
26 Roll of 100, has shinier gum, plate numbers (1111) nearly touch "st-Cl" of "First-Class" on roll of 100, 1998 is ½mm farther to right of perforations as compared to roll of 3,000
27 Rounded corners (all four) are found only on spaced self-adhesive stamps
28 New white paper and shinier gum on $1 Seaplane with plate number 3
29 Process-color plate number digits ordered black, yellow, cyan and magenta
30 Process-color plate number digits ordered black, cyan, yellow and magenta
31 Process-color plate number digits ordered yellow, magenta, cyan and black
32 Luminescent ink
33 Plate number 1 dull gum, plate number 2 low-gloss gum

Notes for self-adhesive panes

1 Selling price was $5, which included a 50¢ surcharge. On September 7, 1990, the USPS announced it was sending 400,000 Eagle & Shield stamps to the U.S. Forces in the Persian Gulf Area. The selling price would be $4.50, thus eliminating the surcharge.
2 Plate numbers are in two positions, upper left and lower right.
3 Also available in coil format.
4 There are two different UPC bar codes on the back of the liner. The correct one is 16694. The other one, 16691, is the number for the African Violets booklet.
5 Also available in coil format with plate number.
6 When originally issued, the selling price was $5 (7¢ surcharge). The Postal Bulletin dated February 18, 1993, announced that beginning March 1, 1993, the new selling price would be $4.93, thus removing the surcharge.
7 The pane contains 17 stamps and one label the same size as the stamps.
8 Originally printed on prephosphored paper with and without a lacquer coating. When reissued with the revised back in October 1992, the panes were tagged on press (overall tagged). See Linn's Stamp News December 7, 1992, issue.
9 The Peach/Pear, Flag Over Porch, and the Pink Rose all have reorder labels in the lower right corner of the pane. To discourage the use of these labels as postage, later printings had a target and x die cut into the label. The Peach/Pear V12131, V33323 and V33333 exist both plain & die cut, while V33353 and higher numbers exist die cut only. The Flag Over Porch V23322 and V23422 exist both plain and die cut, while V12331, V13831, V13834, V13836, V23522, V34743, V34745, V36743, V42556, V45554, V56663, V56665, V56763, V57663, V65976 and V78989 exist die cut only. The Pink Rose S444 exists both plain and die cut while S555 exists die cut only. The 55¢ Love Cherub B2222-1 exists die cut only.
10 In 1996, to lower costs, USPS instructed printers that printing on the inside of the liners was no longer required. Several sheetlets that were originally issued with printed liners had unprinted liners on later releases. The following issues can be found with both printed and unprinted liners: 20¢ Blue Jay (S1111 and S2222 both ways); 32¢ Love Cherub (B2222-1 and B2222-2 both ways); 32¢ Pink Rose (S555 both ways); 32¢ Flag Over Porch (V23322, V23422, V42556 and V45554 both ways; V13831, V13834, V13836, V23522, V34745, V36743, V56663, V56763, V57663, V65976 and V78989 with unprinted liners only). The Flag Over Porch panes of 10 have unprinted liners on any panes with plate number V44322 or higher. The original Midnight Angel (B1111 and B2222) have printed liners while the reissue (B3333) has an unprinted liner.
11 In 1997 the printing on the back of the pane was changed to "NATIONAL DOMESTIC VIOLENCE HOTLINE." The original inscription was "Stamps etc." Plate V34745 exists

with both backings, while V36743, V56663, V56763, V57663 and V78989 exist only with the new backing. All other plates were printed with the original "Stamps etc." inscription.

12 There are three different back printings: "108th Tournament of Roses Parade," "Kids! Start Stampin!" and "Delivering the Gift of Life The National Marrow Donor Program." Both S1111 and S2222 are available with all three printings.

13 There are two different back printings: "Stamps etc." and "NATIONAL DOMESTIC VIOLENCE HOTLINE." Plate number V3333 exists with "Stamps etc." only; V1311, V2222, V2311, V2331, V3233, V3513 and V4532 are found with "NATIONAL DOMESTIC VIOLENCE HOTLINE" only. Plate numbers V1111, V1211 and V2122 can be found with both.

14 Also available in a folded version for vending-machine use: Blue Jay ($2.00), Ring-Necked Pheasant ($2.00), Yellow Rose ($4.80 and $9.60), Statue of Liberty ($4.80 and $9.60), Botanical Prints ($4.80) and American Holly ($4.80 and $9.60), Wreaths ($4.80), Flag Over City ($4.95), Fruit Berries ($4.95), Coral Rose ($4.95) and Deer ($4.95).

15 Each pane contains four plate numbers, in selvage adjacent to corner position stamps.

16 The pane contains 20 stamps and one label the same size as the stamps.

17 The reissue has a different style die cut in the backing paper than the original.

18 There are two different back printings: "Stamps etc." and "National Domestic Violence Hotline." Plate numbers V1111 and V2222 exist with "National Domestic Violence Hotline" only. Plate numbers V1211 and V2122 can be found with both.

19 Stamps are printed on both sides of the pane (single liner between them). Plate number is only present on one of two sides. Also includes a label identifying issue and the price of the pane.

20 Initially, the Breast Cancer semipostal stamp was valued at 32¢ for postage and 8¢ for cancer research. Effective with the 1999 rate change, this changed to 33¢ for postage and 7¢ for cancer research.

21 Exists with and without a special die cut for philatelic purposes.

Booklets with plate numbers

Scott booklet number	Booklet	Scott pane number	Denom- ination	Plate numbers	Notes
137	$3.60 Animals	2 panes 1889a	18¢	1-16	1, 2
138	$1.20 Flag	1 pane 1893a	two 6¢ & six 18¢	1	
139	$1.20 Flag	1 pane 1896a	20¢	1	3, 4
140	$2 Flag	1 pane 1896b	20¢	1, 4	3, 4
140A	$4 Flag	2 panes 1896b	20¢	2, 3, 4	3, 4
140B	$28.05 Eagle	1 pane 1900a	$9.35	1111	2
142	$4 Sheep	2 panes 1949a	20¢	1-6, 9-12, 14-26, 28, 29	1, 2, 5
142a	$4 Sheep	2 panes 1949d	20¢	34	5
143	$4.40 D	2 panes 2113a	D (22¢)	1-4	5
144	$1.10 Flag	1 pane 2116a	22¢	1, 3	3
145	$2.20 Flag	2 panes 2116a	22¢	1, 3	
146	$4.40 Seashells	2 panes 2121a	22¢	1-3	
147	$4.40 Seashells	2 panes 2121a	22¢	1, 3, 5-8, 10	
148	$32.25 Eagle	1 pane 2122a	$10.75	11111	3
149	$32.25 Eagle	1 pane 2122a	$10.75	22222	
150	$5 London	2 panes 2182a	25¢	1, 2	6
151	$1.50 London	1 pane 2197a	25¢	1	
152	$3 London	1 pane 2197a	25¢	1	

Scott booklet number	Booklet	Scott pane number	Denom-ination	Plate numbers	Notes
153	$1.76 Stamp Collecting	1 pane 2201a	22¢	1	
154	$2.20 Fish	2 panes 2209a	22¢	11111, 22222	
155	$2.20 Special Occasions	1 pane 2274a	22¢	11111, 22222	
156	$4.40 Flag	1 pane 2276a	22¢	1111, 2122, 2222	6
157	$5 E	2 panes 2282a	E (25¢)	1111, 2122, 2222	
158	$5 Pheasant	2 panes 2283a	25¢	A1111	
159	$5 Pheasant	2 panes 2283c	25¢	A3111, A3222	
160	$5 Owl/Grosbeak	2 panes 2285b	25¢	1111, 1112, 1133, 1211, 1414, 1433, 1434, 1634, 1734, 2111, 2121, 2122, 2221, 2222, 2321, 2822, 3133, 3233, 3333, 3412, 3413, 3422, 3512, 3521, 4642, 4644, 4911, 4941, 5453, 5955	3
161	$3 Flag	2 panes 2285c	25¢	1111	
162	$4.40 Constitution	4 panes 2359a	22¢	1111, 1112	3
163	$4.40 Locomotive	4 panes 2366a	22¢	1, 2	6
164	$5 Classic Cars	4 panes 2385a	25¢	1	6
165	$3 Special Occasions	1 pane each 2396a/2398a	25¢	A1111	3, 6, 7
166	$5 Steamboat	4 panes 2409a	25¢	1, 2	7
167	$5 Madonna	2 panes 2427a	25¢	1	6, 7
168	$5 Sleigh	2 panes 2429a	25¢	1111, 2111	6, 7
169	$5 Love	2 panes 2441a	25¢	1211, 2111, 2211, 2222	6, 7
170	$3 Beach Umbrella	2 panes 2443a	15¢	111111, 221111	6, 7
171	$5 Lighthouse	4 panes 2474a	25¢	1, 2, 3, 4, 5	6, 7
172	$2 Bluejay	1 pane 2483a	20¢	S1111	7
173	$2.90 Wood Duck	1 pane 2484a	29¢	4444	7
174	$5.80 Wood Duck	2 panes 2484a	29¢	1111, 1211, 2222, 3221, 3222, 3331, 3333, 4444	7, 8
175	$5.80 Wood Duck	2 panes 2485a	29¢	K11111	7, 9
176	$2.95 African Violet	1 pane 2486a	29¢	K1111	7
177	$5.80 African Violet	2 panes 2486a	29¢	K1111	7
178	$6.40 Peach/Pear	2 panes 2488a	32¢	11111	6, 7
179	$5 Indian Headdress	2 panes 2505a	25¢	1, 2	7
180	$5 Madonna	2 panes 2514a	25¢	1	6, 7
181	$5 Christmas Tree	2 panes 2516a	25¢	1211	6, 7
182	$2.90 F	1 pane 2519a	F (29¢)	2222	6

Scott booklet number	Booklet	Scott pane number	Denomination	Plate numbers	Notes
183	$5.80 F	2 panes 2519a	F (29¢)	1111, 1222, 2111, 2121, 2212, 2222	6
184	$2.90 F	1 pane 2520a	F (29¢)	K1111	9
185	$5.80 Tulip	2 panes 2527a	29¢	K1111, K2222, K3333	7, 9
186	$2.90 Flag	1 pane 2528a	29¢	K11111	7, 9
186A	$2.90 Flag	1 pane 2528a	29¢	K11111	3, 9
187	$3.80 Balloon	1 pane 2530a	19¢	1111, 2222	7
188	$5.80 Love	1 pane 2536a	29¢	1111, 1112, 1212, 1113, 1123, 2223	6, 7
189	$5.80 Fishing Flies	4 panes 2549a	29¢	A11111, A22122, A22132, A22133, A23123, A23124, A23133, A23213, A31224, A32224, A32225, A33233, A33235, A44446, A45546, A45547	6, 7, 10
190	$5.80 Desert Storm/Shield	4 panes 2552a	29¢	A11111111, A11121111	7
191	$5.80 Comedians	2 panes 2566a	29¢	1, 2	7
192	$5.80 Space Explorations	2 panes 2577a	29¢	111111, 111112	7
193	$5.80 Madonna	2 panes 2578a	(29¢)	1	6, 7
194	$5.80 Santa Claus	4 panes 2581b-2585a	(29¢)	A11111, A12111	7
195	$2.90 Pledge	1 pane 2593a	29¢	1111, 2222	7
196	$5.80 Pledge	2 panes 2593a	29¢	1111, 1211, 2122, 2222	
197	$5.80 Pledge	2 panes 2593c	29¢	1111, 1211, 2122, 2222, 2232, 2333, 3333, 4444	6, 11
198	$2.90 Pledge	1 pane 2594a	29¢	K1111	7
199	$5.80 Pledge	2 panes 2594a	29¢	K1111	
201	$5.80 Hummingbirds	4 panes 2646a	29¢	A1111111, A2212112, A2212122, A2212222, A2222222	3, 7
202	$5.80 Animals	4 panes 2709a	29¢	K1111	7, 9
202A	$5.80 Madonna	2 panes 2710a	29¢	1	6, 7
203	$5.80 Christmas Contemporary	5 panes 2718a	29¢	A111111, A112211, A222222	7
204	$5.50 Rock 'n' Roll	2 panes 2737a & 1 pane 2737b	29¢	A11111, A13113, A22222, A44444	7
207	$5.80 Space Fantasy	4 panes 2745a	29¢	1111, 1211, 2222	7
208	$5.80 Flowers	4 panes 2746a	29¢	1, 2	6, 7
209	$5.80 Broadway Musicals	4 panes 2770a	29¢	A11111, A11121, A22222, A23232, A23233	7
210	$5.80 Country & Western	4 panes 2778a	29¢	A111111, A222222, A333323, A333333, A422222	7

Scott booklet number	Booklet	Scott pane number	Denom-ination	Plate numbers	Notes
211	$5.80 Madonna	5 panes 2790a	29¢	K1-11111, K1-33333, K1-44444, K2-22222, K2-55555, K2-66666	7, 10
212	$5.80 Christmas Contemporary	1 pane each 2798a, 2798b	29¢	111111, 222222	6, 7
213	$5.80 AIDS	4 panes 2806b	29¢	K111	7, 9
214	$5.80 Love	2 panes 2814a	29¢	A11111, A11311, A12111, A12112, A12211, A12212, A21222, A21311, A22122, A22222, A22322	7
215	$5.80 Flowers	4 panes 2833a	29¢	1, 2	6, 7
216	$5.80 Locomotives	4 panes 2847a	29¢	S11111	7
217	$5.80 Madonna	2 panes 2871b	29¢	1, 2	6, 7
218	$5.80 Stocking	1 pane 2872a	29¢	P11111, P22222, P33333, P44444	7
219	$3.20 G	1 pane 2881a	G (32¢)	1111	6
220	$3.20 G	1 pane 2883a	G (32¢)	1111, 2222	
221	$6.40 G	2 panes 2883a	G (32¢)	1111, 2222	
222	$6.40 G	2 panes 2884a	G (32¢)	A1111, A1211, A2222, A3333, A4444	3, 10
223	$6.40 G	2 panes 2885a	G (32¢)	K1111	9
225	$3.20 Flag Over Porch	1 pane 2916a	32¢	11111, 22222, 23222, 33332, 44444	6, 7
226	$6.40 Flag Over Porch	2 panes 2916a	32¢	11111, 22222, 23222, 33332, 44444	
227A	$4.80 Flag Over Porch	1 pane each 2921a, 2921b	32¢	11111	6, 7, 12
228	$6.40 Flag Over Porch	2 panes 2921a	32¢	11111, 13111, 21221, 22221, 22222, 44434, 44444, 55555, 55556, 66666, 77777, 88788, 88888, 99999	3, 6, 7
228A	$9.60 Flag Over Porch	3 panes 2921a	32¢	11111	6, 7, 12
229	$6.40 Love	2 panes 2959a	32¢	1	6, 7
230	$6.40 Lighthouses	4 panes 2973a	32¢	S11111	7
231	$6.40 Garden Flowers	4 panes 2997a	32¢	2	6, 7
232	$6.40 Madonna	2 panes 3003b	32¢	1	6, 7
233	$6.40 Santa/ Children with Toys	1 pane each 3007b & 3007c	32¢	P1111, P2222	7, 10
234	$6.40 Flowers	4 panes, 3029a	32¢	1	6, 7
237	$2.00 Blue Jay	1 pane each 3048b, 3048c	20¢	S1111	
241	$4.80 Yellow Rose	1 pane each 3049b-3049d	32¢	S1111	

Scott booklet number	Booklet	Scott pane number	Denom-ination	Plate numbers	Notes
242	$9.60 Yellow Rose	5 panes 3049d	32¢	S1111	
242A	$2.00 Ringed-Neck Pheasant	1 pane each 3051b, 3051c	20¢	V1111	
242B	$4.95 Coral Pink Rose	1 pane each 3052a-3052c	33¢	S111	
259	$4.80 Statue of Liberty	1 pane each 3122b-3122d	32¢	V1111	
260	$9.60 Statue of Liberty	5 panes of 3122d	32¢	V1111	
260A	$4.80 Statue of Liberty	5 panes of 3122Eg	32¢	V1111	
261	$4.80 Merian Botanical Plants	2 panes 3128b, 1 pane 3129b	32¢	S11111	
264	$4.80 American Holly	1 pane each 3177b-3177d	32¢	B1111	
265	$9.60 American Holly	5 panes of 3177d	32¢	B1111	
270	$4.80 Wreaths	1 pane each 3248a-3248c	32¢	B111111	
271	($6.60) H Hat	2 panes of 3267a	(33¢)	1111, 2222, 3333	
275	$4.95 Flag Over City	1 pane each 3278a-3278c	33¢	V1111, V1112, V1121, V1122, V1212, V2212	
276	$6.60 Flag Over City	2 panes of 3279a	33¢	1111, 1121	
276A	$4.95 Fruit Berries	1 pane each 3301a-3301c	33¢	B1111, B1112, B2212, B2221, B2222	
276B	$4.95 Deer	1 pane each 3367a-3367c	33¢	B111111, B222222	
280	($6.80) Statue of Liberty	2 panes each 3451b, 3451c	(34¢)	V1111, V1112, V1121, V1122	
281	($6.80) Four Flowers	1 pane each 3457c, 3457d, 2 panes of 3457b	(34¢)	S1111	
281A	$2.00 George Washington	1 pane each 3482b, 3482c	20¢	P1, P2, P3	
282	$2.00 George Washington	1 pane each 3483a, 3483b	20¢	P1, P2, P3	
282A	$2.00 George Washington	1 pane each 3483d, 3483e	20¢	P1, P2, P3	
282B	$2.10 Bison	1 pane each 3484b, 3484c	21¢	P11111, P33333	

Scott booklet number	Booklet	Scott pane number	Denomination	Plate numbers	Notes
282C	$2.10 Bison	1 pane each 3484Ae, 3484Af	21¢	P11111, P33333	
282D	$2.10 Bison	1 pane each 3484Ah, 3484Ai	21¢	P11111, P33333	
283	$6.80 Statue of Liberty	2 panes each 3485c, 3485d	34¢	V1111, V1122, V2212, V2222	
284	$6.80 Four Flowers	1 pane each 2490c, 3490d, two panes 3490b	34¢	S1111	
284A	$6.80 Apple and Orange	1 pane each 3494c, 3494d, two 3494b	34¢	B1111	
285	$6.80 Rose and Love Letter	2 panes each 3498a, 3498b	34¢	B1111	
286	$6.80 Four Santas	1 pane each 3544c, 3544d, 2 panes 3544b	34¢	V1111	
287	$6.80 United We Stand	2 panes each 3549Bc, 3549Bd	34¢	S1111	
288	$2.30 George Washington	1 pane each 3618a, 3618b	23¢	P1, P2, P4	
289	$2.30 George Washington	1 pane each 3619a, 3619b	23¢	P1, P2, P4	
289A	$2.30 George Washington	1 pane each 3619c, 3619d	23¢	P1, P2, P3, P4	
290	$7.40 Flag	2 panes each 3624a, 3624b	(37¢)	S11111	
291A	$7.40 Flag	2 panes each 3634c, 3634d	37¢	V1111	
291B	$7.40 Flag	2 panes each 3636a, 3636b	37¢	S11111	
292	$7.40 Antique Toys	1 pane each 3645c, 3645d, 2 panes 3645b	37¢	V1111	
293	$7.40 Snowmen	1 pane each 3691c, 3691d, 2 panes 3691d	37¢	V1111	
296	**$7.40 Music Makers**	**1 pane each 3828c, 3828d; 2 panes 3828b**	**37¢**	**S11111**	
298	**$7.40 Holiday Ornaments**	**1 pane 3890c, 3890d, 2 panes 3890b**	**37¢**	**S11111**	

Notes for booklets with plate numbers.

1. *Joint lines on some panes.*
2. *Electric-eye (EE) marks on tabs.*
3. *Cover varieties.*
4. *Panes available scored or unscored.*
5. *Plate number either on top or bottom pane.*
6. *Various markings on either the selvage or the panes themselves allow these panes to be plated by position.*
7. *Available as never-folded or never-bound panes.*
8. *Panes issued either overall tagged or on prephosphored paper.*
9. *Panes can be found with cutting lines on either stamp number 5 or 6 (vertically oriented panes) or stamp number 3 or 8 (horizontally oriented panes).*
10. *Each of the panes in these booklets can have different plate numbers on them.*
11. *Shiny and dull gum.*
12. *Pane 2921a has a 1997 year date.*

No-hole panes

The following is a list of those panes that were officially issued by the U.S. Post Office Department and/or U.S. Postal Service as loose panes, i.e., not bound into a booklet and thus not having staple holes. Panes without staple holes can be found that aren't listed below. They aren't listed because they weren't officially issued without staple holes. The lack of staple holes can be caused by the following:

1. Staples passing through the perf holes.
2. Booklets assembled with one staple missing and the other passing through the perf holes or both staples missing.
3. Staple holes at the top of a wide tab that have been trimmed off.

Scott number	Pane	Notes
1035a	3¢ Statue of Liberty (6)	
1036a	4¢ Lincoln (6)	
1213a	5¢ Washington (5 + Slogan 1)	
1278a	1¢ Jefferson (8)	
1278b	1¢ Jefferson (4+2 Labels)	
1280a	2¢ Wright (5+1 Slogan 4 or 5)	
1280c	2¢ Wright (6)	1
1284b	6¢ Roosevelt (8)	
1393a	6¢ Eisenhower (8)	2
1393b	6¢ Eisenhower (5+1 Slogan 4 or 5)	
1395a	8¢ Eisenhower (8)	2
1395b	8¢ Eisenhower (6)	
1395c	8¢ Eisenhower (4 + 1 each Slogans 6 & 7)	2
1395d	8¢ Eisenhower (7 + 1 Slogan 4 or 5)	2
1510b	10¢ Jefferson Memorial (5 + 1 Slogan 8)	
1510c	10¢ Jefferson Memorial (8)	2
1510d	10¢ Jefferson Memorial (6)	
C39a	6¢ Plane (6)	
C51a	7¢ Jet, blue (6)	
C60a	7¢ Jet, carmine (6)	
C64b	8¢ Jet over Capitol (5 + 1 Slogan 1)	

Scott number	Pane	Notes
C72b	10¢ Stars (8)	
C78a	11¢ Jet (4 + 1 each Slogans 5 & 4)	
C79a	13¢ Letters (5 + 1 Slogan 8)	

Never-bound panes

By definition, a never-bound pane is one that was never assembled into a booklet. Loose panes such as Scott 1595a-d that were in booklets have small V-notches in the edge of the tab and traces of adhesive. The other panes in this category that were in booklets will have disturbed gum in the tabs showing that they were attached to either the booklet cover or each other.

Scott number	Pane	Plate number	Notes
1595a	13¢ Liberty Bell (6)		
1595b	13¢ Liberty Bell (7 + 1 Slogan 8)		2
1595c	13¢ Liberty Bell (8)		2
1595d	13¢ Liberty Bell (5 + 1 Slogan 9)		
2581b	(29¢) Santa Claus (4)	A11111	
2582a	(29¢) Santa Claus (4)	A11111	
2583a	(29¢) Santa Claus (4)	A11111	
2584a	(29¢) Santa Claus (4)	A11111	
2585a	(29¢) Santa Claus (4)	A11111	
2718a	29¢ Christmas Toys (4)	A111111, A112211, A222222	
2790a	29¢ Madonna (4)	K1-11111, K1-33333, K1-44444, K2-55555	

Never-folded panes

Scott number	Pane	Plate number	Notes
2398a	25¢ Special Occasions (6)	A1111	4
2409a	25¢ Steamboats (5)	1, 2	
2427a	25¢ Madonna (10)	1	4
2429a	25¢ Sleigh (10)	1	4
2441a	25¢ Love (10)	1211	4
2443a	15¢ Beach Umbrella (10)	111111	
2474a	25¢ Lighthouses (5)	1, 2, 3, 4, 5	3, 4
2483a	20¢ Bluejay	S1111	
2484a	29¢ Wood Duck (10)	1111	
2485a	29¢ Wood Duck (10)	K1111	5
2486a	29¢ African Violets (10)	K1111	
2488a	32¢ Fruits (10)	11111	4
2505a	25¢ Indian Headdress (10)	1, 2	
2514a	25¢ Madonna (10)	1	4
2516a	25¢ Christmas Tree (10)	1211	4
2527a	29¢ Tulip (10)	K1111	5

Scott number	Pane	Plate number	Notes
2528a	29¢ Flag w/Olympic Rings (10)	K11111	5
2530a	19¢ Balloons (10)	1111	
2536a	29¢ Love (10)	1111, 1112	4
2549a	29¢ Fishing Flies (5)	A11111, A22122, A23124, A23133, A23213, A32225, A33213, A33233	4
2552a	29¢ Desert Shield/Storm (5)	A11121111	
2566a	29¢ Comedians (10)	1	
2577a	29¢ Space Exploration (10)	111111	
2578a	(29¢) Madonna (10)	1	4
2593a	29¢ Pledge of Allegiance (10)	1111	
2594a	29¢ Pledge of Allegiance (10)	K1111	
2646a	29¢ Hummingbirds (5)	A1111111, A2212112, A2212122, A2212222, A2222222	
2709a	29¢ Animals (5)	K1111	5
2710a	29¢ Madonna (10)	1	4
2737a	29¢ Rock 'n' Roll (8)	A11111, A13113, A22222	6
2737b	29¢ Rock 'n' Roll (4)	A13113, A22222	
2745a	29¢ Space Fantasy (5)	1111, 1211, 2222	
2764a	29¢ Spring Garden Flowers (5)	1	4
2770a	29¢ Broadway Musicals (4)	A11111, A11121, A22222	
2778a	29¢ Country Music (4)	A222222	
2798a	29¢ Christmas Contemporary (10)	111111	4
2798b	29¢ Christmas Contemporary (10)	111111	4
2806b	29¢ AIDS (5)	K111	5
2814a	29¢ Love (10)	A11111	
2833a	29¢ Summer Garden Flowers (5)	2	4
2847a	29¢ Locomotives (5)	S11111	
2871b	29¢ Madonna (10)	1, 2	4
2872a	29¢ Stocking (20)	P11111, P22222, P33333, P44444	
2916a	32¢ Flag Over Porch (10)	11111	4
2921a	32¢ Flag Over Porch (10)	21221, 22221, 22222	4
2921a	32¢ Flag Over Porch (10)	11111	4, 7
2921b	32¢ Flag Over Porch (5 + 1 label)	11111	4
2949a	32¢ Love (10)	1	4
2973a	32¢ Lighthouses (5)	S11111	
2997a	32¢ Fall Garden Flowers (5)	2	4
3003b	32¢ Madonna (10)	1	4
3007b	32¢ Santa and Children (10)	P1111	
3007c	32¢ Santa and Children (10)	P1111	
3029a	32¢ Garden Flowers (5)	1	4

Notes for no-hole, never-bound and never-folded panes

1 Shiny and dull gum.
2 Electric-eye (EE) marks on tabs.
3 Plate 1 panes available with and without scoring.
4 Various markings on either the selvage or the panes themselves allow these panes to be plated by position.
5 Panes can be found with cutting lines on either stamp 5 or 6 (vertically oriented panes) or stamp 3 or 8 (horizontally oriented panes).
6 Panes from A11111 have been found in 1993 Year sets only. They all had the bottom stamp removed and thus are panes of seven, not eight.
7 Has year date 1997.